DUGALD STEWART

The Pride and Ornament of Scotland

DUGALD STEWART

The Pride and Ornament of Scotland

GORDON MACINTYRE

sussex
ACADEMIC
PRESS
BRIGHTON • PORTLAND

Copyright © Gordon Macintyre 2003

The right of Gordon Macintyre to be identified as author of this work has been asserted in accordance with the Copyright, Designs and Patents Act 1988.

2 4 6 8 10 9 7 5 3 1

First published in 2003 in Great Britain by
SUSSEX ACADEMIC PRESS
PO Box 2950
Brighton BN2 5SP

and in the United States of America by
SUSSEX ACADEMIC PRESS
920 NE 58th Ave   Suite 300
Portland, Oregon 97213-3786

All rights reserved. Except for the quotation of short passages for the purposes of criticism and review, no part of this publication may be reproduced, stored in a retrieval system, or transmitted, in any form or by any means, electronic, mechanical, photocopying, recording or otherwise, without the prior permission of the publisher.

British Library Cataloguing in Publication Data
A CIP catalogue record for this book is available from the British Library.

Library of Congress Cataloging-in-Publication Data
Macintyre, Gordon.
Dugald Stewart : the pride and ornament of Scotland / Gordon Macintyre.
p. cm.
Includes bibliographical references and index.
ISBN (hardcover) 1 903900 34 4   ISBN (paperback) 1 903900 35 2 (alk. paper)
1. Stewart, Dugald, 1753–1828. 2. Philosophers—Scotland—Biography.
I. Title.
B1556.M23 2003
192—dc21
2003000086

Typeset and designed by G&G Editorial, Brighton
Printed by TJ International, Padstow, Cornwall
This book is printed on acid-free paper.

Contents

List of Illustrations   vii

Preface and Acknowledgements   ix

1. Who was Dugald Stewart?   1
2. Family Background and Infancy   6
3. At School and University (1761–1772)   14
4. The Young Stewart, Mathematician (1772–1780)   24
5. Boarders, Travels, Marriage and Change (1780–1785)   36
6. The Young Stewart, Philosopher (1785–1787)   48
7. Stewart and Robert Burns   54
8. Revolutionary France and Remarriage (1787–1790)   65
9. Liberal Philosopher in a Harsh Climate (1790–96)   79
10. Students and Travels (1796–1800)   95

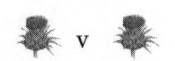

Contents

11	The Stewarts and the Palmerstons (1800–1803)	104
12	Social Life and the Leslie and Ashburton Affairs (1803–1805)	121
13	Towards Retirement (1806–1810)	134
14	The Teacher and the Man	155
15	The Early Years of Retirement (1810–1815)	172
16	Deaths of Friends and the Final Break (1815–1820)	187
17	The Last Years (1820–1828)	205
18	Epilogue	228

Supplement A: The Writings — 246
Supplement B: Stewart's Written Words — 259

Notes and Further Reading — 269

Index — 319

Illustrations

1. (a) Portrait of Dugald Stewart by Sir Henry Raeburn.
   (b) Bronze bust of Dugald Stewart by Samuel Joseph.
2. (i) Paste medallion of Adam Smith by James Tassie.
   (ii) Paste medallion of Thomas Reid by James Tassie.
   (iii) Portrait of Professor Adam Ferguson by unknown artist after Sir Henry Raeburn.
3. (iv) Portrait of Principal William Robertson by Sir Henry Raeburn.
4. (a) Portrait of William Ker, Earl of Ancram, by Sir Henry Raeburn.
   (b) Portrait of Dugald Stewart with his first wife and son Matthew by Alexander Nasmyth.
5. (a) Paste medallion of Dugald Stewart by James Tassie.
   (b) Porcelain medallion of Dugald Stewart by John Henning.
   (c) Medallion (plaster replica) of Mrs Helen D'Arcy Stewart after John Henning.
   (d) Pencil drawing of George Cranstoun, Lord Corehouse, by Benjamin William Crombie.
6. (i) Caricature ("original portrait") of Professor Andrew Dalzel by John Kay.
   (ii) Pencil and water-colour drawing of Professor John Playfair by William Nicholson.
7. Portrait of George and Maria Stewart by Sir Henry Raeburn.
8. (a) Pencil and water-colour drawing of Mrs Helen D'Arcy Stewart by Thomas Heaphy.

Illustrations

    (b) Pencil and water-colour drawing of Matthew Stewart in uniform by Thomas Heaphy.
9 (a) Portrait of Lord Palmerston by Thomas Heaphy.
    (b) Portrait of the Rev. Sidney Smith by Henry Perronet Briggs.
10 (a) Portrait of James Boswell and his family by Henry Singleton.
    (b) Marble bust of the Rev. Archibald Alison by Samuel Joseph.
11   Photograph of Kinneil House, Bo'ness.
12 (i) Portrait of Francis Horner by Sir Henry Raeburn.
   (ii) Portrait of Charles Babbage by Samuel Laurence.
13 (a) Pencil drawing of Dugald Stewart by John Henning.
    (b) Portrait of Professor John Wilson ("Christopher North") by Thomas Duncan.
14 (i) MS letter from Dugald Stewart to Charles Babbage.
   (ii) MS letter from Mrs Helen D'Arcy Stewart to Charles Babbage.
15 (a) Portrait of Archibald Constable by Andrew Geddes.
    (b) Portrait of Mrs Helen D'Arcy Stewart by William Nicholson.
16   Chalk drawing of Dugald Stewart by Sir David Wilkie.

The author and publisher gratefully acknowledge permission to reproduce copyright material, as detailed below, and apologize for any errors or omissions. The publisher would be grateful to be notified of any corrections that should be incorporated in the next edition or reprint of this book.

The British Library: 14(i), 14(ii).
Edinburgh Central Library: 6(i).
Edinburgh University: 3(iv).
Historic Scotland: 11 – Crown copyright reproduced courtesy of Historic Scotland.
National Galleries of Scotland (Scottish National Portrait Gallery): 1(a), 1(b), 2(i), 2(ii), 2(iii), 5(a), 5(b), 5(c), 5(d), 8(a), 8(b), 10(a), 10(b), 12(i), 13(b), 15(a), 16.
National Portrait Gallery: 7, 9(a), 9(b), 12(ii), 13(a), 15(b).
Private collections: 4(a) – in a private Scottish collection; 4(b) – in a private collection – every effort was made to contact the copyright holder.
The Trustees of the National Museums of Scotland: 6(ii).
Cover picture courtesy of Roman Michnowicz (Roman Photography), Glasgow.

Preface and Acknowledgements

I came to the subject of this biography by chance. In 1997 my wife and I moved into a double-upper flat in Edinburgh's New Town. Before long our neighbours in the flats below mentioned that the house had once been the home of Dugald Stewart. I knew that Stewart had been a philosopher of the Scottish Enlightenment, and was curious to learn more. I soon discovered that the information we had been given was incorrect: Stewart had not *lived* at 5 Ainslie Place – he had *died* there, in 1828, apparently while visiting a friend.

I also discovered that although there were many references in academic books to Stewart's writings, there was little, and certainly nothing recent and comprehensive, to be found about his life. His son had written a short memoir of filial piety after Stewart's death.[1] When an edition of his collected works was produced in the late 1850s John Veitch had inserted a rather fuller account which included some letters.[2] But a good deal of the space was taken up with Stewart's philosophy and style, and the biographical material was brief and impersonal. From these and a few other sources, including Cockburn's *Memorials*,[3] Sir Leslie Stephen had compiled an article for the *Dictionary of National Biography* in the 1890s.[4] And these slender resources were the basis for almost every subsequent biographical reference. The absence of a modern life was surprising, for it was clear that in his day and for some time afterwards Stewart had been a famous figure, not only in Scotland but internationally, and I began to wonder whether something might be done to fill this gap in the literature.

Veitch had stated baldly in his mid-nineteenth-century essay, "Materials for a detailed account of the life of Mr Stewart do not exist."[5] This seemed discouraging for any attempt at a fuller version, and his grounds for saying what he did will appear in my final chapter. But I found that paradoxically much more source material is available now than was accessible a hundred and fifty years ago. For example, most of the relevant Palmerston papers came to light only in the 1950s,[6] and surprisingly large numbers of unpublished letters to and from Stewart and his wife have found their way to such collections as those of the British Library, Edinburgh University and the National Library of Scotland. There are also many references to Stewart and his family in the now published journals, letters and biographies of his contemporaries; and though some of these are trivial in themselves, they help to establish a more intimate and rounded picture than Veitch can have thought possible. Nor was Stewart's life by any means – to use his own phrase – "barren of those incidents which furnish materials for biography".[7]

All this might still have been of no more than antiquarian interest, but the further I pursued my researches the more impressed I became by how central a figure Stewart had been in the intellectual life of his time, by the large and varied number of well-known people whom his life had touched, by the respect and affection with which they regarded him, and indeed by what attractive figures he and his second wife had been. So I persevered, and their story is told here as fully, within the bounds of readability, as I have been able to unearth it. As a pioneer in the field, I have been careful to identify all the sources used, and though speculation has sometimes seemed warranted it has always been made clear if conclusive evidence is lacking.

By the time I came to begin a first draft I had lived with Stewart so closely that I felt a degree of intimacy with him. But his was an age of much greater formality than ours in personal address. His wife in her letters normally referred to him as "Mr Stewart" – sometimes, in writing to people who knew them well, as "Mr S." – but never as "Dugald". There is some evidence that a few old friends who first knew him when he was young called him by his first name,[8] but he himself seems never to have employed a more informal signature than "D.S.", and that infrequently. His wife almost always subscribed her letters "H. D. Stewart". I have not felt it appropriate to assume in my text a familiarity which they would probably have found presumptuous, if not offensive.

Spelling in the Stewarts' day was a little temperamental (see, for example, Mrs Stewart's "intreat" in Plate 14 (ii)). I have retained the original versions in my quotations from letters without inserting the rather

Preface and Acknowledgements

irritating "(sic)". Mrs Stewart was much given to abbreviations such as "wd" for "would" and to the use of a squiggle for "and": I have transcribed words in full. Writers also tended to be profligate by modern standards in their use of capital letters and of commas. Again I have retained the original punctuation with the exception of the eighteenth-century habit of sometimes separating sentences by a dash; this would be unnecessarily distracting, and full stops have been substituted.

I have many debts of gratitude to acknowledge. Staff at the libraries where I have consulted – in some cases frequented – have been ever helpful and efficient. These are the various departments of Edinburgh Central Library, the National Library of Scotland, the Scottish National Archives, Edinburgh City Archives, the libraries of the Universities of St Andrews, Glasgow and especially Edinburgh, the Scottish National Portrait Gallery, and the Court of Lord Lyon, King at Arms. Other sources have been consulted, no less helpfully, at a distance – the library of the University of Aberdeen, the Special Collections and Archives of the University of Keele, the Hartley Library of the University of Southampton, the Beinecke Rare Book and Manuscript Library of Yale University, Historic Scotland, the Ayrshire Archives Centre, the Denbighshire Record Office, Consignia (the Post Office group) and above all the British Library, where Dr Christopher Wright and Malcolm Marjoram went out of their way to facilitate me.

Other individuals who have generously helped in a variety of ways include Mr C. G. Angus, Archivist at Monteviot; Mr Hanfried Brockmann, Guest Services Team Leader at Warwick Castle; Dr Allan Carswell, Curator of the National War Museum of Scotland; Mrs Pat Crichton, Archivist at Hopetoun House; Mrs Linda Ducklin, Outreach Co-ordinator at Newbattle Abbey; Mrs Tina Hampson, professional researcher at the Public Records Office at Kew; the Earl of Home (for access to the Douglas-Home archive); members of the Lennox Heritage Society of Dumbarton; Mrs Ann Mitchell, historian of Lord Moray's feu; and Mr Henry Steuart Fothringham of Grantully and Mrs Muriel Walker, both of the Stewart Society. At a fairly late stage in my research I came in contact with Dr Michael Brown of the Department of History at University College Dublin; his shared interest in Dugald Stewart and enthusiasm for assessing his contribution to Enlightenment thought have been stimulating.

Almost since the outset I have had the immense good fortune to be in touch with Mrs Pat Gordon, FSAG, of Vaucluse, NSW, Australia. She is not only a direct descendant of Stewart's sister Janet but a professional

Preface and Acknowledgements

genealogist, and without her expertise I would never have been able to discover and disentangle so much of the family detail of the Stewarts, the Bannatynes and the Millers.

Not being trained in philosophy beyond a fairly elementary level, I was anxious that my references to Stewart's thought, and to that of contemporaries such as David Hume and Thomas Reid, should be subjected to some academic scrutiny. I am particularly grateful to Professor Knud Haakonssen of Boston University for reading a draft version of chapter 12, and to Dr James Harris of St Catherine's College, Oxford for reading chapters 1 and 14 and Supplement A; his comments were most helpful, though obviously I alone am responsible for the use to which I have put them.

In Tony Grahame, Editorial Director at Sussex Academic Press, I found the ideal publisher – knowledgeable, prompt, patient and helpful. I am indeed most grateful for all he has done to assist in bringing this book to life.

Lastly, I have to thank my wife, Nancy Macintyre, for her encouragement and for tolerating so patiently for more than five years my preoccupation with Dugald and his family.

Gordon Macintyre
5 Ainslie Place
Edinburgh
May, 2003

DUGALD STEWART

The Pride and Ornament of Scotland

CHAPTER ONE

Who Was Dugald Stewart?

"The distinguished professor, at whose house we were, is the pride and ornament of the university, and of Scotland."   Benjamin Silliman

On 9 July 1828 a meeting took place in the University apartments of the Royal Society of Edinburgh to consider some form of memorial to an eminent friend of those present who had died four weeks previously at the age of seventy-four. The chairman was a nephew of Robert Adam, the architect: William Adam, now himself aged nearly seventy-seven, had been a distinguished Member of Parliament and in 1816 had launched Scotland's first Jury Court, of which he was the Lord Chief Commissioner. The meeting passed the following resolutions:

> That this meeting is deeply impressed with sentiments of admiration and respect for the talents and virtues which distinguished and adorned the character of the late Mr Dugald Stewart, and with a deep sense of the honour which his genius and learning have reflected on his country, during his long and bright career as an author and public instructor on the most important parts of philosophy.
>
> That this Meeting, in common with many of the friends and admirers of Mr Stewart, is desirous that there should remain to future times some lasting public monument of the high estimation in which he was held by his contemporaries, and of the reverence with which his memory is cherished by all those to whom he was known.
>
> That in the opinion of this Meeting, a monument of an architectural kind

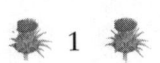

would be the best fitted for the attainment of their wishes. That a Committee be appointed to consider the most proper means of accomplishing the object . . .[1]

The committee selected was a roll-call of the good and the great of the Edinburgh of that time. The chairman was to be the Lord Chief Commissioner himself. Among the members were two earls, three lords, five baronets or knights among whom was Sir Walter Scott, and a list of notabilities which included Francis Jeffrey, Henry Cockburn and William Playfair.

The agreed decisions were to be published in the Edinburgh and London newspapers "in order to afford to those who may approve of the object of this meeting an opportunity of giving their concurrence and aid in its accomplishment". Subsequent developments are recounted in the final chapter, but the outcome was the circular monument on Calton Hill which frequently appears as a foreground feature in photographs and paintings of the view across Edinburgh. Around the base of the monument is carved in bold letters the name **DUGALD STEWART** with the dates of his birth and death; no more.

Who was this man, so eminent in his day, now so nearly forgotten? He was for many years a professor at the University of Edinburgh, where for a quarter of a century he held the chair of moral philosophy. Latterly he was the foremost philosopher in Britain. The range of his academic interests included mathematics, astronomy, ethics, the philosophy of mind, and what we should now call psychology, economics, political science, jurisprudence, philology, aesthetics and literary criticism; he also paid a good deal of attention to the subject of education. His published works extend to several volumes, and include memoirs of three distinguished contemporaries. He was an outstandingly gifted teacher, and among his students were several men who were later to be prominent in various walks of life; two of them became Prime Minister. They all regarded him with reverence and affection. His second wife, to whom he was married for nearly forty years, was a gifted woman and a partner in his work. He was an inveterate traveller. His adult life, throughout which he was a staunch Whig, encompassed the American, French and industrial revolutions, all of which affected it significantly.

He was born in Edinburgh in 1753 in the midst of the Scottish Enlightenment.[2] This period, though it cannot be precisely defined, is usually taken as extending from about 1730 until 1790.[3] "Enlightenment" has not a precise meaning any more than it has a precise location in history. The term indicates a cluster of characteristics which

Who Was Dugald Stewart?

arose in a particularly concentrated form in the intellectual life of many parts of Europe in the eighteenth century. Immanuel Kant, one of its foremost protagonists, attempted to define it not as a viewpoint but as a way of thinking – an approach in which men relied on their own rationality. The period has also been called the age of reason. "Reason" today might be understood as opposed to prejudice or superstition, and in the Scotland of the past there was much of these from which to disengage, but in the eighteenth century the opposition was rather to unquestionable authority. Men were enlightened because they no longer felt obliged to accept, from the state or from the church, limits to what they ought to question or believe: they should think for themselves, and follow their own reason – and, they would have added, 'sentiment' – wherever these might lead.

Freedom was therefore a key issue for the intellectuals of the time. Men must be free to think and to publish. A climate of toleration in which new ideas could be disseminated, discussed and developed implied a state of affairs in which the powers of government were restricted by an independent and principled legal system. The rights of man became a subject of serious debate. Yet social stability was also considered essential for progress to be possible.

The Enlightenment did not emerge from an entirely dark age. The application of human reason had already led to notable advances in science and mathematics. These were enabling improvements to be made in areas such as agriculture, industrial processes and domestic life that were beginning to raise standards of living for large numbers of people. Scientific progress was also raising expectations about what the application of human reason could achieve. Might there not be a comprehensive science of man which could establish mental and moral laws comparable with the great explanatory laws that had been discovered in the natural world? This was a quest to which Stewart and others engaged in academic work at this time devoted their lives. The age of reason was also therefore an age of optimism and of intellectual ferment.

That it should have taken so strikingly brilliant a form in art, literature, science, philosophy, architecture and other fields in the small and relatively poor country of Scotland is a phenomenon that has been much discussed. There were predisposing historical causes in the decline of puritanism in the Church of Scotland and in the stimulus afforded by the Act of Union with England at the beginning of the eighteenth century, though there was loss in this too. Stewart himself adduced Scotland's close intellectual links with the continent of Europe to help explain what he called "the sudden burst of genius, which to a foreigner must seem to have sprung up in this country by a sort of enchantment, soon after the

Rebellion of 1745".[4] He also remarked that in Scotland "the liberal constitution of universities has been always peculiarly favourable to the diffusion of a free and eclectic spirit of inquiry".[5] The well established system of Scottish parish schools provided a valuable underpinning, and it has been suggested that "the really distinctive mark of Enlightenment in Scotland is that its ideas and ideals were very widely diffused, in all areas and among a very wide span of social groups, in what was for the time a remarkably well-educated and highly-literate population."[6]

But essentially what we are looking at is the fortuitous emergence of a significant group of men of outstanding ability and energy in the same place and at roughly the same time – Smollett's "hotbed of genius".[7] That such a happy accident, though rare, is not unique can be seen if one thinks of fifth-century BC Athens, fifteenth-century Florence and Elizabethan London. Reference to these other flowerings of the human spirit suggests an aspect which they had in common: all took place in small and intimate communities. This was critically true in the case of the Edinburgh of Stewart's life-time, for during that period it was pre-eminently, though by no means exclusively,[8] in Edinburgh that the Scottish Enlightenment had its focus. The population of the city when Stewart was born was about 55,000; habitation was almost entirely concentrated on the ridge of land which stretches from the Castle to the Palace of Holyroodhouse and to a few streets on its south side. Even when the population gradually grew, and the "New Town" extended northwards at the end of the eighteenth century, the professional classes who began to move out to this more spacious and salutary environment still lived within easy social distance of each other.

This was the setting for the interlocking and overlapping groups of university professors, churchmen, lawyers and aristocrats who created the Scottish Enlightenment. They were often related, directly or by marriage; they had gone to the same schools, and had been classmates or had taught one another at the University; they attended the same churches; they were members of the same social clubs and masonic lodges; they visited each other's homes; they corresponded and used each other's personal contacts; their portraits were painted by the same artists; they read each other's books; they discussed each other's ideas. They were intensely conscious of being members of a dynamic and progressive society.

The strength and complexity of these networks are well illustrated by Stewart's own life. The son of a mathematician well known in his day, he studied philosophy under the founder of the Scottish school of common sense, Thomas Reid, whose disciple and friend he became, and whose life he wrote. He also wrote accounts of the life and works of Adam Smith, author of *The Wealth of Nations,* and, at his own dying request, of Principal William Robertson of Edinburgh University, historian of European fame and leader of the Moderates in the Church of Scotland; he knew these men well. He was on warm personal as well as professional terms with both his predecessor, Adam Ferguson (one of the first sociologists), and his successor, Thomas Brown, in the Edinburgh chair of moral philosophy, and his circle included all the University men who were his contemporaries, several of them eminent in their fields. He corresponded with men of letters in England, Ireland, France and the United States.

In the world of literature he was a friend of Henry Mackenzie, the Man of Feeling, and he knew James Boswell. He was an early and generous patron of Robert Burns. Walter Scott and the poet Thomas Campbell were both his students and remained his friends. Maria Edgeworth became a warm admirer of Stewart and his wife, and Tom Moore was another acquaintance. The founders of *The Edinburgh Review* had all attended his lectures. In the legal and political world too he had numerous intimate acquaintances, and he was on close terms with many of the aristocracy of his day. He was familiar with scientists, explorers, doctors and mathematicians. At different times he had his portrait painted by Alexander Nasmyth and by Sir Henry Raeburn, James Tassie made a medallion of his head in profile, and Sir David Wilkie drew him as an elderly man. Stewart lived until 1828 – for long enough to become an intellectual bridge from the Enlightenment acrosss the Romantic period to the nineteenth century. Even in death he was associated with the notable men of his age, for he died in a crescent planned by Gillespie Graham, and his monument was designed by W. H. Playfair.

The overwhelming impression left by the many distinguished men who knew him well is that Dugald Stewart was above all an inspiring teacher and a good man. Benjamin Silliman, an American student and future academic who visited Edinburgh in 1806, described him as "the pride and ornament of the university, and of Scotland".[9] This book explores his claim to such a place in the annals of his country at one of the outstanding periods of its history.

CHAPTER TWO

Family Background and Infancy

"The two greatest mathematicians that I have ever had the honour to be known to, and, I believe, the two greatest that have lived in my time, Dr Robert Simson of Glasgow, and Dr Matthew Stewart of Edinburgh, never seemed to feel even the slightest uneasiness from the neglect with which the ignorance of the public received some of their most valuable works." Adam Smith

Dugald Stewart was born in Edinburgh on 22 November 1753 and named after his paternal grandfather. The elder Dugald had been born in 1674,[1] possibly in Campbeltown;[2] he was descended from the Stewarts of Bute by a branch of the family which had settled for some generations in Argyllshire.[3] At Glasgow University he studied divinity, though he appears to have had something of his grandson's breadth of interests, for the University holds a book of lengthy notes which he made very neatly in Latin in 1693 from Professor John Boyd's lectures on physics.[4] At some point he went to live on the Isle of Bute, and it seems that he was a master in the burgh school of Rothesay in 1695.[5] In 1698 he was licensed by the Church of Scotland to preach, and on 11 April 1700 the Rev. Dugald Stewart was ordained as minister of the High Kirk in Rothesay, where he remained for nearly fifty years.[6]

Mr Stewart was described as having the "qualifications of a clergyman and a gentleman", and being "a father to his people and the friend of mankind";[7] but in some respects his long tenure in Bute must have been discouraging. Just about the time when he accepted the call to Rothesay the village of Campbeltown in the Kintyre peninsula was made a royal burgh, and the family of the Duke of Argyll offered substantial inducements to people to settle there. Not a few in Rothesay accepted the tempting offers made to them, and as a result the principal town of Bute lost many of its traders and much of its trade, and the population fell sharply during the first two-thirds of the eighteenth century.[8] Lack of opportunity at home may have been one reason why so many of the Rev. Dugald Stewart's family about whom we have knowledge moved away from Bute.

Like his grandson, the elder Dugald married twice. His first wife was Margaret, daughter of another Church of Scotland minister, the Rev. Robert Stewart. There were two children of this marriage; James, the elder, produced a son, Robert, originally a merchant in Campeltown, who emigrated after his marriage to Prince Edward Island, and there became the first speaker of the Parliament.[9] In 1712 the Rev. Dugald married Janet Bannatyne, one of a family from Kames in Bute, and this marriage produced several children. The eldest son, Robert, became an army surgeon in the Bahamas,[10] and the eldest daughter, Ann, married a bookseller in Edinburgh. After Ann came Matthew, born on 28 June 1717,[11] and it was he who was to become the father of Dugald Stewart the younger.

After attending the grammar school in Rothesay, Matthew was sent to Glasgow University in 1734 to train for the Church. During the course of his studies he received special encouragement from two of the professors.[12] One was the philosopher, Francis Hutcheson, later to be credited by Matthew's son with something like the status which he is now often (though perhaps simplistically) given as the father of the Scottish Enlightenment.[13] He was one of the first professors at a Scottish university – probably the very first – to lecture in English rather than Latin, and he exerted a liberal influence on a whole generation of young men entering the church in the west of Scotland.[14] Born and brought up in Ulster, Hutcheson was described by another of his students, Alexander Carlyle, as "a good-looking man, of an engaging countenance. He delivered his lectures without notes, walking backwards and forwards in the area of his room. As his elocution was good, and his voice and manner pleasing, he raised the attention of his hearers at all times."[15] Matthew's son later recorded that his father had attended Dr Hutcheson's lectures for several years, and "never spoke of them without much sensibility".[16] Hutcheson developed the notion that man is endowed with a moral sense, analogous with our visual sense.

The other seminal influence on young Matthew Stewart was Robert Simson, the eminent professor of mathematics, in whose class he probably met Adam Smith: certainly Smith and Stewart became friends at this time.[17] Simson was a confirmed bachelor who lived in a tavern opposite the College gate, but he was a man of varied interests who "made Glasgow University a centre for the study of classical antiquity".[18] He rarely left the College bounds, except for a Saturday walk to the village of Anderston accompanied by a couple of chosen companions. Alexander Carlyle recorded at the end of his life that "Mr Simson's most constant attendant and greatest favourite was his own scholar, Mr Matthew Stewart".[19] He had discovered that Matthew had a marked ability in mathematics, and the young man was drawn into Simson's particular interest, an attempt to rediscover the geometric knowledge and methodology of ancient Greece.[20] In 1741 Matthew went on to the University of Edinburgh to pursue his studies in divinity under Professor John Goldie (or Gowdie), and also to study under Edinburgh's professor of mathematics, Colin Maclaurin, to whom Simson provided a letter of introduction.[21] Maclaurin had been recommended for the Edinburgh chair by Sir Isaac Newton, and when Newton died Maclaurin wrote an account of his scientific method which helped to establish Newton's huge influence on Enlightenment thinking.[22] Stewart got on well with Maclaurin, and during his time in Edinburgh he maintained contact with his former mentor, Robert Simson, through correspondence about their common interest in ancient geometry, and in particular about the porisms of Euclid.[23]

In May 1744 Matthew Stewart was licensed to preach, and a year later, through the influence of the Earl of Bute and the Duke of Argyll, he became the minister at Rosneath in Dunbartonshire. This was the idyllic spot chosen many years later by Walter Scott for the reunion of Jeanie Deans (supposedly some seven years before Matthew arrived in actuality) with her father and future husband after her heroic journey to London in *The Heart of Midlothian*.[24] But Matthew did not rival his father in the duration of his parish tenure.

Professor Maclaurin, like most of Edinburgh University, had no sympathy with the Jacobite rising under Prince Charles Edward Stuart in 1745. Their opposition was on both economic and political grounds, and sprang mainly from a conviction that the restoration of the Stuarts would entail the imposition of an intolerant and authoritarian government. It was Maclaurin, who included "fortification" and "the theory of gunnery" in his College courses,[25] who organized the defences of the city against the rebel troops. He worked day and night in planning the hastily raised fortifications and superintending their erection. This was to the detriment of his own health, which was not robust. In spite of his efforts the rebels occupied Edinburgh, and Maclaurin thought it wise to flee the city; he took refuge with the Archbishop of York. When he was able to return home, exposure to extreme cold further weakened him.

During May of 1746 Matthew Stewart was in Edinburgh (possibly for the General Assembly of the Church of Scotland), and called once or twice at Maclaurin's house. Word had been given that the professor was not inclined to receive anybody who had not particular business with him, but hearing of Matthew's visit he said that he would be glad to see him for a quarter of an hour. When this meeting took place Maclaurin told him that while he was dangerously ill he had wondered about who might succeed him, and could think of no one more suited than Matthew himself, though since he was now a minister he might not be interested in such a move. He added that if Stewart had taken his advice he would never have become a clergyman, for Maclaurin thought he might have done much better in some other profession. Matthew responded by thanking him for his good wishes, but hoped there would be no occasion to think of a successor soon.[26]

However, the following month Colin Maclaurin died, aged only forty-eight, and the chair of mathematics at Edinburgh University became unexpectedly vacant. During this year Matthew published a book, *General Theorems of considerable use in the higher parts of Mathematics*, which established him as a serious mathematician, and encouraged by Professor Maclaurin's (as it now appeared) dying message, he decided to apply for the post. This was not so bold a move as it would seem today. At this period each Scottish university had only one teacher per subject, and that was the professor. Occasionally a chair might be nominally occupied by two men jointly, but such arrangements were made to accommodate particular circumstances. There were no assistant lecturers, and thus when it was necessary to fill a chair, unless a professor were minded to move from another university, an incumbent had to be recruited externally. As the pool of well educated men was not large, this was not infrequently from the church. On this occasion the Town Council of Edinburgh, as governors of the University, first offered the post elsewhere,[27] but it was declined, and in September 1747, "being amply certiorate of the learning, prudence and good qualifications of the Reverend Mr Mathew Stewart",[28] they appointed him, at the age of thirty, to be the seventh professor of mathematics. They wished him to start at Martinmas[29] (11 November).

Family Background and Infancy

Matthew duly resigned from his charge at Rosneath. In March 1748 the Town Council agreed that since Colin Maclaurin's widow was to vacate her house on Whitsunday, "and as the said lodging was really necessary for the petitioner's accommodation", Mr Stewart should possess it during the Council's pleasure, "he always paying rent for the same as the lodging shall be rated by the Council".[30] At this time Edinburgh University, or the Town's College as it was usually called, occupied a rectangle of old and inadequate buildings on approximately the same site as that of the present 'Old College' on the South Bridge. Within the boundaries of the College was a house for the Principal and accommodation for the holders of six of the university chairs, among them that of mathematics. It was of this house that Matthew now became the tenant. It is thought to have been part of a short two-storey terrace known as the Teviot Chambers, next to the old Senate House or Guard Hall.[31] A Council minute of four years later refers to it as having "six chambers". The context of this minute was that Matthew had laid out £30 (a substantial sum) in repairs; his rent – normally 10 guineas a year – was adjusted accordingly.[32]

In the meantime, in the autumn of 1748, no doubt stimulated by his new appointment and anxious to supplement his rather meagre earnings from the University, Matthew followed the example of several of his fellow professors by advertising private tuition in the press.[33] But his father, the Rev. Dugald Stewart, was over eighty years of age and becoming increasingly frail. In the end he could no longer climb into the pulpit, and according to a descendant he preached his last sermon in Rothesay in October 1747. It would appear that he and his wife Janet retired to live in Edinburgh in May of the following year.[34] Not only had their son Matthew just acquired a house there, but Edinburgh was also the home of Matthew's elder sister Ann and her husband William Sands.[35] Evidence of how the old couple spent their last years is scanty, but it suggests that they went first to live with Matthew, and may later have moved in with their daughter.[36]

This would be consistent with the known fact that on 1 June 1750 Matthew Stewart married. His bride Marjory (like his father's first wife) bore the same surname. She was the only surviving child of Archibald Stewart, a solicitor,[37] and his first wife Janet Craig, who came from Riccarton. Janet had died in her early thirties, when Marjory was only three or four years old; but after an interval of six years Archibald married again, and from that time Marjory was brought up by his second wife, Christian Aird. From a member of the Aird family Archibald bought a small country home in the village of Catrine in Ayrshire, and when he died in April 1752 Marjory, as the only child, inherited the house, which thus became Matthew's. It was to play an important part in his life and in that of his son.

The first child of Matthew and Marjory Stewart was a boy, named Archibald after his maternal grandfather; but little Archie died in infancy. A girl was born on 12 July 1752, and not surprisingly, since it was the name of both of her grandmothers, she was christened Janet, and known familiarly as Jenny.[38] Before the family was enlarged the Rev. Dugald Stewart died, aged nearly ninety, on 24 January 1753.[39] (Mrs Janet Stewart, who received a small annuity from the recently established Ministers' Widows' Fund, lived on until 9 March 1761.[40]) Thus the elder Dugald Stewart never saw the grandchild who was given his name, born ten months later.

The sequel was to prove that the young Dugald had a robust constitution, but as a child he was delicate, and his health gave much anxiety to his parents. He may well have been helped by the fact that Matthew now established the practice of spending the family summers in the country house at Catrine.[41] At this period Catrine scarcely merited the description of a village; it consisted merely of a farmhouse with a mill and adjoining blacksmith's shop[42] on the north side of the River Ayr, some fourteen miles inland from Ayr town. The country home which had come into Matthew's ownership was a small two-storey dwelling built in 1682 about fifty yards from the river on the opposite side, with only a wooden footbridge to link it with the other houses. A historian of Scottish philosophy who went to look at it in the middle of the nineteenth century remembered it as "a whitewashed, broad-faced commonplace old house, situated very pleasantly in what Wordsworth called expressively the 'holms of bonnie Ayr'".[43] The parish minister of the 1790s wrote that the situation of Catrine "is romantic and delightful. The banks on both sides, being well wooded, defend it from almost every wind that blows. Few places in the same latitude and so far inland . . . can boast of a warmer climate. It is generally a fortnight earlier than any other part of the parish."[44]

Here the Stewart family may have spent as much as six months in each year when Dugald was a small child, for the university was in recess from mid-April until early November. Catrine sounds like a safe and healthy spot for a small boy to play with his sister. Before long this word could be used in the plural, for in 1758 the third surviving and last child of Matthew and Marjory was born, a girl named Christian after her mother's stepmother.[45] Little is known of Marjory Stewart. She died aged fifty[46] before any of her children were properly grown up. Many years later Dugald's own son recorded that "His mother was a woman remarkable for her good sense, and for great sweetness and kindliness of disposition, and was always remembered by her son with the warmest sentiments of filial affection."[47]

That his father's business was mathematics must have impinged upon Dugald from an early age. Living during the winter months in the midst of the University, the little boy's life would have been constantly surrounded by student bustle and the calls made upon his father as a respected teacher. When Dugald was two his father published in the *Essays* of the Philosophical Society of Edinburgh a solution, employing only elementary geometrical principles, to the problem involved in Kepler's second law of planetary motion. Five years later Matthew published a number of *Tracts* in which, again relying on geometry, he deteremined "the effect of those forces which disturb the motions of a secondary planet", and enunciated a theorem in which he deduced the motion of the moon's orbits with an accuracy that far surpassed that achieved by Newton.[48] Clearly the nature of this research would have been lost on a small boy, but his father's engagement with it must have been evident, especially since much of it was conducted during the quiet summer months at Catrine. Indeed Matthew sometimes took advantage of being in the west of Scotland on these summer vacations to visit his old friend Dr Simson, who did not retire from his chair at Glasgow University until he was well into his seventies and who lived until 1768. "It was pleasing to observe," wrote Stewart's successor and biographer, John Playfair, "in these two profound mathematicians, the most perfect esteem and affection for each other, and the most entire absence of jealousy, though no two men ever trode more nearly in the same path."[49] Adam Smith considered them "the two greatest mathematicians that I have ever had the honour to be known to, and, I believe, the two greatest that have lived in my time".[50] Something of the father's habits and methods must also have rubbed off on the son. Playfair recalled that Professor Stewart could retain his discoveries in his memory in an almost incredible manner.

> When he discovered any proposition, he would put down the enunciation with great accuracy, and, on the same piece of paper, would construct very neatly the figure to which it referred. To these he trusted for recalling to his mind, at any future period, the demonstration or the analysis, however complicated it might be. Experience had taught him, that he might place this confdence in himself without any danger of disappointment; and for this singular power, he was probably more indebted to the activity of his invention, than the mere tenaciousness of his memory.[51]

Family Background and Infancy

A similar power of intense concentration was a characteristic of Dugald's from an early age.

Like his son after him, Matthew had occasionally to fill in for a colleague, and during the session of 1758–9 he did so for Dr John Stewart, professor of natural philosophy, who had become ill – and died in May 1759. According to one of the students, Professor Stewart, in his supply role –

> confined himself almost entirely to mathematical demonstrations, which few of his students were capable of following . . . Even in his own department, Dr Matthew Stewart, though perhaps the first mathematician of his age, as appears from his publications, was unfortunately found deficient in the qualifications of a teacher. He could not deviate from the standard of consummate science, or accommodate himself to the capacity of his scholars. Besides, he was of a disposition so bashful and sensitive, that the slightest irregularity, or approach to rudeness, in the behaviour of his students, disconcerted him. The misconduct of any of these boys, for such most of his pupils were, instead of meeting with a reproof from the Professor, made him blush like a child. With the exception of those of them who enjoyed the assistance of private tutors, and those who had a decided natural predilection for mathematics, none of the students in my time were masters of the propositions, or derived any considerable mathematical knowledge from attending the public class.[52]

Carlyle described him as "of diminutive stature and of an ordinary appearance, and having withal an embarrassed elocution", and felt that Stewart did not win so secure a place in society in Edinburgh as he had done in Glasgow.[53] So we have a picture of Matthew Stewart as a scholar more than a teacher. Nor, it would seem, did he embrace the range of intellectual interests for which his son was to be so remarkable; his biographer reported that "though extremely studious, he read few books".[54] Yet one might suppose that this gentle, single-minded man was a careful educator of his own children, particularly one who was so apt a pupil as Dugald.

CHAPTER THREE

At School and University
1761–1772

"A public school like the old High School of Edinburgh is invaluable, and for what is it so? It is because men of the highest and lowest rank in society send their children to be educated together." Lord Brougham

It must have been through the care and instruction of his parents that Dugald was able to start at the High School of Edinburgh some weeks before his eighth birthday.[1] Entrants were expected to be able already to read and write, for the curriculum consisted almost entirely of Latin language and literature.[2] Dugald was a year or so younger than the usual age for enrolling at a grammar schoool. At least he did not have far to walk to his school, for it was situated just a few hundred yards to the east of the College, at the foot of what is now Infirmary Street. But the building in use at that time dated from 1578, and a decision to replace it was made in 1775, only ten years after Dugald left, so we may assume that even in the early 1760s the premises were somewhat inadequate.

Hours of attendance were fairly strenuous for children so young. During most of the year school began at 7 a.m., the hour at which Edinburgh shops opened in the eighteenth century. From 9 o'clock there was an hour for breakfast, followed by another two-hour session from 10 a.m. until noon. The afternoon session was from 2 until 4 p.m. in winter and from 3 until 5 in summer. In the 1720s a concession had been won

At School and University (1761–1772)

by the parents that from October until the end of February (when the winter, somewhat optimistically in Edinburgh, was deemed to end) the two morning sessions should be replaced by a single three-hour block commencng at 9 o'clock. This regime applied on Saturdays as well as weekdays, and holidays were very short by modern standards – only about a month in the summer.

The system of organization was that boys (for no girls attended) remained for three years with the master in whose class they were placed on arrival, and then moved to the Rector's class for their final one or two years. There may have been about 60 in each class. Impressions of a fairly brutal form of discipline at the eighteenth-century High School have been created by Lord Cockburn's reminiscences, but Henry Cockburn's time was a generation later, and it seems likely that Dugald was more fortunate. The undermaster to whom he was assigned, and in whose care he remained for three years, was Robert Farquhar. Farquhar had been there ten years earlier when Henry Mackenzie was a pupil, and Mackenzie described him as a native of Banffshire, a sort of 'Parson Adams', and a great favourite of his pupils. Parson Adams appears in Fielding's *Joseph Andrews*, and may be characterized as learned and good-hearted, though somewhat ludicrously naive. For part of Dugald's first two years with Farquhar a fellow-pupil was John Sinclair of Ulbster, the future MP, baronet, and compiler of the *Statistical Account of Scotland*, who was six months younger.

The classical curriculum appears extraordinarily restricted and tedious to modern thinking. The boys began with an initiation into Latin grammar and vocabulary (Greek was not taught), and gradually moved to reading simpler and then more advanced texts. But methods of teaching seem to have been livelier than might have been expected. 'Geography' had been introduced some years before, and though this probably meant no more than maps to make classical literature more intelligible, some history and mythology were also taught. There is an account from a slightly earlier period of a model of Caesar's bridge over the Rhine being constructed by one of the masters.

Each summer a deputation from the Town Council, which ran the school, made a visit of inspection. On these occasions the scholars would recite 'speeches', which were passages from the Roman poets. At the end of Dugald's first year the Lord Provost and magistrates were so pleased by what they saw of the work of the school during their visitation that they increased the number of prize books and made the Rector and masters burgesses of the city. Although Dugald, aged eight, presumably did not play any prominent part in these proceedings, he must have absorbed a sense that his was a well respected school. His son was later to record that "he distinguished himself by the quickness and accuracy of his apprehension", and "the singular felicity and spirit with which he caught and transfused into his own language the ideas of the classical writers attracted the particular remark of his instructors".[3]

As might be expected, the most formal of curricula could not keep active boys in a permanent state of constraint. Walter Scott, a High School boy a little before Cockburn's time, remembered fights (or 'bickers') in the streets of Edinburgh between boys from different districts;[4] and the joint heroes of *Redgauntlet*, who are supposed to have attended the High School, reminisce about such exploits as breaking windows, tormenting the hucksters in the street, climbing dangerously on the Castle rock, throwing snowballs at passers-by from the Cowgate Port and even playing truant on Leith Sands.[5] There is no telling whether the young Dugald Stewart participated in any such unphilosophical activities, but at least he must have observed them. His frend Willie Robertson, writing in later life to another High School contemporary, recalled the "days when we were wandering about Braid and Merchiston".[6] The Braid Hills were certainly a spot to which the adult Dugald Stewart returned, so perhaps his recreation was more apt to take the form of such "wandering" explorations.

The Rector during Dugald's first years in the school was Alexander Matheson, who had studied at Aberdeen and spoke with a marked Aberdeen accent. He was an effective teacher who kept a firm grip on the school. But he did not enjoy good health, and during Dugald's fourth and final year, when he was in the Rector's class, Matheson became unable to carry on.[7] To cover his absence for the rest of the year a 23-year-old named Alexander Adam was appointed. This was not an easy assignment for one so young, but Adam was a gifted teacher and a scholar of Roman antiquities, and three years later he was appointed Rector. He ran the school in a progressive manner for more than forty years. This period included the attendance of Henry Cockburn, who later wrote of him that "he was born to teach Latin, some Greek, and all virtue".[8] Cockburn's contemporary Henry Brougham declared in later life how much he approved the system in the old High School in Edinburgh, and in the University, as invaluable in a free society because it cultivatd and cherished higher objects than mere learning; and he said that from Adam he learned and retained "a strong faith in the power of education to exorcise all the evils of society".[9] Dr Adam had a stroke on 13 December 1809, while teaching his class. "But it grows dark, boys," he said; "you may go. We must put off the rest till to-morrow." He died five days later.[10] Though he can have taught Dugald for no more than four or five months, he seems to have

At School and University (1761–1772)

had a strong influence on his development; Dugald left school with a love of Latin literature, and especially poetry, which lasted all his life.[11]

Another observation of Brougham's (at a dinner in 1825) was this: "A public school like the old High School of Edinburgh is invaluable, and for what is it so? It is because men of the highest and lowest rank in society send their children to be educated together." One of his own fellow-pupils had been the son of a nobleman, while others came from the poorest homes in the Cowgate.

> There they were, sitting side by side, giving and taking places from each other, without the slightest impression on the part of my noble friends of any superiority on their part to the other boys, or any ideas of inferiority on the part of the other boys to them; and this is my reason for preferring the old High School of Edinburgh to other and what may be termed more patrician schools, however well regulated and conducted.[12]

If this was true of the High School, there was no less of a social mix at the University where Dugald was now to go, and where he formed some of his most lasting friendships. As he lived within the College grounds, attendance at the University was an even simpler operation in practical terms than walking down to the High School. Psychologically, too, it must have been a much easier transition than for many boys. His father was a professor, and all the leading figures in the University would have been well known to him by sight and often in person. The Principal was now William Robertson, minister of Old Greyfriars Church in Edinburgh and Moderator of the General Assembly of the Church of Scotland, who had achieved fame throughout Britain a few years previously with his *History of Scotland*.[13] But Principal Robertson can have been no remote figure of authority to Dugald: the Principal's house, which the Robertsons had occupied since Dugald was eight, was nextdoor to his own,[14] and for three years the Principal's eldest son Willie, who was later to become a judge on the Scottish bench and was almost exactly the same age as Dugald, was his fellow-pupil at the High School.

In some respects he must have been a privileged student. In one of his books he was later to refer to a visit to Edinburgh in 1768 (when Dugald was fourteen) by James Ferguson, "author of the justly popular works on Astronomy and Mechanics". He adds: "I had not only an opportunity of attending his public lectures, but of frequently enjoying in private the pleasure of his very interesting conversation."[15] Such opportunities to meet interesting and distinguished visitors may well have arisen not infrequently for a professor's son who lived within the College.

Nevertheless, when Dugald Stewart enrolled in the arts faculty at the beginning of November 1765 he was not quite twelve years old. To embark on higher education at the age of eleven now appears extraordinary, and it was very unusual even then. The normal starting age at the Scottish universities was thirteen or fourteen, which seems youthful enough, though youngsters in their early teens were not unknown at Oxford at this period. However, the age of the student body must have had some bearing on the level of the education provided.

In principle the system was remarkably free.[16] Students wore no kind of uniform, and lived where they pleased (or could afford). They could attend any classes they wished, and in any sequence. There were no examinations, and in most cases there was no set work; teaching was largely by means of a course of lectures, which ran from early November, with only the shortest of breaks at Christmas and Easter, until the second half of April. Like much else in Scotland, this programme was related to the requirements of the agricultural year, as is illustrated by a story passed on many years later by Stewart's wife. Dugald had commented on the late arrival, in December, of a fellow-student who replied, "Ay, I had to stay till the stacks were thacked, and I maun be hame afore the oat-seed; but I'll hae gotten a good lock logic or than [before then]."[17]

A student who wished to graduate was obliged to attend certain classes prescribed by university statutes, but graduation in the arts faculty carried no particular advantage, and was unusual. In practice, however, certain subjects were normally taken early in a student's career, with logic and the moral philosophy for which it was a preparation coming at the end. It may well be that some of the more advanced teaching passed over the heads of many of the students, and it was not uncommon for students to sit through the same course of lectures more than once. But the method by which professors were paid contained a safeguard against excessive tedium or ineffectiveness: in addition to a small basic salary they derived most of their income from class fees paid by each student who wished to receive a class ticket. This could lead to lectures becoming a kind of performance designed to appeal to immature minds, but with the best teachers it was a stimulus to intellectual distinction.

The course of study pursued by Dugald, no doubt with parental guidance, was a sensible one. He took only one class in each of his first three years. His first was 'humanity' under Professor George Steuart, which was little more than a continuation – remedial when required – of the Latin curriculum of the High Schools. In his second year he studied Greek under Professor Robert Hunter. Six months of this subject at the age of thirteen would scarcely have furnished him with the facility in Greek texts which he displayed in his books, and it may be supposed that his class learning was supplemented by his father. Professor Matthew Stewart was now at the height of his powers. In June 1764 he had been elected a Fellow of the Royal Society. During his six years at the University Dugald did not attend his father's classes in mathematics: it must have been agreed between them that the teaching in the subject which he received at home made this superfluous.

In his third year he took logic with Professor John Stevenson, who had occupied the chair since 1730 and had taught Principal Robertson himself. This was an elementary class designed to prepare students for more advanced studies in science and the arts; it met for three hours daily, the last of these being devoted to the history of philosophy.[18] Alexander Carlyle decribed Stevenson as "the most popular of all the Professors on account of his civility and even kindness to his students".[19] Dugald was particularly impressed by Stevenson's teaching, and attended his class again in his fourth year along with Professor James Russell's course in 'natural philosophy', which was a wide-ranging introduction to the physical sciences. Russell encouraged his students to rise above detail and grasp the general principles involved. It was probably through his teaching that Dugald was first introduced to the spirit and method of Francis Bacon, who was to be a major influence on his thinking throughout his life.

There is little direct evidence of his health during his years at school and university, except that he seems to have been able to proceed normally through both. In later life he spoke of having had a slight indisposition which confined him to his room when he was fourteen or fifteen. He was attended by Dr William Cullen, a professorial colleague of his father and one of the foremost doctors in Edinburgh at that time; he was to be seen each morning making his domiciliary visits in a sedan chair. He recommended that his young patient should engage in some light reading, and asked whether he was familiar with *Don Quixote*. When the answer was negative, Cullen turned round to Matthew Stewart and asked that the book should be obtained at once. In all his subsequent visits he examined Dugald on the progress he was making and discussed with him every incident and character, each of which he himself remembered clearly, entering fully into the pleasure Dugald was deriving from the satirical romance.[20] It was no doubt a form of relaxation particulary enjoyed against the normal background of earnest application. Many years later he referred to the book as "one of the happiest and most wonderful creations of human fancy".[21]

Four academic years was a fairly normal period of university study, but Dugald had taken his courses slowly, and was still only fifteen. He

At School and University (1761–1772)

continued as a student at the College for a further two years,[22] taking the same two subjects each time – rhetoric and belles-lettres under Professor Hugh Blair and moral philosophy under Professor Adam Ferguson. Blair's subject has no exact counterpart in the modern academic world. It covered such matters as taste and genius, the use of language, style in writing and speech, eloquence in public speaking and criticism of prose and verse. Blair himself was a prominent figure in the Edinburgh literary circle. Like Robertson he was also a leading churchman, being minister of the 'High Church', part of what is now known as St Giles Cathedral, where he was a popular preacher. This had not prevented him from having a close friendship with David Hume, which they maintained by avoiding the discussion of theology. He was described as an amiable man, full of harmless vanity and simplicity, and always ready to read the manuscripts which young authors brought to him for comment.

Adam Ferguson was also an interesting character. Like Robertson and Blair he had trained for the church, and as he was a highlander and a Gaelic speaker he was qualified to become, in 1745, deputy chaplain to the Black Watch Regiment. In that capacity he was present at the Battle of Fontenoy.[23] He abandoned the clerical profession some nine years later, and after various temporary employments was appointed in July 1759 to the chair of natural philosophy at Edinburgh. In the short space of time before the class met in the autumn he acquired a sufficient knowledge of physics to run the course. Five years later, in a kind of professorial reshuffle, he secured the job which he really wanted, that of professor of pneumatics and moral philosophy, 'pneumatics' then meaning mental philosophy.

He became a popular teacher whose lectures attracted a wide audience. Three years before Dugald first attended them Ferguson published an *Essay on the History of Civil Society*, in which his approach displayed the breadth of his interests and warrants a claim for regarding him as one of the earliest sociologists. His lectures covered what would now be termed anthropology and psychology as well as ancient history, theology, ethics, jurisprudence and politics. They seem to have struck his hearers as eloquent and ennobling, rather in the manner of an ancient Roman. The years he had spent following the fortunes of war gave a severe cast to his mind, and he portrayed the moral life as a kind of battlefield in which the stakes were higher than mere military glory.[24]

Writing many years later about his experience as a student at the University, Stewart cited Ferguson, Russell and Stevenson as the teachers for whom he felt special respect and gratitude,[25] while it seems to have been Stevenson and Ferguson who detected an aptitude for philosophical reflection in Dugald.[26] All three of the Edinburgh professors were quick to appreciate the significance of the work of a colleague who had just succeeded Adam Smith as professor of moral philosophy at Glasgow University. This was Thomas Reid, who in 1764 had published his *Inquiry into the Human Mind*. Reid's book was strongly recommended to Edinburgh students; even Stevenson, at the age of seventy, was prepared to recast what he had been teaching for forty years.[27] To Dugald, Ferguson went further, and urged him to go to Glasgow and hear Reid's teaching at first hand.[28]

At the age of seventeen, Dugald must now have been wondering what to do with his life. At one time he had thought of seeking employment as an engineer with the East India Company. Now his mind had turned towards the Anglican Church,[29] which he may have seen as a means of pursuing a life of quiet scholarship. Thus the idea of going to Glasgow had a double attraction for him, since Glasgow University, through the Snell Foundation, afforded a means of studying at Oxford[30] – a route which had been followed by Adam Smith. It was in October of 1771, the year in which he completed his studies at Edinburgh, that his mother died. The next month found Dugald in Glasgow.

He was only to spend one academic session there, but it was a notable period in his life for two reasons. One was that he formed some of the closest friendships of his life. He shared lodgings with Archibald Alison, the son of a Lord Provost of Edinburgh. Archy was just beginning a university course, and was more than three years younger than Dugald; but till the end of his life he regarded Dugald as his dearest friend.[31] Dugald also got to know one of the many young Ulstermen who came to the Scottish universities at this period. William Drennan,[32] only six months younger than Dugald, was the son of a Presbyterian minister in Belfast who had been a close friend of Francis Hutcheson. He was completing his arts degree at Glasgow and was about to proceed to Edinburgh to study medicine. Both Alison and Drennan were to become well known in later life. But not least in personal significance Dugald became friendly with Dugald Bannatyne,[33] the son of a Glasgow merchant; it seems very likely that it was at this time that he met his friend's younger sister Helen, whom he was later to marry.

The other notable aspect of Dugald's sojourn in Glasgow was his initiation into the academic life of its university. John Millar, professor of civil law, had published *The Origin and Distinction of Ranks* in the year of Dugald's arrival, and this must have widened his intellectual horizons. Still more importantly, he was able not only to attend the lectures of Professor Reid but to form a friendship with him which lasted until Reid's death. Thomas Reid, now in his early fifties, was a small but athletically built man. Another son of the manse, he had studied philosophy and divinity at Marischal College, Aberdeen, and after a spell as librarian there he was presented by King's College to the living of New Machar, twelve miles away. This form of patronage, whereby a minister was foisted upon a parish without any local say, was much resented, and Reid encountered hostility from his parishioners: indeed, according to one account, he was ducked in a pond – a form of initiation to the science of morals comparable with Ferguson's experience on the battlefield. But he gradually overcame the local prejudice, and he remained at New Machar for fourteen years until he obtained an academic appointment at King's College, Aberdeen in 1751. Here he founded a philosophical society nicknamed the Wise Club, and in 1764 he was elected to the professorship at Glasgow vacated by Adam Smith's resignation.

He lectured five days a week for two or sometimes three hours, his subject matter covering natural theology, ethics and political science, to which he added a course on rhetoric. In later life Stewart wrote about these lectures "from personal knowledge", and he did not make Reid sound like the most enthralling of teachers.

> In his elocution and mode of instruction, there was nothing peculiarly attractive. He seldom, if ever, indulged himself in the warmth of extempore discourse; nor was his manner of reading calculated to increase the effect of what he had committed to writing. Such, however, was the simplicity and perspicuity of his style, such the gravity and authority of his character, and such the general interest of his young hearers in the doctrines which he taught, that by the numerous audiences to which his instructions were addressed, he was heard uniformly with the most silent and respectful attention.[34]

Certainly Dugald himself must have been an attentive listener, for though not uncritical of Reid's philosophy he became an admirer and disciple.

Being away from parental supervision for the first time in his life, he may also have engaged in a little more social activity than hitherto. He joined a literary society, the members of which included his old classmate from the High School, John Sinclair;[35] and he read before it a paper on *Dreaming*.[36] Twenty years later he incorporated this almost without alteration in his first major publication.[37] The paper does not, of course, anticipate Freud. The question addressed is the state of the mind in sleep: which faculties continue to operate and which are suspended. Stewart's answer was that in sleep those operations of the mind are suspended which depend on our will – not that the actual power of volition is suspended, but that the will loses its power over the faculties of mind and body which are subject to it when we are awake. Thus, for example, we may dream that in a frightening situation we are trying to escape, but something seems to prevent us; the body cannot obey the will. In the same way the will cannot direct our thoughts as it does when we are awake – cannot discriminate, as it does in consciousness, among the succession of ideas which rush through our minds. Our dreams are influenced by bodily sensations and our temporary mood, but also by our prevailing habits of thought – a mathematician may dream of an interesting problem, and may even fancy that he is solving it successfully, but in sleep the mind cannot distinguish ideas from real existence.

From a biographical point of view the paper shows remarkable assurance and maturity in a young man of eighteen. It also shows how early in Stewart's intellectual career he was preoccupied with questions of the philosophy of the mind, tending to confirm his own observation that he could not recollect the date of his earliest speculation on the "incomprehensible communication between Mind and Matter".[38] There is even evidence of an early concern with methodology, for the paper ends with the claim that in no respect has it "transgressed those rules of philosophizing, which, since the time of Newton, are commonly appealed to as tests of sound investigation". When Lord Chief Commissioner Willy Adam presided over the meeting described in chapter 1 to consider a memorial to Stewart's life, he said he believed he was the only man alive who had been there when Dugald presented his paper in Glasgow fifty-six years before; the vivid impression which it made on him then remained with him still.[39]

Where might Dugald Stewart have gone from here? He might have returned for another year to Glasgow to familiarize himself further with the thinking of Thomas Reid. He might have done as his friend Archy Alison was to do, obtained an exhibition to Balliol and taken orders in the Church of England. But as so often happens in life, it was an unforeseen development which now determined his career.

CHAPTER FOUR

The Young Stewart, Mathematician
1772–1780

"To this season he always referred as the most laborious of his life, and such was the exhaustion of the body from the intense and continued stretch of the mind, that on his departure for London, at the close of the academic session, it was necessary to lift him into the carriage." Matthew Stewart

When Dugald Stewart left Glasgow in the early summer of 1772 – probably to join his father at Catrine in the first instance – the situation which confronted him was that Matthew Stewart's health was deteriorating. It is not known what form his illness took, but it is possible to suggest two psychological factors that might have made him physically vulnerable. The death of his wife in the previous autumn, closely followed by his son's departure for Glasgow, may have left him grieving. Also, he had suffered something of a setback in his professional life. In 1763 he had published a theorem entitled *The Distance of the Sun from the Earth determined by the Theory of Gravity*. His reasoning made this distance to be 119 million miles. A pamphlet issued in 1769 had pointed out the nature and magnitude of his error, and in 1771 another mathematician had published an independent refutation of his conclusions. Though Stewart's calculations were elegant and ingenious, he followed Maclaurin in preferring geometrical methods, and his essential mistake was in supposing that so complex a subject could be treated in this way. Reacting as his son might have done,

The Young Stewart, Mathematician (1772-1780)

he declined to enter into controversy on the subject, saying that if his investigation was right it could never be contradicted, and if it was wrong it ought not to be defended.[1] Nevertheless, his confidence may have been shaken by this *contretemps,* and in fact he never published again.

As November approached it became clear to Matthew Stewart that he could not undertake another year's teaching, and he decided that the best course of action was to delegate his academic responsibilities to his son. It may be that Matthew, who was still only fifty-five, did not at first expect his withdrawal to be permanent; but the step which he took was a rather extraordinary one, considering that Dugald was not yet nineteen. However, it was normal practice that when a professor was unable to teach he found his own substitute, and the Town Council as 'Patrons' of the University were not consulted. They knew that Matthew Stewart was a man of European eminence,[2] and as an early historian of the University suggested,[3] this may have led them to accept his judgment. At any rate, at the beginning of the session 1772-3 Dugald Stewart took over the full range of duties which belonged to the chair of mathematics. He soon became *de facto* professor. His father retired to the country home at Catrine, and although he lived on for more than twelve years, amusing himself for as long as he was able with geometric research, he never lectured again in the University.[4] In the meantime his confidence in his son's abilities was fully justified. Though probably the youngest person who ever discharged the duties of a professor, at least at Edinburgh, Dugald's students stood in some awe of his abilities, and treated him respectfully.[5] When asked how it was that he, who had not made a special study of mathematics, had succeeded in teaching the subject better than his father, he replied, "If it be so, I can only account for it by the fact that during the whole session I have never been more than three days ahead of my pupils."[6] He continued to live in the house that had been leased to his father in the College.

At approximately the same time as he took up his mathematical duties another new member of staff joined the University. This was Andrew Dalzel, appointed professor of Greek. He had studied arts and divinity at Edinburgh, though he was never licensed as a minister. He acted as tutor in the Lauderdale family, and most recently had been assisting Dr Adam of the High School in preparating a Latin grammar book. The study of Greek was at a low ebb in the University, and Dalzel proceeded to develop his subject by combining scholarship with cultivation of a taste for Greek literature. Cockburn described him as "mild, affectionate, simple, an absolute enthusiast about learning" who spoke in "a slow, soft, formal voice" – "a great favourite with all boys, and with all good men".[7] Though

The Young Stewart, Mathematician (1772–1780)

he was eleven years older than Stewart, the two newcomers to the College staff became life-long friends.

Another outlet for Stewart's social inclinations was membership of the Speculative Society. This was a private debating club, founded by six students a few years previously, which met weekly during College terms. It enjoyed a privileged position, for the Town Council had granted it a site within the College on which to build its own rooms.[8] In some ways, by providing a forum for debate and discussion, it served as a substitute for aspects of higher education which would now be considered intrinsic but which the formal system of instruction through lectures did not offer. Meetings took the form of general discussion of any literary topic followed by a debate on a subject previously agreed, which was opened by one of the members in rotation.[9] Stewart read his Glasgow paper on *Dreaming* to the Speculative Society, and titles of other papers which he presented to the Spec. during his first three years on the University staff were *The Causes and Effects of Scepticism; Taste;* and *The Conduct of Literary Institutions with a view to Philosophical Improvement.*[10] Clearly these were not contributions from someone whose sole interest was in mathematics.

Stewart's success as a teacher soon became established. According to his own son, in spite of "Dr Matthew Stewart's well merited celebrity, the number of students considerably increased under his son".[11] Since it was clear that Matthew would never be able to resume his professorial duties he might have formalized his retirement sooner, but there were legal obstacles to anyone being appointed as a professor before attaining the age of twenty-one.[12] This Dugald Stewart did on 22 November 1774. In June of the following year a procedure was followed whereby Matthew resigned his office and on the same day he and Dugald were unanimously elected joint professors of mathematics. The formula was a device not uncommonly adopted at a time before retirement pensions were available. It meant that the senior partner in the arrangement continued to receive the professorial salary (which was small, even in the values of the time, but provided a basic subsistence), while the person actually carrying out the duties received the class fees paid by students. Dugald, the Council Minute declared, had given the strongest proof of his ability to discharge the duties of the office "by teaching the class for some time past to the utmost satisfaction of the Professors of the University and students, and likeways of his loyalty and affection to his Majesty's Person and Government".[13] (It was still only thirty years since Prince Charles Edward's Jacobite rising.) A kind of academic succession in mathematics thus led to Stewart from the great Sir Isaac Newton: Newton had recom-

The Young Stewart, Mathematician (1772–1780)

mended Maclaurin, who encouraged Matthew Stewart, who brought in his son.

And so in 1775, in his twenty-second year, Dugald Stewart became a professor of the University of Edinburgh and a member of its Senatus Academicus, responsible for all the internal affairs of the College. A week after his election he was made a burgess of the City along with Andrew Dalzel and John Hill, professor of humanity, whose appointment was also fairly recent.[14] He spent the rest of the summer in the west – writing in mid-September from Catrine to Willie Robertson, who had become an advocate in January:

> My life since I saw you has been a continued scene of Dissipation. About a fortnight after I left Edinburgh I set out on a jaunt to Bute where I spent near a month, and since my return home I have been almost constantly employed in visiting my friends in Ayrshire. Any short intervals of study that I have had have been entirely devoted to Mathematicks.[15]

While in Bute he thought he had found good evidence for the existence of the Kraken, supported by affidavits from seamen, and he had also come upon a Viking wall on a small island at the north end of Bute which interested him. The stones appeared to have been welded together by great heat, producing a form of vitrification: he was going to bring a sample back to Edinburgh with him. He had been appointed to give the first paper of the winter season to the Speculative Society, and asked his friend's advice about a suitable subject. He added that he longed for College news.

Although in this letter he referred to the country house at Catrine as 'home', and he must have felt it to be so, his entitlement to the house in Edinburgh which went with the mathematics chair was now confirmed. But the repairs which his father had effected in 1752 had evidently not been sufficient to put the old building to rights, and tenancy may have been a mixed blessing. Less than a year after his appointment Stewart petitioned the Council that "the house which he inhabits has fallen into such disrepair as to be unfitt for accomodation of a family". A committee set up by the Council to investigate "found the dwelling house in very bad repair". The Council agreed that he should possess it rent free for three years from the following Whitsunday "on his satisfying the Council at the end of the said three years that he has expended to the amount of the whole rent upon repairing the house".[16]

Teaching accommodation also presented problems in the very inadequate and unsuitable buildings of the College. A report prepared by the Senatus some forty years later to guide the architects for a new college indicates what some of these problems were – noise from streets and passages, poor lighting, difficulties for students in seeing and hearing, and not least heating:

> A few persons near the fire have a great deal too much of it, while the greater part of the class have no benefit from it. This inconvenience is particularly felt by the Professor, who, in some instances, is roasted by a large fire close at his back or side; and, in others, is absolutely starved with cold.[17]

For obvious reasons it was regarded as necessary that at least an hour should elapse between classes in the same room, and this added to timetabling difficulties. However, Stewart's friendship with Andrew Dalzel seems to have stood him in good stead. In June 1777 the two professors made a joint application, supported by a plan of proposed alterations, to have the Greek classroom fitted up to allow it to be used for mathematics also. The Council agreed to carry out the work at a cost not exceeding £20.[18]

Though thrust at such an early age into senior responsibilities, Stewart was not without friends of his own age. The son of Principal Robertson was clearly one. Another was his Irish companion from Glasgow, William Drennan, who had come to Edinburgh in 1773 to begin a course in medicine. For much of his life Drennan exchanged frequent letters with his older married sister in Belfast, Martha McTier, and those written from the beginning of 1776 have survived.[19] In their references to Dugald Stewart they show Martha anxious that Will should maintain his friendship with the professor, whom she perhaps regarded as a steadying influence. On 30 November 1777 Drennan replied to one of her enquiries:

> I indeed forgot to mention Stewart particularly in my last. He has showed me the most unfriendly civility since I came to Edinburgh – I have dined and breakfasted with him repeatedly, and I admire him more than ever. He has only committed a Scotticism in the course of our correspondence with each other; and I pass it over, for it was a bull [a self-contradicting proposition] on my side to suppose that a person could be all head and all heart at the same time. If you were an anatomist you would discover that the human heart supplies *itself* with blood, before it parts with a single drop for the rest of the body – a striking picture of what goes on in the mind of man.[20]

This is interesting as one of the few critical observations recorded about Stewart, and even that is qualified by the evidence which it contains of persistent hospitality and by the fact that friendship between the two men continued for many years – indeed less than a fortnight after writing this letter Will was passing on to Matty an amusing anecdote which Stewart had just told him[21] – and they were both members of the Speculative

The Young Stewart, Mathematician (1772–1780)

Society. Perhaps Drennan's somewhat cryptic observation reflected as much as anything a clash of Scottish and Irish cultural expectations – what in Edinburgh would seem only decent reserve looking to Irish eyes like a lack of warmth and spontaneity.

By this time a major issue of national policy was agitating the nation – Britain's relations with its American colonies. During the previous year leaders of the colonists had signed the Declaration of Independence (a document which owed a good deal to the thinking of the Scottish Enlightenment,[22]) and there were many, such as Irish Presbyterians like Drennan, who had considerable sympathy with their position. After hostilities commenced, and General Burgoyne surrendered at Saratoga, Will wrote, a little inelegantly, to his sister: "I am persuaded that the event of the war will turn on this great event, and it is probable that future historians will date the fall of the British Empire, from the 16th of October 77."[23] In January 1778 he wrote further on the subject:

> Nothing is going on here at present but raising regiments, to be devoted to destruction in America. Every order of men from the highest to the lowest are emptying their pockets (and what more could be asked from Scotchmen?) in the support of the war . . . The greatest part of the professors have given ten guineas, Stewart but two . . .[24]

Drennan did not say whether Stewart's lack of generosity was due to a corresponding lack of enthusiasm for the cause of colonial subjugation, but since Drennan's information presumably came from Stewart himself, and especially in view of the strong indication of Stewart's views recounted below, it seems clear that he shared his friend's scruples and deliberately made only a token contribution to the war funds. After France signed a treaty of alliance with the colonists in the following month, and Spain came into the war in 1779, it became more difficult to express doubts about the wisdom of British policy. In September 1778 alarm was occasioned in Edinburgh when a small squadron of ships commanded by John Paul Jones appeared in the Firth of Forth and threatened Leith. Strong west winds soon forced them out to sea, but the incident must have added to the war psychology.

In the meantime Stewart continued to involve himself in University affairs. On 7 April 1778 he and Andrew Dalzel together with John Bruce, the professor of logic, and four others attended a graduation ceremony to take their degrees.[25] As has been said, this was then unusual in the arts faculty, but there must have been seen to be some advantage in professors being formally graduates. The experience brought home to Stewart and

Dalzel how shabby a place the common hall of the University was, so much so that, as the latter remarked, "it is mortifying for the University or Senatus Academicus to appear in it". Stewart suggested that in the following session his friend should give a course of lectures on poetry and charge two guineas a ticket to raise money for repairs. Dalzel would prepare these lectures during the summer. Then, Andrew wrote to a friend, "I propose to open the hall after it is repaired with a Latin harangue. Dugald and I see many advantages from all this."[26]

Stewart must also have become a member of the Philosophical Society of Edinburgh, for in the early summer of 1778 he was among some active members who formed a sub-group to be known as the Newtonian Club. Other Newtonians were medical professors such as Dr James Gregory, and meetings of the Club were to be held immediately after those of the Philosophical Society. At its second meeting, on 18 June, the Newtonians, arguing that "a multiplicity of laws has a direct tendency to produce confusion instead of order", proclaimed that "as this club consists entirely of Philosophers, it would therefore be ridiculous to make any laws for its internal police". Sadly for those who cling to a belief in the wisdom of philosophers, there are no records of any later meetings of this high-minded organization.[27]

While at Catrine that summer Stewart found time to reply to a letter which he had received at the beginning of April from the eccentric judge and scholar Lord Monboddo,[28] whom Stewart had known well for many years.[29] Monboddo believed that everything in nature was either body or mind, and though only fragments of this letter survive he appears to have been arguing that consequently no true philosopher could believe in Newton's theory of gravitation among the celestial bodies. Stewart told him that he had had not had time to reply when the letter arrived because of "some private business which required the whole of my attention".[30] It may be that this related to a decision he had reached to add to the two classes in mathematics which he had been conducting at the University (one mainly on Euclidian geometry, and the other, more advanced, on algebra and trigonometry[31]) a third, to be concerned with optics and the now popular subject of astronomy.[32] This had been touched upon by Colin Maclaurin in the course of his general lectures on mathematics, as it was by Professor Matthew Stewart;[33] but Dugald appears to have been the first person at Edinburgh University to have devoted a specific course to the subject.

If preparation for this new class was the business which preoccupied him, it equipped him well to respond to Lord Monboddo's letter with a firm and lucid defence of Newton's position. Newton's account of plan-

The Young Stewart, Mathematician (1772–1780)

etary motions was, Stewart maintained, the only theory that could explain them. He added the neatly epigrammatic retort: "I have no objection to your Lordship's doctrine 'that every planet is under the guidance of a particular Mind'; provided you will allow that all the exertions of this Mind are in straight lines directed to the sun."[34] (Monboddo remained unconvinced, and told an English correspondent two years later that although Stewart was "a young man of excellent genius, and very happy in a clear distinct elocution, which makes him the best lecturer of our University", he was sadly deficient in Greek Philosophy, and thus a prey to mistaken notions about the power of gravitation on celestial bodies.)[35]

Although Stewart had thus already taken on a heavy teaching load for the ensuing academic year, he found when he returned to Edinburgh that the American Revolution was about to add to his burdens in an unexpected way. The British Government had decided to send commissioners, led by the Earl of Carlisle, to try to negotiate a settlement with the rebellious colonists, and Adam Ferguson was asked to accompany them. Ferguson had recently published proposals for bringing the conflict to an end; they involved conciliatory measures from Britain, but also demanded concessions from the colonists, and his approach had found favour with the Government. When the Commissioners arrived in Philadelphia at the beginning of June they found that their designated secretary was not available and they elected Ferguson to this position.

When he left for America in the spring of 1778 Ferguson expected to be back in time for the recommencement of classes in November, but very late in the day he sent word that it now appeared some part of the winter might elapse before he could return and resume his professorial duties. Joseph Black, the professor of chemistry, who acted as Ferguson's trustee in his absence, reported this to the Council and expressed the hope that some other person should be appointed to teach his class since his delay was "occasioned by causes which Mr Ferguson neither could foresee nor prevent".[36] According to John Veitch, who wrote a short life of Stewart in 1858 to acompany his collected works, Ferguson asked Stewart to be his temporary replacement,[37] and although Stewart had only just given notice of his proposed new class in astronomy, he agreed to do so, feeling perhaps that it was an opportunity which he could not afford to turn down. (It may be added that the rather inadequate diplomatic mission proved to be in vain, for George Washington refused Ferguson a passport with which to proceed to Congress with the British terms, and in due course the Commissioners came home empty-handed.)

The minute of the Council recording Stewart's appointment was dated 4 November.[38] His son later recorded:

The Young Stewart, Mathematician (1772–1780)

although the proposal was made to him and accepted on Thursday, he commenced the Course of Metaphysics the following Monday, and continued during the whole of the season to think out and arrange in his head in the morning, (while walking backwards and forwards in a small garden attached to his father's house in the College) the matter of the lecture of the day. The ideas with which he had thus stored his mind, he poured forth extempore in the course of the forenoon, with an eloquence and a felicity of illustration surpassing in energy and vivacity (as those who have heard him have remarked) the more logical and and better digested expositions of his philosophical views, which he used to deliver in his maturer years. The difficulty of speaking for an hour extempore every day on a new subject for five or six months is not small, but when superadded to the mental exertion of teaching also daily two classes of Mathematics, and of delivering for the first time a course of lectures on Astronomy, it may be justly considered as a very singular instance of intellectual vigour. To this season he always referred as the most laborious of his life, and such was the exhaustion of the body from the intense and continued stretch of the mind, that on his departure for London, at the close of the academic session, it was necessary to lift him into the carriage.[39]

According to a letter written by Andrew Dalzel in mid-February 1779, Stewart was in fact basing his moral philosophy lectures on Ferguson's own writings so that the transition should be as easy as possible for the students if Ferguson returned during the session, but this makes his achievement little less remarkable. Dalzel reported that "Dugald Stewart . . . is making a wonderful figure . . . The great fluency and distinctness with which he speaks, and the extent of his knowledge upon the different subjects of the course, are amazing . . . The students like him even better than Ferguson."[40] What we know of the University societies in which he was interested suggests that he was already thinking of moving away from mathematics if an occasion arose; and the success with which he performed his supply role may well have confirmed him in that ambition, as well as staking a sound claim when the chance did come.

It so happens, also, that one of the records of Stewart's lectures that have survived is a neat summary of his philosophy course in 1778–9 written up by an able student named Josiah Walker,[41] who had attended his mathematics classes in 1775 and 1777. According to Walker's notes, Stewart was bravely forthcoming with his own liberal views on a number of issues. He expressed doubt about the justification for capital punishment in the present state of society, and he concluded an analysis of slavery by asking with fine scorn, more than half a century before slavery was abolished in the British Empire, "Is it lawful that we should reduce such numbers of our fellow creatures to a state infinitely worse than that of the brutes because we must have sugar and tobacco?" Most remarkably, on the morning of Saturday, 3 April 1779, in the middle of the war with America, he declared in the course of a lecture on contracts:

> The right of the Sovereign to govern does not resemble the right of a master over a servant, which tends chiefly to the interest of the former. It rather resembles the right of a tutor to command his pupil, for the good of the latter. When we have a persuasion that the present state of government is inconsistent with the natural liberty of man, and that society would be better by being thrown into anarchy, it is not only lawful, but it is incumbent on us to resist the reigning power. Perhaps the rebellion of our American colonies is the only instance where people have taken arms merely on a speculative principle.

On the following Monday evening, having referred to the reign of James I, he added:

> It is our fate to live in an age when the Rights of Man are better known. To the allowance of resisting despotic kings we owe our freedom. One of our tyrannical monarchs was slain by his subjects; another on account of his stretch of power was deprived of his crown. It is the Revolution from which we may date the era of British liberty.

In February 1779 Stewart must have been disturbed, both personally and politically, by one of the more inglorious episodes in Edinburgh's history at this time – rioting (which anticipated the Gordon riots in London in the following year) in opposition to a Government bill for the removal of penalties from Scottish Catholics. At one point a Protestant mob made towards the home of Stewart's neighbour, Principal Robertson, because he had prevented the General Assembly of the Church of Scotland from protesting against the proposed legislation. Henry Dundas, the Lord Advocate, had to deploy troops to protect him. But ten days later the Government announced that the bill would be abandoned. The following year Robertson stepped down from the position of Moderator of the General Asssembly which he had held since 1763, though he continued to act as Principal of the University.

There are no records of what Stewart may have done during the visit to London for which he had to be helped into the carriage. He had written to Archy Alison: "I have now a good prospect of visiting London about the beginning of May, and perhaps of *going a little farther*. Don't mention this to a mortal."[42] This sounds rather mysterious, but perhaps he had in mind only a trip to Oxford to see Archy, who was then studying at Balliol.

It was probably at the close of this summer that he sent an apology to the Rev. Archibald MacLea, who had succeeded as minister in the Rev. Dugald Stewart's old church in Rothesay, for not getting to Bute that year. "I have protracted my stay in England so long," he wrote, "that I find myself under a necessity of spending the remainder of the Harvest at home, which I propose to do without paying a single visit."[43]

In 1780 it was events in Stewart's private life that were dominant. The first was clearly a sad one. Of all Stewart's contemporaries when he was a student the one who took most of the same classes in the same years as himself was a certain Matthew Stewart. It does not appear that Dugald and Matthew were related, but they became close friends, and Matthew was about to take orders in the Church of England when he died at the age of twenty-eight. A letter written by Dugald Stewart to Archibald Alison in April 1780 vividly reflects the emotions of a young man coming to terms with such a bereavement.

> My dear Archy,
> I would have written you sooner, but have not been able to summon up sufficient resolution. When I recollect the many happy days I have spent in company with you and Matthew Stewart, my mind is perfectly overpowered. You knew how I loved him, and how completely all my habits were formed to his. Never, I am persuaded, were two men more dependant on each other. I now feel myself solitary and helpless, and deprived of the friend who knew every secret of my heart, and directed me in every step of my life. Oh, Archy, I could not have believed that it was possible for me to have survived him, far less that I should have been able, within a few days after his death, to have engaged in my usual business. Indeed I am astonished at my want of sensibility, and often reproach myself when I feel, in company, a disposition to cheerfulness. But his death has left an impression on my mind, that I am persuaded will never leave it, and which has almost entirely destroyed my relish for all my former pursuits. I can fix my attention on nothing; and the only satisfaction I enjoy, is in lamenting over him with his mother and sisters. Pray write me soon, and believe me most affectionately yours, D.S.[44]

The second personal event of 1780 may be presumed to have been a happier one, for it was the marriage of his elder sister Janet on 2 June.[45] Her husband was the Rev. Thomas Miller, son of an Edinburgh bookseller and minister of Cumnock in Ayrshire. He was only a couple of weeks short of his fortieth birthday on the day of his marriage, and thus twelve years older than his bride. Cumnock is about four miles south-east of Catrine, and as Janet had probably gone to live with her father when he retired there this would readily explain how she came to know Thomas

The Young Stewart, Mathematician (1772–1780)

Miller. For Dugald Stewart the proximity of his married sister and the children who soon began to arrive must have provided an added attraction to his summer holidays in Catrine.

A third development, which came at the beginning of the new academic year in November, may conveniently be postponed to the next chapter.

CHAPTER FIVE

Boarders, Travels, Marriage and Change 1780–1785

"I am somewhat in low spirits at the prospect of winter, particularly at the thought of teaching Euclid for the thirteenth time." Dugald Stewart

We have it from Stewart's son that –

> In the year 1780 he began to receive some young noblemen and gentlemen into his house as pupils, under his immediate superintendence, among whom were to be numbered the late Lord Belhaven, the late Marquis of Lothian, Basil Lord Daer, the late Lord Powerscourt, Mr Muir Mackenzie of Delvin, and the late Mr Henry Glasford.[1]

There can be no certainty about the order in which these young men were received, or how many were in residence with Stewart at one time. We know that when he resumed the practice of having resident students at a later period in his life he would take only two or three simultaneously.[2] It is also possible to say that the order in which Stewart's son lists the second batch of resident students is chronological, so there might be a presumption that this is also the case with the group just named. But the evidence of the matriculation roll does not quite bear that out. Henry Glasford does not appear there at all. Of those who do, the earliest is Alexander Muir Mackenzie, who took classes between 1780 and 1784; Lord Ancram (courtesy title of the eldest son of the Marquess of Lothian) and Lord Daer were both enrolled for the sessions 1781–2 and 1782–3; Richard

Boarders, Travels, Marriage and Change (1780–1785)

Wingfield (the future Lord Powerscourt) took two classes in 1782–3; and William Hamilton (the future Lord Belhaven) may have been the last – in 1783–4 and possibly the year after that as well. For a reason which will shortly appear, Stewart's first period of taking resident students may have begun to phase out, if it did not end altogether, in 1783.

The way the system worked is reasonably clear. It was well established at Glasgow University when Stewart was himself a student there. The parents of these young men paid a substantial fee which covered their board and lodging plus general advice and supervision in their academic studies. Stewart would of course have had servants to housekeep and cook. The educational guidance might have been more or less direct. At least two of the students – Muir Mackenzie and Daer – attended Stewart's own maths class,[3] and supplememtary tuition would therefore have followed naturally. His help with other studies might have been less specific but perhaps no less useful. In a general way he would have provided a stimulating and educative environment, and support which might be compared with that of an elder brother rather than that of a father. His motivation was no doubt partly financial, as he was otherwise in receipt of only student fees from his maths classes; but all his life he had a genuine interest in education in a broad sense, and he clearly enjoyed the company of young men.

What do we know of those who lived with Stewart at this time? William Hamilton, later the 7th Lord Belhaven, was born on 13 January 1765, served in the army, and died at the age of forty-nine. The Powerscourts had their seat in County Wicklow in Ireland and their family name was Wingfield. Richard Wingfield, who became the 4th Viscount Powerscourt on the death of his father in 1788, was a little older than William Hamilton. He became a strong opponent of the union of Ireland with Great Britain, and was one of five Irish peers who voted against it. Here there was a historical parallel with William Hamilton, for the latter's rather distant forebear, John, the 2nd Baron Belhaven, had been a vigorous opponent of the union of England and Scotland in 1707. Richard's second son, John Wingfield, was Lord Byron's fag at Harrow, and he himself died at Powerscourt in 1809, aged forty-six. Alexander Muir became an advocate. He assumed the name of Mackenzie when he succeeded to the estates of his great-uncle, John Mackenzie of Delvine in Perthshire; a baronetcy was conferred on him in 1805. In December 1792 Stewart proposed him for membership of the Literary Class of the Royal Society of Edinburgh.[4]

Henry Glassford was an exception in this group of minor aristocrats. His father, John Glassford – described by the fictional Matt Bramble in

Boarders, Travels, Marriage and Change (1780–1785)

Smollett's *Humphry Clinker* as "one of the greatest merchants in Europe"[5] – was certainly one of the wealthiest of the Glasgow tobacco lords. He had made his money first in domestic business and then through trade with Maryland and Virginia. He used his fortune to build an impressive country mansion, Dougalstown in Dunbartonshire. He knew Adam Smith, and corresponded with him (a possible connection with Stewart). Henry Glassford inherited his father's estates when John died in 1783; some years later he became the sole owner of the Oil and Vitriol Works of Prestonpans, and in 1807 Member of Parliament for Dumbarton.[6] He was thus a child not of old money but of trade and the industrial revolution.

But the two members of Stewart's original group of resident students with whom he later maintained the closest relations were Lord Daer and Lord Ancram. Basil William Hamilton, Lord Daer, was the second and oldest surviving son of the 4th Earl of Selkirk. At the beginning of the 1781–2 session he was eighteen years old. He later made an issue of the political position of the eldest sons of Scots peers, who were at that period allowed neither to sit as MPs nor to vote in parliamentary elections. He spent a good deal of time in France, where he knew and sympathized with several of the leaders of the revolution. His radical views commended him to Robert Burns, as we shall see in chapter 7. Ancram was just a few months younger than Daer, and also eighteen when the academic year began in November 1781. As William Ker, he was heir to the 5th Marquess of Lothian, whom he did not succeeed until he was over fifty, so that he was known for most of his life as the Earl of Ancram. The Lothian family owned Newbattle Abbey near Dalkeith, and also (as they still do) Monteviot near Jedburgh in the Scottish borders.

In the early autumn of 1782 Will Drennan, now practising as a doctor in Belfast, came to Edinburgh with his sister Martha to consult Dr Cullen about her health. On one of their four days in the city they supped with Principal Robertson and his family. By chance Dugald Stewart, who at some point during this year was made an honorary burgess of Dumfries,[7] had come back from Ayrshire on business on the previous day, and he joined the party. "He is in good health and high reputation," Drennan reported to his brother-in-law, "is at present tutor to Lord Ancrum, eldest son of the Marquis of Lothian, a genteel young man for which tuition he gets £250 [nearly £20,000 in present values] and it was obtained by Dr Robertson's interest with the Marquis". Drennan took this as confirmation of what "the world says", that Stewart was going to be connected with Robertson's elder daughter, to whom in Drennan's observation he "paid his attentions chiefly" that evening. "Miss Robertson," he added,

Boarders, Travels, Marriage and Change (1780–1785)

"is a sensible handsome girl with at least £1,000 fortune, paints well (herself I mean) and will no doubt render Dugald the happiest of men."[8] But either Will Drennan misread the situation or the romance fell through. In due course Mary Robertson married Patrick Brydone, a pioneering student of electricity who had become famous for his book *A Tour through Sicily and Malta*[9] and who was some years older than either Stewart or herself. Their eldest daughter, Mary Brydone, married the 2nd Earl of Minto and became a close friend of the Stewarts in later life.

During the summer of 1783, which may have marked the end of Ancram's period as a student at Edinburgh University, he and Stewart set out together on an extended tour of the Low Countries and northern France. Such arrangements were not uncommon: the sons of well-to-do families would be sent off on a more or less grand tour in the company of an older man who was qualified to act as companion, supervisor and cultural guide. In this instance Stewart was now twenty-nine and Ancram nineteen. In Stewart's own circle, Adam Smith had gone to France and Switzerland with the young Duke of Buccleuch in the years 1764–6, Adam Ferguson had travelled on the continent with the Earl of Chesterfield in 1775–6, and Andrew Dalzel had accompanied Lord Maitland, the future Earl of Lauderdale, to Paris in 1774. Stewart may well have received some advice from Dalzel in preparation for his own excursion. He set off with Ancram towards the end of May, and first of all spent some days in London, where Stewart had been at least once before, in 1779. On this occasion the highlight of his stay in the capital seems to have been hearing the eloquence of the young William Pitt, which he did on two occasions and wrote about at length to his friend Willie Robertson. In every respect except originality he considered Pitt far superior to Charles James Fox.[10] Since it was by this route that they eventually returned, it is likely that they crossed the Channel from Dover to Calais; and they made their way (probably through Cambrai) to Douai. It was from here on 4 June, a few days after their arrival, that Stewart wrote to Robertson:

> I believe the cheapness of the living, the slender state of our finances and above all the civilities of Principal Grant [of the Scots College] will induce us to remain for several weeks. We have got very comfortable lodgings both for ourselves and servants at about 3 Guineas Sterling a month and dine every day at a Table d'Hote for 2 livres a head. Our company at the Table d'Hote has consisted hitherto chiefly of lawyers who have business before the Parliament of Flanders which meets here. They all talk a great deal, and altho' as yet I understand very little of their conversation, I feel myself every day sensibly improving in the language. My principal defect arises from not having been accustomed to hear the language spoken by natives . . .[11]

Boarders, Travels, Marriage and Change (1780–1785)

The main source of information about the remainder of the tour is Ancram, who, as was commonly done by young men in his situation, kept a journal to record where he had been and what he had seen.[12] The first of the three notebooks which he used for this purpose has been lost. The second begins on 1 July, "a monstrous hot day", by which point they had gone north as far as Lille. Their route from here is shown on the map on page 41. In Flanders they travelled for the most part in their own chaise, and Ancram sometimes recorded whether they changed horses on their way from one place to the next. At Asse, between Ghent and Brussels, they acquired a drunk postilion who nearly overturned them several times. They often started out early, which enabled them to make intermediate halts at places of interest along the way. It may also have been designed to take advantage of the cooler part of the day, for throughout July they experienced a heatwave: "insufferably hot weather", the diarist described it at one point. They took a break from their horse-drawn progress when they left their chaise at Utrecht and proceeded to Leiden and Delft by barge.

Everywhere they were assiduous in their sight-seeing, visiting numerous cathedrals, abbeys and churches. From Tournai they went to be shown the battlefield of Fontenoy, where Adam Ferguson had seen action. In Leiden they saw a woman publicly whipped – "though not with much severity," Ancram noted; "she cried however a good deal" – he thought it was for stealing. "It was expected that a person guilty of forgery was to have his hand struck off, this has been putt off." They looked at a great many paintings – many by Rubens, but also by Rembrandt, Van Dyck and others. They called upon various British residents and visitors, to some of whom they had letters of introduction. In what they termed North Holland the objects of their inspection became more varied – they looked at the Great Dyke; in Amsterdam they visited a prison, where they were shocked by the severity of the regime; and they went to see a sect of Moravians. Though they were struck by the civility with which they were met in Flanders, at one place in Holland they encountered "the most violent antipathy against the English", and passed themselves off as Americans. The quality of their lodgings varied considerably: at Tournai they slept in a room where the Emperor Joseph of Germany had once lodged, but in Somme they had "a disagreeable night passed among fleas".

They reached Paris on 8 August and remained there in lodgings until 8 October. Here there were more members of the British nobility and gentry to be called upon and dined with. On their first day in the city they met Lord Daer, and they saw him several times during their stay. It appears that Willie Robertson was also to come to Paris while Stewart and Ancram

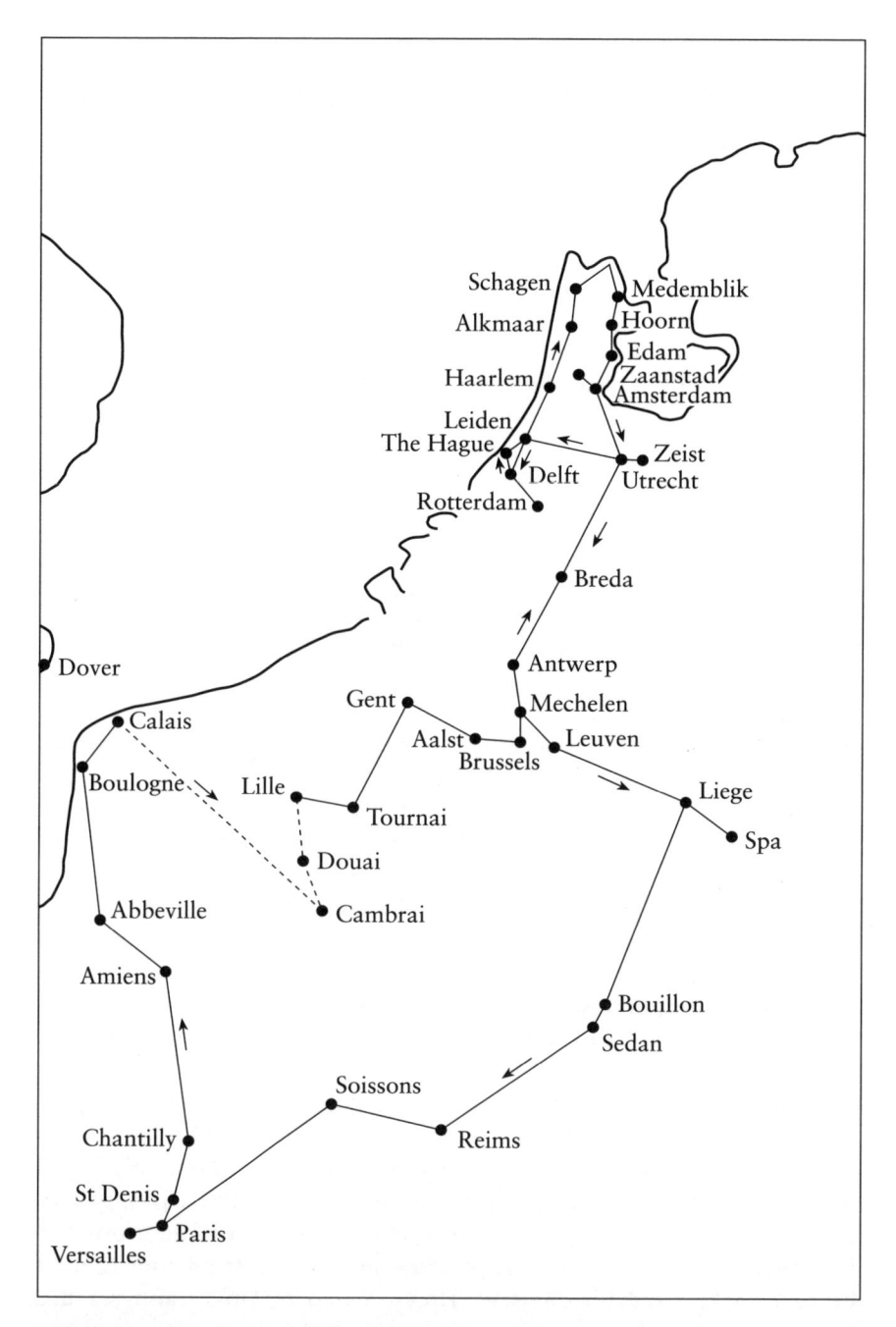

Route followed by Stewart and the Earl of Ancram during their tour of the Low Countries and northeastern France in the summer of 1783.

Boarders, Travels, Marriage and Change (1780–1785)

were there. On three occasions they were entertained by "Dr Franklin" at Passy. This was the seventy-seven year old Benjamin Franklin[13,] prominent Freemason, signatory of the Declaration of American Independence and future President of Pennsylvania. He had recently been appointed American minister in France, and took up residence in the Hotel de Valentinois in what was then a small suburban village on the route from Paris to Versailles. Once they dined in the company of Lafayette, and they may have taken advantage of an introduction sent on their behalf to the American minister (and future first Chief-Justice of the United States Supreme Court) John Jay,[14] who was engaged, along with Franklin, in negotiations with the British. (On 3 September the Treaty of Paris recognized the independence of the United States of America.) They visited St Germain, where, as Ancram noted, the Pretender had lived, and went twice to Versailles, where they saw the King and Queen and other members of the French royal family. They also visited a home for foundlings and a school for the dumb and were much impressed by the children's progress.

As they became settled in Paris Ancram's notes more frequently used the first person singular rather than the habitual "we" of the earlier part of the journal, and it is not clear whether all the excursions which he recorded included his tutor, who may have spent some time in the bookshops.[15] The young man seems to have been much taken with the theatre, and at times went to plays or the opera almost every evening. He also attended three experiments with balloons, including one constructed by M. Montgolfier which was launched in the presence of the King and Queen: unhappily it didn't stay in the air for more than two minutes. Once he went for a day's shooting with Lord Daer. But he did not neglect to see more paintings, in several private collections, and one may assume that Stewart was with him then. A visit was made to a church to witness the ceremony of a virgin of sixteen-and-a-half taking the veil ("a most melancholy sight", Ancram thought), and on the day before their departure they saw Notre Dame.

They left Paris on 8 October and made their way to Chantilly, where they spent a night and did some final sightseeing, and thence through Amiens and Boulogne to Calais, where they arrived at Dessein's Inn. It may have been from there that they had hired their carriage; M. Dessein had become rich and famous through being mentioned in Laurence Sterne's *Sentimental Journey*, for it was from him that its hero, Yorick, hired his chaise.[16] They crossed to Dover and reached London about half-past eight on the evening of Saturday, 12 October. Before he left Paris, Stewart had written to Archy Alison, now in his final year at Balliol College, Oxford, to propose a meeting at the Adelphi Hotel.[17]

Ancram was going on the next morning "to the Country", and it may be supposed that Stewart lost no time in getting back to Edinburgh. Not only was the new university year about to begin, but on 4 November he was married to Helen Bannatyne.[18] Veitch described Helen as "the object of an early and prolonged attachment",[19] so it does seem likely that their relationship dated back to Stewart's winter at Glasgow University in 1771–2. It is possible that Neil Bannatyne, the father of Dugald and Helen, who was already deceased at the time of his daughter's marriage, had some connection with Stewart's grandmother, the Rev. Dugald Stewart's second wife Janet Bannatyne, but of that there is no known confirmation. Helen was twenty-seven at the time of her marriage.

Around this time Stewart appears to have moved his place of residence in Edinburgh. The city Directory for 1784 to 1785 gives his address as Hay Street,[20] which was then a small passage linking Potter Row with the north side of Nicolson Square, so he was still only a few hundred yards from the College. The move was a temporary one, and while it may have been connected with his marriage it may also have been due to work being carried out on the Teviot Chambers houses. It seems reasonable to suppose that his personal supervision of young students terminated at about this time.

An arrival in Edinburgh while Stewart was on the continent was the Swiss-born future author and politician in France, Benjamin Constant de Rebecque. His name was later to be linked with that of Madame de Staël, and in later life, after the second restoration of the Bourbons, Constant became leader of the liberal opposition in the Chamber of Deputies. During his two years in Edinburgh he attended Andrew Dalzel's Greek class[21] and was an active member of the Speculative Society, thus moving in some of the same circles as Stewart.[22]

Another event which occurred during Stewart's absence was the founding of the Royal Society of Edinburgh. Principal Robertson was always jealous of the prestige of Edinburgh in relation to London, and he was instrumental in obtaining a Royal Charter for the existing Philosophical Society. This body had been established half a century before for the improvement of medical knowledge. Its scope had been enlarged on the initiative of Colin Maclaurin to include philosophy and literature, and David Hume had been its joint secretary in the 1750s. It had lapsed for a time, but revived in 1777 with Stewart as one of its members.[23] The new body, "for the advancement of learning and useful knowledge",[24] held its first general meeting towards the end of June 1783, and appointed John Robison, professor of natural philosophy, as its secretary. At its second meeting it elected a number of "foreign members", including Benjamin Franklin, whom Stewart had met in France. The Royal Society (RSE) soon divided into two groups, a Literary Class and a Physical Class – an arts section and a science section, as they might have been called in later times. Stewart joined both groups, and in March 1784 he read to the Literary Class papers on the idea of cause and effect and on the nature and object of natural philosophy, again displaying interests well beyond mathematics. He was active in proposing new members for both groups, often eminent people from outside Scotland such as Nevil Maskelyne, the Astronomer Royal. Members of the RSE contributed papers on a large array of topics reflecting their eager curiosity about every aspect of the world, past and present, that new thinking and investigation might illuminate. Stewart was for many years a regular attender at RSE meetings.[25]

In April 1784 he was involved in a flurry of activity concerned with a visit to Scotland by Edmund Burke. In the previous November the Irish Member of Parliament, who was then best known for his eloquent opposition to Government policy towards the American colonists and more recently for his campaign against abuses by the East India Company, had been elected Rector of Glasgow University, and he now came north for his official installation. He went first to Edinburgh to meet his old friend Adam Smith. Smith and Andrew Dalzel took Burke to the town house of Dalzel's former travelling companion Lord Maitland, heir to the Earl of Lauderdale and at that time a rising Whig politician. Three years previously Maitland had made his maiden speech in the House of Commons in support of the second reading of Burke's Bill for the Regulation of the Civil List Establishments. On Thursday, 8 April, the party was joined by Stewart, now clear of his teaching commitments at the College for the Easter weekend, and they went on to Hatton, the old Earl's country seat in Midlothian, four miles out from East Calder and on the way to Glasgow.[26] On the following day Stewart made a note of some of the conversation. Dalzel wrote to a friend, "We got a vast deal of political anecdote from him".[27] (A general election campaign was in progress.)

On a separate slip of paper Stewart amusedly added later, "Mr Dalzel's great anxiety was to prevent an old horse shoe that lay on the Library table being noticed. Lord L. had found it himself, and attached much value to it as infallibly bringing good luck."[28] This might stand as a defining Enlightenment anecdote. During the previous year Dalzel had been one of the founder members the Royal Society of Edinburgh, and had become Joint Secretary of the Literary Class. Here he was, at the centre of affairs in progressive Edinburgh, terrified that this eminent visitor to Scotland should observe something so blatantly *unreasonable*.

On the following day, Good Friday, the party proceeded to Glasgow, and had supper with Professor John Millar. Stewart would almost certainly have known Millar in Glasgow, and Maitland was reputed to be his favourite pupil, while Millar himself had been a student of Adam Smith's. He was an outspoken advocate of liberal causes such as American independence and the abolition of the slave trade.[29] On the morning of Saturday, 10 April, James Boswell, another former student of Adam Smith's, rode in from Kingswells and presented himself at the Saracen's Head where Edmund Burke was staying. Burke invited him to join his group for breakfast, which of course Boswell did, in spite of finding himself in such Whiggish company. He recorded in his journal that in addition to Burke and Lord Maitland, "Lord Daer, Professor Dalzel, Professor Dugald Stewart, Professor Millar, and Dr Adam Smith were all of the party. I was a little flustered from the consciousness of my being in the midst of opposition. But I conducted myself very well."[30]

Burke had to be at Glasgow University by ten. As part of the installation ceremony he gave an address which he tactfully prefaced by declaring that he had never before addressed so learned a body; and there was a service in the College chapel. On the Sunday, Stewart and Dalzel returned to Edinburgh to be ready for their classes on the following day, while Smith and Maitland took Burke on a short tour to see Loch Lomond and the Carron Ironworks, that wonder of newly industrializing Scotland, before returning to Edinburgh for a farewell dinner at Smith's home in Panmure House off the Canongate.

That summer at Catrine Stewart reflected that he had now been carrying out the duties of the chair of mathematics for twelve years. He seems to have done the job competently, but his heart was never wholly in it. Although he was later to become a prolific writer, he had published nothing of a mathematical nature, nor did he read any papers on the subject to the Royal Society. His interest in mathematics, it was suggested by Veitch, was "more in a philosophical point of view, as filling a place in the scheme of human knowledge, than from any strong predilection for them as an independent object of study".[31] Writing to Archy Alison in the autumn, he observed with obvious feeling, "I am somewhat in low spirits at the prospect of winter, particularly at the thought of teaching Euclid for the *thirteenth* time".[32] To Willie Robertson at around the same date he described himself as heartily sick of his present profession; "the Moral

Phil. is as favourite an object as ever."[33] How long his mind had been fixed in that direction is impossible to say, but probably at least since the time when he had substituted for Ferguson.

The possibility of a new professor of moral philosophy being required did not seem remote, for Adam Ferguson was in poor health, and Stewart begged of Robertson from Ayrshire: "If a vacancy should take place I would have you to start me without delay, and take such steps as appear to yourself to be most prudent without waiting a moment to consult me". Robertson should seek the advice of his father, the Principal. "Consult with whom you please." And he suggested a few who might be approached. "As to the mathematical class I should certainly wish it to be disposed in such a way that my father might continue to draw the salary during his life." From a conversation which Ferguson had broached with him in the spring he was satisfied that Ferguson "wished me to succeed him rather than anyone else"; if necessary Stewart would undertake the duties of both chairs during the ensuing winter. But he recognized that there would be other candidates, of whom Professor Bruce would certainly, he thought, be one. If Bruce were successful, Stewart was so unsettled that he declared he would go for the chair of logic which Bruce would vacate.[34]

However, the opportunity for change did not arise quite so quickly as then seemed possible; Adam Ferguson soldiered on for another year. But on 23 January 1785 a death did occur – that of Professor Matthew Stewart, aged sixty-seven. He may have lived just long enough to see the birth of his grandson, for it was towards the end of 1784 or early in 1785 that Helen Stewart gave birth to the son who was to be her only child. In the Scottish tradition, the little boy became another Matthew.

His father's death meant an increase in Stewart's income, for he now received the salary attached to the maths chair as well as the student fees; but this did not diminish his desire to switch to philosophy, and at last the chance came. Adam Ferguson was sixty-two, and although he lived for another thirty years, his health was at this point so poor that he was obliged to give up teaching. Exactly how the solution was engineered is not clear, but on 16 May 1785 Ferguson and Stewart both resigned their offices, and two days later the Town Council appointed Dugald Stewart to be professor of moral philosophy and Dr Adam Ferguson and the Rev. John Playfair to be joint professors of mathematics.[35] It may be relevant to note that the Lord Provost who had been elected in September 1784 was Sir James Hunter Blair, the son of an Ayr merchant, who was much interested in the improvement of Edinburgh.

For an individual to be both a mathematician and a philosopher is not so unusual as it might seem; indeed some of the greatest philosophers have also been mathematicians.[36] Adam Smith for one considered that the changes were beneficial. "I . . . have no hesitation to recommend the University of Edinburgh in preference to any other," he had told a Lincolnshire rector in February. "It is at present better provided in Professors than any other Society of the kind that I ever knew; and it is likely soon to be still better provided than at present."[37]

On the maths side the arrangement was similar to that which had applied to Matthew Stewart and his son: Ferguson was to enjoy the salary of the post as a form of pension with no duties attached, while the new member of academic staff would do the teaching and be entitled to the student fees. The sociable and outstandingly able John Playfair was then thirty-seven. In 1783 he had resigned his living in order to act as tutor to two brothers named Ferguson of Raith, one of whom was to become a radical MP for Kirkcaldy. Some years before that he had applied for the chair of natural philosophy at St Andrews; he was unsuccessful, but he had now become secretary of the Physical Class of the RSE. Along with Andrew Dalzel he was to become Stewart's closest friend and ally in the University of Edinburgh.

On the philosophy side, Dugald Stewart, aged thirty-one, now entered on his true vocation. The American historian Professor Arthur Herman has recently written: "For the next quarter-century he would influence the mind of Europe and the English-speaking world to a degree no Scotsman ever equalled, before or since."[38]

CHAPTER SIX

The Young Stewart, Philosopher 1785–1787

"I may truly say that it is not easy to conceive a university where industry was more general, where reading was more fashionable, where indolence and ignorance were more disreputable. Every mind was in a state of fermentation." Sir James Mackintosh

The chair of moral philosophy which Stewart occupied from 1785 was one of the most important in the University, for the whole arts curriculum was concerned to inculcate a general philosophical approach.[1] Moral philosophy, according to John Gibson Lockhart, was "the favourite science of this country";[2] it was essential for those who intended to graduate (albeit a small minority, as has been said) or to enter the church.[3] Stewart always permitted divinity students to attend his lectures without paying a class fee if their parish minister certified that payment would be difficult.[4]

The principal method of teaching was the formal daily lecture, though to start with Stewart sometimes also set essay topics for those students who wished to test their thinking in this way. Most students, as we have seen, entered the University at fourteen or fifteen, but they tended to take philosophy towards the end of their studies, so that by that time they might have been three or four years older. Usually, too, they had already taken the class in logic, which provided, from a different point of view,

The Young Stewart, Philosopher (1785–1787)

an introduction to the theory of knowledge. Thus the presentation of philosophy needed to make relatively few concessions to the youth or inexperience of the students.[5] Nor does it seem likely that, like his father, Stewart had any problems with what we might now call 'discipline'. Many of his students testified to his air of innate authority, and the barrister and politician Sir James Mackintosh, who began to study medicine at the College in 1784, wrote in later life: "I may truly say that it is not easy to conceive a university where industry was more general, where reading was more fashionable, where indolence and ignorance were more disreputable. Every mind was in a state of fermentation."[6]

In the first year in which Stewart occupied the chair there were 102 students, and the average number thereafter was 138, with a peak of 196 in 1807–8.[7] His successor but one gave this account of those who attended his class:

> The Moral Philosophy class is composed of several very different orders of students . . . perhaps two-thirds of my students are students in Divinity, or call themselves students in Divinity . . . Of the remaining third part of the Moral Philosophy class, some are gentlemen who have finished their education, and many who attend this or that class as it may suit their taste or convenience; some are officers in the army or navy, others men of fortune, or strangers who are remaining a few months in Edinburgh . . . Some gentlemen likewise attend my class who are apprentices in writers' [solicitors'] chambers. They are generally among the best of my students, both in regard to regularity and talent; but at the commencement of the session they frequently tell me that they cannot count upon daily attendance, for that their time is not their own . . . There are not many instances of their attending my class two years. That happens almost always in the case of my ablest students, from a desire to master some difficulties that have occurred to them in the previous session.[8]

This was in 1826, some years after Stewart had retired but while he was still alive; there is no reason to think that the situation had changed greatly since he was conducting the class. It was to this varied audience that he had to learn to address himself. He began from the course plan of Adam Ferguson,[9] which he had used as his starting-point in 1778–9, and gradually adapted it to his own ideas until, after eight years, he was sufficiently confident to publish his own textbook as a guide for his students.[10] But in the meantime much had happened in his private life.

The Edinburgh Directories for the years 1786 to 1790[11] give his address as being again the College. Many years later, when he submitted his effective resignation from the moral philosophy chair, the Town Council noted that the house enjoyed by him, "which belongs to the Chair of Mathematics", should revert to the maths professor.[12] It would seem from this that though his father's old house was not for most of the time the main residence for Stewart and his family, it remained his to use when he wished to do so, and it was presumably there that he did live with his wife and baby son when he first became professor of moral philosophy. As we shall see, he later referred to living at Drumsheugh during the winter of 1788–9,[13] so by then the house at the College may have served only as a *pied-à-terre*.

At this time, too, his residence in Edinburgh was still broken by his summers at Catrine. It was from there that he wrote in September 1785 to Ancram's elderly relative, Lady Jane Home, with an ominous report about his young wife: "Mrs Stewart is no better since we left Edinburgh. She is indeed somewhat stronger, but her cough and spitting are worse than ever."[14] This sounds very much like tuberculosis.

In the autumn of 1785 he also wrote from Catrine to his Ayrshire neighbour, James Boswell. Although Boswell makes little reference to Stewart in his voluminous writings, it seems likely that they knew each other fairly well. Boswell was thirteen years older than Stewart, and had attended Professor Matthew Stewart's mathematics class while a student at Edinburgh. He was a Freemason, and, like Stewart, a member of the Canongate Lodge. On this occasion Stewart added at the end of his note, "I shall hope for the honour of your company on Monday";[15] and in a book published near the end of his life Stewart refers to Boswell in a manner that suggests some degree of intimacy:

> his stories, which I have often listened to with delight, seldom failed to improve wonderfully in such keeping as his memory afforded. They were much more amusing than even his printed anecdotes; not only from the picturesque style of his conversational, or rather his convivial diction, but perhaps still more from the humorous and somewhat whimsical seriousness of his face and manner.[16]

In 1773 Boswell had caused a stir in Edinburgh by persuading Dr Samuel Johnson to come for the tour which took them to the Western Isles. He arrived in the capital in the middle of August, and Principal Robertson took them to see the College, but Stewart may well have been at Catrine at that time. It seems that he also missed seeing Johnson when he and Boswell spent nine days in the city on their return in mid-November. Johnson lost no time in publishing his account of the journey,[17] but it was only now, in the year after Johnson's death, that Boswell had published his own version, the Dedication being dated 20

The Young Stewart, Philosopher (1785-1787)

September 1785.[18] He must have sent a copy to Stewart, for the latter said in his letter:

> I return your *Tour* which I have read with great pleasure. Before Dr Johnson's death, I had often wished to see him, but the picture you have drawn of his character and manners is so lively and expressive, that I shall have much less reason for the future to regret that my curiosity was not gratified. I cannot help being sorry that you have recorded the anecdote about my friend Tytler, p. 405, as I am sure it will disturb him much.[19]

The anecdote in question showed Alexander Fraser Tytler, professor of universal history at the University, being put down rather brutally by Johnson in conversation, and Stewart was right in thinking that he would find its publication upsetting. Boswell was most anxious to make amends, and at his request, when Stewart got back to Edinburgh, he acted as an intermediary. An exchange of letters, and an assurance that the identity of Johnson's verbal target would be disguised in future editions, was sufficient to settle the matter to both men's satisfacion.[20]

A name which appears on the roll of Stewart's first philosophy class is John Wedgwood.[21] This was the name of the eldest son of the founder of the great pottery business. John certainly spent a year in Edinburgh, and though he worked for some time in the London showroom during 1786[22] that might have happened after the end of the academic year. It is also possible that the name on the register was a mistranscription of "Josiah", the second surviving son, who is known to have been at Edinburgh University that year as he was enrolled for both natural philosophy and universal history. The youngest brother, Tom, who was the ablest and most outgoing member of the family and was to become a pioneer of photography, studied in Edinburgh from 1786 until 1788. The Wedgwoods were nonconformists, which would account for their presence in Edinburgh. While in the city, Jos and Tom stayed with the blind poet, Dr Blacklock,[23] who was a friend of Stewart's, so it is likely that he knew them outside the lecture-room.

One acquaintance whom the brothers made in Edinburgh was John Leslie, the protagonist in the events described in chapter 12. Leslie was a few years older than the Wedgwoods, and had turned from theology to the natural sciences. In 1790, with his father's permission, Tom invited him to stay in Etruria for a couple of years to help them in their scientific studies and assist in the Wedgwood laboratories. The Wedgwood brothers' liberal education left them ill prepared for dealing with the business when their father died in 1795. They established themselves as country gentlemen – John near Bristol, and Josiah in Dorset, of which he became Sheriff in 1803. Eventually Jos reluctantly accepted the succession for which his father had tried to prepare him, became known in the history of the pottery as Josiah II, and oversaw the first production of bone china. In due course he sent his own son, Josiah III, to Edinburgh, where he studied under the guidance of Professor Playfair from 1812 until 1814, and therefore was very likely to have come in contact with Playfair's close friend Dugald Stewart, though by then retired. Three other grandchildren of Josiah I followed Joe to Edinburgh, so that seven Wedgwoods studied there altogether.

Stewart continued to be an active member of the RSE, and must have been a particularly interested listener at two meetings which he attended in the early part of 1786, for they both referred to his father. In February a paper was read about a number of theorems which Dr Matthew Stewart had published forty years previously, and in April John Playfair, the new occupant of the maths chair, read an account of Matthew Stewart's life and writings.[24]

At the end of his first session's philosophy teaching Stewart and his wife may have attended the wedding of Andrew Dalzel, which took place on 28 April 1786. His bride was Anne Drysdale, whose mother was a sister of Robert and James Adam, the architects, and a cousin of Principal Robertson. After this date the Stewarts set out for Northamptonshire,[25] where Archy Alison was now the incumbent at Sudbury, near Thrapston. He too had made a well connected marriage, for in 1784 he became the husband of Dorothea, a daughter of the late Dr John Gregory, professor of medicine at Edinburgh, and therefore one of the first recipients of Dr Gregory's then famous plan for female education, published in 1774 as *A Father's Legacy to his Daughters*. After her father's death Dorothea Gregory had lived for ten years in London and Paris with his friend Elizabeth Montagu, and met many of the outstanding figures of the day. She was a sister of Stewart's somewhat flamboyant University colleague, contemporary and family doctor, James Gregory, the originator of Gregory's Mixture.

On 19 May, having got as far as Berwick, Stewart sent a letter to Benjamin Vaughan in London. Vaughan, the son of a West India merchant, had studied medicine at Edinburgh, when it is likely that he and Stewart came to know each other. Subsequently he had become a friend and confidential agent for Lord Shelburne, who, when he became Prime Minister, employed him to assure Benjamin Franklin that Britain would recognize the independence of the United States. It was Vaughan who had written to John Jay in Paris in the summer of 1783, describing Sewart as "the most remarkable among the literary young men in Scotland . . . there

The Young Stewart, Philosopher (1785–1787)

is no knowing where he will stop."[26] At the end of 1784 Stewart had seconded the nomination of Vaughan as a member of the Royal Society of Edinburgh. He now wrote:

> [Mrs Stewart] is very far from being well so that I find it necessary to proceed by very short stages, and indeed I am somewhat apprehensive that the state of her health may put it out of my power to pay the short visit which I proposed to London. I shall write you again as soon as we are at the end of our journey, and inform you what effect it has produced, and whether or not I shall be able to leave her.[27]

Before the end of July they were back at Catrine, and Stewart wrote to the Rev. Mr MacLea in Rothesay:

> The very unsettled state I have been in the whole of this spring and summer in consequence of Mrs Stewart's illness will I hope be some excuse to you for my delay in acknowledging the receipt of your letter and the barrel of excellent herrings which accompanied it. We returned very lately from England, and I am sorry to add that our journey has not been attended with so much benefit to her health as I expected. She has indeed gained both in point of strength and spirits, but her cough and spitting continue nearly as bad as ever. We had some thoughts of trying the goatwhey in Arran, but have now laid that scheme entirely aside.[28]

(In another of the fictitious letters of Matthew Bramble in *Humphry Clinker* he records having consulted Dr John Gregory, the father in real life of Dorothea Alison with whom the Stewarts had just been staying, "who advises the highland air, and the use of goat-milk whey".[29])

After he returned from Rome to Scotland in 1785 Alexander Nasmyth, who knew Stewart through Freemasonry, painted an outdoor family portrait – probably in 1786 or 1787, for it includes little Matthew as a black-haired infant, still 'unbreeched' in a child's dress. He stands with an arm on his mother's knee, while she sits with a hand touching him protectively. The background is the Kinneil estate, which was to be Stewart's home at a much later period in his life. Helen Stewart appears as a dark, attractive young woman, on whom and on their child Dugald gazes fondly. [Plate 4 (b)][30] And that is really all that is known about her. During 1787 she died,[31] leaving Stewart a widower at thirty-three with a small son to bring up.

CHAPTER SEVEN

Stewart and Robert Burns

"Mr Stewart's principal characteristic is . . . that sterling independence of mind, which, though every man's right, so few men have the courage to claim, and fewer still the magnanimity to support . . . unseduced by splendor, and undisgusted by wretchedness, he appreciates the merits of the various actors in the great drama of life, merely as they perform their parts." Robert Burns

The Stewart home at Catrine was only about three miles from Mossgeil, the farm of which Robert Burns and his brother Gilbert became tenants in the spring of 1784.[1] This proximity brought Stewart into contact with Burns, and he recognized his merit, both as a man and as a poet, before such recognition was at all widespread. He helped him in several significant ways at the start of his public career, and Burns came to have a warm regard for him.

It was on 31 July 1786 that the first collection of poems by Robert Burns ("chiefly in the Scottish dialect") was published in the now famous Kilmarnock edition. One of its early readers was the minister at Loudoun, a few miles north of Mossgeil, the Rev. Dr George Lawrie, who sent a copy to his friend Dr Thomas Blacklock. Blacklock was a contemporary of Burns's father and the son of a bricklayer in Dumfriesshire; he had lost his sight at the age of six as the result of smallpox. From an early age he wrote poetry, and as a young man he was befriended by David Hume. In his late thirties he studied successfully for the ministry, but when his prospective parishioners in Kirkcudbright complained that he could not carry out his duties properly because of his blindness he withdrew to Edinburgh, where he and his wife supplemented his small annuity from the Church by taking pupils, such as the Wedgwood brothers, to board in their house. He had considerable classical and scientific learning, and he was an accomplished musician as well as a poet. His Augustan verse is not read today, but it was popular and well regarded during his life-time. Lawrie asked Blacklock to bring Burns's book to the notice of people of influence, for at this time Burns was so depressed by his situation that he had made up his mind to emigrate to Jamaica.

Blacklock acknowledged Lawrie's gift in a letter in which he expressed his admiration for Burns's work in warm and generous terms. He added, "Mr Stewart, Professor of Morals in this University, had formerly read me three of the poems, and I had desired him to get my name inserted among the subscribers; but whether this was done, or not, I never could learn." He had been told that the whole first impression was already exhausted, and he gave it as his advice, "for the sake of the young man", that he should lose no time in bringing out a second and enlarged edition.[2] Lawrie arranged for this letter from Blacklock to be shown to Burns, who read it with surprise and delight. "The Doctor," he wrote less than a year later, "belonged to a set of Critics for whose applause I had not even dared to hope."[3] He abandoned his idea of leaving Scotland, and in a few weeks' time he was emboldened to make his first visit to Edinburgh to explore the possibilities of a second edition being published there.

Before this happened Stewart invited him and their common friend Dr John Mackenzie to dinner at Stewart's house in Catrine on 23 October. This must have struck Burns as almost as great and unexpected an honour as the commendation of Dr Blacklock. In his poem *The Vision*, a monologue on the cultural achievements of Scotland and in particular of Ayrshire, he had referred to Stewart and his father in these lines:

> With deep-struck, reverential awe,
> The learned Sire and Son I saw,
> To Nature's God and Nature's law
>   They gave their lore,
> This, all its source and end to draw,
>   That, to adore.[4]

This stanza had not been incorporated in the poem as published in the Kilmarnock edition, and was added along with several others in the version which appeared in the Edinburgh edition of April 1787; but there is evidence from the poet's own account that it was part of the poem as he had originally written it in 1784 or 1785.[5] Another poem, *The Brigs of Ayr*, was certainly written before the dinner-party, for it was sent to its dedicatee (John Ballantine of Ayr) towards the end of September, although it too did not appear in print until the Edinburgh edition. It concludes with a visionary procession down the river. Among the abstract participants –

> Learning and Worth in equal measure trode,
> From simple Catrine, their long-lov'd abode.[6]

It is clear from these respectful references that Stewart was already known to Burns by reputation as a personage in whose distinction Ayrshire had a special claim.

Stewart may have known John Mackenzie, who was very slightly his junior, when they were both students at Edinburgh Univesity. Mackenzie was now a physician in nearby Mauchline. He had attended Burns's father during his final illness, and had got to know Robert at that time; their friendship had grown after the Burns family moved to Mossgeil. Giving an account of these events after Burns's death, Stewart described the dinner-party as the first occasion on which he had met Robert Burns. He continued:

> I cannot positively say, at this distance of time, whether, at the period of our first acquaintance, the Kilmarnock edition of his poems had been just published, or was yet in the press. I suspect that the latter was the case, as I have still in my possession copies, in his own handwriting, of some of his favourite performances; particularly of his verses *On Turning up a Mouse with his Plough*, *On the Mountain Daisy*, and *The Lament*.[7]

The Kilmarnock edition had in fact been in print for nearly three months by the time of Burns's visit to Catrine, so it seems unlikely that it was on this occasion that Stewart was given the manuscript poems which he mentions. Another sequence of events is possible, and it is one which might account for the slight confusion in Stewart's mind ten years later. The wording of Blacklock's letter to Lawrie ("Mr Stewart had formerly read me three of the poems") implies that Stewart had introduced Blacklock to Burns's poetry before Blacklock received his copy of the Kilmarnock edition; and the coincidence of Blacklock's mentioning three poems with there being three titles listed by Stewart suggests that it was these poems that Stewart read to Blacklock in Edinburgh before the Kilmarnock edition was published at the end of July.

How might Stewart have come by these handwritten copies? The explanation could lie in the fact that Stewart, Mackenzie and Burns were all Freemasons (as, incidentally, was Blacklock). In July 1784 Burns had become Depute Master – *de facto* chairman – of the Lodge St James, Tarbolton, of which Dr Mackenzie was also a member, and the records show that he attended half a dozen meetings of that Lodge during the summer of 1786.[8] Tarbolton was at that time a small Ayrshire village dependant on silk-weaving, but with a strong, intelligent and radical interest in the issues of the day.

At least once in the following year, while residing at Catrine, Stewart attended a meeting of the Tarbolton Lodge as a guest,[9] and he may have done so on other occasions. In spite of his later recollection, Mackenzie may even have introduced Burns to him at a Lodge meeting, for he also wrote that he was indebted to Mackenzie for Burns's acquaintance. It does at any rate seem plausible that Mackenzie passed specimens of Burns's poems to Stewart before their publication, with or without the poet's knowledge, as productions which the professor might think remarkable. The fact that Stewart brought them to the attention of his friend Dr Blacklock suggests that he did at once realize that they were the work of an exceptional talent. For this insight he deserves the more credit in the light of widespread efforts by the Edinburgh literati of this period to eliminate Scotticisms from their speech and writing, and adopt what they saw as 'correct' English.

Certainly the dinner party at Catrine took place. (Dinner at this period was generally taken at four or five o'clock.) In Stewart's account he states that Lord Daer happened to arrive at Catrine on the same day, and so made a fourth at the table.[10] Daer, who was four years younger than Burns, had just returned from another visit to France, where he had met Condorcet (another Freemason) and others who were soon to be involved in the early stages of the Revolution. His prepossessing appearance together with his pleasant manner and liberal ideas made a strong impression on Burns, who had never met a member of the nobility on terms of social equality before. So excited was he by the occasion that when he got home he wrote some light-hearted stanzas to commemorate the day when he "dinner'd wi' a Lord". They appear among his works as *Lines on Meeting with Lord Daer*. In mock self-deprecation he describes his awkward nervousness at this unexpected encounter. "To meet good Stewart little pain is" –

> But 'Burns!' – 'My Lord!' – Good God! I doited:
> My knees on ane anither knoited
> As faultering I gaed ben.

He looked for "the symptoms of the Great", but –

> The fient a pride, nae pride had he,
> Nor sauce, nor state, that I could see,
> Mair than an honest ploughman.
>
> Then from his Lordship I shall learn,
> Henceforth to meet with unconcern
> One rank as well's another;
> Nae honest, worthy man need care
> To meet with noble youthfu' Daer,
> For he but meets a brother.[11]

Two days after the dinner party Burns sent these "extempore verses" to Dr Mackenzie with the following note:

> I never spent an afternoon among great folks, with half that pleasure, as when in company with you I had the honour of paying my devoirs to that plain, honest, worthy man, the Professor. I would be delighted to see him perform acts of kindness and friendship, though I were not the object, he does it with such grace. I think his character divided into ten parts, stands thus – four parts Socrates – four parts Nathaniel – and two parts Shakespeare's Brutus.
>
> The foregoing verses were really extempore, but a little corrected since. They may entertain you a little, with the help of that partiality with which you are so good as [to] favour the performances of, Dear Sir, Your very humble servant, Robert Burns.[12]

It may be supposed that before they parted on that Monday evening some words were exchanged between Stewart and Burns about the latter's plan to visit Edinburgh. Stewart must have gone back there soon afterwards in order to be ready for the start of the academic year. In his later account he wrote: "On my return to Edinburgh, I showed the [Kilmarnock edition], and mentioned what I knew of the author's history, to several of my friends, and among others to Mr Henry Mackenzie."[13]

Henry Mackenzie was a lawyer, some eight years older than Stewart, who had become famous as a young man through his short book *The Man of Feeling*, a title by which he was now often known himself. This episodic novel of sentiment, in which many tears are shed, was a favourite of Burns, who habitually carried a copy with him. Mackenzie had subsequently written a couple of other novels and a number of plays, and he edited two periodicals; he was generally regarded as the doyen of the Scottish literary scene. At this time he was bringing out a weekly paper called *The Lounger*, to the appearance of which each Saturday the cultivated classes of Edinburgh looked forward with keen expectation.[14] Prompted by Stewart, he wrote a review of Burns's poems in the edition of 9 December. This was not quite the earliest notice of Burns's work to appear in print, but it represented a breakthrough for serious consideration of his poetry. Though somewhat patronising in tone (the title was *Surprising effects of Original Genius, exemplified in the Poetical Productions of Robert Burns, an Ayrshire Ploughman*), it was generous in its praise, and it certainly strengthened the case for a second edition. "I trust," Mackenzie wrote, "that I do my country no more than justice, when I suppose her ready to stretch out her hand to cherish and retain this native poet."[15]

Burns had arrived in Edinburgh at the end of November, and was soon reporting in letters to his friends in Ayrshire how quickly he had been received by members of the *Noblesse* and the Literati. He told Dr Mackenzie that "our worthy friend Mr Stewart, with that goodness truly like himself, got me in the periodical paper, *The Lounger*; a copy of which I here inclose you".[16] A few days later he sent another copy of the weekly to his patron and friend John Ballantine with a similar acknowledgement of Stewart's role.[17] Henry Mackenzie later wrote that Stewart had introduced Burns to him personally,[18] and Stewart may well have secured similar useful contacts.

In part this must have been through Freemasonry. On 13 January 1787 Burns was present at a meeting of the St Andrew Lodge, and was taken aback when the Grand Master proposed a toast to "Caledonia and Caledonia's bard, Brother Burns",[19] thus showing how rapidly his standing was being established among reputable people. (Those present that evening included Principal Robertson and Adam Smith.[20]) On 1 February he attended a meeting of the Canongate Kilwinning Lodge, the home lodge of Stewart as well as of Henry Mackenzie, and was introduced by Henry Erskine, Dean of the Faculty of Advocates and future Lord Chancellor who was to become famous for his defence of the radicals in the treason trials of 1794. Erskine, he told a friend, was one of those who "have taken me under their wing".[21] There is a story which has become part of Burns mythology that a month later he was installed as 'Poet Laureate' of this Lodge. It was given currency by a painting done fifty years after Burns's death by W. Stewart Watson which purports to depict the scene, and shows Stewart among the members present; but the tale is almost certainly a fiction.[22]

About this time, however, Stewart was present at, and may have been indirectly responsible for the famous and only occasion when words were exchanged between Scotland's two greatest literary figures, Burns and

Walter Scott. Adam Ferguson, possibly prompted by Stewart, invited Burns to one of the weekly open days which he held in his home at Sciennes Hill House, a building that still stands about half a mile south of the University. Not only Stewart but Joseph Black and James Hutton, the geologist, were among the company. Scott, then only fifteen years old, was a friend of Ferguson's son, also named Adam, and the two boys were present at the time. Forty years later Scott recorded having seen Burns "one day at the late venerable Professor Ferguson's, where there were several gentlemen of literary reputation, among whom I remember the celebrated Mr Dugald Stewart. Of course we youngsters sat silent, looked and listened." Burns was moved by a print in the room, and the only person who was able to give him the name of the writer of some lines of verse attached to it was young Scott. Burns "rewarded me," he recalled, "with a look and a word, which though of mere civility, I then received, and still recollect, with very great pleasure".[23] The incident at Adam Ferguson's house became the subject of another well known posthumous painting in which Stewart is made to appear – this by Charles Martin Hardie.

The poet was now so much engaged that Stewart saw less of him than he would have wished, but on one or two occasions in the spring he invited Burns to join him for an early morning walk on the Braid Hills, where they were able to admire the view across the city and the Firth of Forth to Fife. Stewart wrote that "he charmed me still more by his private conversation than he had ever done in company".[24]

Burns left Edinburgh on 5 May 1787 to tour the Borders. A week or so later he sent a jocular piece from Selkirk to his Edinburgh publisher, William Creech (one of the founders of the Speculative Society), which referred to –

> Mackenzie, Stewart, such a brace
> As Rome ne'er saw.[25]

After a second excursion, which took him into the West Highlands, he was back on his farm in July. Stewart as usual spent some weeks in Ayrshire during the summer, and saw Burns occasionally. On 25 July he "was led by curiosity to attend for an hour or two a mason lodge in Mauchline, where Burns presided". This was in fact the St James's Lodge, Tarbolton, which sometimes met at Mauchline.[26] The Lodge took the opportunity to admit Stewart as an honorary member, and he was struck by the fluent and appropriately complimentary manner in which Burns was able to speak without any premeditation.[27]

The poet was briefly in Edinburgh again in August before setting off for another Highland tour; Stewart may still have been at Catrine at this time. Burns returned to the capital city towards the end of October and stayed there until the middle of February 1788. He spent a good deal of time working on contributions to James Johnson's *Scots Musical Museum*, an attempt to collect the words and music of all the old Scottish ballads. (Stewart had lent him a collection of songs by Dr Aiken, which "he read with unmixed delight".[28]) Latterly he was also much preoccupied by his philandering affair with "Clarinda" (Mrs McLehose). In general he seems to have mixed less with the 'Noblesse' and the Edinburgh literati than during the previous winter, and there is no specific record of his meeting with Stewart. It seems likely, however, that they saw each other from time to time, for in November Burns wrote to his patroness Mrs Dunlop of Dunlop, "It requires no common exertion of good sense and Philosophy in persons of elevated rank, to keep friendship properly alive with one much their inferior". He went on to describe Stewart as the only man he knew who truly valued people for their intrinsic merits and not for their rank; and although he refers to him as "Professor Dugald Stewart of Catrine",[29] the timing suggests that this tribute may have been prompted by recent experience of Stewart's friendship since Burns returned to Edinburgh.

It would appear that the two men met in Ayrshire in the spring of 1788. A few days later, writing from Mauchline, Burns sent Stewart "one or two more of my bagatelles" together with his good wishes for the latter's forthcoming visit to the continent, on which he had in fact already set out when the letter arrived. Burns added:

> Wherever I am, allow me, Sir, to claim it as my privilege, to acquaint you with my progress in my trade of rhymes; as I am sure I could say it with truth, that, next to my little fame, and the having it in my power to make life more comfortable to those whom nature has made dear to me, I shall ever regard your countenance, your patronage, your friendly good offices, as the most valued consequence of my late success in life.[30]

In the early summer of 1788 Burns left his Ayrshire farm at Mossgeil, and for the rest of his short life his homes were in Dumfriesshire. In January 1789 he wrote from there to Stewart with "a few more of my productions", one of which "I have not shown to man living till I now send it to you . . . please let it be for your single, sole inspection". Again he added a flattering paragraph:

> Need I make any apology for this trouble to a gentleman who has treated me with such marked benevolence and peculiar kindness, who has entered

into my interests with so much zeal, and on whose critical decisions I can so fully depend? A Poet as I am by trade, these decisions are to me of the last consequence. My late transient acquaintance among some of the mere rank and file of Greatness, I resign with ease; but to the distinguished Champions of Genius and Learning, I shall ever be ambitious of being known. The native genius and accurate discernment, in Mr Stewart's critical strictures . . . I shall ever revere. I shall be in Edinburgh some time next month.[31]

Unfortunately no record of Stewart's critical comments survives. However, in the letter to Currie referred to in the final paragraph of this chapter he made an interesting general observation: "all the faculties of Burns' mind were, as far as I could judge, equally vigorous; and his predilection for poetry, was rather the result of his own enthusiastic and impassioned temper, than of a genius exclusively adapted to that species of composition. From his conversation, I should have pronounced him to be fitted to excel in whatever walk of ambition he had chosen to exert his abilities."[32]

Burns's final visit to Edinburgh, a brief one, took place at the end of February 1789. It seems also to have been the occasion of his final meeting with Stewart, who recorded that "the last time I saw him was during the winter of 1788–9, when he passed an evening with me at Drumsheugh, in the neighbourhood of Edinburgh, where I was then living. My friend, Mr Alison, was the only other person in company. I never saw him more agreeable or interesting."[33]

In July 1790 Burns was able to do Stewart a favour by sending him a letter of introduction to Captain Francis Grose, a voluminous antiquarian who had met Burns and whose acquaintance Stewart had told him he greatly coveted.[34] In his letter to Grose he described Stewart as "a Man of the first parts, and what is more, a Man of the first worth". His principal characteristic was a "sterling independance of Mind"; and Burns repeated the substance of his earlier comment about Stewart: "he appreciates the merits of the various Actors in the great Drama of Life, merely as they Perform their Parts".[35]

Burns's last surviving letter to Stewart was written from his farm at Ellisland near Dumfries at the end of July 1790, when he sent him some further poems, expressing regret that he had not the opportunity of hearing his criticisms:

> I will not pretend to say, whether it is owing to my prejudice in favor of a gentleman to whom I am so much indebted, or to your critical abilities; but in the way of my trade, as a Poet, I will subscribe more implicitly to *your*

strictures, than to any Individual on earth . . . I shall have leisure soon, to write off for you, several of my pieces.

I have the honour to be, Sir, your oblidged humble servant
Robt Burns.[36]

It was during this month, as we shall see, that Stewart remarried. As Helen Cranstoun, the second Mrs Stewart had written a song to which Burns added four lines "to make all the stanzas suit the music", and he sent the piece to Johnson's *Scots Musical Museum*, in which it was published in August 1792. He refers to it in his note as being by "a Miss Cranston",[37] but he could hardly have been unaware who the poetess was, and it seems likely that he had some communication on the subject with Stewart's wife, before or after her marriage.

In April 1792 Burns still regarded Stewart as one whose advice could be sought. Writing to William Creech about new material which he might supply for publication, he mentioned Stewart as one of three men whom Creech knew "and whose friendly patronage I think I can trouble so far". This was to seek their criticism of the new poems and their assessment of the value of books which Burns might ask for by way of payment. However, he understood that Stewart and Henry Mackenzie were "busy with works of their own", and therefore preferred that his third nominee, Fraser Tytler, should be approached.[38] In due course he asked Creech for three books; one of these was "D. Stewart's *Elements of the Philosophy of the Human Mind*".[39]

When Burns died in July 1796 at the age of thirty-seven an immediate concern of his friends was to make provision for his widow Jean and his children. One of Burns's closest friends was the Edinburgh solicitor and Freemason Alexander Cunningham, a nephew of Principal Robertson, and Stewart accompanied him to seek (successfully) the assistance of his own banker[40] Sir William Forbes, also a Mason, about collecting subscriptions. But the going was not easy. "The truth is," Cunningham wrote to another Burns associate in Dumfries, "the poor Bard's frailties – excuse this vile word – were not only so well known here, but often I believe exaggerated, that even the admirers of his genius cannot be prevailed on to do what we all ought – to forget and forgive."[41]

It may be that Stewart was one of those who had become disappointed in Burns. At some point he told Henry Mackenzie that the poet's conduct and manners had become so degraded that decent people could hardly take any notice of him. Mackenzie recognized that Stewart might have "been deceived by exaggerated accounts of his irregularities";[42] but what he had heard may have had some influence on a decision he had shortly to make. Another plan to raise money for the Burns family was to commission a biography of the poet, and Stewart was considered as one who might take this on. It is not clear whether he even knew of this idea; if he did, however, the most obvious reason for declining may well have been the predominant one: he was too busy with his academic work. He was not a man to undertake a responsibility to which he could not do full justice, and he must have realized that writing an adequate account of Burns's career would be a time-consuming assignment.

The first *Life of Burns* was in the end produced by Dr James Currie of Liverpool, whom Stewart had known well when he was a medical student in Edinburgh and had kept in touch with since. He provided for Currie a letter of some two and a half thousand words to help him with his task.[43] That statement has been drawn upon at several points in this chapter. Apart from its factual information, it contained a generous and perceptive assessment of the man Stewart had known and encouraged so helpfully, and it has been heavily quarried by innumerable writers about Robert Burns. In September 1800 Stewart wrote to Currie to congratulate him on his biography.[44]

CHAPTER EIGHT

Revolutionary France and Remarriage 1787–1790

"We saw together Louis XVI led in triumph by his people thro' the streets of his capital." Thomas Jefferson

Stewart's reaction to his wife's death in 1787 seems to have been to throw himself into work and activity. During the ensuing winter, only his third in the philosophy chair, he undertook in addition to his own duties to supply the place of Professor Robison, who suffered from ill health.[1] However intensive his preparations for this additional responsibility, he must have shared the general dismay at the sensational break-in to the University Library on the night of 30 October and the theft of the ancient silver College mace. This was the latest in the series of daring raids in the city which had begun in August of the previous year and were eventually traced to the well-known town councillor and deacon, William Brodie.[2] But even without a mace the new session got under way, and it was for Stewart another remarkable feat of intellectual energy and versatility. During the course of the year he wrote to Archy Alison:

> The Natural Philosophy goes on beyond my expectation. I have already finished the Mechanics and Hydrostatics, two parts of the course to which I looked forward with some apprehension, and I have performed every experiment (even the Hydrostatic ones) with my own hands, and without breaking a single jar. I am sure I could not have done it in the presence of *two* or *three* friends, but in my public exhibitions I have found myself just

as cool and collected as if I had been alone. To-morrow I proceed to Pneumatics, and am just now employed in premeditating two lectures – the one on the Air-Pump, and the other on the Immortality of the Soul.[3]

At the beginning of April 1788 he had another consignment of "most excellent herrings" to acknowledge from the Rev. Mr MacLea in Rothesay, who seems to have considered the inhabitants of urban Edinburgh to be in need of wholesome food. Stewart added: "I had flattered myself with the hopes of paying a visit to you and my other friends in Bute in the course of next summer, but I find I must delay it till another year, as I have agreed to spend a few months on the Continent with a son of Mr Ramsay the Banker."[4]

It may be that the prospect of a long summer at Catrine with neither father nor wife for company was not very attractive. Moreover, Catrine itself was ceasing to be the quiet village of Stewart's boyhood holidays. The industrial revolution in Scotland began with the advent of the cotton textile industry. After a visit to Glasgow by Richard Arkwright in 1784 an arc of water-frame factories grew up, and in 1787 a cotton-twist mill was built in Catrine to take advantage of the power afforded by the River Ayr.[5] The mill was visible from the Stewart home, and its arrival on the scene began a process which was soon to convert Catrine into a 'new town'.

Stewart had once before told Lady Jane Home of leaving his son with his mother-in-law in Glasgow;[6] on this occasion he left little Matthew in the care of his brother-in-law, Dugald Bannatyne,[7] who had married in 1781 and now had two small children of his own,[8] and he set out on tour with George Ramsay. In this very year George's father, "the banker", bought the joint estate of Barnton and Cramond Regis, the grounds of what is now Davidson's Mains Park, and proceeded to demolish an old house which stood there and build a much grander one, getting Queensferry Road realigned to the south of its original position.[9] He thus became known as William Ramsay of Barnton, and he was indeed a very wealthy man, being the dominant figure in one of Edinburgh's two major private banks and a very substantial shareholder in the Royal Bank of Scotland.[10] It is possible that Stewart was introduced to the Ramsay family through his erstwhile boarder, the future Lord Belhaven, for Belhaven's sister, Jean Hamilton, eventually married George Ramsay and the two families may already have known each other.

We may reasonably assume that Stewart did not lose financially by acting as travelling tutor to young George. But the youth was described by at least one observer in a less than flattering light. Stewart and he began

Revolutionary France and Remarriage (1787–1790)

their journey early in May and spent some time in London. They also visited Windsor and met there with Josiah Walker, the Ayrshireman who as a student had transcribed Stewart's philosophy lectures in 1778–9 and who eventually became professor of humanity at Glasgow University. Walker told a friend in June: "About a month ago [D. Stewart] came here with his lubberly charge. What an uncongenial companion! Yet he seems extremely good humoured and tractable."[11]

The Rev. John Home, author of the renowned tragedy *Douglas*, was with them at this stage, and one day when walking on Windsor Terrace they fell in with that other Edinburgh notable, Lord Monboddo, who always attended the court while he was in London and was received with special favour by George III. Home was also well known to the monarch, for he had been his tutor when he was Prince of Wales. It thus happened that Stewart and his companions were at hand when Monboddo was in conversation with the King. George III's quick-fire manner of speaking was currently being so well hit off by the physician John Wolcot in his serial satirical cantos, *The Lousiad*, which he wrote under the name of Peter Pindar, that Stewart could hardly hold back his laughter at hearing the real thing. While in Windsor he called upon the Edinburgh-trained Dr James Lind, physician to the royal household, and on the astronomer William Herschel (on whom Edinburgh University had conferred an honorary degree two years previously), at whose home in Slough he "had a peep through the telescope".[12]

In London in early June, Stewart managed to hear the first two days of the lengthy speech made by Richard Brinsley Sheridan in Westminster Hall as manager of the impeachment of Warren Hastings: he was disappointed in his eloquence, which he did not consider comparable with that of Fox, Pitt or Burke.[13] It may have been at the impeachment hearing that he met James Mackintosh, who also attended them; having studied medicine at Edinburgh, Mackintosh was thinking of going to Russia as a phyisician. Although at this time they hardly knew each other, Stewart gave him a letter of recommendation;[14] but Mackintosh did not proceed with this idea, and presently decided to go to the bar. Stewart also introduced Josiah Walker to "some of his London friends",[15] and it seems likely that one of those with whom he was in touch while in London was Bernard Vaughan. Vaughan's diplomatic activities in behalf of Lord Shelburne had brought him into contact with the leaders of the embryonic United States, and on 6 June he furnished Stewart with a flatteringly worded letter of introduction to Benjamin Franklin's successor as Minister Plenipotentiary from the States of America in Paris, Thomas Jefferson.[16]

Revolutionary France and Remarriage (1787–1790)

By 18 June Stewart and his pupil were in Douai, and Stewart had time to write to Archy Alison:

> We have now been ten days on the Continent; but I was so busy in seeking out a comfortable house to board in, and in arranging our little affairs, that I have hardly been able till now, to command an hour to myself. And even at present, I write this, with Ramsay sitting by me, in a room adjoining to mine, and repeating over *avoir* and *etre* to his French master, so that I scarcely know what I have been writing. We are lodged in the house of a Benedictine monk. All the abbeys in this neighbourhood have houses belonging to them in some of the fortified towns, to which they may retire in case of war. Such a house is called the *refuge* of the abbey, and is commonly inhabited by one of the monks, who keeps it in order. *That* in which we are boarded at present belongs to the rich abbey of St Amand. It is at least as large as Heriot's Hospital, and is inhabited only by the monk, Mr Ramsay, myself, and a few servants. It is in the environs of the town, and has a very large and excellent garden, in which the monk spends most of his time, and where we have an opportunity of enjoying his conversation. He keeps an excellent table, which he enjoys very much himself, and has constantly some of his friends with him, so that, on the whole, we are very comfortably situated. I think we shall continue here at least three weeks, during which time I request of you to write to me more than once.[17]

A few days later Stewart wrote again, enclosing a letter for Dr James Gregory, who was on his way to visit the Alisons. It related to a young man about whom Stewart added for Alison's private information: "his leaving the Abbé Goval's house was not entirely a matter of choice, as I understand he had given that reverend gentleman some offence by taking improper liberties with his maid." With regard to his own adventures, he continued:

> I like our monk better and better every day. He speaks the language well, and is very willing to impart to us any knowledge he has. You may believe it is not very extensive, for he had never once heard of Montesquieu's name in his life, and I am afraid he has had some suspicions about my veracity ever since I attempted to describe to him Franklin's Apparatus for Securing Houses from Lightning. [Benjamin Franklin had invented the lightning conductor shortly before Stewart was born.] By the way we have had the most dreadful thunder storm I ever heard (which Ramsay did not much like) ... Write instantly. God bless you – and Mrs Alison and all with you. Yours ever aff'ly, D.S.[18]

Stewart and Ramsay were still in Douai in early July when they met with another travelling tutor and his pupil – Hugh Cleghorn, professor of civil history at St Andrews University, and Alexander, 10th Earl of Home. Home and Ramsay already knew each other, as did Cleghorn and Stewart, who had attended several classes in common as students,[19] and the latter pair called together on Principal Gibson of the Scots College and attended mass. (It is clear from his relations, on this and his previous visit to the continent, with the Scots College – an institution for training Catholic priests – that Stewart had no strong sectarian prejudices.) The next day, 13 July, there was another tremendous thunderstorm; in his journal Cleghorn recorded the sudden darkness, with lightning as "one long uninterrupted sheet" and rain accompanied by pieces of ice "the smallest of which were larger than pigeon's eggs".[20] These storms had peculiar significance, for they ruined the harvest, and the resultant food shortages in the following year contributed to the discontents that culminated in the French Revolution.

It is not possible to trace the details of the itinerary which Stewart and Ramsay followed thereafter. They were certainly in Paris, and when Stewart wrote to Dugald Bannatyne on 4 August 1788 it was from Marseilles

> where [we] arrived the day before yesterday, after a very pleasant journey, in the course of which we visited the Roman antiquities at Nimes and in the neighbourhood. Indeed the whole of our journey from Paris (which has employed us nearly a fortnight), has been most delightful, making allowance for the intolerable heat of the climate, and the swarms of flies, which give me little rest, night or day, and which, I hope, will reconcile me for the rest of my life to the cold and wet weather of Ayrshire.

A resident of Marseilles at this time was the Abbé Raynal, famous for his history of European activities in the East and West Indies which had first appeared in 1770. Actually a compilation of contributions by several hands including his own, the book was strongly anti-religious in tone, and had caused such displeasure to Louis XVI that Raynal had been obliged to live abroad for several years. He had returned to France in 1787, and Stewart went to see him.

> I spent some hours yesterday with the Abbé Raynal . . . ; and I think I never saw a man whose conversation forms a more remarkable contrast [with] his writings. He is good-natured and communicative, but the most trifling, *clavering* creature I ever met with. He is now seventy-six, but still in good health and still writing . . .
>
> I begin to long very impatiently to [see] my little man, who, I hope, continues to be a good boy, and to enjoy the same health as before. I have spent the summer as agreeably as I could have wished, and yet I don't think

it would be an easy matter to persuade me to leave him for six months. Believe me ever, dear D,. your affectionate brother, D.S.

We set out this afternoon for Geneva, and shall probably pay a visit on our way to the *Grande Chartreuse* in Dauphiné. I think it likely that we shall remain nearly a month in Switzerland.[21]

As usual he put his time to good use. It seems very likely that during this period in Geneva Stewart got to know Pierre Prévost, the Swiss physicist and man of letters, with whom he was to correspond at intervals for the rest of his life and who translated one of Stewart's books. It must also have been during his time in Switzerland that he made the visit, mentioned in his lectures on political economy, to two villages "in a small district, which forms part of the principality of Neufchatel" that were a centre of the watchmaking industry. These, he remarked, he "had once an opportunity of observing with some attention".[22]

However, Stewart and Ramsay's stay in Switzerland must have been a little less extended than the former expected, for on 27 August he was writing to Archy Alison from Paris, referring to their arrival there two days earlier, too late in the day to witness "the wonderful revolution which has taken place here".[23] The reference is to the collapse of the last attempt to save the old regime in France brought about by the bankruptcy of the treasury and the appointment of the popular Swiss banker, Jacques Necker, as Principal Minister to restore calm until the Estates-General should meet. This is the first evidence of Stewart's keen interest in political developments in France. A surviving letter shows that he was still in Paris on 11 October, when he mentions another travelling Scottish tutor, Mr Arbuthnot, "a very particular friend of mine", who was then in the city "with Sir John Hunter Blair, the son of our late Provost".[24] Soon after this Stewart and Ramsay must have returned to Edinburgh for the new College year.

Prompted no doubt by his contacts in Paris, Stewart proposed two names for membership at a meeting of the Physical Class of the RSE at the beginning of December.[25] One was that of M. Guyot, whom he had first known in Edinburgh a few years previously when he acted as tutor to two brothers de Lessert who had both attended his mathematics class.[26] The other was Thomas Jefferson, principal drafter of the American Declaration of Independence.

Early in the following year an event occurred which must have saddened Stewart. His elder sister Janet, Mrs Miller, died on 19 January 1789 at the age of thirty-six, leaving five small children in the manse at Cumnock, the oldest only seven and the youngest not quite two.[27] Nearly forty years later Stewart's second wife was to tell Lord Minto that the young Millers "were all bred up as our own children".[28] This cannot have been literally true, but relations between the families were certainly close throughout their lives, and some of the Miller children seem to have lived with the Stewarts at various periods.

In spite of his having missed Matthew so much during the previous summer, Stewart decided to spend more time on the continent in 1789. It appears that this time he left Matthew with Archy Alison and his wife. On 30 May he wrote to him from Paris, saying: "I received your letter to-day, and along with it a letter from Mr Miller, which makes my mind perfectly easy for the present with respect to Matthew and the children at Cumnock."[29] There is an obvious ambiguity here as to which of the two letters set his mind at rest about his little son, but it seems more likely that he left him with the Alisons on his way south than that he would have imposed him on Thomas Miller, who had to care for his own young family so soon after Janet's death. The question seems to be settled by a footnote to a later and lengthy letter to Alison which, he said, "you owe in part to most agreeable accounts which I have just received of Matthew. God bless you!"[30]

It would seem that on this occasion Stewart did not go abroad as a tutor. He set out as usual through London. On 4 May he met Richard Price, who was a Unitarian minister, a political radical who supported the American and French revolutions, and a moral philosopher. Price gave him a letter to give to Thomas Jefferson in Paris. "This letter will, I hope, be convey'd to you by Mr Dugald Stewart, Professor of Moral Philosophy at Edinburgh and a very able man who is this day setting out for Paris with Lord Dare in order to be present at the time of the meeting of the three estates."[31] Two days later Stewart wrote to Adam Smith saying he had been so hurried during his short stay in London that this was his first opportunity to write. He had done some business on Smith's behalf with his publisher, Thomas Cadell, and on this he reported, adding "I write this from Dover which I am just leaving with a fair wind, so that I hope to be in Paris on Thursday."[32]

Whether Lord Daer actually accompanied him on the journey is unclear, for shortly after his arrival in Paris he mentioned, in writing to Alison, Daer's "dilatoriness" in trifling away his time in London with his brother John and thus losing the chance to see the three estates together.[33] There can be little doubt that Stewart's own prime reason for this visit to France was his fascination with the political situation there. References in his letters to "we" and "our tour"[34] most likely refer to Daer, though at one point he noted that "Mr Ramsay is perfectly well",[35] as if his pupil of

1788 might have been with him again, at least at that point. In another letter he mysteriously referred Archy Alison "for particulars to a letter from A. to his father".[36] In September he reported having just made "a little expedition to the country with Arbuthnot",[37] and a note by Veitch suggests that "Arbuthnot" was "probably Robert Arbuthnot, Esq., Edinburgh, elder brother of the late Sir William Arbuthnot, Bart."[38] The latter was Lord Provost of Edinburgh in 1815–17 and again at the time of George IV's visit to the city, and Robert may have been the same Arbuthnot as Stewart mentioned being in Paris during the previous summer. But whatever company he had, his correspondence confirms that his own overriding interest was in the rapidly developing situation in France.

On 10 May he was writing to Alison to report his safe arrival in Paris after a journey through Kent and northern France in delightful weather and "the greatest possible beauty". In spite of his haste he had missed the ceremonial convention of the Estates-General on the 5th, but he began immediately to report on political developments.

> The States-General were opened *two* days before my arrival . . . I have read the King's speech, which I think excellent. [He goes on to comment on the quality of the deputies elected to the Third Estate.] I am much mortified to hear that no strangers are to be admitted to [the] deliberations [of the Estates-General]; but I have not as yet given up all hopes.[39]

Three weeks later he was giving Alison a long account of the state of affairs in the Estates-General, and added a postscript on 4 June:

> Of late the *Tiers Etat* have admitted strangers into the gallery, which they are always to do for the future, and I accordingly went to Versailles the day before yesterday to hear one of their debates. The subject . . . was not very interesting, but on the whole I was very well pleased with what I heard . . . They have accepted all our Parliamentary expressions, to a degree which is sometimes ludicrous . . .[40]

Clearly Stewart's command of French was now sufficient for him to follow even animated debates with comprehension.

Two days prior to this, he had been invited to *souper* with the Duc de La Rochefoucauld and his mother.[41] In his life of Adam Smith, Stewart refers to "a friend [of Smith's] who happened to be then at Paris"[42] conveying a message to the Duke; this was about a reference Smith had made to La Rochefoucault's more famous grandfather, the writer. Elsewhere in Stewart's writings he makes it clear that he was himself the friend,[43] so there seems little doubt that this was the occasion. The contemporary Duke was a progressive and a Freemason who had just been elected to the Estates-General as a representative of the *noblesse,* and it was he who was to describe the events of 14 July to Louis XVI.

On 18 June Stewart sent an apologetic letter to Archy Alison. "I have found it impossible of late to write you as often as I could wish, as I have been almost constantly at Versailles attending the debates in the *Chambre des Communes,* which have been so long and so interesting that it was pefectly out of my power to give you any idea of their proceedings."[44] Nevertheless he gave some account of what had been happening, adding, "You may expect a Supplement in two or three days". Unfortunately this has not survived, but we know that Stewart was a witness to the dramatic events of July 1789. Soon after his arrival in Paris he had delivered Richard Price's letter to the American Minister, Thomas Jefferson. More than thirty years later Jefferson told John Adams:

> I became immediately intimate with Stuart, calling mutually on each other almost daily, during their stay at Paris, which was of some months. Ld. Dare was a young man of imagination, with occasional flashes indicating deep penetration, but of much caprice and little judgment . . . Stuart is a great man, and among the most honest living.[45]

Stewart and Jefferson were together three days after the storming of the Bastille, when they watched the French King pass through Paris wearing a tricolour cockade on his hat after endorsing the changes in power which had taken place.[46]

No comments by Stewart on these events have survived, but his general sympathy with the aims of the revolution clearly remained unqualified. Since he expounded each year to his philosophy students the admirable balance which the British constitution achieved through the division of the legislature,[47] he must have shared the general approval felt in Britain at this time for the steps by which France appeared to be moving towards a constitutional monarchy and a similar state of harmony. On 17 September he was still in Paris, writing again to Alison. After a paragraph about the latter's affairs he continued:

> I have spent my time very pleasantly since I came here, and have seen a good many extraordinary men, and some still more extraordinary women.
> The pleasantest woman, by far, whom I have seen here, and the most respectable, is Madame de Lessert, the mother of two young gentlemen of that name who sudied some years ago at Edinburgh. She, too, was a very intimate friend of Rousseau's, and it was for her daughter that he wrote his introducton to botany; but she is a woman perfectly free from every sort of pretension, and occupied entirely with the education of her children. M.

Guyot, who had charge of the young men when they were in Scotland, and who is one of their nearest relations, still lives with them, and has been of more use to me than any person I have met with at Paris.

I am just returned from a little expedition to the country with Arbuthnot, in the course of which we visited Ermenonville, where I need not inform you that Jean-Jacques is buried. I was miserably disappointed to find everything in such disorder, partly in consequence of the negligence of the proprietor, and partly of the winter's floods . . .

He went on to comment on the very latest political development – a decision that under a revised constitution the monarch should have only a temporary veto on legislation passed by Parliament. This he described as

an event which has given great joy to the populace here. For some days past they have been testifying their satisfaction by throwing squibs and crackers, and by playing all the other pranks of a London mob. I passed the Pont Neuf this forenoon, where they were assembled in great numbers, and where they forced every passenger to pull off his hat to the statue of Henri IV.[48]

Stewart may have remained in France for long enough to witness the bread riots in early October and the enforced move of the royal family from Versailles to Paris; but not long after these stirring events we must assume that he returned to England, reclaimed little Matthew from Northamptonshire and was back in Edinburgh for the start of another academic year.

Early in the new session, on 16 November 1789, a notable event took place for Edinburgh University – the laying of the foundation stone for a new College building.[49] This was the culmination of more than twenty years' campaigning by Principal Robertson to rehouse the College on its original site (which at that time was still open to the west and north) in a building suited to its needs and worthy of its reputation. There was support both from the Town Council and from Henry Dundas in the government in London, and the Principal's cousin, Robert Adam, recently concerned both with building the new Register House at the east end of Princes Street and with the South Bridge scheme, had been given the job of designing the new university.

There is no certainty about the location of the foundation stone: an inscription on a wall inside the quadrangle now suggests where it is likely to have been laid. But a detailed description of the ceremony appeared in the press at the time, and it was a splendid occasion which Stewart almost certainly attended. Watched by a huge crowd (the High School took a special half-holiday), a procession made its way from the Parliament Close behind St Giles Cathedral down the High Street and then up the new South Bridge to the back of the old College buildings. First came the Lord Provost (a merchant named Thomas Elder), the magistrates and council, preceded by their sword and mace, and next the University Principal and professors, wearing black gowns and hats, and students – though not as many as there might have been, since some took offence at a rather belated invitation – each with a sprig of laurel in his hat. Before them went a new mace, presented by the Council on the day after Deacon Brodie was hanged to replace the one that he had unceremoniously removed in 1787.

The stone was laid by Lord Napier, Grand Master of the Freemasons in Scotland. In reply to his speech of congratulation Principal Robertson attributed much of the University's eminence to the generosity of successive sovereigns, and he also paid tribute "to his colleagues who had attracted students not only from every part of the British dominions, but also from almost every nation in Europe and every state in America". This was a significant point to make on a public occasion, as the Town Council's support for the Town College was based in no small measure on the honour and prosperity which its reputation brought to Edinburgh.[50] No meeting of the literary class of the RSE was held that day, "most of the members of the Society being present at a grand Entertainment given on that occasion by the Lord Provost and Magistrates".[51]

It was partly because of the financial strains imposed by the War of American Independence that the project had been delayed so long, and as it turned out the pressure of another war was to delay its implementation far beyond what those present that day hoped and expected. The whole of Dugald Stewart's professional life was spent working in the inadequate premises in which he had himself been a student, and it was not unitl several years after his retirement, and under a differenet architect,[52] that the rebuilding work was completed.

One of the students who appeared that year in Stewart's philosophy class was the slightly lame young man who had been able three years earlier to provide Robert Burns with the name of the obscure poet whose lines attracted his attention. Walter Scott was now studying for a legal career, and later told Lockhart that at the College, "I was farther instructed in Moral Philosophy at the class of Mr Dugald Stewart, whose striking and impressive eloquence riveted the attention even of the most volatile students."[53] Being himself one of the more conscientious students, Scott produced several essays as part of his course work. One, which he had already delivered to the Literary Society, was on the origins of the feudal system, and another, which displayed a wide range of reading, he entitled *On the Manners and Customs of the Northern Nations*. This particularly attracted Stewart's notice, and a classmate of Scott's remembered his saying impressively, "The author of this paper shows much knowledge of his subject, and a great taste for such researches."[54] This encouragement was perceptive, and must have been welcome to a youth of eighteen. It is likely that Stewart already knew Scott slightly, for apart from the incident at Adam Ferguson's, the Scott family had lived in the College Wynd, just ouside the University walls, until Walter was about three, before moving to George Square. Whatever acquaintance there had been was strengthened during Scott's period in Stewart's class.[55]

Writing to a professor at Glasgow University in 1794, Andrew Dalzel recalled that "many years ago", which might have been about this period, Principal Robertson had offered him and Stewart an LLD. They had declined it "for certain reasons which I could mention to you in conversation, but which will not do in writing".[56] This mysterious reference is all we can know about the episode. Dalzel added that if he were to be given an honorary degree from Glasgow he would prefer it to be in company with Dugald Stewart.

The origin of the next major development in Stewart's life is the subject of an anecdote which appeared in the *Quarterly Review* some years after his death.[57] It assumes, as was almost certainly the case, that Stewart continued to be on friendly terms with the Earl of Ancram whom he had accompanied to the continent in 1783.[58] A sister of Ancram's great-grandfather, the 3rd Marquess of Lothian, had become the wife of William, the 5th Lord Cranstoun, and their seventh son, George, had married an Ayrshire woman, Maria Brisbane, and produced a family of two boys and three girls. Helen, the youngest of the daughters, occasionally wrote poetry. Her best piece was the one which Burns supplemented by four lines and contributed to *The Scots Musical Museum*. Without the Burns addition it reads as follows:

> The tears I shed must ever fall.
> I mourn not for an absent swain,
> For thought may past delights recall,
> And parted lovers meet again.
>
> I weep not for the silent dead,
> Their toils are past, their sorrows o'er,
> And those they lov'd their steps shall tread,
> And death shall join to part no more.
>
> Though boundless oceans roll'd between,
> If certain that his heart is near,

Revolutionary France and Remarriage (1787–1790)

> A conscious transport glads each scene,
> Soft is the sigh, and sweet the tear.
>
> Even when by Death's cold hand remov'd,
> We mourn the tenant of the tomb;
> To think that even in death he lov'd
> Can gild the horrors of the gloom.
>
> But bitter, bitter are the tears,
> Of her who slighted love bewails;
> No hope her dreary prospect chears,
> No pleasing melancholy hails.
>
> Hers are the pangs of wounded pride,
> Of blasted hope, of wither'd joy;
> The prop she lean'd on pierc'd her side,
> The flame she fed, burns to destroy.
>
> Even conscious virtue cannot cure
> The pangs to every feeling due:
> Ungenerous youth! thy boast how poor,
> To steal a heart, and break it too!
>
> In vain does memory renew
> The hours once ting'd in transport's dye;
> The sad reverse soon starts to view,
> And turns the thought to agony.
>
> From hope, the wretched's anchor torn,
> Neglected, and neglecting all,
> Friendless, forsaken, and forlorn,
> The tears I shed must ever fall.[59]

The story is that Ancram showed Stewart this production by his distant cousin, and that Stewart was much impressed; Ancram of course passed his complimentary comments back to Helen Cranstoun. This led to a meeting, and thence to love and marriage. It is not possible to know how literally to take this pretty tale, but it is a fact that on 26 July 1790 Dugald and Helen were married.[60]

Helen D'Arcy Cranstoun had been born on 13 March 1765, so that she was twenty-five at the time of her wedding, eleven years younger than her husband. Everyone must have been struck by the coincidence of both Stewart's wives being named Helen, and it may have been in part to establish her own identity that the second Mrs Stewart now signed her letters "H.D. Stewart"; certainly this is the practice which she maintained almost uniformly throughout her life. Her father, the Hon. George Cranstoun, had recently died,[61] though her mother survived until 1807. Ten years previously her eldest sister, Margaret, had married William Cunninghame, the son of a wealthy tobacco lord like John Glassford. In 1779 William Cunninghame senior had purchased the estate of Lainshaw in Ayrshire, which he set about 'improving', and his town house in Glasgow was a splendid building which is now the core of the Gallery of Modern Art in Queen Street.[62] Other members of the Cranstoun family strengthened Stewart's connection with Walter Scott. Both the middle sister, Jane, and the younger brother, George (who had taken Stewart's maths class in 1784), knew him well; George Cranstoun was born in the same year as Scott, also made law his profession, and remained a close friend until Scott's death. Like his youngest sister, George amused himself with writing, and while practising at the bar he wrote a skit called *The Diamond Beetle Case* in which he caricatured several of the judges of the day. The eldest member of the Cranstoun family, Henry, became a neighbour of Scott's at Abbotsford when he retired from the Navy Pay Office in London.[63]

Although the reviewer in the *Quarterly* described Helen as "the least beautiful of a family in which beauty was hereditary", the poet Thomas Campbell, who knew her well, wrote that "in her youth, she was stately and handsome".[64] Certainly her intelligence was not in doubt. Stewart was later to say that he never considered anything he wrote to be finished until she had reviewed it: though she probably did not understand the abstract points of his philosophy as well as he did, she helped him to illustrate his reasoned arguments by a play of feeling and imagination.[65] She had an exceptional gift for friendship, and a warmth and vivacity exactly suited to complement, and perhaps to modify, Dugald's slight formality and reserve. Their friends seem to have been well aware of this contrast between them. "One cannot write to bid her hide one's letters," Campbell once remarked to a friend, "and though she writes nonsense most deliciously, I am always afraid of the wise Professor seeing nonsense from me!"[66]

When Helen Cranstoun married she acquired not only a husband but a five-year-old son (Matthew was never a 'stepson'). Writing after Stewart's death, Matthew described his father's second marriage as "a union to which he owed much of the subsequent happiness of his life".[67] After many years of that union had passed, Helen wrote to Archibald Constable, who had just remarried, to congratulate him on his good fortune "in the most important, and most awful of lottery's – on which all life depends. You seem indeed to have drawn a prize."[68] So, indeed, had Stewart.

CHAPTER NINE

Liberal Philosopher in a Harsh Climate
1790–1796

> "The lectures of my friend Professor Stewart on moral philosophy are in the highest estimation. They are, indeed, of first-rate excellence, being the production of one of the few learned men who in these extraordinary times have not allowed their minds to swerve from the true principles of science, and to be overwhelmed with prejudice, intolerance, and, I may say, insanity." *Andrew Dalzel*

After their wedding in 1790 the Stewarts went to Ayrshire. On 5 August Mrs Dunlop of Dunlop wrote to Robert Burns, "Your friend Mr Dugald Stewart has just brought home his wife to Catrine."[1] The 60-year-old Frances Dunlop knew Mrs Stewart's sister Margaret Cunninghame, and she had met "the youngest Grace" among the Cranstoun girls and named her Euphrosyne; she was curious to see Helen's husband, especially in the light of what Burns had told her of him. She lost little time in making her way from Loudoun Castle, where she was staying with her daughter, to "go and congratulate a new-married pair", as she told Burns two weeks later. She was not disappointed in Stewart: "I never saw more modest, gentle, mild manners in a man."[2] On her return she sent "Euphrosyne" twenty lines of rhyming couplets.[3]

But Catrine was changing rapidly, and from now on it was used less by

Liberal Philosopher in a Harsh Climate (1790–1796)

Stewart and his family as a summer retreat. The cotton-mill had been built by David Dale of Glasgow[4] in partnership with a wealthy local laird.[5] Dale employed mainly women and children, for his mills required only unskilled labour and no great strength. He was a relatively enlightened employer, who provided red sandstone houses of a good standard[6] and a school for the child labourers; but the effect was of course to transform a tiny village into a small but busy industrial town. A brewery was built in 1793, and by that year the population had grown to 1600.[7] Catrine and New Lanark between them were consuming 20 per cent of the raw cotton imports into Scotland.[8]

As usual with the middle period of Stewart's life it is impossible to be exact about his permanent residence in Edinburgh. As we have seen, he referred in his letter about Burns to living at Drumsheugh during the winter of 1788-9,[9] and the Edinburgh Directory for 1790-2 gives Drumsheugh as his address. (Though Drumsheugh is now a central district of the city, just off the West End, when Boswell went to live there in 1781 he referred to his new home as "our country-house".[10]) For the years 1793-6 the Directories locate Stewart in Argyle's Square,[11] which no longer exists but was then a small area about a quarter of a mile west of the University; he may have moved there after his period at Drumsheugh.

According to Veitch he later occupied Stewartfield House, "in the neighbourhood of Edinburgh", for several years[12] during a period prior to others which can be dated more exactly and which began in the later 1790s. Certainly letters were addressed to and from him at Stewartfield in early 1794.[13] The house was demolished a hundred years after this to make way for a railway line, but it was one of several small mansions built to the south of the then rural Water of Leith. A picture shows it to have been a square three-storeyed building with a high-pitched roof surmounted by an enormous chimney.[14] Stewart himelf referred to it as "a small house on the road to Leith by Bonington".[15] The eponymous Stewart had nothing to do with Dugald, but was James Stewart, a magistrate, merchant and banker in Edinburgh who bought the estate in 1746. The area now called Stewartfield comprises a small housing and industrial estate west of Newington Road. To the south, across what would then have been open ground, there is a good view of Arthur's Seat. It is too far from the University for easy winter commuting in the eighteenth century, and it therefore seems likely that while Stewartfield was the family home during the early years of Stewart's second marriage, he used Argyle's Square or the old house in the College as *pieds-à-terre* during the working week.

It seems to have been in 1791[16] that Stewart and some other professors began to run summer courses between the middle of May and the end of July. This was done, he wrote some years later, "with a view chiefly to accommodate those students whom the situation does not permit of so long an interruption to their studies as is occasioned by our six months' vacation".[17] However helpful to the students, and presumably remunerative to their instructors, these courses must have added to the wear and tear of an already strenuous life.

On 26 June 1791 the first child of Stewart's second marriage was born. He was named George after Mrs Stewart's father.[18] Although he was to prove a gifted boy, it appears that he was never very robust. In October Stewart was ordering books from Cumnock,[19] for even if the attraction of Catrine had diminished he must still have been drawn to this part of Ayrshire to see his brother-in-law Thomas Miller and his late sister's children, and perhaps this year the country air was judged good for the baby. Miller claimed that the parish was very productive of butter and cheese. (He also reported that a leading object of the inhabitants was "to converse and dispute about religious subjects and church government, concerning which there is a considerable diversity of opinion among them".[20])

When Stewart returned to Edinburgh it was to a College where building work was now in progress. Robert Adam had been on hand to supervise it since May, and he remained in Edinburgh until the beginning of 1792. On at least one winter evening he recorded taking a chair to Professor Stewart's.[21] He was distantly related to Mrs Stewart, as his grandmother had been a daughter of the 3rd Lord Cranstoun. However, soon after his return to London, on 3 March, Adam died. His death, which was soon followed by that of his elder brother John Adam, was a setback for the construction of the new College; and before long serious financial problems brought about by the war with France caused work to grind to a halt, with a substantial part of the new building incomplete and unroofed. A petition in 1799 stated that the situation now subjected the students "to greater inconveniences than were felt during the miserable state of the old buildings".[22] Stewart had to work in such unsatisfactory conditions until he retired.

In January 1792 it fell to Mrs Stewart to acknowledge another barrel of herrings from the Rev. Mr MacLea in Bute. She did so, she told him, on behalf of Mr Stewart, for "since their arrival he has been so busy that he never has had one moment to himself, and ... there is no prospect of his having any more leisure for some weeks".[23] Stewart was in fact completing his first book, Volume I of *The Elements of the Philosophy of the Human Mind*, which he dedicated, "in testimony of the respect and affection of the author" to his old teacher, Thomas Reid, whose comments he had obtained on an early draft.[24] He dated the *Advertisement* (Preface) from the College of Edinburgh on 13 March 1792, saying that he hoped at some time in the future to supplement this analysis of man's intellectual powers with volumes concerned respectively with man as an active and moral being and with man as a member of a political society.[25]

As soon as Volume I of *The Elements* was off his hands he must have become heavily engaged with his next project. His father's old friend, and his own, Adam Smith, had died on 17 July 1790, shortly before Stewart's second marriage; and now arrangements were being made by his executors to publish a collection of his *Essays on Philosophical Subjects*. Early in January 1792 Cadell, the publisher, wrote to Edward Gibbon, "I forgot to inform you that Dr Stewart [sic – Stewart never took a doctorate] is to prefix Memoirs of the Life of Adam Smith before the intended publication."[26] The preparation of this short biography must have occupied a good deal of Stewart's time during the remainder of the year, though he told Cadell in the middle of August, "I am just now setting [out] on a little Tour to the country",[27] and at the end of October he was writing to Archy Alison from Lainshaw,[28] the estate of his new brother-in-law, William Cunninghame.

He read the first part of his *Life of Smith* to the literary class of the Royal Society of Edinburgh in January 1793.[29] In the middle of March he reported to Cadell that the *Life* was ready to send to the press, and since it was probably now too long to appear in the *Transactions* of the RSE except in an abridged form, he wondered whether it could be considered as a separate publication. If so, he hoped that it "may make my name a little more known in England, and may perhaps quicken the sale of my former work".[30] He read the remainder of the *Life* to the RSE during that month,[31] and the text did appear in full in their *Transactions* in 1794. Though he told the liberal-minded English lawyer Samuel Romilly, whom Stewart had probably first met in France in 1788 or 1789, that he had dealt with *The Wealth of Nations* more briefly than he had once intended,[32] his account of Smith devotes more attention to his philosophic and economic theories than to his life as such. But Smith's most recent biographer observes that "He collected useful facts on Smith's life and background, and preserved otherwise unavailable materials"; "his portrait of Smith is affectionate and balanced".[33]

As soon as Stewart had done with Adam Smith, the occasion for another biographical exercise was becoming imminent. Principal Robertson was now over seventy and his health was failing. During 1792 he moved from his official residence in the College to Grange House, then on the outskirts of the city, which betokened a kind of retirement. On 31

Liberal Philosopher in a Harsh Climate (1790-1796)

March of that year Stewart and Andrew Dalzel (who was to take over the Principal's house) proposed at a General Convention of the College that Robertson should be requested "to sit to Mr Raeburn for his protrait, to be hung up in the Library".[34] Robertson's international fame as a historian now rested not only on his *History of Scotland,* but on his later *History of Charles V, History of America* (an account of the discovery of the new world), and *Historical Disquisition concerning the Knowledge which the Ancients had of India.* There was a special significance in mentioning the proposed location for the portrait, for one of Robertson's major achievements had been to build up the College Library. Stewart had already had dealings with Henry Raeburn, for he had commissioned from him a portrait of his friend Lord Ancram[35] which now hangs at Monteviot [Plate 4 (a)]. For the portrait of Robertson, Raeburn was paid thirty guineas, and he charged an additional seven for the frame in which it is still mounted in Edinburgh University. The cost was divided among the twenty-seven professors.[36] [Plate 3]

Stewart often visited the old man at Grange, conversing with him through his ear-trumpet and usually finding him in his orchard, where he continued to wear the cocked hat that had been his habitual attire in the city. Robertson died of jaundice on 11 June 1793. A few days before this, no doubt aware that he had not much longer to live, he specifically sent for Stewart and asked him to write his life.[37] This further heavy assignment may have been received with a heavy heart, but it was one which in these circumstancs, and coming from a man whom he had known and been befriended by throughout his life, he could hardly refuse. He received much help from Andrew Dalzel, now joint librarian of the College, in respect of University records, and from his boyhood friend, the Principal's son, William Robertson.[38] But he was too busy to rush the job, and it was nearly three years before he completed his *Life of Robertson.*

Two matters in particular must have preoccupied him considerably during the remainder of 1793. One was the arrival on 10 April of another baby – this time, a girl.[39] She was named Maria D'Arcy Stewart after Mrs Stewart's mother, the former Maria Brisbane. The little girl was familiarly known in the family as Mia; she was Stewart's third and last child. The other preoccupation was the preparation of Stewart's second published work, intended as a philosophy textbook. Nevertheless, he found time for some travel: when he wrote to Cadell towards the end of August he mentioned that "I have been in the country" (where of course he may have been working on his book), and "I propose to leave town soon".[40] However, in September Samuel Romilly told Dumont of Geneva that among the men of letters in Edinburgh he had spent most time with was

Liberal Philosopher in a Harsh Climate (1790–1796)

"our friend Dugald Stewart whom the more I know the more I esteem for the qualities of his heart, and the more I admire and respect for his knowledge and his talents".[41]

Outlines of Moral Philosophy was complete by the beginning of the new College year. Stewart dated the Preface 8 November 1793, and the first paragraph explains his purpose.

> My principal object, in this Publication, is to exhibit such a view of the arrangement of my Lectures, as may facilitate the studies of those to whom they are addressed. In a course which employs more than five months, and which necessarily includes a great variety of disquisitions, it is difficult for a hearer to retain a steady idea of the train of thought leading from one subject to another; and, of consequence, the Lectures, by assuming the appearance of detached discourses, are in danger of losing the advantages arising from connexion and method. The following Outlines will, I hope, not only obviate this inconvenince, but will allow me, in future, a greater latitude of illustration and digression, than I could have indulged myself in with propriety, so long as my students were left to investigate the chain of my doctrines by their own reflections.[42]

Adam Ferguson had produced a similar classroom text.[43]

Stewart had not lost interest in the developing situation in France. His continued optimism about the way events were shaping is reflected in letters to Archy Alison. "The affairs of France," he wrote in November 1791, "are going on more and more every day to my satisfaction . . . The little disorders which may now and then occur in a country, where things in general are in so good a train, are of very inconsiderable importance . . . ."[44] Almost a year later (after the September massacres and the vote by the National Convention to end the monarchy and declare a Republic): "France goes on well . . . My hopes on the subject are much confirmed by a good deal of private information I have received of late . . . ."[45]

Early in January 1793 Stewart had to respond to the arrival of Archibald Alison junior on the 29th of the previous month and to Archy's invitation to Dugald to be his son's godfather. He replied:

> My dear Archy, – I rejoice at the birth of your son, and still more at the good accounts you give of Mrs Alison. I don't know what duties your Church imposes on a godfather, but I promise to do all I can to make him a Philosopher and an Economist; and I engage, as soon as he begins to snuff (which, I suppose, he will do in a dozen years hence), to make him the present of a very handsome box which I received lately, with the 'Rights of Man' inscribed on the lid.[46]

The reference, of course, was to the book by Tom Paine of which the first part, written as a response to Edmund Burke's *Refections on the*

Liberal Philosopher in a Harsh Climate (1790–1796)

Revolution in France and dedicated to George Washington, had been widely read when it was published in March 1791. The second part, which appeared in February 1792, was fiercely anti-monarchical, and called for an English version of the aims of the French Revolution. In December, Paine, who had gone to France, was tried *in absentia* and found guilty of sedition; the Government then suppressed his book, and booksellers who stocked it were threatened with imprisonment. As often happens with measures intended to be repressive, this was counter-productive, for the effect was to boost the book's readership considerably. It may be doubted whether Stewart went along with the cry that revolution was the order of the day, but the semi-jocular allusion suggests that he and his Anglican friend shared some degree of sympathy with Paine's position.

So, of course had done many others in Britain. The exclamations of William Wordsworth and Charles James Fox in relation to the early stages of the revolution in France are too well known to need repeating.[47] In December 1791, when Edinburgh University Dialectic Society debated the question "Will the Revolution in France be of more advantage than disadvantage to Europe?" the vote was unanimously affirmative.[48] But opinion seems to have swung against the revolution during the summer of 1792, especially among the propertied classes, who were badly frightened by what was happening across the Channel. These events were divisive of British public opinion, but as the Government's reaction to Tom Paine showed, national policy was moving towards suppression of any dissenting voice. In Scotland there was the notorious case of the promising young advocate Thomas Muir who had been active at the end of 1792 in establishing north of the border Societies of the Friends of the People corresponding to that formed in London by the Whig politicians Grey and Sheridan. Their aim was change by constitutional means. At one meeting Muir read a letter of support for parliamentary reform from the United Irishmen. Early in 1793 he was arrested on a charge of sedition and in August subjected to a highly partisan trial before Lord Braxfield as a result of which he was sentenced to fourteen years' transportation to Botany Bay. Romilly attended this trial and was horrified by it. (An appeal for royal clemency by William Adam was unsuccessful.)

To Stewart also this kind of policy was abhorrent. There was now talk of war between Britain and France (which had already declared war on Bohemia, Hungary and Prussia), and in his letter to Alison of early January 1793 he continued:

> I tremble at the thought of war, because it appears to me to be risking the prosperity and tranquillity of this country on the throw of a die. If we engage

in it, it will open a new source of political events, the final issue of which is beyond all calculation; but I think, in general, we may venture to predict, that it will not be agreeable to those who are most anxious to promote it. Is it not melancholy that the occurrences of the last twenty years [he is clearly thinking of British policy towards the American independence movement] should have taught statesmen so little wisdom? The infatuation of this part of the country is beyond belief. A few weeks have turned the tide most effectually, and all freedom, both of speech and of the press, is for a time suspended. But things cannot long continue in their present state, and Government will undoubtedly miscalculate its strength if it counts much on newspaper declaration. The late shocking barbarities in Paris, have furnished the means of inflaming popular passions; but if order were established in that country, or if the events of next campaign should be as contrary to the expectations of our politicians as those of the last, I am afraid to look forward to the consequences. I own I am still in hopes that the storm may blow over, and that the mercantile interest of the country may have the sense and spirit to come forward as they ought.[49]

These opinions were being expressed in private letters, but in a situation when political events were so much in the forefront of everyone's mind, most people's general views must have been pretty well known, and teachers may have had a particular difficulty about concealing them, even if they wished to do so. Stewart had made some observations in his *Life of Smith* which seem indirectly self-defensive. Smith's speculations, he wrote, "have no tendency to unhinge established institutions, or to inflame the passions of the multitude".[50] But other remarks were open to misconstruction in the new climate of fear,[51] and a whole section in *Elements of the Philosophy of the Human Mind* was reformist in tone, however guardedly – for instance:

> The danger, indeed, of sudden and rash innovations cannot be too strongly inculcated; and the views of those men who are forward to promote them, cannot be reprobated with too great severity. But it is possible also to fall into the opposite extreme, and to bring upon society the very evils we are anxious to prevent, by an obstinate opposition to those gradual and necessary reformations which the genius of the times demands. The violent revolutions which, at different periods, have convulsed modern Europe, have arisen not from a spirit of innovation in sovereigns or statesmen; but from their bigoted attachment to antiquated forms, and to principles borrowed from less enlightened ages. It is this reverence for abuses which have been sanctioned by time, accompanied with an inattention to the progress of public opinion, which has, in most instances, blinded the rulers of mankind, till government has lost all its efficiency, and till the rage of innovation has become too general and too violent to be satisfied with changes, which, if proposed at an earlier period, would have united in the

Liberal Philosopher in a Harsh Climate (1790–1796)

support of established institutions, every friend to order and to the prosperity of his country.[52]

He had, moreover, quoted with approval from Condorcet,[53] then known to him as a mathematician and one of the last of the *philosophes*; and though the force of the quotation was *against* the recovery of liberty by force of arms, in some eyes it was dangerous enough to express any agreement with one of the leaders of the Revolution.

One whose suspicions were aroused was George Jeffrey, a Depute-Clerk in the Court of Session. He was the respectable father of the much more famous Francis Jeffrey, future editor of the radical *Edinburgh Review* and later a judge in the courts where his father had worked. Having left Edinburgh High School, Francis went at the age of fourteen to Glasgow University, where he studied for two years. But though a career in the legal profession was envisaged, his father forbade him to attend the lectures of Professor Millar, who, as was noted in chapter 5, was a Whig well known for his support of liberal causes. In 1792 young Jeffrey attended lectures at Edinburgh University, but they did not include those of Dugald Stewart. His biographer, Lord Cockburn, had no doubt that Stewart's "class door . . . was shut to Jeffrey by the same prejudice that had shut John Millar's".[54]

It is possible that Stewart may also have suffered from a degree of guilt by association. His friend Lord Daer formed a branch of the Friends of the People in Wigton, and wished to be known as Citizen Douglas. Another radical with whom Stewart had been friendly was the Irishman, Will Drennan. After completing his medical studies at Edinburgh, Drennan had practised in Belfast and Newry, and there he began to take an interest in politics. At the end of 1784 he wrote a pamphlet entitled *Letters of an Irish Helot* in which he addressed his countrymen as "Fellow-Slaves" and urged them to elect delegates to a Dublin convention of the Irish Volunteers. Early in 1785 he wrote to his sister Martha, "If an opportunity happens, enclose a copy of the Helot to Dugald Stewart of Edinburgh";[55] and a year later he wrote of having sent pamphlets to Stewart, who, he presumably thought, would sympathize with his views.[56]

In 1789 Drennan moved to Dublin, and there grew more deeply involved. He became a friend of Thomas Emmet and was one of the leaders of the United Irishmen, writing the society's original prospectus. Having an eloquent style, he was chosen to write various proposals and addresses advocating Catholic emancipation, parliamentary reform and universal male suffrage. It was he who wrote the fraternal letter to the Scottish Friends of the People. In December 1792, in an *Address to the*

Volunteers, he went so far as to call upon "Citizen-Soldiers" to take up their arms and demand reform – language which could clearly be construed as seditious. He was in fact put on trial in 1794, and though he was acquitted he withdrew after that from active participation, and played no part in the rebellion of 1798.

Nevertheless, there must have been people in Edinburgh in the early '90s who heard of these events and remembered that as a student Drennan had been a close friend of the man who now occupied the chair of moral philosophy. In early 1794 Stewart was aware that in one of his circle, the judge Lord Abercromby, there appeared to be "a change in his sentiments" towards him. Abercromby, it may be said, was no advanced progressive. In the autumn of the previous year he and another judge had tried Thomas Palmer, an English unitarian preacher who was consideed to be making mischief among the working classes, and sentenced him to seven years' transportation. In his summing-up, Abercromby told the jury, "Gentlemen, the right of universal suffrage is a right which the subjects of this country have never enjoyed; and were they to enjoy it, they would not long enjoy either liberty or a free constitution."[57] Stewart asked a common friend, Will Craig, also a judge, to speak to Abercromby and discover if some misrepresentation by a third party had led him to suppose that Stewart did not adequately appreciate the kindness he had received from him.

Lord Craig undertook this mission, and reported back to Stewart in a letter dated 15 February 1794. It was not as Stewart feared; the coolness which he had observed arose from the passages in Stewart's writings to which reference has been made. After the massacres in France such opinions ought to be explicitly disavowed.

> The *triumph of Philosophy and Reason* daily exhibited in France [Abercromby had declared ironically], ought to have satisfied every thinking and every virtuous man of the danger of unhinging established institutions, even tho' such institutions should appear when considered abstractedly in the closet, to be less perfect than the Theories of ingenious and speculative men ... *after* the Massacres of Paris, he flattered himself from the high opinion he entertained of your character that you would embrace the earliest opportunity of retracting in an open and a manly manner, every sentiment you had ever entertained, and every word you had ever uttered, in favour of doctrines which have led to so giant a mishief, and above all he trusted that you would have exerted all your talents to impress upon the minds of our youth, a love and a veneration for the British constitution, upon the preservation of which it is now too evident, that not the public welfare alone, but the safety and happiness of every individual in his little domestic circle necessarily depends. Disappointed in these hopes, and

knowing with absolute certainty, that there exists at this moment a party among us, who wait only for a favourable opportunity to repeat here the same scenes of Horrour, which have been acted in France, he owns that he cannot esteem any man, who in any shape whatever gives the smallest countenance to opinions, which in *these times* and under the *circumstances* in which we are now unhappily placed, tend directly to destroy the peace and happiness of Society, and to deprive us of every thing that is valuable and dear to us in Life.[58]

The whole business had given Lord Craig "much vexation", and Stewart lost no time in thanking him for the trouble he had taken. To Abercromby's attack he responded firmly and reasonably. His own views may by now have been modified by the execution of Louis XVI and Marie Antoinette and the start of the Terror, but clearly he saw no need for apology or retraction.

> With respect to my writings, they are now before the world and I must abide by the consequences. That I differed widely from some of my friends, in rejoicing at the prospect of an extension of my own political happiness to other nations, I am not ashamed to acknowledge; but the Chapter your Lordship alludes to, bears ample testimony in my favour, that even in the most despotic governments in Europe I was aware of the mischiefs to be apprehended from the spirit of innovation and from sudden changes in established institutions . . . no reference has once been made to my opinions (so far as I have been able to learn) by any of the inflammatory writers of the times . . . as to the French Philosophers in general, and the tendency of their sceptical doctrines to corrupt the morals, and to poison the happiness of mankind, your Lordship will do me the justice to ackowledge that I opposed them with zeal, at a time when the profession of scepticism was not quite so unfashionable as it is at present. Whoever may be called upon to retract their former admiration of their principles (which have indeed *led to a giant mischief*) I certainly am not among their number.
>
> I shall ever regret that I dishonour'd some of my pages, by mentioning with respect the name of Condorcet. But when my papers were sent to the Press, he was quite unknown in any public capacity, and he enjoyed the friendship of the most respectable men in Europe. The passage I have quoted from him . . . breathes a spirit of moderation, which if it had proceeded from any other pen, would be read not only without censure but with high approbation. It is for this passage alone that I am responsible, and not for anything else in his writings – far less in his subsequent conduct. I shall only add that ever since I was Professor of Moral Philosophy, I have concluded my course with a set of lectures on the English Constitution, the peculiar excellencies of which I have always enlarged upon in the warmest and most enthusiastic terms . . . Of the utility of my labours as an Instructor of Youth, it does not become me to judge, but I may be allowed to say, that I have long enjoyed,

and that I continue to enjoy, every testimony of approbation which the public can give.

I hope you will forgive me for troubling you with these details. I have no view in stating them to court the friendship of any man – but to do justice to myself. Your Lordship has had some knowledge of my habits in private life, and I believe are satisfied that my *little domestic circle* gives me as deep an interest in the tranquillity of my country, as any individual can profess however elevated his station.[59]

This dignified rejoinder may be presumed to have silenced, if not entirely to have appeased, Lord Abercromby. Mrs Stewart wrote across Craig's acknowledgement: "Scotland in the 1794. From 2 persons who were at least 3 even'gs in the Week in our house."[60] The atmosphere of over-reactive suspicion, designed to silence all but the boldest advocates of any kind of reform, was to persist for many years, not least in a Scotland effectively governed by Henry Dundas. Stewart, together with Andrew Dalzel and John Playfair, were the leading Whigs in the University. Lord Cockburn wrote later:

> Of these three, mathematics, which was his chair, enabled Playfair to come better off than his two colleagues; for Dalzel had to speak of Grecian liberty, and Stewart to explain the uses of liberty in general; and anxiously were they both watched. Stewart, in particular, though too spotless and too retired to be openly denounced, was an object of great secret alarm.[61]

A conspiracy to overthrow the government was discovered in Edinburgh in May of 1794, and a man named Robert Watt was convicted of high treason and publicly hanged. In July the militia of Royal Edinburgh Volunteers was formed. In September Mrs Dunlop of Dunlop told Robert Burns that his goddess, Liberty, "has behaved in such a way as to injure her reputation . . . she is too much attached of late to the society of butchers".[62] France's declaration of war early in 1793, bringing fears of imminent invasion, had further aggravated the situation. In Scott's novel *The Antiquary,* set in the 1790s, the following dialogue occurs:

> "And what news do you bring us from Edinburgh, Monkbarns?" said Sir Arthur; "how wags the world in Auld Reekie?"
>
> "Mad, Sir Arthur, mad – irretrievably frantic – far beyond dipping in the sea, shaving the crown, or drinking hellebore. The worst sort of frenzy, a military frenzy, hath possessed man woman and child."
>
> "And high time, I think," said Miss Wardour [the heroine of the novel], "when we are threatened with invasion from abroad, and insurrection at home."[63]

Liberal Philosopher in a Harsh Climate (1790–1796)

Such was not an atmosphere in which liberal opinions could easily flourish. But in 1798 Andrew Dalzel wrote:

> The lectures of my friend Professor Stewart on moral philosophy are in the highest estimation. They are, indeed, of first-rate excellence, being the production of one of one of the few learned men who in these extraordinary times have not allowed their minds to swerve from the true principles of science, and to be overwhelmed with prejudice, intolerance, and, I may say, insanity.[64]

It may be noted that in 1817 Stewart advised Macvey Napier that he should have a set of Condorcet's works in the Signet Library: "it is a book which ought certainly to be in such a collection."[65]

During these years a number of students who were later to become well known attended Stewart's philosophy class.[66] Walter Scott has already been mentioned. One who entered Edinburgh University in 1790 was James Mill, the future politician, historian, utilitarian philosopher and father of John Stuart Mill; he wrote that he attended Stewart's lectures as often as he could, and regarded them as "a high treat".[67] Others in the early 1790s were John Leyden, the shepherd's son from the Borders village of Denholm who became a friend of Scott and a scholar of Oriental languages; Francis Horner, Whig politician and expert on economic affairs, who was to be a family friend; Henry Duncan, who became minister at Ruthwell in Dumfriesshire, founded the first savings bank in 1810 and continued for many years to correspond with Mrs Stewart;[68] and Duncan's close friend Henry Brougham, a great-nephew of Principal Robertson and future Lord Chancellor of England.

A student who was to play a greater part in the life of Stewart himself was a precocious boy named Thomas Brown. He lingered behind after one lecture to ask the professor a question: if memory depends on voluntary attention, as Stewart maintained, how is it that we remember dreams? It so happened that this objection had recently been put to Stewart by Professor Prévost of Geneva; Stewart was impressed by his young critic's acuteness and took him under his friendly wing.[69] Brown went on to study medicine, but he maintained his interest in philosophy and literary matters, and eventually was to become Stewart's effective successor in the chair of moral philosophy.

Writing about his father after his death, Matthew Stewart recorded that about this time –

> he rendered his house . . . the resort of all who were most distinguished for genius, acquirements, or elegance in Edinburgh, and of all the foreigners who were led to visit the capital of Scotland. So happily did he succeed in

assorting his guests, – so well did he combine the grave and the gay, the cheerfulness of youth with the wisdom of age, and amusement with the weightier topics that formed the subjects of conversation to his more learned visitors, – that his evening parties possessed a charm which many who have frequented them have since confessed that they have sought in vain in more splendid and insipid entertainments."[70]

No doubt his young, intelligent, well connected yet self-effacing wife played a considerable part in the success of these occasions, which were, according to Veitch, "for many years the source of an influence that most beneficially affected the society of the capital. Those meetings, moreover, embraced, even when political zeal was at its highest, men of varied shades of opinion, and thus contributed not a little to soothe the bitterness of party feeling in Edinburgh."[71]

One such gathering took place during a visit to Edinburgh in the autumn of 1795 by Anna Barbauld.[72] Mrs Barbauld had published several popular volumes of prose for children along with her brother, John Aikin, and she was a supporter of radical causes such as the freedom of Corsica and the abolition of slavery. During her evening at the Stewarts' she read, with great effect, an unpublished translation by William Taylor of Norwich of a German ballad which had recently come much into vogue, *Lenore* by Gottfried August Burger.

This incident had a sequel involving Walter Scott, then twenty-four years old, and two members of the Cranstoun family. Scott, as he wrote afterwards, "was not present upon this occasion, although he had the distinguished advantage of being a familiar friend and frequent visitor of Professor Stewart and his family". But when he returned to Edinburgh he heard enthusiastic reports from his friends, including Mrs Stewart's brother, George Cranstoun, who was able to quote from Mrs Barbauld's performance the lines –

> Tramp, tramp across the land they speede,
> Splash, splash across the sea.

Scott was seized with a desire to make his own translation of the poem (which was actually based on a Scottish ballad), but it was the spring of the following year before he was able to obtain a copy of the original German. One evening he promised his own version to his friend and mentor Jane Cranstoun, who kept house for her brother in Frederick Street, and Scott finished it by daybreak the following morning – incorporating, with acknowledgement, two lines very similar to those of Taylor which George had remembered. Before breakfast he delivered his manuscript to Jane, who was astonished and delighted. "Upon my word," she wrote to a friend, "Walter Scott is going to turn out a poet." Knowing that Scott was about to meet the young lady to whom he was then paying court, she quickly arranged for a few copies of his translation to be elegantly printed by Robert Miller, the bookseller, and sent one to him with which to impress Williamina Belsches. Some time later Jane Cranstoun told Scott of an occasion when Stewart was reading the Scott translation to a certain Mr Greenfield (possibly William Greenfield, Hugh Blair's successor as profesor of rhetoric and belles lettres): "he look'd up and poor G. was sitting with his hands nail'd to his knees and the big tears rolling down his innocent nose in so piteous a manner that Mrs S. burst out laughing".[73]

Once again it is difficult to be sure in which house it was that the Stewarts entertained Mrs Barbauld. In the Edinburgh Directory for 1796–7 Stewart's address changes from Argyle's Square to Callander's Entry, which was on the north side of the Canongate; and in 1797–8 it becomes Lothian House, Canongate.[74] At some point in the mid-90s, therefore, the family must have moved from Stewartfield to Lothian House,[75] which was to be their home for about ten years. Sometimes known as 'Lothian Hut', this was a small but magnificent town mansion of the Lothian family which had been built in 1750. It stood where the Scottish Parliament building is now, surrounded by a pleasant garden. The 4th Marquess of Lothian seems to have been the last to use it, and it then became the home of his widow for some twenty years. It may well be that after the dowager marchioness died Stewart's friendship with the 5th Marquess, and in particular with his heir, Lord Ancram, together with Mrs Stewart's kinship with the family, secured them the tenancy. A masonic factor is also possible: there is no evidence whether Stewart continued as an active mason during these years, but presumably he was still in membership, and in the years 1794–6 the Earl of Ancram was Grand Master of Freemasons in Scotland. The house had a particularly splendid dining-room that must have lent itself to the large-scale entertaining in which the Stewarts engaged at this period.

Certainly it was from "Canongate" that Stewart wrote to Walter Scott in 1796 to acknowledge four copies of "your beautiful Translations", which included that of *Lenore*. He and his wife would keep two of these as "both set a high value on them as gifts from the Author"; the others he would send to a friend in England who he hoped would make their merit more widely known. "In a few weeks, I am fully persuaded, they will enjoy the public attention to the utmost extent of your wishes, without the aid of any recommendation whatever. – I ever am, dear Sir, yours most truly . . ."[76]

On 21 March 1796 he had read the first part of his *Account of the Life and Writings of Dr Robertson* to the Royal Society of Edinburgh (second and third instalments being read to meetings in May and June respectively of 1799),[77] and in the summer of 1796 much of his time was taken up with another elderly friend. This was Dr Thomas Reid, who came through from Glasgow, accompanied by his daughter, to stay with Dr James Gregory, who was a relative. The old man's regard for his former student had been demonstrated in 1785 when he dedicated his *Essays on the Intellectual Powers of Man* jointly to Stewart and Gregory. Reid was now eighty-six. In 1792, a few weeks after his wife's death, he had written to Stewart: "I have more health than at my time of life I had any reason to expect. I walk about; entertain myself with reading what I soon forget; can converse with one person, if he articulates distinctly, and is within ten inches of my left ear; go to church, without hearing one word of what is said."[78] In fact he was still active in mind and body. In the following year he added slyly, in writing to Stewart: "Have you read *A Vindication of the Rights of Woman*? [Mary Wollstonecraft's book was first published in 1792.] I think a Professor of Morals may find some things worthy of his attention, mixed, perhaps, with other things which he may not approve."[79]

Now he was in Edinburgh, and Stewart recorded:

> As Dr Gregory's professional engagements . . . necessarily interfered much with his attention to his guest, I enjoyed more of Dr Reid's society than might otherwise have fallen to my share. I had the pleasure, accordingly, of spending some hours with him daily, and of attending him in his walking excursions, which frequently extended to the distance of three or four miles. His faculties (excepting his memory which was considerably impaired) appeared as vigorous as ever; and, although his deafness prevented him from taking any share in general conversation, he was still able to enjoy the company of a friend . . . In apparent soundness and activity of body, he resembled more a man of sixty than of eighty-seven.[80]

However, not long after his return to Glasgow, Dr Reid became seriously ill, and he died on 7 October 1796. "I hate biography," Stewart wrote to Archy Alison in 1797 with reference to his own *Life of Robertson*,[81] and it is not clear at what point he decided to make Reid the subject of his third and last essay in that art – writing to Dr Samuel Parr in May 1801 he said that in doing so he was yielding "to the wishes of some of my friends", and he hoped with it "to close for ever my attempts as a biographer".[82] His *Account of the Life and Writings of Thomas Reid, DD* was read to meetings of the Royal Society of Edinburgh during 1802.[83] After Reid's death "he was . . . the only writer of recognised authority upon philosophical topics in the island".[84]

CHAPTER TEN

Students and Travels
1796–1800

"Ward was evidently a man who deeply needed sympathy, and especially a woman's sympathy – one to whom he could pour out his heart and his thoughts, and to whom he could look for comfort and advice. Such a woman he found to perfection in Mrs Stewart."   S. H. Romilly

"In 1796," in the words Stewart's elder son, whose life as a boy must have been much affected by this development, "he was induced once more to open his house for the reception of students".[1] There were several differences from the time when he took in resident students during the early 1780s. He was now living in the elegant accommodation of Lothian House, and he was an older man (almost forty-three at the beginning of November 1796), though he had the support of his still youthful wife. Moreover, whereas the first group came mainly from the Scottish gentry and nobility, the second was predominantly from the Whig aristocracy of England. In part this reflected the relatively low esteem in which Oxford and Cambridge were held at this time, and the closure of the continent during the war with France, but it was also a positive tribute to the high reputation of Edinburgh University and the fame of two or three distinguished professors, of whom Stewart himself was one.

The initial move seems to have come from the rather unpopular Whig grandee, the Marquess of Lansdowne, who, as Lord Shelburne, had been

Prime Minister for some eight months in 1782–3 and had overseen the negotiations leading to peace with the American colonies. During this period his confidential adviser had been his friend the Chancellor of the Duchy of Lancaster, the first Baron Ashburton. As John Dunning, Ashburton had been a barrister and the MP who in 1780 moved the famous motion that "the influence of the crown has increased, is increasing, and ought to be diminished". Ashburton died in 1783, aged fifty-one, and his title was inherited by his infant son, Richard Barré. In due course Richard had gone to Westminster School, but now that he was about fourteen Lansdowne was concerned about his higher education, and advised his mother to send him to a Scottish university. He wrote to Stewart for advice about this.[2]

In March 1796 Stewart sent him detailed information concerning College terms, the availability of lodgings, and the courses which young Ashburton might follow. He added: "I should have wished Lord A. to have been a year or two older before coming here, for if our Scotch Universities have any advantages, I sincerely think that it is in those branches which commonly conclude an Academical Education."[3] This letter led to a proposal from Ashburton's mother and guardian that the boy should stay with the Stewarts while studying at Edinburgh University. Stewart agreed to take him for "a fortnight's trial", and he arrived around the middle of June.[4] He was a rather odd youth, but on the 26th Stewart wrote to Lady Ashburton to report "that everything I have hitherto seen of his temper and disposition has prepossessed me much in his favour, and that, if I am not greatly deceived by appearances, there is every prospect of our going on very comfortably together".

To occupy his time until the College term should begin in November, Stewart had engaged private tutors in classics, French and drawing, "and he has consented to take lessons from a dancing master whenever I shall think proper". Stewart concluded:

> Mrs Stewart, who enters perfectly into your Ladyship's anxiety about your son, begs me to assure you that every attention shall be paid to his health while he remains here. And (as I have mentioned her name) your Ladyship will forgive me when I add that I don't know any person in the country from whose conversation and society he has a fairer opportunity of deriving improvement.[5]

In the middle of July Lady Ashburton told Lord Lansdowne that "my son writes me every week in the highest spirits and desires me to inform all his friends how much happier he is than with the system at Westminster".[6]

In September Lord Lansdowne wrote to Stewart again, this time about his own son by his second marriage, Lord Henry Petty. Henry, who was a couple of years older than Ashburton, had also been attending Westminster School, where he was under the special care of a private tutor, the Rev. Mr Debarry. He had been educated very much with a view to the career in public life on which he was soon to embark, and now his father had decided that rather than attend public lectures in London, where at this period there was no university, he too should come to Edinburgh with his tutor. Lansdowne hoped that Henry might acquire some knowledge of scientific principles, and envisaged an establishment "liberal enough to enable him and Mr Debarry to cultivate the acquaintance of such men of letters and such professional men as you may perhaps have the goodness to point out to them". He asked for Stewart's views on these plans, adding, "I cannot forego this opportunity of expressing the great satisfaction it has given me to hear from Lord Lauderdale of your goodness to Ashburton. It gives me great pleasure that passing through your hands his heart cannot fail of being enlarged as well as his understanding."[7] Stewart again expressed his readiness to help, and assured Lansdowne that "if Lord Henry arrives here before the end of October, he will have the choice of the best lodgings in the neighbourhood of the College, before the town begins to be crowded". He suggested a comfortable hotel in the New Town where they might stay for a few days while they looked round.[8]

Thus when the new College year began in November 1796 the Stewarts had Lord Ashburton in their home as a resident student, and a form of proxy guardianship of Lord Henry Petty. Petty obviously knew Ashburton well, and he spent much time with the family at Lothian House, where the Stewarts soon came both to respect and to be fond of him.[9] He attended Stewart's own lecture course in his first year,[10] and in January 1797, no doubt with Stewart's encouragement, he joined the Speculative Society.

Among his fellow-students in the moral philosophy class were George Birkbeck, the future pioneer of popular education; Lovell Edgeworth, brother of Maria Edgeworth, the Irish writer; and the Austrian Count Wenceslaus Gottfried Purgstall.[11] Presumably it was at Lothian House that the Count met Mrs Stewart's sister Jane Cranstoun: he married her in June 1797. After their wedding they went to live in one of his properties, Schloss Riegersburg in Stiermark (Styria), which reminded Jane of Stirling Castle. The Count suffered during the Napoleonic wars, and died in 1812. Despite the entreaties of her friends Jane Purgstall did not return to Scotland, but remained in Austria until her death at Schloss Hainfeld in 1835.

Within a short time the Stewart household was further enlarged. In mid-February 1797 Stewart was writing to Lord Lansdowne: "I am much indebted to your Lordship for the very agreeable information you have been so good as [to]convey to me about Lord Dudley and his connections. Everything is now settled between us, and I expect the young Gentleman at Edinburgh before the end of March." He went on to refer to Lord Henry's talents as "of the very first order", and reported that "Lord Ashburton continues to behave to my entire satisfaction in every essential respect. Your Lordship is well acquainted with his peculiarities; but I have always found him perfectly good natured and tractable, and possessed of an uncommonly acute and active mind. I have seldom seen a more decided turn for Mathematics, in which he has already made a very considerable progress for his age."[12]

The son and only child of the third Viscount Dudley and Ward, to whom Stewart referred, came to Lothian House in March 1797 and was another for whom the Stewarts became virtual foster-parents. Before he arrived in Edinburgh, John William Ward had had an unhappy childhood. His rather eccentric though enormously wealthy father had allowed him neither sports nor playmates, but had insisted on a regime of unremitting study. While still a young boy he had been set up in a separate establishment from his parents and put in the hands of an Oxford tutor. Thirty years later he was to serve as foreign secretary under both Canning and the Duke of Wellington, but at this time he was a shy though clever and sensitive young man of seventeen, sadly lacking in self-confidence, and craving the care and affection which Mrs Stewart gave to him generously. The subsequent editor of his letters wrote:

> Ward was evidently a man who deeply needed sympathy, and especially a woman's sympathy – one to whom he could pour out his heart and his thoughts, and to whom he could look for comfort and advice. Such a woman he found to perfection in Mrs Stewart. She was sufficiently his senior in point of years for him to be guided by her experience of the world, and yet not too much so for his intense admiration for her to be untinged with a certain element of romance. In his earliest letters from Oxford [where he matriculated in October 1799] he writes to her as to one who had supplied the place of a mother to him; she is his 'dearest mama'; then, as a young man entering upon public life, the 'mama' is dropped, and the tinge of romance becomes more apparent in the pet name of 'Ivy'. In his later letters this form of address also disappears, but his expressions of devotion when they occur show that his love for his divinity remained as strong as ever, though the tone is no longer that of a boyish lover, but of one writing to an old and very dear friend. This love and respect were unbounded, and continued to the end.[13]

Ward remained with the Stewarts for two years, attending Stewart's own class in 1798–9.[14] The Earl of Dudley, as he became in 1827, died unmarried, predeceasing Mrs Stewart by some five years. At the beginning of the twentieth century his letters to her, which were thought to have been destroyed, were published under the title *Letters to "Ivy" from the First Earl of Dudley*. A possible clue to the origin of this nickname occurs in a letter which Mrs Stewart wrote to a later boarder, Lord Palmerston, when she told him, "Great Ash's, little Oaks, and large Ivys all salute the Palm."[15] Lord Ashburton was familiarly known as Ash, and this may have given rise to a household joke about trees; the little oaks may have been Matthew and George Stewart, and ivy is of course known for clinging to other growths.

Stewart took advantage of the long summer vacations to travel. In 1797 he set out through the Scottish borders (Melrose and Dryburgh) to Carlisle, the Lake District and Barnard Castle, where he noted that he "parted here with Lady A." This probably implies that Ashburton's mother had joined Stewart and her son for part of an educational tour. Hence he proceeded by Ripon, Fountains Abbey and Boroughbridge to York. The impressions of York Minster which he recorded in his journal reflect an active mind alert to both aesthetic and technical interest and the interdependence of the two.

> saw [the Cathedral], for the first time, more than 20 years ago, and now (after all that I have seen since) more struck with it than ever – both in considering the simple grandeur and majesty of the whole fabric, and the beauty and elegance of its parts in detail. The west elevation (which first presents itself in going from the inn) most admired, and I think justly. Two towers, with a beautiful window between them. The principal tower rising from the centre of the church, grand from its height, and at the same time perfectly beautiful in all its proportions. The inside of the church unites all the perfections of which Gothic architecture appears susceptible, without the disadvantages commonly attending it – grand and solemn without gloom – perfect illumination of every corner. The columns light and airy, yet manifestly equal to the weight they have to support – partly from the striking solidity of the masonry, and partly from the lightness and beauty of the roof, conveying even to the most ignorant eye, some general conception of the manner in which it is supported. The distribution of the pressure among the different columns, by means of the vaulted compartments of the roof, and the systematic connections and mutual dependencies of all the different parts of the edifice. The slightest survey is sufficient for comprehending as much of the general principles on which the stability of the building depends as is necessary for the satisfaction of the spectator, while at the same time the skill is so refined, that an attentive examination only encourages the wonder.

I am inclined to think that this constitutes the chief superiority of Gothic over Grecian architecture, that, in the latter, the means employed are too obvious, neither furnishing any employment to the spectator's ingenuity nor conveying any high idea of the skill of the designer. A great edifice accordingly in the Grecian style only suggests the notion of immense labour and expense, without leading up the imagination to one comprehensive mind which embraced the whole design and contained the means of carrying it into execution.

Very few minute ornaments in the style of Melrose, excepting a few specimens here and there, which seemed intended to shew, that the artists were perfectly equal to this species of work, if they had chosen to indulge their dexterity. Obscene variations in various places – chiefly levelled at the *regular* clergy . . . ?[16]

In the summer of 1798 the circle of Stewart's younger friends was again enlarged, this time by the arrival of the Rev. Sydney Smith, who was then curate at Nether Avon on Salisbury Plain. The squire of the parish, Michael Hicks Beach of Williamstrip Park in Gloucestershire, had taken a great liking to Smith, and asked him to act as travelling tutor to his eldest son, Michael. Since the war prevented their going on the continent, Edinburgh University was chosen as the base for their studies, and at the end of June, within a week or two of reaching the city, Smith reported to his pupil's father that Stewart was one with whom they had already become friendly.[17]

Stewart recorded in his travel journal that in the summer of 1798 he visited Wales.[18] He wrote down no details of his trip, but it would seem that one thing he and his wife did was to visit the two women, Lady Eleanor Butler and Miss Sarah Ponsonby, who had famously left their respective homes in Ireland to establish a joint ménage and become known as the Ladies of Llangollen. With such financial support as they could importune, they read together, cared for a garden and often dressed in male clothes. In their gothicized cottage they received a number of distinguished visitors, and Miss Ponsonby recorded in her tiny handwriting that on 19 October they paid ten shillings and sixpence "to Mr Green for a drawing for Mrs Stewart".[19] Mr Green was in all probabilty one of three artistic brothers who flourished at this time, possibly Amos Green who was among other things a landscape painter, and the drawing is likely to have been a topographical print.[20] This may well have been given in reciprocation for some tribute which visitors to the Ladies were expected to provide. Contact between them and the Stewarts was maintained thereafter.

When the new academic year began, another young man became a frequent guest at Lothian House. This was Thomas Campbell, who had recently come to Edinburgh from Glasgow with a view to studying law. He was already writing some minor verse, and the Stewarts took a parental interest in him.[21] In the spring of 1799 Campbell produced his first major poem, *The Pleasures of Hope*, which immediately made him famous.

In the summer of that year Stewart received a letter from Lord Henry Petty, now nineteen years old, who had left Edinburgh to go to Trinity College, Cambridge. In his reply to "Dear Lord H.", Stewart assured him how much interest Mrs Stewart and he would always feel in whatever concerned him.

> I am particularly anxious to know in what manner you are likely to employ the precious years that remain to be passed before you enter on public life, and I sincerely wish on your account as well as on many others that the state of the continent may soon admit of your carrying into execution the plan you had formed of visiting Europe at a period when it presents a spectacle so singularly interesting.

Petty did in fact set out on a short "grand tour" when he left Cambridge after the Peace of Amiens in 1802. Stewart continued:

> We continue to go on at Edinburgh in our old uniform way – nor do I recollect a single incident since you left us worthy of notice . . . In a few weeks Mrs S. and I with Lord A. set out for Shropshire to meet his mother, leaving Ward in Northumberland with a friend of his father's, Col. H. Paul. I could have wished to proceed as far to the south as Wiltshire, and also to pay a visit to Warwick Castle, but I am limited in my absence to three weeks, of which I must devote a few days to my old friend Alison.[22]

In fact Stewart's holiday journal shows that after visiting Kenley in Shropshire, where Archy Alison had his curacy (and studied natural history as a disciple of Gilbert White of nearby Selborne), he did manage in that summer of 1799 to get to Bath and across the Wiltshire border to Bowood House, the home of Henry Petty's father, the Marquess of Lansdowne. Here Lord and Lady Holland found them as part of "a numerous company" when they arrived at Bowood on 25 September.

Elizabeth, Lady Holland recorded in her Journal: "Dugald Stewart and his wife, from Edinburgh, were here; he is reserved, and I did not hear him speak, but he is supposed deservedly to enjoy a high reputation. She is clever, well-informed, and pleasing."[23] While they were all at Bowood the Stewarts may have been asked to dine with the Hollands in London, for they did so, either in Mayfair or at Holland House, on Sunday 13 October, and on the following day the two couples went to the theatre together.[24] At Holland House at this period Lady Holland presided over social gatherings of literary and political figures of the Whig persuasion. Stewart was becoming closely acquainted with a growing number of this circle.

However, his reference to Warwick Castle shows that his reputation stood high not only among fellow Whigs. Another of his resident students at this time, after leaving Winchester, was Henry Richard, Lord Brooke, heir to the Tory George Greville, second Earl of Warwick.[25] Spending time in Edinburgh had become something of a tradition in this family. The Earl himself had been educated under the care of Principal Robertson, and his younger brothers, Charles and Robert Greville, had lodged with Adam Ferguson in the mid-1760s.[26] After leaving Edinburgh, Lord Brooke became Tory MP for Warwickshire from 1802 until 1816, when he succeeded to the title and also succeeded his father as Recorder of Warwick. He lived until 1853. But the absence of evidence of subsequent visits or correspondence suggests that he did not remain on as close terms with the Stewarts as others of their former students. Roughly contemporary with Brooke and with John Ward as a resident at Lothian House, which he left in 1799, was Laurence Sulivan.[27] Sulivan's grandfather had been Chairman of the East India Company, and his father was a private secretary to Warren Hastings. Laurence will figure again in this narrative in connection with the most famous of all the Stewarts' resident students.

The social life of which the Stewarts made their home the focus during these years was closely connected with their role as temporary guardians to the young men under their roof, for they justly believed, as Matthew Stewart put it, "that the formation of manners, and of taste in conversation, constituted a no less important part in the education of men destined to mix so largely in the world, than their graver pursuits".[28] A number of students other than their own residents were frequently guests at Lothian House. As well as Francis Horner and Henry Petty, these included the scholarly and well loved Lord Webb Seymour, a brother of the Duke of Somerset, who came to Edinburgh in 1797 and made it his home until the end of his life.

Sydney Smith, whose wit and lively disposition made him friends wherever he went, was another frequenter of Lothian House. Along with his pupil, Michael Hicks Beach, he attended Stewart's lectures in moral philosophy. During his stay in Edinburgh he also took occasional services at the Charlotte Chapel in Rose Street, and it is clear that Stewart did not value him only as a stimulating social companion, for he declared that the original and unexpected ideas in Smith's preaching gave him "a thrilling sensation of sublimity never before awakened by any other oratory".[29] In the summer of 1800 Smith returned to England to marry Catherine Pybus, the daughter of a London banker. Michael Hicks Beach junior had now ceased to be his pupil, but he was succeeded in that capacity by his younger brother William, who lived with the newly married couple in Edinburgh's George Street. Smith's friendship with Stewart, based on mutual respect between the two men, now included their respective wives, and was to last for many years.

CHAPTER ELEVEN

The Stewarts and the Palmerstons
1800–1803

"I like Mr and Mrs Stewart amazingly, it is impossible for anybody to be kinder than they both are." Hon. Henry Temple

In June 1800 Stewart received a letter from the 2nd Viscount Palmerston.[1] Because his title was an Irish one, Palmerston was eligible to serve as a Member of Parliament, and he had done so, in the Whig interest, since 1765. Though not a prominent politician, he was a highly sociable man, possessing country estates at Sheen in the Derbyshire Peak District and at Broadlands near Romsey in Hampshire, besides a town house in Hanover Square where he entertained lavishly; he knew practically everyone of consequence in his time. He was also a notable collector of paintings. To Stewart he wrote:

> My son, who was fifteen years of age last October, has risen nearly to the top of Harrow School and has given me uniform satisfaction with regard to his disposition, his capacity and his acquirements. He is now coming to that critical and important period when a young man's mind is most open to receive such impressions as may operate powerfully on his character and his happiness during theremainder of his life. At this time, therefore, I think it of the greatest consequence that he should be judiciously directed through such a course of studies as may give full exercise to his talents and enlarge his understanding, and that he should converse as much as possible with persons to whose opinions he must look up with deference, and in whose

society his manners would be improved and his morals secured. These objects I have always thought unattainable by boys remaining in the upper class of a public school, who can only pursue the common routine of classical instruction, and who must associate principally with companions from whom they can derive no improvement. It has therefore always been my intention to place my son, when he should attain the period to which he has now arrived, in some intermediate situation between school and an English university, if that should be his future destination: and after much consideration and enquiry, it is the united wish of Lady Palmerston and myself, with a direct view to all those points I have enumerated, to place him under your direction, and in the family of yourself and Mrs Stewart, whose character, you will, I am sure, allow me to say, has very considerable weight in our determination.[2]

The Stewarts were pleased to realize that the Palmerstons' decision must have been influenced by good reports from the Earl of Warwick and Lord Brooke. Stewart must have been conscious, too, of the compliment to the Scottish universities implicit in this northern migration of the English aristocracy; no doubt he was aware that in 1799 the Earl of Lauderdale had prevailed upon Professor John Millar to accept William Lamb, the future Lord Melbourne, and his brother Frederick as pupils in his home in Glasgow. Stewart replied to say that he would be honoured to receive Mr Temple (the Palmerston family name) as proposed, though it would suit him best if the young man's arrival were deferred until the beginning of the academic year in November.[3]

In the latter part of the summer the Stewart family spent some time in Burntisland across the Firth of Forth, described by one who knew it well at this period as "a small quiet seaport town" bounded on the east "by a beautiful bay with a sandy beach".[4] It would have been an appropriate place to go with two young children. By 6 October Stewart was back in Edinburgh, for he wrote from there to the army son of Charles Hutton the mathematician, passing on some advice from his friend John Playfair, who was then working on his *Illustrations of the Huttonian Theory of the Earth*,[5] concerning the geology of Schiehallion.[6]

The Palmerston family reached Edinburgh in October, and Lord Palmerston recorded in his journal for the 7th, 8th and 9th of November: "During these days we remained at Edinburgh and finally settled Harry, much to our satisfaction, in the house of Professor Stewart, under whose care he is to pursue his studies and attend the lectures of some of the professors in the University of Edinburgh." Before Harry's parents left the city, Palmerston made a few notes which provide a partial account of the kind of service which Stewart provided for his young boarders.

The Stewarts and the Palmerstons (1800–1803)

> Lectures are read in the College at Edinburgh in various branches of science, by the respective professors, to all who choose to attend them. No students reside in the College, nor are they under any kind of regulation or discipline. Mr Stewart is the only professor who receives pupils. He has never had more than two or three at a time. He has at present Lord Ash[burton] and Harry, besides his own son, who is about Harry's age, and pursues the same course of study. [Matthew Stewart had in fact started at Edinburgh University in 1799.] We understand that he has lately declined taking any additional pupils, but we have no certain knowledge of the fact, or what his intentions really are. Mr Stewart takes considerable pains with the young men under his care, if they are disposed to be industrious and, in that case, they may, by his assistance, get much forwarder and draw much more advantage from the lectures of the other professors than they could otherwise do. He sometimes, as an evening amusement, encouraged the young men in his house to debate before him upon some subject previously agreed upon.
>
> Mr Stewart's terms are £400 per annum, for board and for his own instruction. The payment to other professors, which are inconsiderable, and the expenses of masters, are not included.[7]

The inflation which had taken place since the beginning of the war with France meant that £400 in 1800 was worth rather less in purchasing power than the £250 that Will Drennan recorded Stewart as charging in 1782; but since Stewart had told Lord Lansdowne four years previously that good lodgings in Edinburgh for a student and his tutor could be had for a guinea and a half per week,[8] £400 a year for a student on his own, even if it included stabling for a horse, was still a substantial charge. On the other hand, as Harry Temple's experience bears out, Stewart took his responsibilities very seriously and gave generously of his time. As well as supervising his students' educational and social life, he and his wife were ready to look after them for a considerable part of the long holiday, and often took them on summer excursions, as they had done with Lord Ashburton.

Harry's room in Lothian House looked towards Arthur's Seat, and he found the house "perfectly quiet and pleasant". In addition to Mr and Mrs Stewart and his contemporary, Matthew, there were the two younger Stewart children; Harry reported escorting George ("an amazingly nice little fellow") to the High School, to which, it seems, he crept somewhat unwillingly. He thought Lord Ashburton "the most singular compound of oddities" he had ever seen; his short legs made him resemble "a young hippopotamus or seacow", and Harry thought him, though good humoured, "on the verge of madness".[9] Also in residence was a nephew of Stewart's; this was probably Peter Miller, Janet's eldest son, who would

The Stewarts and the Palmerstons (1800–1803)

then have been eighteen. Since he eventually became a doctor, he may well have been studying medicine at this period. His younger brother William Miller, known in the family as Willy, also frequented the Stewart home while Harry Temple was there. Before the end of November Harry wrote to his father:

> I like Mr and Mrs Stewart amazingly, it is impossible for anybody to be kinder than they both are. Lord A improves upon acquaintance, though his oddities and whims are surprising. He has a surprising dread of squinting and he thinks that the study of optics must bring it on; therefore as Mr Stewart in his lectures about the sense of seeing described the anatomy of the eye, he would not go to college that day . . .
>
> My hours at college are from 9 to 10, 12 to 1, 2 to 3; Mr Playfairs's, algebra or second class; Mr St., Moral Philosophy; and Mr Tytler's historical lectures. The hours are rather awkward, as no two lectures come together. In general the students manage it so that once going up to college serves for all, but as I breakfast before nine, I have the two hours from 10 to 12 perfectly free. The only part of the day which is lost is from 1 to 2, for in a bad day if I return to Lothian House, I have no time to do anything before it is time to go back again to Mr Tytler's lecture. I intended to have employed that hour three times a week in riding, but as that does not seem to answer, Mr Stewart proposed my taking a lesson of drawing. There is a very good master who lives very near the college, and he can give me from one to two twice a week, Tuesdays and Thursdays. I believe he would give me an hour on Saturday, but as that is our holiday, I would rather have it perfectly unengaged. I like the plan very much if you have no objection . . . Three times a week you know I read Latin and Greek with Mr Williamson from 3 to 4 . . . I get on very well with Mr Stewart in Euclid, I am nearly through the first book. I should have been through it already if we had gone on regularly every night, but when my headaches were bad he would not let me do any . . .[10]

Lord Palmerston replied: "I am rejoiced to find that you are so well pleased with Mr Stewart. His character stands so very high in the world, and both he and Mrs Stewart appeared to us so thoroughly amiable and kind, that I had no doubt but that you would all be equally well satisfied with each other. I approve very much of the disposition of your time . . ."[11] Harry also wrote to his mother, mentioning again his disinclination to have drawing lessons on Saturdays, as he liked to keep them "disengaged, either for skating, shooting or walking".[12] His father had permitted him to begin shooting while he was still at Harrow, and he was to remain a keen sportsman all his life. Evidently it was not a pursuit of which Stewart disapproved, for early in the new year Harry told his father: "Last Saturday I was out shooting with Mathew and another boy of the name of Brown. It was a terrible day. When we set out it was snowing very hard, and nothing would have tempted me to have gone out, but that I had a terrier upon trial . . . we killed between two and three dozen of [small birds], of which we afterwards had an excellent pie made."[13] The terrier, facetiously named Seizer, was kept in the attic along with a variety of livestock belonging to Ashburton.

But Harry's reference to headaches had not escaped his anxious parents, and a letter rejecting one explanation which Lord Palmerston must have suggested throws further light on daily life in the Stewart home.

> I do not think that my headache was at all due to wine, as I hardly ever drink any at dinner, and never more than two glasses after, indeed in general but one, for we never sit after dinner. I think we generally leave the eating room an hour and a half after we sat down to dinner, sometimes sooner. I think however it is very likely in part owing to eating supper, or rather to drinking a glass of that ale, for I never eat more than a potato. It is a great nuisance that there is always supper at ten, and it seems unsociable not to come down when everybody else does and when one is there it is difficult to hinder oneself from taking a potato and a glass of ale . . .[14]

In another letter Harry explained that after dinner, which, it should be remembered, was usually taken around four o' clock at this period, he went for a walk (perhaps to exercise Seizer). It was when he returned that he had his remedial hour of geometry with Stewart before tea at eight.[15] The young men in the household had also the opportunity to meet the Stewarts' interesting and distinguished guests. One of the first to appear for dinner after Harry arrived at Lothian House was the Selkirkshire explorer Mungo Park, who had become famous during the previous year through the published account of his highly hazardous attempt to find the source of the River Niger.

In April 1801 Harry reported that he was reading the newly published *Moral Tales* of Maria Edgeworth.[16] He thought that one of the characters, an Englishman who comes to Edinburgh to continue his studies, must be based on his fellow-boarder, whom Miss Edgeworth's brother Lovell had known when he was in Edinburgh: "it is him exactly, only he is much more eccentric and differs in many respects from Ash, especially in his contempt for gentlemen, as Ashburton has very high notions of rank and old families."[17] It is not clear whether the household realized that the character of Dr Campbell in *Forester* – tolerant, benevolent, calm and courteous – was based on what Maria Edgeworth had gleaned from her brother about Stewart himself.[18]

The Stewarts and the Palmerstons (1800–1803)

It was during the winter of 1800–1 that Stewart began to give a separate course of lectures three times a week on "political economy". This was the first university course on economics in Britain, and as such it created a considerable stir. The writings on the subject by David Hume and Adam Smith were not yet well known, and the very terminology was unfamiliar. Some thought the subject beneath the dignity of an academic lecture, and Lord Cockburn, who attended the second presentation of the course, recorded that "the word 'corn' sounded strangely in the Moral Philosophy class, and 'drawbacks' seemed a profanation of Stewart's voice".[19]

The content of the course bore little resemblance to a contemporary class in economics. Stewart discussed the doctrines of Adam Smith and the Physiocrats, but he talked in terms of general principles rather than using graphs or statistics; as Lord Cockburn put it, "he certainly did not involve his hearers in intricacies".[20] But because of the course's groundbreaking nature it was highly influential. Not only undergraduate students attended the lectures; the audience included many members of the Scottish bar[21] and all the founders of the *Edinburgh Review* which burst upon the world with its new style of journalism in the autumn of 1802 – Sydney Smith, Francis Jeffrey, Henry Brougham and Francis Horner. For them, Stewart was a direct link back to Thomas Reid and Adam Smith. "We who live in these days," Veitch wrote thirty years after Stewart's death, with reference to his course on political economy, "can hardly appreciate the debt we owe to the political teachings of Stewart."[22]

Little more than a month after Harry Temple joined her household Mrs Stewart wrote to the Palmerstons that he was "the idol of the whole family",[23] and the evidence suggests that he became her favourite among all the young men who came to her home. He was indeed a very agreeable and good-looking youth – when he later went to Cambridge he was nicknamed 'Cupid'. Early in 1801 Stewart himself explained, somewhat more formally, that he too would have written if he "had had anything to mention of Mr Temple, but the uniform and exemplary propriety of his conduct . . . "[24] In a report on Harry's first year in Edinburgh sent to Lord Palmerston in May he made an observation on the relative standards of the British universities at this time, at least as seen from the north.

> If I were to be consulted hereafter about the plans of any young man who wishes to unite the advantages of an English and a Scotch University, I should strongly recommend the example of Lord Webb Seymour, who after remaining for several years at Oxford, has finished his academical studies at Edinburgh. The uncommon maturity of Mr Temple's mind will I am persuaded, render in his case a departure from this plan of immaterial conse-

quence, more particularly as I flatter myself that his classical knowledge, if not increasing so rapidly as it might have done if it had been his chief object, had not been suffered to decline since he left England.[25]

This may sound like Scottish prejudice, but more than fifty years later the former Harry Temple was reported as telling the House of Commons that "he was bound in frankness to say that any information which he might have acquired at Edinburgh was infinitely more useful and general than at Cambridge; and that the two years which he spent at Cambridge he passed very much in forgetting what he had learned at Edinburgh".[26]

Certainly under Stewart's tutelage few opportunities for acquiring information were lost. When the winter courses ended in the spring of 1801 he encouraged Harry to attend the early morning summer class of the professor of botany, partly because he thought the walk to the Botanical Gardens (then near the top of Leith Walk) would be good for him; and he occupied some other spare time for Harry and Matthew by going over with them the lectures on natural philosophy which he had given when substituting for Professor Robison and by working on Harry's weakness in mathematics. In his second year Harry had private lessons in handwriting and fencing as well as classics, and in his third year he undertook dancing and double-entry book-keeping – all presumably facilitated by Stewart.

Stewart arranged for Harry and Ashburton to spend part of the summer of 1801 at St Mary's Isle, outside Kirkcudbright. This was the grand country home of the Earls of Selkirk, which Stewart had visited as a guest of his student and friend, Lord Daer, the heir to the title. Daer had died of consumption in 1794, aged only thirty-one, and on the death of his father five years later Daer's younger brother Thomas had now succeeded as 5th Earl of Selkirk. Stewart evidently knew him well, having referred to him in the year before Daer's death as Tom Douglas.[27] His house had an excellent library. Stewart recorded in his holiday journal that he himself visited St Mary's Isle in the summer of 1801.[28] This may have been in part to collect the two young men, for although he left Harry Temple at Carlisle at the beginning of August to make his own way home, he then set off with Ashburton on a tour of the Highlands and the north of Scotland which was his other major excursion for that summer.

James Mackintosh, visiting Edinburgh, was sorry to miss him, but he told Stewart from London a year later, "though I could not *see* you, I *felt* your influence in the taste, the knowledge, and the eager and enlightened curiosity, which you had diffused among the ingenious young men with whom I had the pleasure of conversing".[29] Stewart was back in Edinburgh at latest by 2 November, the date he put on a postscript to his Preface for a second edition of the *Outlines of Moral Philosophy*.[30] He now omitted the sections on political economy, since this had become the subject of his separate course.

His boarding students for 1801–2 were the same as in the previous winter – Lord Ashburton and the Hon. Henry Temple. His son Matthew attended his moral philosophy class this year, as did Gilbert Elliot,[31] whose father was a couple of years older than Stewart and had for two years been a fellow-student with him at the College. Elliot senior had become a prominent Whig politician and diplomat, and had recently been raised from baronet to be Baron Minto of Minto, taking his title from the family seat in Roxburghshire. Stewart and Minto had remained friends, and Minto was one of the closest friends of the Palmerstons, so young Gilbert was another who frequented Lothian House during his years at the University; he and Harry Temple got on well together. Early in January 1802 Mrs Stewart sent a note to Lord Minto at Charlotte Square referring to an entertainment they had all attended that morning and hoping that he and Lady Minto could give "the happiness of your company an evening before you go [back to London]"; she added that if there was anybody in Edinburgh they had "any curiosity to see" she would ask them too.[32] Lord Minto wrote to Lady Palmerston reporting that "Harry is as charming and as perfect as he ought to be . . . On this subject I do not speak of my own judgment alone. I have sought opportunities of conversing with Mr and also Mrs Stewart on the subject . . . "[33]

About the same time Harry was writing to his father to tell him about his workload in his second year. "I have a good deal to do at home, in writing out the notes I take at the chemistry and at Mr Stewart's lecture, and doing the algebraic exercises Mr Playfair gives us, and reading Latin and Greek for Mr Christison . . . " He added, implying, like the animals in the attic, a fair degree of tolerance on the part of Mrs Stewart: "Ashburton, Mathew and myself are deeply engaged in chemistry, and burn our fingers and tables with acids most delightfully . . . "[34]

Indeed, life at the Stewarts' home was not all earnest. Lord Buchan, son of Henry Erskine, remembered being taken as a boy to Lothian house and meeting – presumably on different occasions – Henry Brougham and Henry Petty. He believed it was Harry Temple "who beat them all at jumping on the lawn after dinner".[35] Jumping may indeed have been one of his specialities, for the story was also passed down in the Minto family that at one of the Stewarts' parties Harry sprained his leg as a result of leaping over Mrs Stewart's gothic couch in the middle of her drawing-room.[36]

The Stewarts and the Palmerstons (1800–1803)

The young poet Thomas Campbell had recently returned from some months in Germany. He had written to the Stewarts about political events and military operations on the continent, though these letters have not survived.[37] While abroad he also wrote several short poems, including *Ye Mariners of England*. His father's death brought him back to Edinburgh, where his experiences in Germany were the object of much interest. Stewart introduced him to Archibald Alison, who had recently moved to Edinburgh as minister of the episcopal church in the Cowgate and whom Campbell came to regard as his intellectual father, and also to Lord Minto, who befriended him in both Scotland and London. In February 1802 Campbell sent Mrs Stewart "my latest fugitive pieces", among which was the subsequently much anthologized *Hohenlinden*.[38] He was to remain an admirer of Mrs Stewart until the end of her life; "my dear Mrs Stewart", he described her in a letter to a friend in 1808.[39]

But misfortune of an unexpected kind was about to strike the Stewart household. On 14 April Harry Temple was sent for because his father had become ill. Mrs Stewart had just left home on a visit to her sister Margaret Cunninghame at Lainshaw, and as soon as she heard what had happened she wrote to Harry at Hanover Square to express her anxious concern. She was pleased that Gilbert Elliot had volunteered to accompany Harry on his journey south.[40] But on the 16th, before the boys arrived, Lord Palmerston died, and Lady Palmerston asked Lord Minto to meet them with the sad news. Though Harry was now the 3rd Viscount Palmerston, he was still only seventeen years old. As soon as she was able, his mother wrote to another member of the Whig aristocracy (and Minto's brother-in-law), the Earl of Malmesbury, who became his guardian:

> I wish Harry to return into Scotland with Lord Minto to make a tour, and return into England if he likes in the summer, but the next winter to pass with Mr Stewart, such I know being the wishes of his dear father, and when the classes are over to come up and be entered for Cambridge. With respect to William [Harry's younger brother], I wish him to remain at Harrow till he is sixteen, which will be in February twelve month, then to go for three years to Mr Stewart's, but as he would lose the classes he must quit Harrow the end of October to be in time for the opening of the classes in November.[41]

In fact Harry decided to return to Edinburgh before the end of May. Mrs Stewart wrote to tell him of "the unfeigned happiness" of everybody at Lothian House that they would see him again so soon, and asked only for a line on the way so "that we may be certain of not a single stranger to plague us, being in the way when you arrive".[42] Before long Harry began a daily routine of fencing with Matthew, which he told his mother he liked very much.[43]

Early in June, Stewart was thrown into a state of considerable agitation, and he wrote to his London printer to express it.

> It was not till yesterday that I became acquainted with the mangled shape in which my *Account of Dr Robertson* has been prefixed to the new Edition of the *History of Scotland*; and I really cannot express the astonishment I felt at the sight of the book, nor the heart-felt vexation it has given me. In republishing an author's works (at least during his life-time) I took for granted that the Edition corrected under his own eye, would have been considered as sacred from all intentional alterations either in matter or form; nor can I conceive any possible reason, in the present instance, why a step in which I was so very deeply interested, should have been taken without the slightest communication with me . . . If you will only take the trouble, yourself, to look into the volume, I am persuaded you will agree with me in pronouncing it . . . so completely ludicrous, that, if such a publication were to go abroad under my sanction, it would justly expose me, after what I have said on the subject, to the charge of insanity.

He then detailed the errors which he had detected, adding:

> The truth is, that trifling as these particulars may perhaps appear to others, they affect me so seriously, that I am anxious to dismiss as soon as possible so unpleasant a subject. If I were not detained here by indispensable engagement, I would instantly have set out for London to save the trouble and time of our correspondence.
>
> In these circumstances, no alternative is left but to suppress the whole impression; and I only tremble, lest some copies may have got into circulation, before this letter reaches you.
>
> I shall expect to hear from you in course of post, and entreat you will inform me, how this incomprehensible accident has happened . . .[44]

It may well be that Stewart needed a holday. In April, writing to Lord Henry Petty to congratulate him on his success at Cambridge, he had referred to "the constant hurry" in which he had been kept during the preceding winter by his second course of lectures on political economy[45] – an extended version of the first presentation – and in May he had read to the Royal Society of Edinburgh the first part of his *Life of Thomas Reid*.[46] The indispensable engagement to which he referred may have been one of his summer courses, and he was now in his late forties. Some relaxation was on the way, however, for in June Sydney Smith, whose wife had just given birth to their daughter Saba, was writing from Burntisland to

Francis Jeffrey, "Just now I am expecting Dugald Stewart and his spouse".[47]

During 1802 Stewart was one of several Scottish literati who responded to news that Nassau Hall at Princeton in the United States had been destroyed by fire, further depleting the library which had already lost a number of books during the Revolution. He sent copies of his *Elements of the Philsophy of the Human Mind* and *Life of Reid* and Reid's own *Inquiry into the Human Mind*.[48]

In August Lady Ashburton came to Edinburgh, and took the Stewarts' nine-year-old daughter away with her – presumably to stay for a time at the Ashburton home in Devon. Mrs Stewart had some misgivings ("a fearful distance"), but "Lady A. was so kindly anxious to have Maria with her, and is so fond of her, that it would have been sadly selfish to rob the little creature of the unspeakable advantage of going".[49] Later in the month the rest of the family, including Lord Ashburton, set off for the neighbourhood of Carlisle. On 1 September Stewart was writing letters from an inn in Keswick where he told one correspondent that he had been "enjoying a few days leisure, after a long course of very fatiguing business".[50] This correspondent had proposed translating his *Life of Robertson,* and Stewart suggested that he should follow the second edition, which had appeared as a separate volume, and not the mangled version attached to Robertson's *History of Scotland*, so it would appear that he did not succeed in stopping its circulation entirely. He also wrote that day to "Lord H." – Henry Petty – to ask if he might be in town during October.

> I am at present on a short tour through some of the Northern Counties with Mrs Stewart, your old friend Ashburton, and my eldest son; and I have some thoughts before I return to Edinburgh, of stepping into the London mail, and leaving my party for a few days, to amuse themselves in Yorkshire. If I could flatter myself with the prospect of seeing you, were it but for an hour or two, it would decide my plans with respect to this excursion.

He asked for a reply to York, "where I expect to be about the beginning of October". (He added some comments about Bentham, saying that "in my next course of lectures I think I shall have much to say to his fundamental principle of *Utility* considered in connection with the Theory of Morals".[51])

During the first half of September, while in neighbourhood of Keswick, the Stewarts made a call to see the writer Elizabeth Hamilton and her sister, who were then staying in Bowness. In the previous year Stewart had written to congratulate Miss Hamilton on her *Letters on Education*, and he now encouraged her strongly to proceed with her new project, a historical novel based on the life of Agrippina, wife of the Roman general Germanicus. The Stewarts also urged the Hamilton sisters to come to Edinburgh for the winter, which they did, anxious, as Elizabeth put it, to obtain "the advantage of literary conversation, in a very chosen circle of society" and "much improvement, even from the casual hints of such a man as Mr S—". A few months later she had given him a draft of most of the first volume of *Agrippina*, and he assured her that it was her *forte*.[52] Mrs Hamilton (as she later styled herself) lived until 1816, and devoted much of her time to writing and philanthropic work in Edinburgh.

In the meantime it seems unlikely that Stewart's projected visit to London took place. Mrs Stewart must herself have had it in mind to go farther south than York, for she wrote to Palmerston from that city on 5 October lamenting that they would not be able to get to Broadlands. She had become ill in Scarborough, had been confined to bed for ten days, and was still "weak and uncomfortable". She had hoped that Stewart and Matthew might have made the visit without her, but "you know Mr S.'s sad anxiety when anybody's finger aches – to get him to leave me now is impossible". So she had to defer the pleasure of getting to Broadlands until the following year. In the meantime John Ward had come to meet them in York, and she attempted some elaborate plans about how they might meet up with Palmerston on his journey back to Edinburgh and have his company for part of the way.[53]

When the new teaching year began the Stewarts still had the same two resident students. Harry Palmerston, as part of another busy schedule, began to attend Stewart's class in political economy; many years later the careful transcriptions he made from his shorthand notes became one of the bases for establishing a text of Stewart's lectures.[54] Before the end of November Harry received an approving letter from Lord Malmesbury.

> Political economy is a very important and interesting subject. From everything I hear of Mr Stewart I have no doubt he will teach it on its right principles and in the way which can the best tend to qualify you to act as becomes in you in the rank you hold in life and in the part you will probably be calld upon to act. The classics should never be forgotten . . .[55]

In March 1803 Malmesbury again commended Harry's course of studies as likely to provide "a store of useful and amusing information". He added:

> I only fear when you get to Cambridge you will find yourself with nothing to learn, or rather that your tutors will know nothing with which you will

not be previously acquainted. I, however, hear from every quarter St John's so well spoken of that if it should only provide a quiet and comfortable residence for a year or two which you may dedicate to reading, it will answer the going there perfectly.[56]

In December 1802 Stewart had completed reading to the RSE the last of his three biographical essays, that concerning Thomas Reid. James Mackintosh read it three years later in Bombay and felt it to "breathe a consolatory calm over me".[57] But as in the case of Stewart's other lives, more space is devoted to the subject's writings than to biographical detail. He ended on an unusully intimate note.

> In concluding this Memoir, I trust I shall be pardoned, if, for once, I give way to a personal feeling, while I express the satisfaction with which I now close finally my attempts as a Biographer. Those which I have already made were imposed on me by the irresistible calls of duty and attachment; and, feeble as they are, when compared with the magnitude of subjects so splendid and so various, they have encroached deeply on that small portion of literary leisure which indispensable engagements allow me to command. I cannot, at the same time, be insensible to the gratification of having endeavoured to associate, in some degree, my name with three of the greatest which have adorned this age . . . But I, too, have designs and enterprises of my own; and the execution of these (which, alas! swell in magnitude as the time for their accomplishment hastens to a period) claims at length an undivided attention.[58]

In March 1803 Maria Edgeworth made her first visit to Edinburgh. She and her father had spent the winter in Paris, but they decided to come to Scotland as a result of alarming reports about the health of Maria's young brother Henry for whose early education she had been made responsible and who was now studying at Edinburgh University. Stewart had "acted as a teacher, host and father-figure"[59] to him and to his elder brother Lovell. (Harry Palmerston considered the Edgeworths to be the only exception to his observation that all the Irish in Edinburgh were blackguards.) Henry's father and sister were relieved to find him in better health and spirits than they had expected, and they were delighted to find him affectionately included in Stewart's circle of friends. Maria recorded:

> From the time he came to Edinburgh, to the hour he left it, Henry was received at Lothian House, where Mr and Mrs D. Stewart then resided, as if he had been one of their own family. There all his holidays, all the hours that could be spared from study, were delightfully spent; and there, in health and in sickness, he received all the counsel and sympathy, and all the tender

care, which the best of parents could have bestowed . . .

May I? Yes I *must* be permitted to name Mrs Dugald Stewart, for whom he always felt the gratitude of the most affectionate son to the kindest of mothers. To her maternal care, and to Mrs Alison's, we owe it, that Henry got through two severe seasons in Scotland, and that a few years longer of his life were preserved. [Henry Edgeworth lived only until 1813, when he was thirty-one.]

We spent some weeks with him, and among his friends in Edinburgh, in delightful society. The evening parties at Lothian House appeared to us (though then fresh from Paris) the most happy mixture of men of letters, of men of science, and of people of the world, that we had ever seen . . .

We left Edinburgh with sentiments of public admiration and private gratitude, regretting, that we must quit such society, and part from such friends.[60]

At the end of their stay Miss Edgeworth, who was thirty-six at this time, wrote to her aunt:

Mr and Mrs Stewart surpassed all that I had expected, and I had expected much. Mr Stewart is said to be naturally or habitually grave and reserved, but towards us he has broken through his habits or his nature, and I never conversed with any one with whom I was more at ease. He has a grave sensible face, more like the head of Shakespeare than any other head or print that I can remember. I have not heard him lecture; no woman can go to the public lectures here, and I don't choose to go in men's or boy's clothes, or in the pocket of the Irish giant, though he is here and well able to carry me. Mrs Stewart has been for years wishing in vain for the pleasure of hearing one of her husband's lectures. She is just the sort of woman you would like, that you would love. I do think it is impossible to know her without loving her; indeed she has been so kind to Henry, that it would be doubly impossible (an Irish impossibility) to us. Yet you know people do not always love because they have received obligations. It is an additional proof of her merit, and of her powers of pleasing, that she makes those who *are* under obligations to her forget that they are bound to be grateful, and only remember that they think her good and agreeable.[61]

In the spring the Stewarts again changed their place of residence. The move was a very short one, almost directly across the road from Lothian House, to Callander House on the north side of the Canongate.[62] This building, which still stands, is part of Whitefoord House, now a residence for Scottish naval and military veterans. On the site of a much older mansion, it was built in 1769 by Sir John Whitefoord, who had been the owner of the Ballochmyle estate in Ayrshire. Sir John had suffered financially as a result of the collapse of the Ayr Bank, and had been compelled to sell Ballochmyle and come to live in Edinburgh, where he was one of those who befriended Robert Burns. During the year of the Stewarts' move a family connection was established, for his eldest daughter, Mary Anne, became the second wife of Mrs Stewart's elder brother, Henry Cranstoun.

Sir John now moved to St Andrew Square, and at this point Whitefoord House was divided into two parts. The central section, with the original entrance from the Canongate, became the home of a judge, Lord Bannatyne, while the Stewarts took possession of the rather smaller west wing, which was entered from the rear. They had an association with Lord Bannatyne as well, for he had inherited the estate of Kames in Bute from where Stewart's paternal grandmother had come, and Bannatyne's sister Isabella had married Dr Archibald MacLea, the donor of fresh herrings from Rothesay. Bannatyne had also been a member, along with Stewart, of the Young Poker Club in 1786–7. Whatever the reason for the Stewarts' move (Lothian House survived until 1825 when it was demolished to make way for a brewery), the property would have been the more attractive in that it possessed the remains of an old orchard.

It may seem surprising that the Stewarts did not follow so many of their professional contemporaries to live in the more spacious and salubrious area of Edinburgh's New Town, which had begun to develop in the 1760s. Probably Stewart set a high priority on being within fairly easy walking reach of the University, and the residences which he chose (Stewartfield House, Lothian House, Callander House) all had some grounds round them. Although the last two were in the Old Town they were far from being the cramped and overcrowded tenements which were by this time increasingly deteriorating into slums.

Initially, however, the move had unfortunate consequences, for Mrs Stewart became ill through over-exerting herself. Lord Ancram arrived during May from a visit to Paris and persuaded the family – which as usual included Ashburton, though Palmerston, having now finished his third year at Edinburgh University, was off on a tour of Scotland – to stay at Newbattle Abbey until she was fully recovered. Matthew and (less skilfully) Ash amused themselves by shooting crows. Reporting on these matters to Palmerston at Inveraray, Matthew asked him particularly for a few lines "as my father has been in the fidgets for three days on your account".[63]

Towards the end of June Matthew and George (now twelve years old) proceeded as an advance party to the home of Matthew's uncle, Dugald Bannatyne, who was now an enterprising Glasgow businessman, prominent in the Chamber of Commerce of which he and his father had been founding members in 1783; the Stewart boys were followed a few days later by their parents and Ashburton.[64] Shortly afterwards they met up with Palmerston at Inveraray. Also of the party was Francis Chomeley, the son of a 'bluestocking' friend of Lady Palmerston who had been studying at Edinburgh since January 1801. From Inveraray they went down the Mull of Kintyre to Campbeltown (on Stewart's part a search for his roots?), stopping at Lochgilphead in both directions. From the inn there they admired the view of Arran, which Stewart thought even finer than from Ayrshire, and they sailed for about three miles on the Crinan Canal. They then proceeded as far north as Oban, Stewart beng particularly impressed by the mass of Ben Cruachan. On their way back through Arrochar they made a detour to see Glen Shira.[65]

Stewart set off again from Edinburgh at the beginning of August with Ashburton and a Miss Scott on a four-day excursion through Fife, visiting St Andrews, Cupar, Falkland and Dunfermline.[66] On 10 August, after another short turn-round in Edinburgh, the Stewarts with Ashburton and Mrs and Miss Scott (Mrs Scott seems to have been known in the household as "the Lady") began a long journey down the west side of Britain.[67] According to Sydney Smith, this tour was "to see Lord Ashburton come of age".[68] They proceeded through Hamilton and Moffat to Carlisle, where they stayed for a few days, and from there to Gilsland, where they spent what Mrs Stewart called "a most charming fortnight" away from all contact with the outside world: "we have almost forgot that Buonaparte exists". They all drank the water, including their servant Robert: "rather a new occurrence in his life to prefer water to whisky", as Mrs Stewart remarked to Palmerston, who was spending some time at Minto before returning to Broadlands.[69]

On 5th September they resumed their journey south, reaching Penrith, where they parted with Mrs Scott, and thence through Lancashire to Liverpool, Knutsford and 'Ashburn', where they stayed at the Blackamoor, "an excellent inn", and visited Dovedale. At Sudbury they met and may have stayed with Lord Vernon, whom Stewart had probably got to know while visiting Archy Alison when he was the incumbent there in the late 1780s. (His second wife, was a daughter of Sir John Whitefoord.) From here they went through Birmingham and Worcester to Great Malvern, where they saw the Ladies Douglas, the two unmarried sisters of the Earl of Selkirk. Thence to Cheltenham, where they made another short halt; and then by Oxford, Newbury and Andover to Salisbury, from where at the end of September they proceeded through the New Forest and arrived at last at the Palmerston seat at Broadlands near Romsey. Here, as well as meeting again with Harry and his mother,

The Stewarts and the Palmerstons (1800–1803)

they made acquaintance with William Temple, who was to take his elder brother's place in Edinburgh in November.

They stayed in this area for ten days or so, crossing from Southampton to Portsmouth by water, and spending a night at Cowes on the Isle of Wight. By way of Winchester and Windsor they then made their way to London, which they reached on 12 October. Here they saw something of Sydney Smith, who had now removed there,[70] and also called on Thomas Campbell, who had recently married.[71] This visit to the capital seems likely to have been the occasion of an incident recounted by Frances Allen, two of whose sisters married John and Jos Wedgwood respectively. Tom Wedgwood and Stewart were both present at a party in London to see "a painting of Christ" by Leonardo da Vinci. This was probably *The Virgin of the Rocks*, which is now in the National Gallery; in 1786 it had been bought by the Marquess of Lansdowne, and he may have been responsible for the party. Stewart's impressions of the Leonardo were not recorded, but he was much struck by Tom's profile, which he had probably not seen for fifteen years, as Tom looked intently at the picture, exclaiming that "it is the finest head I ever saw".[72]

However, the Stewarts' stay in London must have been brief, for later in the month Matthew was writing a friendly letter to Willy Temple from Langholm. They had come north through York, where John Ward, as in the previous year, had joined them for a day or two, and were about to pursue their journey homewards to be back for the start of the College year. Willy was advised to arrive in Edinburgh not later than 10 November.[73]

Lord Palmerston in the meantime was starting his new life at St John's College, Cambridge. He sent a gift of china to Mrs Stewart so that "sometimes in your delightful evening parties" she might think of him. His letter was probably awaiting her when she reached Edinburgh.

> I can assure you my dear Mrs Stewart that the moment in which I took leave of you and Mr S. was far from being one of the happiest of my life. The uniform and unceasing kindness I experienced from you for the three years I was an inmate of your house (and during part of that time, alas, I had need for all the soothing attention of friendship) it is impossible for me to forget. Indeed I shall ever feel for you and Mr S. the affection of a son, for sure I am that had I been related to *you by the ties of blood* you would not have been more kind and attentive to me than you were.

At Cambridge he had for the first time met his predecessor at Lothian House, Laurence Sulivan, whom, he told Mrs Stewart, "I like uncommonly".[74] The two men were to be intimate for the rest of their lives.

CHAPTER TWELVE

Social Life and the Leslie and Ashburton Affairs 1803–1805

"I never saw Mr S. so roused as by the shameless profligacy of these persecuting Clergy – they got quite the better of his patience, and his joy at the victory was very great." Mrs Stewart

Edinburgh in the second half of the eighteenth century and the early nineteenth was a city replete with clubs and societies. This partly reflected the Enlightenment ideal of eagerly disseminating new ideas and discoveries, but it also had a practical basis: while most people still lived in the confined quarters of the old town there was very little space at home for entertaining friends, and meetings in taverns, oyster-cellars or public rooms were a necessary alternative.

We have already found evidence that Stewart was a clubbable man. He joined a literary society when he was a student in Glasgow, and the Speculative Society when he returned to Edinburgh as a young teacher of mathematics. At least during the period of his friendship with Robert Burns he was an active Freemason, and masonic meetings in those days were essentially convivial evenings. He was a member of the rather more serious-minded Philosophical Society, and of its curious though short-lived offshoot, the Newtonian Club. When the Philosophical Society became the Royal Society of Edinburgh Stewart was for long a regular attender at its meetings and he served for many years on the committee of the Physical Class.[1]

Social Life and the Leslie Ashburton Affairs (1803-1805)

Along with John Playfair he was co-opted to the Oyster Club, a convivial society of the older generation (Joseph Black; Adam Ferguson; James Hutton, the founder of modern geology) which usually met at an inn in the Grassmarket.[2] In 1786 he was one of those who attempted to revive the Poker Club.[3] The original Poker Club had been formed early in 1762 by a group of Edinburgh literati who wished to support the establishment of a militia force in Scotland corresponding to one which existed in England, and resented the fact that the London Government was unwilling to countenance such a development so soon after the Jacobite rising. Adam Ferguson, who felt strongly on the matter, had suggested the name of this club as one which was intelligible to its originators (pokers being used for stirring things up), but "was an impenetrable mystery to everyone else". Its last recorded meeting was in January 1784. However, the new group, in spite of including Lord Daer, John Playfair, William Robertson junior and Henry Mackenzie as well as Stewart, never really took off, although it was not until 1793, in the context of the war with France, that a militia was authorized in Scotland.

Now, in June 1803, another social group was formed, largely on the initiative of Walter Scott. Known as the Friday Club, it initially met weekly on the evening indicated by its title. The chief qualifications for membership, according to Lord Cockburn, who soon became the Club's secretary and was to act as its historian, were a taste for literature, agreeable manners, and above all "perfect safety". Vices to be avoided were "conversational exhibition", religious narrow-mindedness, and as far as possible political party spirit. Stewart and Archy Alison, described by Lord Cockburn as "a most excellent and agreeable man; richly imbued with literature; a great associate of Dugald Stewart", were both present at the inaugural meeting of the Friday Club, as was Stewart's brother-in-law, George Cranstoun. Other founder-members, in adition to Scott, included John Playfair, Sydney Smith, Francis Jeffrey, Henry Brougham, Henry Mackenzie and Thomas Campbell. "We sit chatting every week till two in the morning," Jeffrey wrote at the time.[4]

In its second year Andrew Dalzel, Lord Webb Seymour and the Earl of Selkirk joined the Club. The weekly meetings were gradually replaced by dinners held on a Sunday in a tavern once a month from November until July. Brougham and Sydney Smith, in Cockburn's view, predominated for the short time before they left Edinburgh, but John Playfair "was unquestionably at our head". For their staple drink the members moved from punch to iced punch, then to claret. After 1814, Cockburn recorded, when the Continent was opened again, "we soared above prejudice, and ate and drank everything that was rare and dear". By this time Stewart's appear-

Social Life and the Leslie Ashburton Affairs (1803–1805)

ances are likely to have been less frequent, but the Club was still in being when he died, and Cockburn wrote that his "memory will ever be cherished by those who knew him as a member of this association. It is an honour to us to have it in our power to say we lost such a man."

In the autumn of 1803 Stewart may have been especially glad of such social amusements, for his household was now smaller than it had been for several years. Early in January 1804 Mrs Stewart sent new year greetings in a letter to Palmerston, observing that "for the last three years I could do it in person", and enviously imagining the "rehearsing and sporting and painting" that must be going on at Broadlands, where apparently Lord Ashburton was also present, "busier than a bee in a bottle", she supposed. "Here we are more dismal, more doleful than words can paint. That innocent creature your brother I wish he may not go melancholy mad for there is not a creature here that one knows." Stewart was reported to be pining sadly for Lady Minto "and swears all parties are impossible when he has not her to chat with".[5]

But as usual with Stewart such distractions were set against a background of continuous hard work. In the early part of 1804 his friend Andrew Dalzel became ill, and in addition to his own two courses Stewart supplied for Dalzel twice a week in the Greek class.[6] (On other occasions he took Playfair's mathematics classes, Finlayson's logic, and belles lettres for Hugh Blair's successor.[7] He did not retain the class fees during these spells of supply work, but returned them to the professor who normally took the class.[8])

William Temple settled well in Edinburgh, and by February Mrs Stewart told his elder brother that he was "really a darling".[9] In the early summer, however, the Stewarts were alarmed by a letter from Willy's mother, Lady Palmerston, intimating that she was ill. In fact she had discovered that she had cancer of the womb, though she concealed her condition for as long as she could. Mrs Stewart wrote with anxious good wishes to Palmerston in August from St Mary's Isle, where the family were staying with the Earl of Selkirk. She was pleased to learn that Palmerston had been touring Wales with Laurence Sulivan, and even more satisfied that he still preferred Scotland. Stewart's nephew, Willy Miller, who was in the army, was to be assigned to Edinburgh Castle during the ensuing winter, and Mrs Stewart hoped that this would "make the house less dreary than it was the last season".[10]

In the meantime, in London, Sydney Smith began his first course of ten lectures on moral philosophy at the Royal Institution on 10 November 1804. Three weeks later Francis Horner wrote to John Murray: "I have just been to hear Smith lecture ... There was a very affectionate and a very

Social Life and the Leslie Ashburton Affairs (1803–1805)

eloquent passage about Dugald Stewart, which produced a great effect."[11]

On New Year's Day, 1805 Mrs Stewart wrote to Palmerston at Broadlands to say how pleased she and Stewart were by the way Willy was maturing and developing; she hoped that this would be gratifying to his mother.[12] No doubt it was, but later in January news reached Edinburgh that Lady Palmerston had died. Her younger son had been confined to the house with a cold, and Mrs Stewart was much concerned about his undertaking the journey south. However, he was determined to go, and Willy Miller undertook to accompany him, as Gilbert Elliot had accompanied Harry in similar circumstances three years before.[13] The Stewarts, who had come to feel that they knew Lady Palmerston well, were of course much upset on her account and on behalf of the Temple family, who were now without both their parents; "I never saw Mr S. so much overwhelmed," his wife wrote to Palmerston. They were anxious to welcome William back to Edinburgh.[14]

There had been another death in their immediate circle: Marjory Miller, the eldest child of Stewart's late sister Janet, died on 25 January aged twenty-three.[15] These events cannot have been helpful to Stewart, who, according to his wife, was at the beginning of the winter "far from well, and in very bad spirits". Then George had become seriously ill with scarlet fever, which lasted for several weeks. After that Stewart was confined to bed with a sore throat, and he had scarcely recovered when Mrs Stewart received an urgent summons to Lainshaw, where her sister Margaret's husband William Cunninghame was dangerously ill; he died on the day she arrived. When she returned home she found that Maria had been "seized with a rheumatic fever", which took some time to pass.[16]

But another death in January had set in motion the events which were to dominate the early part of 1805.[17] John Robison, the professor of natural philosophy, passed away at the end of the month. The Town Council, with general approval, lost no time in offering the vacant chair to John Playfair. There was little financial advantage for Playfair in moving from his mathematics post, but natural philosophy provided a broader and more varied field of activity, and so on 6 February he transferred to that professorship, thus creating a vacancy for the chair of mathematics.

One of the first candidates to appear in the field was the Rev. Thomas Macknight, minister of Trinity Church in Edinburgh, whom Professor Robison had occasionally used as an assistant when he was ill. He spoke to Stewart, who told him he thought well of his abilities, though he could not commit himself until he knew who else would be in the field. He added his firm opinion that if Macknight were to be appointed to the mathematics chair he ought to resign from his church appointment. Macknight appeared to agree with this, but Stewart subsequently discovered that there was a party in the Church, supported by a prominent Town Councillor named Rankin, maintaining that he ought to hold both offices simultaneously.

There was a certain irony in the fact that these clergy were the Moderates, a party which had long been dominant in the Church of Scotland, and which had been very effectively led in the 1760s and '70s by Principal Robertson. At that time to be a Moderate was to be in reaction against the puritan school of hell-fire preaching that had been all too prevalent in the Church for more than half a century; the Moderates were polite and cultivated gentlemen. Many, like Stewart's father, had been influenced by Francis Hutcheson in Glasgow. They advocated good works, civic virtues and social relationships – what Stewart once referred to as "the manly duties of social life".[18] In short, they were men of the Enlightenment: theirs was a rational religion, far removed from the bigotry of the past. But after Robertson's death the Moderate leaders in the Church tried to maintain their ascendancy through patronage, and in face of the social strains produced by the French Revolution they sought to uphold the balance of the *status quo* and thus became associated with William Pitt and his powerful agent in Scotland, Henry Dundas. Now, by advocating the joint occupancy of university chairs and city church livings, although there was a respectable argument in terms of supplementing professorial incomes and thus keeping down student fees, they were seeking to place the Town's College under the effectual control of one presbytery.

Stewart was convinced that this policy threatened ruin for the University since in his view the practice would be bound to lead to neglect of one job or both. He called to see the Lord Provost, Sir William Fettes, whom he knew slightly, but did not find him at home. His sore throat prevented him from returning, and he wrote to the Provost to express his concerns. While accepting that theological professorships should be held by ministers in Edinburgh, he said he could think of no argument for any other chair being held jointly either with another professorship or with an ecclessiastical living. He pointedly claimed "an interest in the literary fame of the University, which cannot be supposed to operate in an equal degree with those who either consider their academical station as secondary objects, or who may be disposed to employ them in subserviency to particular views of ecclessiastical policy".[19] Shortly afterwards Professor Playfair also wrote to the Lord Provost and expressed his opinion "about the degree of effort and application necessary for the discharge of duties, in which I have been long exercised".

It appeared to Stewart and Playfair that their case would be greatly reinforced if there were a candidate stronger than Macknight whose appointment they could positively advocate. Such a man was at hand in the person of their friend John Leslie, whom they had both supported in three previous attempts to obtain a chair at a Scottish university. Leslie had gone at an early age to St Andrews, and subsequently attended Edinburgh University as a divinity student in the mid-1780s. However, he discovered that he preferred science to theology, and for a few years he obtained employment as a private tutor. He had then spent two years in Staffordshire with the Wedgwood family, as already mentioned, and became a regular traveller on the Continent. In 1804 he had produced an important book on the properties of heat which had just been awarded a prize by the Royal Society in London. He was thus a considerably more distinguished scientist than Macknight. Like Stewart and Playfair, he was also a Whig; but the Town Council's offer of the natural philosophy chair to Playfair showed that at least under the influence of Sir William Fettes this was not an insuperable barrier to someone of proven merit as a teacher and a researcher. Nevertheless, in the reference which he supplied for the Town Council, Stewart thought it prudent to observe "that the most intimate friends he has had in both parts of the Island have been men distinguished no less by their loyalty to Government than by their literary attainments".[20]

However, the Presbytery of Edinburgh, led among others by James Finlayson, the professor of logic, decided to contest Leslie's fitness for appointment. They did so on the grounds that in his book Leslie had included a footnote claiming that David Hume had been the first to treat causation "in a truly philosophical manner". Hume's contention was that it is not valid to infer any causal connection from factual observations: our belief in the causal regularity of the world is the result of habituation. This doctrine could be seen as a form of scepticism, for if Hume, a known atheist, were correct it would not be possible to argue from the evidence of nature to the existence of God as a first cause. The Presbytery reminded the University Senate that its members were obliged, if required, to sign the Westminster Confession of Faith. The Senate responded that the last occasion on which a professor had been asked to do so had been in 1758, and in practice the requirement had been allowed to lapse by the former leader of the Moderates, Principal Robertson himself (who in his day would probably have found it difficult to defend every article).

The reaction of the Town Council to these pressures either was a little

Social Life and the Leslie Ashburton Affairs (1803–1805)

devious or laid itself open to that construction; but in the end they made the courageous decision. One of the Moderate leaders had warned the Lord Provost that the clergy would oppose Leslie's appointment, and had been told that the election would take place on 13 March. The ministers met on the previous day. Leslie had written to Dr Hunter, the professor of divinity, to explain his position, and the meeting had before it a letter from Hunter expressing his view that Leslie's statement was sound and that opposition to his appointment should be abandoned. However, this did not satisfy the Presbytery. Just as they had reached this conclusion they learned that the Council was then in session on other business, and to avoid meeting again on the following day was proceeding to fill the University post. Four of the clergy were appointed to hasten to the Council Chamber with an agreed statement, but when they got there they were informed that the Council, with several testimonials to Leslie's orthodoxy and good character before them, was about to appoint him; and this, fifteen minutes later, they proceeded to do. (On the advice of the Lord Provost they wrote the letters of support for Leslie into their minutes.)

At around this time Mrs Stewart was writing a chatty letter to Lord Palmerston, and her view of the situation, though expressed with her usual slightly incoherent emotionalism, probably reflected her husband's pretty closely.

> There is much mischief in the College about the Mathematical Professor. Mr S. who seldom meddles wrote to the Provost on the new system of giving Professorships to Clegymen *holding livings* in Edinburgh as it was altogether an innovation, and made the College entirely subservient to the views of the Clergy who only used it as an engine to manage church-politics, so that all the classes were likely to grow [i.e., become] sinecures. The Provost has behaved very well and very firmly, but the Clergy are making a great uproar. However there seems to be but one opinion in the Town, for every one sees that it is time to do something for the College, as the *last four* Professors have about *eleven* students among them. Mr S. made no objection to Mr Macknight if he would resign his church as Dr Stewart [Mrs Stewart is probably referring to her father-in-law] and Mr P[layfair] had done, but Rankin the Taylor whose daughter Mr M. means to marry did chuse him to do so – wisely forseeing that his class would never equal his stipend. So much for college politics.[21]

The "great uproar" reflected the fact that the Town Council's *fait accompli* split the Presbytery. The Evangelicals among them – those who believed the Church should be playing a more active role, especially in relation to the new industrial working classes – were prepared to accept the appointment, but the Moderates were determined on a fight. On 27 March, by a majority of two votes, they had the matter referred to the next higher Church court, the Synod of Lothian and Tweeddale, and the Synod in turn passed it up to the supreme court, the General Assembly of the Church of Scotland. During the interval between the meeting of the Synod and the annual General Assembly a campaign was mounted against Leslie, in the newspapers and otherwise, designed to damage his reputation by putting the worst possible construction on his note about causality.

Stewart was so outraged by this attack on his friend, on sound philosophy and on what he saw as the public interest, that he hastily wrote a substantial pamphlet entitled *A Short Statement of some important Facts relating to the Election of a Mathematical Professor in the University of Edinburgh*, which he dated 15 May and which was published a few days before the Assembly met. In this, as well as reviewing the events which had taken place, he defended the theory of causality that Leslie had approved, and showed that Hume was not by any means the only philosopher to have treated the kind of causation which is the object of physical investigation as a matter of invariable sequence. As he pointed out, he had said the same thing at some length in his own book more than ten years previously.[22] In a note he had quoted a number of writers, adding: "The strong prejudice which has been entertained of late against Mr Hume's doctrine concerning the connexion among physical events, in consequence of the dangerous conclusions to which it has erroneously been supposed to lead, will, I hope, be a sufficient apology for multiplying so many authorities in support of it."[23]

He had also sought to show that this doctrine did not lead to sceptical conclusions concerning a first cause. Yet this was what the ministers appeared to be arguing. Stewart analysed at length and with considerable scorn the key sentence in their letter to the Council, which read: "That Mr Leslie having, along with Mr Hume, denied all such necessary connection between cause and effect, as implies an operating principle in the cause, has, of course, laid a foundation for rejecting all the argument that is derived from the works of God, to prove either his being or his attributes." What Stewart was really setting out were the limits of scientific investigation: as he saw it (and this was what Leslie meant), all that can properly be looked for in natural philosophy are physical causes – the uniform recurrence of one phenomenon following another. The nature of causality in the sense of what actually brings about change is a separate question.

By the time the Leslie affair reached the General Assembly on 22 May

Social Life and the Leslie Ashburton Affairs (1803–1805)

it had become a *cause célèbre*. Members of the public had to be turned away from the galleries, and the debate lasted for a full two days. Stewart, who was a member of the Assembly as an elder representing the University, was perhaps unfortunate in not being called until almost the end of the second day, for members were becoming impatient for a vote. However, the Moderator observed, "The house, I am sure, will be happy to hear him, and I do not think he will be tedious" – whereupon profound silence was at once restored.

Stewart began calmly, but if the published report of the Assembly's proceedings is accurate his language soon became emotional. "The secret history of that persecution, of which Mr Leslie has been the object for some months past, is completely laid open to the view of the public; and while the recollection of that history shall be preserved, a *stigma*, an indelible stigma, is fixed on the names of the principal actors, from which no vote of this house can save them!"

At this point, according to the contemporary report, there was a loud cry of "Order! order!" from the opposite side of the house. But Stewart continued for a few more sentences, concluding: "But, in so far as the merits of private parties are concerned (on the one hand, the vindication of Mr Leslie's character, and, on the other, the humiliation and disgrace of his accusers) nothing more could have been wished for, than such a disclosure of facts as has been already obtained, to complete the triumph of justice!" The vote shortly took place, and the Assembly determined by 96 votes to 84 to take no further proceedings against Leslie's appointment. The announcement was greeted by cheers from the gallery. It was not an overwhelming victory, but it was decisive. Stewart's friend Sir Harry Moncrieff, minister of St Cuthbert's Church, presided over a victory dinner.

Nevertheless, the controversy rumbled on for some months. One of the Moderate leaders produced a detailed response to Stewart's *Statement*, and John Playfair wrote a scathing refutation of the response. Thomas Brown also entered the fray with a defence of Hume's philosophic position. All these were published in book form, and a later edition included a verbatim account of the debate at the General Assembly.

The Leslie affair was a significant episode in several ways. First, it marked the end of the Moderate party's long period of political and theological dominance within the Church of Scotland. The Moderates now appeared obscurantist, while the Evangelicals, who had supported Leslie in the Assembly debate, were in alliance with the lay and intellectual world represented by Stewart and Playfair. Secondly, the coarse-looking but outstandingly able John Leslie, at the age of thirty-nine, was at last launched on a distinguished academic career in which he eventually followed Playfair to the chair of natural philosophy.[24] One of the students on whom he had a powerful influence was Thomas Carlyle, and he contributed several scientific articles to the *Edinburgh Review*. He lived until 1832, having been knighted earlier in that year on the recommendation of Stewart's former student, Lord Brougham. Near the end of his life, Stewart described Leslie as "one of my best friends".[25] Thirdly, the publication of Stewart's *Statement* brought him for the first time into association with Archibald Constable, who had undertaken the publication of the *Edinburgh Review* in 1802 and who was to be a friend as well as a profesional collaborator with Stewart for many years.

And finally, the episode showed that Dugald Stewart, though normally averse from controversy, was prepared to come out and fight when he believed that important principles were at stake. "I never saw Mr S. so roused," Mrs Stewart told Lord Henry Petty (whose father, the Marquess of Lansdowne, had died in May), "as by the shameless profligacy of these persecuting Clergy – they got quite the better of his patience, and his joy at the victory over them was very great. Contemptible as it is in some respects, yet for Scotland and the University of Edinburgh it was of the greatest importance . . . Mr S. has made many enemies by this business, but that cannot be helped."[26]

Lord Minto, to whom Stewart had shown a postscript to his *Statement* in draft, replied at the beginning of January 1806: "I share most cordially every sentiment you have expressed, not only in this note, but in every other part of the controversy; and I shall ever consider it as a great addition even to your titles to [?] heartfelt respect, that you placed yourself in the breach, for the defence of so many valuable interests, against an attack, which, if opposed with less energy, might have been successful."[27] Sydney Smith, of course, took matters rather more lightly. In June 1805 he told Francis Jeffrey from London: "I wrote to Stewart, to tell him of a report which prevailed here that the General Assembly had ordered him to drink a Scotch pint of hemlock, which he had done, discoursing about the gods with Playfair and Darcy."[28]

In July George Cranstoun's intimate friend, the advocate Thomas Thomson, told Francis Horner that he had spent two days with Stewart while he was "living about eight miles from Edinburgh on the banks of the Water of Leith".[29] Soon afterwards the Stewarts must have moved a little farther south, to Bankhead in Lanarkshire, where they were delighted to hear of an impending visit from Palmerston and Laurence Sulivan – "one of the most delicious incidents that ever occurred," Mrs Stewart declared when she heard they were coming. The family would

Social Life and the Leslie Ashburton Affairs (1803–1805)

return to Edinburgh at the end of August to meet their guests. They would then plan a return to Bankhead, which, she explained to Palmerston, "is surrounded with muirs and ditto corn fields filled with partridges and will of course be more beautiful in your eyes *after* the 1st of September than before it".[30]

However, a less delicious incident was about to occur. Although the peculiar Lord Ashburton was no longer a student, he seems not to have detached himself entirely from the Stewarts or from Palmerston. During the previous summer Mrs Stewart had told the latter, "Honest Ash is bathing in the sea in Leith because Leith is the *only* place where one can bathe comfortably".[31] In the middle of September 1805, shortly after Palmerston's visit to Scotland, she wrote to tell him the latest news. As usual when Mrs Stewart is agitated it is a little difficult to work out exactly what had happened, but there is no mistaking her feelings.

> I am totally overwhelmed with the thunder stroke. Lord Ashburton is to marry Anne Cunninghame [her niece]. Good God how miserable I am – and the comments of the world how *just* they must appear. Alas who will believe that I was deceived by his solemn assurances ten thousand times repeated and still more by the fatal conviction that nothing of that kind could be seriously thought of without my being told of by her or her family. Nor could I dream that any one would not have preferred beggary to such a marriage. You know my sentiments and will judge of my agony. Mr S.'s indignation knows no bounds. He had warned me and I weak and confident in my high opinion of those so unworthy of it *assured* him it was impossible. I am unable to write . . . It strikes me that perhaps your suspicion of the blow awaiting us assisted in bringing you here, it would be so kind so delicate so like yourself . . . none knows so well as your brother my blind confidence in those who have deceived me. Mr S. and I have taken our resolution from which nothing shall ever induce us to depart. We shall never behold either Lord A. or his wife. The total break this made between my sister and me is indeed heavy heavy on my heart but I am not to blame in it.[32]

The marriage took place on the day after this letter was written. Palmerston must have replied sympathetically, for Mrs Stewart wrote to him again a few weeks later to thank him and provide a little more insight into what had upset her.

> You can well imagine, how while the nine days wonder lasts, all the different opinions that are going, and everybody blaming us for opposite faults – some that we contrived it, others that we have no business to resent it etc. etc., but that is all little. It is the *heart* affliction I lament, the break in a fond family – but no more of this, for I can only grieve you by dwelling on irreparable misfortunes.

Social Life and the Leslie Ashburton Affairs (1803–1805)

Since Ashburton respected Palmerston's opinion more than anyone's, she hoped that if opportunity ever arose he would make Ash understand how he had injured them by his deceit. She added: "To you I must with grief own, that *he* is not the party I blame."[33] This hint received confirmation more than ten years later from that somewhat acerbic observer of the social scene, Elizabeth Grant of Rothiemurchus, who came to know the Ashburtons in Edinburgh in 1816. Evidently the story of the strange marriage was still being told.

> He was ungainly in person, disagreeable in habits, some years younger than Miss Cunninghame, who would have him, despight both uncles; [George] Cranstoun felt it was a throwing away of a fine girl, Dugald Stewart took it as a reflexion on himself that in his house, while under his care, a very wealthy nobleman should be while so young engaged to his niece. The niece did not care; she was cold and she was ambitious, so she married her Lord, and they had a fine country house and a beautiful town house – two houses thrown into one, which gave her a spendid suite of apartments for the grave style of receiving company that suited her taste; a dinner party every week, and in the evening her rooms thrown open to an assemblage that filled them. Her intimate acquaince had cards for the season . . . Lord Ashburton delighted in company, and in people that were fat . . . He went about smiling, though saying little except to himself; he had a trick of soliloquising, so very oddly . . .[34]

The habit of 'soliloquy' was one that he shared with John Ward, which perhaps lends credence to the suggestion that the latter acquired it from Stewart himself. The Ashburtons had no children, and when Richard Ashburton died in 1823 the title became extinct. He had written a book which was published two years after his death. In keeping with the mild eccentricity which characterized him it was entitled *Genealogical Memoirs of the Royal House of France*. His widow Anne resided for some time in Edinburgh; in 1826 she remarried, her second husband being Ranald George Macdonald, the Chief of Clanranald.

Mrs Stewart's feelings seem to have softened slightly with the passage of time. Relations with the Cunninghames of Lainshaw may have cooled for a while, but Margaret Cunninghame certainly stayed with the Stewarts in 1826.[35] Even in the summer after the marriage, writing to Lady Minto, Mrs Stewart was able to sound a little more dispassionate: "Lord Ash is at Menton [Menstrie?] in Stirlingshire . . . I believe the same as ever, busied about his rabbits . . . He is very angry with me I understand and says it is *my love of power* which led me to be angry at his marriage . . . "[36] In 1822 she told the Marquess of Lansdowne that "poor Ld. Ashburton has been

Social Life and the Leslie Ashburton Affairs (1803–1805)

dangerously ill, and I fear not yet safe . . . I do pray for his recovery heartily."[37] When he died in the following year he left the substantial sum of £8,000 to his widowed aunt by marriage, the Countess Purgstall.[38]

Willy Temple was the last young man to board with the Stewarts while attending classes at the University. Looking back in later life at the extended family she had acquired over these years, perhaps Mrs Stewart would not have wished to change what she wrote to Lord Palmerston in the summer of 1804: "How vain I am of *all* my Children. See who can turn out *ten* such excellent Bairns. Some of them may have little failings, but on the whole I do not know their equals."[39]

CHAPTER THIRTEEN

Towards Retirement
1806–1810

"I am very much comforted by the account you give me of Mr Stewart's health. And, on every public as well as private account, I rejoice at the resolution he has formed to quit the college after this winter." Francis Horner

On 23 January 1806, in the middle of the war with Napoleonic France, the Prime Minister, William Pitt, died in office. This event was to affect Stewart and his family in a number of ways. Pitt had been one of the two representatives in the House of Commons for Cambridge University, and so the first consequence of his death was a by-election for that constituency. Lord Henry Petty already held a family seat in Parliament, but he decided to contest Cambridge as a Foxite Whig. Some of his friends promptly wrote to Stewart asking him to drum up support among those of Petty's old Edinburgh associates who were Cambridge men.[1] This must have been slightly embarrassing, since it soon emerged that the Tory candidate was to be none other than young Harry Palmerston, who was anxious to embark on a public career and who remained at least nominally a Tory until 1829. However, it seems unlikely that Stewart was diverted from his Whig allegiance, and when polling day came on 7 February, although the Whig vote was split by the intervention of a third candidate, Petty won the seat comfortably, with Palmerston in last place.

Pitt's death brought down the government. A good deal of political

Towards Retirement (1806–1810)

manoeuvring ensued before a new administration emerged under Lord Grenville. This was the government which became known as 'the Ministry of all the talents', for it included representatives of several parliamentary groupings, but it was predominantly Whig. Henry Petty was no doubt helped in his by-election campaign by report that he was to be Chancellor of the Exchequer in the new government – not then such a very senior position as it has become in modern times, but nevertheless an important office. Stewart's friend Samuel Romilly was appointed Solicitor-General and given a knighthood, while Charles James Fox was made Secretary of State for Foreign Affairs.

People like Stewart who had fretted for so long under what they saw as Tory misrule were naturally pleased by these developments, but there were still anxieties about the situation in Scotland. To Francis Horner, who wrote to Stewart with the news of Henry Petty's success at Cambridge, he replied:

> the satisfaction which this, and the general aspect of our domestic concerns has given me, is not a little damped by the apprehensions which I have all along felt, that we, on this side of the Tweed, may not be destined to share in the good fortune which seems now to await the other parts of the empire ... My principal, and indeed my only hope, is founded on the good sense and the justice of the present ministry, who, I trust, after the triumph which they have gained for the country at large, will not deliver us over, with additional mortification and disgrace, into the hands of our old oppressors ... Should, however, these hopes be disappointed, my resolution is already formed – not to enter again, at my time of life, on a new term of servitude, if I should be reduced to the necessity of burying myself in Wales, or of emigrating to America.[2]

Happily, however, things did not come to such a pass; and indeed Stewart's personal fortunes were about to be materially improved by the change of government. After more than twenty years in the political wilderness the Whigs took steps to reward many who had loyally supported them through this lengthy period. A word to the new Lord Chancellor from Holland House was sufficient to obtain for Sydney Smith the living of Foston-le-Clay in Yorkshire, where he remained until 1829. In Scotland, Dugald Stewart was a notable example of loyalty to the Whig cause, and the new administration awarded him a sinecure by appointing him, for a period of twenty-one years in the first instance, to the created office of 'Writership of the Edinburgh Gazette'. The duties were purely nominal, for the work continued to be done by Alexander Lawrie, the printer, but the post carried a salary of £300 a year,[3] equivalent to about £12,500 today.

Not everyone, of course, applauded this step.[4] Walter Scott was rather resentful that the Tories, when in office, had made no such provision for him,[5] and when a new administration came to power in the following year Stewart had the embarrassment of having his appointment cited in the House of Commons by the new Chancellor, Spencer Perceval, as an example of malpractice by the Whigs.[6] No one could believe, he argued, that the post had been created with any other purpose than to give the place to its present possessor. Lord Henry Petty defended his action when in office by declaring that it –

> had been given to an individual who had devoted a long life of disinterested service to the public, and who had in the University but an income of £135 per annum. It had been thought a better mode to provide for this distinguished and meritorious gentleman, Mr Dugald Stewart, by giving him that place, which had before been enjoyed by three Newspaper Writers, than by a pension.

But he did not explain why. The case against what had been done was perhaps most forcefully put by the new Foreign Secretary, George Canning.

> He acknowledged the high literary merit of Mr Dugald Stewart, who had besides the merit, and he thought it no light one, of having educated the noble lord [Petty]. He acknowledged and lamented the general insufficiency of the rewards bestowed on literary merit in this country; but he highly condemned the mode of reward here applied, by constituting a new sinecure, and bestowing it on Mr Stewart and assignees for twenty-one years.

However, the appointment had been made, and the Stewarts must now have felt themselves to be fairly comfortably off. Mrs Stewart wrote a letter of profuse gratitude to Lord Henry Petty for his part in the affair, hinting that there were circumstances which her husband could bring out to shame his enemies.

> My dearest Lord Henry may Heaven reward you . . . I wished Mr S. to write, but he insists it is needless, he says you know every feeling of his heart, and would perfectly understand all that passes in his mind, that he would only do injustice to it by putting it in words. I believe he is right but I cannot be silent to you, and as you know that my heart generally gets the better of my head you will not wonder either at my writing or my inability to do justice to my sentiments.[7]

A not inconsiderable item of expense for the Stewarts must have been their hospitable entertaining. The future barrister and professor at Yale,

Towards Retirement (1806–1810)

Benjamin Silliman, attended one such evening with two American friends in the early spring of 1806. In his journal he desribed the occasion thus:

> There was a circle of ladies and gentlemen, but the formality of mixed parties was entirely banished by the manner in which this was conducted. Instead of sitting down in a solemn circle, the company sat, stood, or walked, as they pleased, without the smallest embarrassment or restraint, and thus every person had an opportunity of conversing with every other. Two or three tables, in different parts of a large room, were spread with a cold collation. Each person partook of the refreshments when he pleased, and thus conversation was made the principal entertainment.

Stewart had spoken "in terms of the highest respect" of his meetings in Paris with Benjamin Fanklin; and though Silliman noted the company's lack of familiarity with his country's poets, the topic of American literature "was treated with much delicacy and politeness".[8]

Eighteen months later, "on a dark evening in December 1807", the literary autobiographer Robert Gillies remembered being entertained at Whitefoord House (there were only four guests that night) with –

> the drawingroom lighted only, but quite sufficiently, by a blazing fire, for the professor had enough of work before dinner time, and was then willing to repose himself over the most common-place chit-chat. The impression derived from this far-famed author's fire-side was materially deepened by, or, I should say in geat measure depended on, the demeanour and conversation of Mrs Stewart . . . The prevalent impression left on the mind of a visitor to Whitefoord House was that of the domestic happiness, the unaffected cheerfulness and perfect unanimity which existed among the inmates.[9]

In the meantime the domestic political scene in early 1806 was dominated by the impeachment of Lord Melville, the former Henry Dundas. This could not be attributed to the change of government, for the situation had begun to develop while his close associate Pitt was still alive and in office, and the Stewarts had watched his impending downfall with eager impatience.[10] For nearly thirty years Dundas had been the most powerful man in Scotland. His use of that power had not all been malign – he had, for example, adopted a fairly enlightened stance towards the Scottish universities – but he had restricted freedom of expression with considerable vigour, and in 1802 he had managed the general election in Scotland so effectively in the interests of the government that only two Whigs were returned from the forty-five seats.

In 1805 the House of Commons received a report from a commission which had been investigating irregularities in naval departments, and this gave rise to suspicions of abuse on the part of Dundas when he had been Treasurer of the Navy in the early 1780s. Stewart told Francis Horner how much he hoped for the end of Melville's political career – "an event which I consider as synonymous with the emancipation and salvation of Scotland".[11] After some hesitation the House resolved to impeach him, and his trial began on 29 April 1806. At its end it fell to Romilly to sum up the evidence. The House of Lords acquitted Lord Melville of all charges, though in some cases by relatively small majorities; the general view was that while he had been culpably negligent, he was not guilty of embezzlement.

These proceedings had of course been a major sensation in Scotland, and the verdict was greeted with jubilation by Dundas's friends and political supporters. A public dinner was organized to celebrate, and Walter Scott composed two songs, both of which made reference to public figures, one with the boisterous line, "Tally-ho to the Fox."[12] For many of Melville's opponents this was hard to take, and Scott's (perhaps uncharacteristic) partisanship was held to be in specially bad taste since Charles James Fox had become ill. The Countess of Rosslyn was said never to have forgiven Scott to her dying day. The Stewarts had been staying at Minto early in June, and after their return Stewart wrote to the Countess:

> I send you Walter Scott's song, my dear Lady Minto. There was another written by him and sung likewise, but he seems to have taken fright about it, for he won't give any copies. The chorus was: 'Since Melville's got justice may the Devil take *Law*!' The applause that followed the song was so great that it was quarter of an hour before silence could be restored.[13]

Lady Minto replied, "There never was anything more wrong-headed or wrong-hearted."[14]

Relations between the Stewarts and Scott cooled from this time on. In 1820 Scott wrote about Stewart in a personal letter: "The fact is I was at one period of my life very intimate with the said philosopher which happy state of things was interrupted by his conducting himself (as I then thought and still think) unworthily on a particular occasion towards the late Lord Melville."[15] It is not clear what form this supposedly unworthy behaviour actually took, but clearly Scott had a side to the story, though it did not prevent him from retaining a respect for Stewart which became evident after Stewart's death.

International as well as domestic affairs had an impact on Stewart at this time. Fox, now at the foreign office, had long been an opponent of

Towards Retirement (1806–1810)

the war with France. He could not deny the danger represented by the power that Napoleon had acquired by his victory at Austerlitz in December 1805, but he regarded the situation as a direct result of the hostility originally shown to the revolution. The war was close to stalemate, and was not popular. Addington as Prime Minister, with support from Pitt, had negotiated the Peace of Amiens in March 1802, and although as a result of Napoleon's actions in Europe peace had lasted for little more than a year, Fox was anxious to try again. Soon after he came to the foreign office he was approached by a Frenchman with a plan to assassinate Napoleon, and with cabinet approval Fox revealed it to the French government. This may have been intended as an olive-branch, and Russia began to discuss with Britain the basis for possible negotiations with France.

Then Napoleon made a move. He had been holding as prisoners of war those British adults who were stranded in France when the war resumed in 1803. One of these was the Tory MP the Earl of Yarmouth, son and heir of the Marquess of Hertford. Yarmouth had been arbitrarily imprisoned in the fortress of Verdun for more than three years. Napoleon now took advantage of an exchange agreement to send him to London with a secret message that France was willing to open negotiations.[16] He arrived early in June 1806. Fox found it hard to believe the interpretation that Yarmouth put on the French position, but he sent him back to Paris to continue talks.

However, the French position did change, a Russian envoy signed a separate peace treaty with France, the negotiations became complex, and Yarmouth was no match for France's foreign minister, the wily Talleyrand. The British government began to lose confidence in their accidental emissary, and the Prime Minister decided to send a second plenipotentiary. Fox's illness had now set in, but Lord Grenville chose for this role one of Fox's friends and a member of his political circle, the 8th Earl of Lauderdale. This was the Lord Maitland who along with Stewart had accompanied Edward Burke to Glasgow in 1784; he had succeeded to the title five years later. When the Whigs came to power Fox had offered Lauderdale the post of Governor-General of India (to succeed Marquess Wellesley), but the Directors of the East India Company opposed his appointment so strongly that Lauderdale was obliged to wihdraw. Although he had then accepted the post of Lord High Keeper of the Great Seal of Scotland, he remained a senior figure in the Whig hierarchy without a corresponding position. Grenville may also have thought that Lauderdale would be acceptable to the French because of his early enthusiasm for the revolution and his strong opposition to the war with France

Towards Retirement (1806–1810)

ten years earlier. He had once appeared in the House of Lords in Jacobin dress, and for a while, after the manner of Lord Daer, he styled himself 'citizen Maitland'. He was indeed a rather strange man: he had a violent temper, a cumbersome style of writing and a notorious lack of humour – as Sheridan once said, "a joke in the mouth of Lauderdale is no laughing-matter".

But he was a friend of Stewart's, and he had recently attended and been much impressed by the professor's lectures on political economy.[17] He now asked Stewart to accompany him on this mission as his private secretary. It may be that he in turn thought Stewart would be an acceptable figure in Paris as a result of his well known support for the revolution in its early years; it may be that he thought Stewart's fluency in French, though perhaps a little rusty after seventeen years, would be useful, for he himself spoke with so strong a Scots accent as to be barely comprehensible; it may be that he simply valued Stewart's support and advice. On Stewart's side it was a chance to resume some of the personal contacts in France which had been in abeyance for so long, and perhaps he found the prospect of observing international affairs at first hand too intriguing to decline. At any rate, he accepted the offer.

Before he set off on his diplomatic mission he may still have been at home when Lord Palmerston visited Edinburgh to collect his brother Willy, and so bring to an end the years during which the Stewarts were hosts and foster-parents to so many well-born young men. William Temple went up to St John's College, Cambridge in October. In 1814 he joined the diplomatic service, and thereafter was rarely in England. He served on the legation staff in Stockholm, Frankfurt, Berlin and St Petersburg, and in 1833 was appointed by his brother as Minister in Naples, where he remained for twenty-three years, returning home to die in 1856. He was knighted for his services, but never married.

It seems that Mrs Stewart accompanied her husband as far as London, for one of John William Ward's "letters to Ivy", written in July, expressed great delight at the prospect of "receiving under my own roof the persons whom I love as my other parents . . . I shall count the days till you come." Stewart was to be assured that his being there would not occasion the smallest inconvenience.[18] He is recorded, presumably from this base, as having dined at Holland House at the end of the month. A Mrs Stewart appears in the Holland House dinner book on three occasions in August and once in late October, so it is possible that Stewart's wife remained in London, seeing her friends, while her husband was in Paris.[19]

He and Lauderdale arrived in Paris at the beginning of August. The identity of Lauderdale's secretary apparently caused much amusement to

Talleyrand, who had spent a couple of years in London in the early 1790s and must have known Stewart's reputation as a philosopher, especially since he became friendly with Lord Henry Petty's father, the Marquess of Lansdowne. The new British negotiator soon found the situation even worse than had been imagined. Not only was Yarmouth out of his depth, he was a gambler and a heavy drinker, and his wife was reputed to be having an affair with one of Talleyrand's intimates. Anything transmitted to him soon found its way to the French. Within a week Lauderdale advised the Prime Minister, "You should not lose a moment in recalling Lord Yarmouth from this country"; and Grenville acted on his advice.

But Lauderdale did not make much better progress. Probably neither side was entirely serious: at this time the French were in such a strong position militarily that they did not feel obliged to make concessions, and there were limits beyond which even Fox was not prepared to go in pursuit of peace. Moreover, another blow was about to fall: Fox's physical condition had deteriorated, and on 13 September he died in office. Napoleon later claimed that the best hopes for peace were while Fox was alive, but before his death Fox was becoming disillusioned with French tactics, and at the beginning of October, as conflict between France and Prussia was about to begin, Lauderdale left Paris. As a parting gift he presented one of the French negotiators with an English sword "to show the high state of perfection that has been reached in the manufacture of arms". It was back to war – and to what Scott had called "military frenzy" – for another nine years.

Stewart's personal records of this episode have not survived, and it is impossible to know how active a part he played in the diplomatic exchanges which took place. According to his son, his visit to Paris did provide "an opportunity not only of renewing many of the literary intimacies which he had formed in France before the commencement of the Revolution, but of extending his acquaintance with the eminent men of that country, with many of whom he continued to maintain a correspondence during his life".[20] In September he wrote asking Lord Holland's intimate, John Allen, to obtain books in London for two of his French contacts.[21] Stewart himself mentioned in one of his writings that he saw much of the Abbé Morrelet,[22] who translated Smith's *Wealth of Nations* into French; and on a number of occasions in future years he wrote, in particular to the philosopher Marie Joseph de Gerando, introducing friends who were about to visit Paris.[23]

Stewart was not long home again before he suffered the loss of one of his old friends in Edinburgh. After a long illness Andrew Dalzel died on 8 December 1806, aged sixty-four. He had written a history of Edinburgh

University which was published posthumously and contains many warm references to Stewart.

It was Matthew Stewart who was most directly affected by the last of the consequences of the change of government to concern Stewart and his family. Matthew, who had been awarded an MA by Edinburgh University in November 1803,[24] decided on a career in the army. A few years later, writing to his Irish friend Will Drennan, Stewart remarked: "The line which he has chosen is very different from mine, but I believe it to be the best suited to his active disposition as well as to the bent of his genius which was always strongly turned to those branches of science which are connected with the business of an engineer."[25] In September 1803 Matthew had become as Assistant Engineer attached to the Trigonometrical Survey (map-making), and in March 1804, at the age of nineteen, he joined the Royal Engineers as a 2nd Lieutenant.[26] The family do not appear to have had any regrets. "Mat," his mother wrote at the beginning of 1804, "is in a situation where he is [natura]lly formed to shine, and where he will be a cred[it to] his family, and be completely happy himself."[27] In 1805 he sat in his new uniform for a pencil and water-colour drawing by Thomas Heaphy, who had used the same medium to draw Mrs Stewart three years earlier [Plates 8 (b) and 8 (a)].[28]

Now an opportunity arose for Matthew to go to India. After Lord Lauderdale's nomination as Governor-General was withdrawn, the government appointed Stewart's old friend Lord Minto, who after the Whigs came to power had been made President of the Board of Control, responsible for government policy in the sub-continent. There is some evidence to suggest that it would have been Lauderdales's intention to take Matthew with him to India as an aide-de-camp,[29] but certainly Minto agreed to do so. The change of appointment caused delay, which Matthew partly put in by spending some weeks at Broadlands with the Palmerstons. "What a relief it will be when they are fairly off," Mrs Stewart wrote, "for Mat poor dog has had a dreary time of it."[30] The party sailed for Calcutta early in February 1807.[31] The Stewarts must have had mixed feelings about this development. Clearly it was a splendid opportunity for a very young officer, and they knew that Minto would keep a fatherly eye on their son. But communications at that time were very slow: the journey by sea took nearly six months, and letters could be exchanged only when some part of the fleet was sailing. It was April 1808 before Mrs Stewart had two letters from Matthew to acknowledge:

> My Beloved M. – . . . they are balm to our hearts. You cannot conceive the joy they have given especially to your fond F. who cannot divest himself of

Towards Retirement (1806–1810)

anxiety wherever he fondly loves, and to be assured that you are alive and well makes him happier than any other worldly good ... Lady Minto writes us many kind things, and gives us sweet hopes of your finding more employment than merely as an Aide de Camp and that she hopes *soon*, not that I am sanguine, but it supports your dear F—— Mia wrote 2 letters she bids me say. G[eorge] is very proud of his from you ... Heaven bless you my darling ...[32]

Not long after the Earl of Minto sailed, the Government of Lord Grenville resigned because the King would not accept their proposal to open all ranks in the army to Roman Catholics. The Whigs were back for another long spell in the political wilderness. The Duke of Portland became Prime Minister at the end of March 1807, and though Lord Melville never held office again, his son, Robert Dundas, became president of the board of control (for India). He could have cancelled Minto's appointment, but chose not to do so, and the two men worked together for the next five years. Minto was a wise and tolerant Governor who by principle and example kept the situation in the sub-continent calm and well ordered.

The change of administration had consequences for another of the Stewarts' circle. An offer came to young Lord Palmerston of his father's old place as a junior Lord of the Admiralty, and in May 1807, with the assistance of his mentor Lord Malmesbury, he at last secured a place in the House of Commons as the MP for Newport in the Isle of Wight. Mrs Stewart wrote at once with a mixture of personal pleasure and political remonstrance:

> If I were to say that I rejoiced at the late Ministry going out, and the present coming in, I would *poshitively* [a joke apparently based on a favourite expression of the family servant, Robert] tell a great fib – but much as I may lament these events in general, it is impossible for me not to feel unfeigned delight at anything which *individually* affects your happiness. Your welfare and your prosperity must ever be the objects of our anxiety and prayers. No parents can feel more pride or pleasure than Mr S. and I do in your talents and virtues being shewn and acknowledged. Were you at my elbow though, how I would scold you for being taken by our Scottish Tyrant [Melville] who has ruled over this poor enslaved corner so long with a rod of iron. Be assured that if you knew the manner in which Scotland has been governed, your mind would revolt at some of your coadjutors. You see I am not yet appalled by your dignity, but keep up my good old way of scolding and lecturing my children.[33]

Two years later Palmerston became Secretary at War and asked Laurence Sulivan, who had been called to the bar, to become his private secretary. Shortly afterwards an opportunity arose for him to bring Sulivan into the War Office, where in due course he became the most senior civil servant, remaining there until his retirement in 1851. In 1811 he married Palmerston's younger sister, the Hon. Elizabeth Temple, and the two men remained close friends and correspondents throughout their lives.

The subsequent career of the handsome and charming Lord Palmerston is of course part of British history. He remained a minister at the war office for nearly twenty years; he was foreign secretary almost continuously for eleven years from 1830 under five Prime Ministers, and again for five years under Lord John Russell from 1846; he was home secretary in Lord Aberdeen's government from 1852 until 1855, when he finally became Prime Minister himself at the age of seventy. He held this office until 1858, and then formed his second administration in the following year, dying in office in 1865, two days before his eighty-first birthday.

He kept in close touch with the Stewarts for the rest of their lives, and as will appear did Stewart a particular service before the latter's death. In 1830 he wrote that in Edinburgh "I laid the foundation for whatever useful knowledge and habits of mind I possess."[34] Evidence for the nostalgia which he retained for his years there is provided by a story of his visit to the city in the year of his death. He was disappointed to find the brewery on the site of Lothian House, but had been told that an old woman named Peggie Forbes, who had been a servant there, remembered him well from his time under the Stewart's roof. The eighty-year-old Prime Minister, in spite of his gout, took the trouble to visit her in her home in Rankeillor Street. She reportedly greeted him with the words. "Eh, Maister Harry, hae ye come back at last?"[35]

On 28 May 1807 Stewart was granted armorial bearings by the Court of the Lord Lyon,[36] a fairly standard procedure for men of his standing. In his application he described himself as "Stewart, Dugald Esq. of Catrine in the County of Ayr, Professor of Moral Philosophy in the University of Edinburgh ... " Only a few days before the grant of arms he had been writing to a Mr Thomas Greenfield as tenant in Catrine House, and he did so again in 1812,[37] so the Stewarts must effectively have ceased to use it by this period; but it was not unusual for claimants to represent themselves as landed, and Stewart may have thought his association with Ayrshire sounded well. It may also show – like his choice of residences in Edinburgh – that in a way he always saw himself as a countryman.[38]

The shield and the devices which the armorial bearings carry are described thus: "Bears Or a fess checky Azure and Argent for Stewart, within a Border Gules charged with three Crescents of the third for Craig" – Craig having been the surname of Stewart's maternal grandmother. The crest is "the rising sun issuing out of a cloud all proper", the visible part of the sun having two eyes and a nose with rays emanating from it; and the Latin motto is *Sol tibi Signa Dabit*. This translates literally as, "The sun will give you signs" – rather more freely, "Sunlight will show you the way".[39] Whether or not this had any personal meaning for Stewart, it was a fairly conventional neo-humanist maxim.

During May the Stewarts went into the country for the summer, taking Mrs Stewart's mother with them. They stayed at Cairnmuir near West Linton, from where Mrs Stewart reported to Lord Palmerston at the end of June: "We are delightfully situated here – a comfortable house with excellent dry walks, and a fine wild and *solitary* country. We scarce remember that the world exists. Mr S. is deep in the most abstract part of his volume [he had presumably embarked on his *Philosophical Essays*]. G. and Mia perfectly happy as there is a nice poney, and good fishing."[40]

But this idyllic period was soon clouded by Mrs Cranstoun's health beginning to decline. "She is now confined to bed constantly," Mrs Stewart told Palmerston at the beginning of October, apologising for her failure to write since for the past two months her attention had been entirely taken up with her mother. "It would be folly," she added, "not to see that all hope is vain." The old lady's mind was quite active, but she was emaciated and had to be lifted and turned in the bed.[41] At the end of the month Mrs Stewart wrote again with the news that "my dear Mother is released from much suffering".[42] On the day of her funeral Stewart received a letter from Dr Will Drennan in Belfast, and when they were back in Edinburgh Mrs Stewart acknowledged it on his behalf, saying that nothing but these circumstances could have prevented him from replying at once.

> It was the very day on which he left home, to attend the funeral of one who loved him as her own son, and to whom he had been the most affectionate of sons . . . you who know him can imagine all that he felt on such an occasion, more especially for me and for the children. He returned only to remove us to Town, where we arrived the evening before his lectures began. During the first week of his college labours he has literally not a moment to himself . . .

She was writing to relieve his frustration at not having time to do so. It must have been a good many years since Stewart and his old friend had met. In 1800 Will Drennan had married a wealthy Englishwoman, and in

1807 he left Dublin and settled at Cabin Hill (now a preparatory school) on the eastern outskirts of Belfast. He gave up his medical practice and devoted himself to literary pursuits. He had already published a number of poems, and is credited with being the first Irish poet to have referred to Ireland, in *When Erin first Rose*, as the Emerald Isle. Mrs Stewart added:

> It is above seventeen years since I became his wife and your name, your verses, all you ever did and said I feel as well acquainted with as if you were my Brother. With what anxiety and agony we at one time felt for your much injured country, I need not say . . . Although my acquaintance with him is not quite of so old a date as yours, I believe I may venture to say, you will find him much the same as you left him. His few hairs are indeed gray, and perhaps the sad history of the world for the last twenty years may have made his manner more serious and reserved in company than it was when you knew him but it is only in company [and] if I may borrow Prior's words, "at home with his friends Lord! how merry is he." You see I take the privilege of an old acquaintance and write nonsense without scruple. I flatter myself the time shall come when you and Mr S. shall have leisure to talk over all stories old and new, while Mrs Drennan and I shall amuse ourselves with speaking ill of our husbands . . .[43]

A couple of days after Christmas Stewart was afflicted by "a severe illness",[44] but he seems to have recovered fairly quickly; he was writing letters[45] and attending meetings of the RSE.[46] The spring weather appears to have been unusually dismal, since Mrs Stewart blamed it for another lapse in her correspondence. "It is impossible for Mr S. even to walk to and from College so he drives there and returns instantly and then we shut up shop for the day. I write for him if we can get quiet, or if not, the everlasting visitors hunt us out, and waste every moment."[47]

The summer was again spent at Cairnmuir in Tweeddale, and in September Stewart got round to replying personally to the letter from Will Drennan. He was able to speak of good reports about how Matthew was doing in India, but part of what he had to say struck an ominous note:

> Since we came here, however, our youngest son, a most promising and amiable boy of 17 has given us a sad alarm by spitting blood and other symptoms equally unpleasant, and I have really had no heart to think of anything else. His disorder, thank God, seems at last to have taken a more favourable turn, and Gregory is of opinion that his lungs are sound; but he is still in a state of great weakness, and although I have every disposition to hope the best, I cannot look forward to the approaching winter without extreme anxiety.

He had hopes that "if our boy shall be in tolerable health" they might in the following season go as far as Portpatrick in the hope of meeting with the Drennans.[48]

But Stewart's hopes for George's recovery were not to be realized. The situation at the end of 1808 was conveyed by Lord Minto in a letter to Matthew Stewart, who had by now left Calcutta to become agent for the manufacture of gunpowder at Allahabad, and had reported – though "giving up the opportunity of making a very large fortune" – what appeared to him to be a network of corruption.[49] The Governor-General had intended responding to the Lieutenant's business letters, but:

> I must undertake a more unpleasant duty in sending you very uncomfortable accounts of your brother George's health. As no letters addressed to yourself have reached us I presume your Father has not himself written, but from some passages in a letter from Minto I have reason to think he would wish you to be informed of your brother's illness, and of the anxiety entertained on his account at the latest date of my letters, which was the 23rd December from Minto. The complaint appears to have been connected with weakness of the stomach and for some time he could not retain any food. By the latest accounts, however, he both eats and slept well, but I am sorry to add that there did not appear to be at that time any real amendment. I do not know the exact time when he was taken ill, but the disorder must have been of some standing (I conceive, several months) and the cause of apprehension was, his gradual and continual loss of strength and flesh. He was emaciated as well as enfeebled to the greatest possible degree. It is not said that his case is despaired of, but I cannot conceal from you the very serious light in which it was viewed both by Dr Gregory and your family . . . Mr Stewart as you will easily believe, is deeply afflicted. Mrs Stewart appears to have encouraged hopes in him which she scarcely entertained herself. Yet hope was not entirely renounced by anyone.[50]

A few days later Matthew replied from Allahabad:

> My dear Lord Minto,
> Let me beg that you will accept all the little return that my warmest gratitude can give for the kindness with which you have softened one of the heaviest afflictions which heaven could bestow. The loss of my only brother (for I know his constitution too well to have a hope) has indeed overwhelmed me. The difference of our age and the superintendence of the earlier part of his education had established a connexion more intimate than even what generally subsists among brothers and he possessed in the warmth of his heart and the loveliness of his disposition all that could win affection or engage esteem. But it is not for myself that I have alone to feel.

> We have hitherto as a family seen very little real sorrow, and the delicate state of my mother's health and the nervous complaints to which she is constitutionally subject, give me the most gloomy apprehensions as to her safety . . .[51]

Matthew was right about his brother's prospects, and the slow progress of mail imposed its own cruelties. By the time Lord Minto wrote his kindly letter on 19 June 1809, George Stewart had already been dead for more than five months. On 7 January Francis Horner had written from Lincoln's Inn to Lord Webb Seymour:

> I was not prepared to expect that poor George Stewart would be so soon relieved from his sufferings, though I looked upon the melancholy event as inevitable. You will believe that I should be anxious to hear now and then of Mr and Mrs Stewart. Her sorrow will be more lasting, I fear, and incurable; for no distress or calamity can be greater than hers. But I am apprehensive about the first excesses of his grief in a constitution of such strong and sanguine affections . . .

Horner hesitated to write to them directly in the midst of their mourning, and asked his friend for guidance as to when some London news might be welcome.[52] But on 25 January he received a letter from Mrs Stewart herself, written from Monteviot,[53] where the Stewarts must have accepted an invitation from Lord Ancram and his wife to stay with them. Even if the house was not then, as it now is, surrounded by one of the loveliest gardens in the country, its peaceful location by the River Teviot must have made it an ideal spot for gentle recovery in the care of the kindest of friends. Stewart arranged for Thomas Brown to supply for him at the College.

And when Horner replied to Mrs Stewart he referred to something else in her letter: "I am very much comforted by the account you give me of Mr Stewart's health. And, on every public as well as private account, I rejoice at the resolution he has formed to quit the college after this winter . . ."[54] He expanded on this a little two days later in writing again to Lord Webb Seymour:

> [Mrs Stewart] informs me, that he has at last determined, and openly declared his intention, of lecturing no more after the present winter. I think this resolution quite right. Thirty-eight years of service would justify him, even if he were retiring from all public duty; but he has engagements to the public and to posterity, which he ought no longer to delay fulfilling, and for which he will thus secure himself an ample command of leisure. I am pleased, besides, with the hope, that he may be tempted to employ some part of it in England, and that I shall have some opportunities of seeing him.[55]

It is not possible from these references to be sure whether Stewart's decision was made in the immediate aftermath of his son's death, but this seems likely; in practice he seems soon to have reacted to grief as he did after the death of his first wife, by throwing himself more energetically than ever into his work.

But his emotional state is perhaps reflected in an incident reported at the beginning of March by Archibald Alison. Thomas Campbell had sent a much appreciated letter of condolence to the Stewarts, and now he had produced a long narrative poem, *Gertrude of Wyoming*. Alison was favourably impressed by it, and sent it at once to Callander House. "You all know," he wrote to Thomas Telford, "what must be the tone of feeling there, at this moment. The effect, however, was greater than even our own Poet could have wished. Mr S. insisted upon reading it first by himself, and he returned to them as pale as a ghost, and literally sick with weeping."[56] Campbell himself understood how to interpret this: "Poor Stewart's tears are at present no certain test; his great, but always suseptible mind is reduced, I dare say, to almost puerile weakness, if I may say it with due reverence to his name."[57]

Brown's undertaking of the moral philosophy course was a brief one,[58] and when the teaching year was over Stewart continued with the preparation of his next book, *Philosophical Essays*. In the final text, published in the middle of 1810, he wrote that some of the work was "committed to writing, for the first time, during the course of the last summer and winter . . . The business of composition was begun at a time when I had recourse to it occasionally as a refuge from other thoughts. . ."[59]

But in the summer of 1809 the Stewarts did have a holiday. It included some time at Kinnaird, and to judge from a letter of Mrs Stewart's to Lady Minto it did them good:

> Mr S. and Maria have gained all, and more than even all I hoped, from our northern jaunt. To see her well and occupied with her favourite companions, was the only thing I was certain that could allow his mind to return with keenness to his studies, and the great object was to interest him again completely in them. All this has happened to a wish, and he is as busy as possible. The occupation of this new place is now very fortunate to all of us.[60]

The "new place" was Kinneil House.[61] Before they left on holiday they had decided on what what was to be their last change of residence. This was to move some twenty miles west of Edinburgh, to a property just outside Bo'ness made available to them by the Duke of Hamilton. It had been built in the mid-sixteenth century, and still stands today, an imposing

Towards Retirement (1806–1810)

square edifice flanked by two towers, although the main part of the building is now no more than a shell. Only a wing remains floored and roofed, and the walls of its two rooms bear some interesting decorations, though these were probably covered by plaster in the Stewarts' time. The house faces down an entrance drive, and is surounded by a wooded estate. In a cottage at the rear James Watt, who had received encourgement from Adam Smith and was known to Stewart (he was a guest of the Friday Club in 1805),[62] had tested the prototypes of his revolutionary steam engine. The Stewarts' predecessor in Kinneil House was his original partner, Dr John Roebuck, co-founder of the Carron Ironworks. Kinneil is only half a mile from the Firth of Forth, and from its upper windows it commanded extensive views across the river to the hills of Stirlingshire and Perthshire. Visiting it a few years after the Stewarts had moved there, David Wilkie described it as "the same kind of house that I should think Voltaire must have lived in while in Switzerland".[63] As long before as in 1792 Stewart had told the Earl of Buchan of his "favourite wish of retiring to the country".[64] Now he had achieved it at a location which cannot have been new to him: it was in the Kinneil estate that Aexander Nasmyth had painted him with his first wife and little Matthew more than twenty years before.

In her letter to Lady Minto, dated 3 August 1809, Mrs Stewart reported their safe arrival: "We are now fairly fixed up in our new abode, and did not come to it [from Montrose] by Edinburgh but made the furniture meet us here. I hope we shall be very comfortable. The House promises to be warm and dry and the oddity of it is no objection to us. The beauty of the situation enchants Mr S———" She finished the letter with a reference to the Rev. Thomas Malthus, the English economist, famous for his *Essay on the Principle of Population* which Stewart apparently found persuasive.[65]

> Mr S. insists I shall tell you a misfortune that befell him. He had staid a week longer, from this, to avoid asking Mr *Malthus* in our first confusion, and heard he was gone. On Saturday last week when but three days here, the roofs still whitewashing and the kitchen ditto, we dined in a closet on a cold leg of lamb, which had been baked in an oven. Just as the bones were going away Mr Malthus sent up his card and begged merely to *see* Mr S. The scene that followed no words ever can describe. He had to make his way through brushes and all sorts of crockery ware. He staid two hours however and Mr S. liked him much but I took a headache with despair.[66]

The Stewarts did not have long to wait for the first of the stream of visitors whom they were to receive at Kinneil for almost twenty years. Archy

Alison's son, who had attended Stewart's moral philosophy class during the preceding winter, recalled in his autobiography that that autumn he and his brother made their first visit of any length away from home on their own by going to Kinneil, and remained there for a fortnight.

> This visit, and many others of a similar nature which we made for several years afterwards to Kinneil House, proved a source of unbounded gratification. The admirable simplicity and unaffected *bonhomie*, joined to the delicate taste and feeling heart, of Mr Stewart; the mingled genius and elegance of Mrs Stewart; and the talents of their daughter, who united the judgment and penetration of the one to the accomplishments and feeling of the other, – rendered this abode a scene of attraction which, for a long course of years, was eagerly sought after alike by the great, the able, and the learned from every part of the country.[67]

The move to Kinneil must have been planned as part of the process of retirement; but in fact Stewart seems to have intended to conduct his two classes once more when the College year began in November. He had probably retained a foothold at Callander House (or his old house in the College) where he could stay during the week. But on 13 November he wrote to Archibald Constable, "I expected to have been in Edinburgh before this time, but the state of my health makes it prudent for me to remain for another fortnight in the country . . . "[68] Thomas Brown would again have been called upon to fill the breach. Stewart must have made it to the city shortly after this, but a few days before Christmas he felt obliged to decline an invitation to speak at the funeral of Dr Adam of the High School, whose death was described in chapter 2. He wrote:

> The state of my health has made it necessary for me to leave Edinburgh at present, and to try the effects of leisure and country air. I hope to be able to return in a week or two; but in the meantime, I feel myself quite unequal to the task which Mrs Adam has so kindly requested me to undertake. I hope you will have the goodness to state to her . . . the impossibility of my joining the procession in this inclement weather; and to assure her from me of the sincere regret it gives me, to be deprived of paying the last duty of respect to one of my oldest and most valued friends.[69]

On the penultimate day of the year he contacted Thomas Brown: "As the state of my health at present makes it impossible for me to resume my lectures on Wednesday next, I must again have recourse to your friendly assistance, in supplying my place for a short time. *Two* lectures or at the utmost *three* in the week will, I think, be sufficient during my absence."[70] Brown read this letter to the class at its first meeting in January 1810: it may have been the review of Stewart's thirty-eight years of university teaching which the future Sir Henry Holland described to Maria Edgeworth as "most pathetic and impressive".[71] Brown pronounced an "eloquent panegyric" on Stewart and said he would give three lectures a week for as long as was required. He carried out this undertaking so successfully that many of the church and the legal profession, and other professors such as John Playfair, came to hear him.

When it was made known that Stewart was returning, the class appointed a committee of their most distinguished members under Holland's chairmanship to draw up an address expressing their admiration for Brown's efforts and also congratulating Stewart on the recovery of his health.[72] It was dated 1 March.

> We have had the honour of being deputed by a very numerous meeting of the Students of Moral Philosophy in the present session of the College to express to you in the warmest terms their unfeigned satisfaction in seeing you resume your public station. They long witnessed with a painful interest your generous struggles in a very delicate state of health to continue the discharge of your fatiguing duties. They could not contemplate these exertions, which you supported with an amiable disregard both of your convenience and safety, without being desirous of offering some expression of their gratitude for so great a sacrifice . . .[73]

Selected to present this to Stewart on behalf of the class was the chairman of the little group, the diminutive Lord John Russell. Lord John's father, the Whig Duke of Bedford, had been told that "nothing was learned in the English Universities" and decided to send his son to Edinburgh. This had not at first been well received by the young man, whose reaction was, "The thing I should most dislike . . . would be an endeavour to acquire Scotch knowledge in a Scotch town." But he had arrived in November 1809 at the age of seventeen, and for the three years he studied in Edinburgh he lodged with Professor Playfair. He was soon a convert to Edinburgh life, and was greatly taken with Stewart's lectures. A few weeks before the occasion of the formal address, he had written to Lady Holland, "The lectures of Dr Brown are but a poor substitute for Stewart."[74]

But clearly neither Stewart's health nor his inclination permitted him to continue beyond this academic year. His last endeavours were devoted to ensuring that he should give way to the successor of his choice, and Thomas Brown had made so favourable an impression during his spells of substitution that there was little opposition to his appointment.

Towards Retirement (1806-1810)

Nevertheless, Stewart exerted himself personally to solicit the support of every member of the Town Council on Brown's behalf. At the beginning of May he wrote to the Magistrates:

> As the state of my health has, for some time past, rendered it impossible for me to discharge the duties of my Professorship, without availing myself of the occasional assistance of my friends; and as I am extremely anxious that the Public should suffer no inconvenience from my indisposition, I beg leave hereby to resign the said Office into the hands of the Magistrates and Council of Edinburgh. In doing so, I presume there can be no impropriety in expressing my wish to be re-elected in conjunction with a Colleague qualified and disposed to co-operate with me cordially, in carrying on that very important department of Education to which I have devoted the best part of my life.[75]

The Council then moved the joint appointment of Stewart and Thomas Brown as professors of moral philosophy in the same form of arrangement which Stewart had experienced before as the junior partner: the understanding was that Brown would carry out the duties of the post.

And so, at the age of fifty-six, Stewart effectively concluded his College career. He wrote to Dr Samuel Parr, the sociable English Whig churchman, schoolmaster and scholar:

> I have now retired completely from the University, and have even quitted Edinburgh as a place of residence . . . I propose henceforth to devote the whole of my time in preparing my works for the press. Our house is about twenty miles from Edinburgh, where we are within reach of the advantages of the public libraries, and can enjoy from time to time the society of our friends.[76]

Five years later, Thomas Campbell, visiting Kinneil, reported:

> Stewart's residence is an old chateau of the Dukes of Hamilton, agreeably situate near the sea, opposite the classic Benledi, and surrounded by fine groves that resound with the songs of birds, the cawing of rooks, and the sweeter cawing of wood-pigeons . . . I slept in a room haunted by a Lady who, two hundred years ago, was tossed over the battlememnts by her husband for being naughty! But knowing me to be a most modest and virtuous man, she had not the assurance to come into the chamber, while I occupied it . . . I found this seat of the Philosopher more splendid, perhaps, than seemed to accord with philosophy; but he is easy and prosperous, and lives in a style that somewhat, though very agreeably, surprised me.[77]

In the meantime the general reaction to the end of an era was recorded by Lord Cockburn: "Stewart's retirement made a deep and melancholy impression. We could scarcely bring ourselves to believe that that voice was to be heard no more."[78]

CHAPTER FOURTEEN

The Teacher and the Man

"To me Stewart's lectures were like the opening of the heavens. I felt that I had a soul. His noble views, unfolded in glorious sentences, elevated me into a higher world." Lord Cockburn

The point in the narrative at which Stewart retires may be a good one at which to survey the evidence of his impact as a teacher, an attempt which is difficult to separate from consideration of his character as a man. The intimacy of the connection is well illustrated by the concluding couplet of some lines which Lord John Russell composed about Stewart in the garden at Kinneil House when he visited there in the early summer of 1812.

> 'Twas he gave rules to fancy, grace to thought,
> Taught virtue's laws, and practiced what he taught.[1]

Stewart was perceived as being an effective and inspiring teacher of *moral* philosophy in large part because he was a good man. Writing many years after his death, Robert Gillies thought his memory still cherished "for the sincerity of his friendships; for his humane, indulgent, and kind disposition".[2] Gillies remembered that in 1807 "his class-room was usually so crowded that without going before the hour it was not possible to find a seat".[3] A number of tributes from his students have already been referred

155

The Teacher and the Man

to along the way. Perhaps the most famous was paid by Lord Cockburn:

> To me Stewart's lectures were like the opening of the heavens. I felt that I had a soul. His noble views, unfolded in glorious sentences, elevated me into a higher world. I was as much excited and charmed as any man of cultivated taste would be, who, after being ignorant of their existence, was admitted to all the glories of Milton, and Cicero, and Shakespeare. Stewart's views changed my whole nature. In short Dugald Stewart was one of the greatest of didactic orators.[4]

Cockburn attended the moral philosophy class in the mid-1790s when Stewart was in his prime, but similar comments were made by Archy Alison's son, the future Sir Archibald, who, as has been noted, was his student in 1808–9, the year of the illness and death of George Stewart. Alison went to Playfair's natural philosophy class in the same year, and wrote of the dual experience:

> Next to the conversations and instructions of my father, I regard that as the most fortunate event which occurred in my education. It was impossible to imagine two men more completely fitted to convey the sublime principles of moral and physical science, or whose character exhibited a more perfect commentary on the doctrines which they taught. Simple in his manners, unostentatious in his habits, but ardent in his enthusiasm, Mr Stewart warmed in the professor's chair into a glow of eloquence which, combined with the beautiful quotations in prose and verse interspersed in his lectures, entranced his hearers and produced an indelible impression on the mind.[5]

Dr John Thomson, whose career culminated as professor of general pathology at Edinburgh, said that the two things which most impressed him in the course of his life were the acting of Mrs Siddons and the oratory of Dugald Stewart.[6] Stewart's own son Matthew declared after his death:

> As a public speaker, he was justly entitled to rank among the very first of his day, and, had an adequate sphere been afforded for the display of his oratorical powers, his merit in this line alone would have sufficed to assure him an eternal reputation. Among those who have attracted the highest admiration in the senate and at the bar, there are still many living who will bear testimony to his extraordinary eloquence.[7]

"I have heard Pitt and Fox deliver some of their most admired speeches," wrote James Mill; "but I have never heard anything so eloquent as some of the lectures of Professor Stewart."[8] Nor was this acclaim confined to one side of the Atlantic. An anonymous young American who had attended Stewart's lectures in Edinburgh wrote in an American journal that he could not remember or mention these lectures "without feelings of the most enthusiastic respect, and of the liveliest gratitude. I have never found any public speaker, in any situation, more eloquent in manner and in language, and never have been made to feel more sensibly, by any orator, the dignity of human knowledge, – the beauty of human genius – or the elevation of human virtue."[9]

A twenty-first-century reader is likely to be struck not only by the warmth of these recollections but by what they reveal about Stewart's lecturing style. Nowadays we do not expect academics to be eloquent and uplifting, and the evidence of Stewart's students points to a need to understand what teachers like him were about. The principal aim of professors of philosophy and history in the eighteenth century was not to develop tools of impartial analysis but to make their students wiser and better men and so help to improve the social order. Professors studied oratory, and used it consciously as a means of fostering virtue. Moral philosophy had for long had pride of place in the curriculum of the Scottish universities because it involved the discussion and defence of those principles on which a good society must be founded, though fashion was gradually changing; at the time of Stewart's retirement a reviewer suggested that through the interest and attraction engendered by his eloquence he had helped to rescue his subject at a time when there was a danger of its being excluded by more practical ones such as agriculture and civil engineering.[10]

One of Stewart's students during the session 1793–4 recorded that the professor concluded his final lecture with these words:

> We have thus exhausted all the subjects comprehended under the Science of Moral Philosophy. To say anything of the importance of these subjects is hardly necessary. Not only their own intrinsic beauty and excellence, but their general and extensive application to other subjects of science, and to the common affairs of life sufficiently recommend them. They are studies which afford to every man an engaging and interesting subject of pursuit. They give him an insight into his own mind, and lay open to him all its most secret laws and operations. Their consideration sharpens his reasoning and reflective powers, and enable him equally to throw off the chains of superstition and to combat the fallacies of scepticism. And while they hold out to his view the purest precepts of religion and morality, they enable him to put these difficult lessons in practice by their influence in subduing the passions, refining the ideas, and exalting the mind above a slavish regard to the empty and feeble allurements which this world can hold out to estrange him from the paths of duty and rectitude.[11]

The corresponding record of another student eight years later shows that while the words may have changed, the spirit remained the same. During the preceding five months Stewart had "endeavoured to direct your attention to studies susceptible to practical application to the concerns of life; whether providence may have called you to fulfil the obscure but important duties of private business or to take part in the great concerns of public life".[12] Even if the student's notes were not completely accurate, this seems to have been a pretty explicit statement of what Stewart saw as his mission. Veitch described his object as "to develop all that is distinctive in man, and thus to give dignity, elevation, even grandeur, to the commonplace of every-day life, by intermingling with it a permanent love of truth, beauty, and virtue . . . "[13]

At the end of his course on political economy he addressed his students in a similar vein, hoping that their studies "may contribute, under various vicissitudes of fortune that may yet await you, to fortify your virtuous resolutions, to elevate your views above the pursuit of vulgar ambitions, and to cherish in your minds those habitual sentiments of religion, of humanity, of justice, and of fortitude, which can alone render talents and accomplishments . . . a source of permanent happiness and honour . . . "[14] Yet Stewart's head was not in the clouds; Sir Archibald Alison recalled an expression he was often heard to use of someone whose talents were not of the highest order, "but they are of a very *marketable description*";[15] coming from a disciple of Adam Smith, the expression is unlikely to have been intended ironically.

His actual course on economics appears also to have been pitched at a high moral level. In his *Journal* for 17 December 1800 Francis Horner recorded:

> I now attend Stewart's lectures on Political Economy, which he delivers three times a week . . . it is not so much from the detail of particulars that I derive improvement from this amiable philosopher's lectures, as from the general manner and spirit with which he unfolds his speculations, and delivers, in chaste and impressive language, the most liberal and benevolent sentiments, the most comprehensive and enlightened views . . . Stewart insisted this morning, with great elegance and force, on his favourite remark, that the general principles of internal economy and regulation, are far more worthy of the interest and attention of the political philosopher, *because more intimately connected with the public happiness* [biographer's italics], than discussions with regard to the comparative advantages of different constitutions.[16]

A student who took the course three years later recorded Stewart as saying, "Every step which has been made in Political Economy has found error counteracting happiness." "Every addition to knowledge augments happiness."[17] In the published version of his lectures he explicitly enlarges the scope of 'political economy' to cover "all those speculations which have for their object the happiness and improvement of Political Society".[18]

His view of his role may well have been incompatible with the detailed study of texts or the teasing out of fine distinctions; but even among Stewart's contemporaries and admirers there was a feeling that his teaching, while free "from pedantry and one-sidedness",[19] was a little *too* general and insubstantial. Less than a month after the entry just quoted, Francis Horner noted in his *Journal*:

> I ... attend Stewart's lectures, and strive to imbibe some portion of that elegant taste and comprehensive spirit which are diffused over his speculations. At the same time, I confess that I begin to suspect him of excessive timidity on the subject of political innovation, and the practicability of improvement by individual exertion. And I am not sure, if the great eloquence and sensibility of his compositions have not in some degree an unfavourable effect in the investigation of truth and the communication of knowledge; in so pleasing a dress, error and involuntary sophistry might insinuate themselves undetected, because without suspicion; and even truth itself finds admission too easy, when the severities of attention have been lulled into reverie by the charms of the most select diction and the most attractive imagery.[20]

Archibald Alison junior was less impressed by Stewart's lectures on political economy than by those on moral philosophy, observing of the former that he "began to suspect that he either had not gone to the bottom of the subject, or was not gifted with an original mind".[21] When Walter Scott learned of Stewart's death he observed in his *Journal*, "There is much of water-painting in all his metaphysics, which consist rather of words than ideas."[22] In 1801 Thomas Chalmers, the future leader of the Free Church of Scotland, had written:

> I attended his lectures regularly. I must confess I have been rather disappointed. I never heard a single discussion of Stewart's that made up one masterly and comprehensive whole. His lectures seem to me to be made up of detached hints and incomplete outlines, and he almost uniformly avoids every subject which involves any difficult discussions.[23]

Cockburn was probably suggesting much the same thing when he wrote:

Stewart dealt as little as possible in metaphysics, avoided details, and shrank, with horror which was sometimes rather ludicrous, from all polemical matter. Invisible distinctions, vain contentions, philosophical sectarianism, had no attraction for him; and their absence left him free for those moral themes on which he could soar without perplexing his hearers, or wasting himself, by useless and painful subtleties.[24]

It is to Cockburn that we owe a physical description of Stewart in action:

Stewart was about the middle size, weakly limbed, and with an appearance of feebleness which gave an air of delicacy to his gait and structure. His forehead was large and bald, his eyebrows bushy, his eyes grey and intelligent, and capable of conveying emotion, in which they were powerfully aided by his lips, which, though rather large perhaps, were flexible and expressive. The voice was singularly pleasing; a slight burr only made its tones softer. His ear, both for music and for speech, was exquisite; and he was the finest reader I ever heard. His gesture was simple and elegant, though not free from a tinge of professional formality; and his whole manner that of an academical gentleman.[25]

The American scientist and educator Benjamin Silliman provided another word drawing.

With a countenance strongly marked with the lines of intellect; with an expression of thought, approaching almost to severity, but, in conversation, softened with great benignity; and with manners, uniting every thing of dignity and ease, he, even at first sight, impresses a stranger forcibly with an idea of his superiority.[26]

We are not dependent solely on verbal description to know something of Stewart's appearance, for several representations were made during his lifetime.[27] The portrait by Nasmyth with his first wife and the infant Matthew, which is in private hands, has already been mentioned. In 1794 and again in 1797 James Tassie made medallions showing his face in profile in white enamel on a blue background [Plate 5 (a)]. Henry Raeburn, who had also done a double portrait of George and Maria Stewart [Plate 7], made a portrait of Stewart in 1808 [Plate 1 (a)]; it appears to have been painted for Stewart's friend Alexander Fraser Tytler, Lord Woodhouselee, and is now, like the Tassie medallions, in the Scottish National Portrait Gallery (SNPG). A mezzotint engraving of it was made by Charles Turner. In 1811 John Henning did two pencil drawings, one of which is in the SNPG and one in the National Portrait Gallery in London [Plate 13 (a)]. (Mrs Stewart mentioned in a letter to Lady Minto

The Teacher and the Man

that Henning had arrived at Kinneil "and we were busy keeping Mr S. quiet while he sat to him".[28]) Either then or two years later Henning also made a medallion which is now in the SNPG [Plate 5 (b)], and he also made a medallion of Mrs Stewart [Plate 5 (c)]. Edinburgh University possesses a marble bust by Samuel Joseph, made in 1827, and a bronze version is in the possession of the SNPG [Plate 1 (b)]. Finally, as will be described in its place, Sir David Wilkie made a chalk drawing of Stewart as an elderly man. Apart from the bald head mentioned by Cockburn, the most evident feature in these portayals is a rather prominent, slightly Roman nose.

An early historian of Edinburgh University noted that:

> About the year 1790 or 1791, he discontinued the practice of extempore speaking. He had formerly delivered his lectures standing, but when he determined to read them, he did it sitting, and persisted in this, as long as he held the professorship. One would have expected, that this alteration must have materially affected his mode of delivery, and that the reading of what he had committed to writing would not have been so pleasing to his audience, and diminished the effect upon them. But this was not the consequence. It is an undeniable fact, that there was very little difference even in the manner . . .[29]

This writer surmised that the reason for his not reading his lectures from the outset was that they were not complete in his mind; a more likely explanation for the change is that the suspicions aroused by the French Revolution made him anxious to avoid misrepresentation and to be able to refer exactly to what he had said. Cockburn, who attended his lectures in the mid-1790s, gives a different account of his posture when lecturing: possibly it was advancing years rather than the practice of reading from notes that caused him a little later to speak from a sitting position.

> Stewart lectured standing; from notes which, with their successive additions, must, I suppose, at last have been nearly as full as his spoken words. His lecturing manner was professorial, but gentleman-like; calm and expository, but rising into greatness, or softening into tenderness, whenever his subject required it. A slight asthmatic tendency made him often clear his throat; and such was my admiration of the whole exhibition, that Macvey Napier told him, not long ago [Cockburn was writing in the 1820s], that I had said there was eloquence in his very spitting. "Then," said he, "I am glad there was at least one thing in which I had no competitor."[30]

The notes to which Cockburn refers do not seem to have been of the most systematic, even at the end of his teaching career. Thomas Brown's biographer remarked:

In general, it is very easy for a Professor to find a substitute. Nothing more is necessary than that the manuscript lecture should be committed to a friend, by whom it is read to the class. In Mr Stewart's case, however, it was otherwise. His habits of composition, the numerous transpositions that were to be found in his pages, and the many illustrations of which he sketched merely the outline, trusting the filling up to his extemporaneous powers of discourse, rendered his papers in a great measure useless in any hands but his own.[31]

Stewart's dislike of controversy, which Francis Horner and Lord Cockburn both detected in his lectures, seems to have been displayed also in his private life. During Harry Temple's first year at Lothian House he was at first much stimulated by the debates which Stewart organized, and looked forward to one on suicide that Matthew was to lead as "sure of producing a good deal of arguing afterwards which is what we want". But before long he was reporting, "our debate about ghosts ended exactly as all our debates have as yet and I fancy always will, when we had exhausted all our arguments on each side of the Question, the debate was over, and we each retired more strongly than ever confirmed in his own opinion, and more convinced that the other was wrong".[32] At about this time, in April 1801, Horner recorded in his *Journal* an afternoon spent at Stewart's home with several of his friends: "The general conversation after dinner was of that rambling, light, literary kind, which Stewart seems studiously to prefer; he never will condescend in company to be original or profound, or to display those powers of observation which he possesses in an eminent degreee, but shuns the least approach towards discussion."[33]

As we have seen, Robert Gillies described conversation at Whitefoord House as "the most common-place chit-chat";[34] and David Wilkie, visiting Kinneil House, said of Stewart, "you never would dream that he had written a book . . . he in no instance leads the conversation to his own particular studies. You never see him trying to say a good thing or a smart thing, but with all this," Wilkie did, however, add, "you never lose sight of his superiority in learning and information, and never forget that you are in the presence of a judge, and of an uncommon man."[35] Referring to the "democratical tendencies" for which at one period Stewart was an object of suspicion, Lady Minto added, "which, however, he never brings forward in conversation".[36] And Sydney Smith, in his facetiously exaggerated way, recorded of a visit by Stewart in 1811:

"We spoke much of the weather and other harmless subjects. He became once, however, a little elevated, and in the gaiety of his soul let out some opinions which will doubtless make him writhe with remorse. He went so far as to say he considered the King's recovery as very problematical."[37]

It may also have been dislike of anything approaching the polemical which accounts for the perhaps surprising fact that Stewart never contributed to the *Edinburgh Review*, since anything he might have submitted would no doubt have been more than welcome to the editors. But five years after his death his son Matthew mentioned to Macvey Napier, referring to the critical journals, "a strong injunction from my father not to write in them (which it would not be pleasant to me to violate)".[38]

One can only speculate on the reason for this aversion to serious discussion. It may be that a form of fastidiousness made him unwilling to expose in conversation opinions which he knew he could express more accurately in writing. And his reticence cannot have been total. Silliman recorded: "When he speaks, whether in his lecture room or in conversation, he draws forth the resources of a highly enriched and polished mind; he charms the hearer by the beauty of his language and the fine cadence of his voice, and arrests his attention by the energy and boldness of his eloquence."[39]

Certainly he did not appear formidable or intimidating in a social setting. The Earl of Dudley remarked that "as to petty victories in argument – sharp turns upon weak and unprepared adversaries – minute and philosophical accuracy in that ordinary discourse when men chiefly seek repose and recreation – this is a sort of superiority which he never sought – which he never thought of seeking – and which could never have afforded him the smallest pleasure."[40] Stewart's son wrote:

> In general company, his manner bordered on reserve; but . . . he was ever ready with a smile to acknowledge the happy sallies of wit, and no man had a keener sense of the ludicrous, or laughed more heartily at genuine humour. His deportment and expression were easy and unembarrassed, dignified, elegant, and graceful. His politeness was equally free from all affectation, and from all premeditation . . . From an early period of life, he had frequented the best society both in France and in this country, and he had in a peculiar degree the air of good company. In the society of ladies he appeared to great advantage, and to women of cultivated understanding, his conversation was particularly acceptable and pleasing.[41]

The last statement is borne out by the striking testimony of Maria Edgeworth, who was notably shy with people she did not know well: "I never conversed with anyone with whom I was more at ease."[42] Matthew continued with reference to his father's private behaviour (he was not an impartial witness, but not all men would speak thus of their parents):

> In his domestic circle, his character appeared in its most amiable light, and by his family he was beloved, and venerated almost to adoration. So uniform and sustained was the tone of his manners, and so completely was it the result of the habitual influence of the natural elegance and elevation of his mind on his external demeanour, that when alone with his wife and his chidren, it hardly differed by a shade from that which he maintained in the company of strangers; for although his fondness, and familiarity, and playfulness were alike engaging and unrestrained, he never lost anything either of his grace or his dignity . . .[43]

To modern taste this may sound a trifle pompous or self-important. But Lord Dudley wrote of Stewart's reserve that "the warmth of his feelings, and the kindness of his disposition, were continually visible beneath this, perhaps necessary, garb".[44] And Robert Burns recorded in his private papers that "his wit, in the hour of social hilarity, proceeds almost to good-natured waggishness; and in telling a story he particularly excels".[45] A recorded incident corroborates the occasional playfulness. The Stewarts often visited Woodhouselee in the Pentland Hills, the home of Alexander Fraser Tytler who was professor of universal history at the University and in 1802 was elevated to the bench as Lord Woodhouselee. His daughter Ann, who became a writer of books for children, recalled of her own childhood:

> Other frequent guests at Woodhouselee were Dugald and Mrs Stewart. He was of graver cast [than Walter Scott, who took the children for walks and told them stories], yet he was no deep philosopher to the younger branches of the family. In one of those visits, on some one going into the drawing-room after breakfast, they found him alone with my brother Peter, running round the room, each balancing a peacock's feather on his nose. Sometimes, on our return from walking, Mr Stewart would compliment us on our blooming complexions. Peter would then never fail to say: 'Now, young ladies, don't be puffed up; remember Mr Stewart probably sees your cheeks quite green.' This was in allusion to a natural optical defect in Mr Stewart's sight: to him, the cherries and leaves on a tree were the same colour; and there was no distinction of hue between the red coats of the soldiers marching through a wood and the green trees themselves.[46]

(Many years later *The Scotsman* published a review of the first volume of the *History of Scotland* by Patrick ("Peter") Fraser Tytler in the same issue as that which carried Stewart's obituary.[47])

Another aspect of his social demeanour may have been that everything was grist to Stewart's philosophic mill. "I am making the character of my host a special study," Thomas Campbell wrote while staying at Kinneil in 1815: "he is very fond of anecdotes; nothing pleases him so much as listening for hours together to the most minute details of human character. I have been telling him all I could remember of the prominent characters of the day; and there he sits, with his intelligent eyes fixed upon me, listening in mute attention. Yet, be it remembered, Dugald is no gossip; but as the bee collects its honey from every flower, he extracts matter for reflection and edification from every variety of human knowledge."[48]

At least by Sydney Smith, he was capable of being teased, as when Smith persisted in assuring him that he was generally considered to be the author of the sensational but anonymous *Plymley Letters*[49] which made a powerful ironic case for Catholic emancipation – and which Smith had in fact written himself.

That Stewart had a sense of humour and that there was quite a strong emotional side to his nature has already emerged. The avoidance of any danger that he might become a dry scholar must have owed much to his second marriage. Helen Stewart may have been, or become, a little 'highly strung', but her personality – her liveliness, her intelligence, her warmth – stand out from every letter she wrote. A writer in the *Quarterly* after her death described her thus:

> Though the least beautiful of a family in which beauty is hereditary, she had the best essence of beauty, expression, a bright eye beaming with intelligence, a manner the most distinguished, yet soft, feminine, and singularly winning . . . she was free from the slightest tinge of pedantry; the world, for anything she displayed, knew nothing of her deep acquisitions, so gracefully did her long-draped robes conceal even the suspicion that aught lurked beneath of azure hue [i.e., she was not a 'bluestocking']. No one felt this more than Lord Dudley, who thus expresses himself . . . : "She has as much knowledge, understanding, and wit, as would set up three foreign ladies as first-rate talkers, in all their respective drawing-rooms, but she is almost as desirous to conceal as they are to display their talents." No wonder, therefore, that her saloons were the resort of all that was best of Edinburgh, the house to which strangers most eagerly sought introduction.[50]

"Her manner," wrote Robert Gillies, "was at all times best indicated by the Scotch word 'couthie' [plain, homely, unsophisticated]; and there was a remarkable contrast between the low, quiet, equable tones of her voice, and the enthusiastic, poetical, romantic sentiments which she so frequently expressed."[51] Great was John Ward's glee when he heard that

Walter Scott, on being pressed by a female acquaintance for comment on Dugald Stewart's wife, had replied that indeed she was a *nice little woman*. In recounting this to "Ivy" herself he added, "You may easily imagine how I laughed when she repeated to me this authentic description of the immeasurable Ivy".[52]

From before her marriage Mrs Stewart had been a close friend of the wife of Lord Woodhouselee, and Ann Tytler recorded:

> Mrs Stewart was a very accomplished person also, and with a voice in speaking peculiarly sweet and musical. They seemed a very happy couple; but my mother would sometimes remark that this happiness was in some danger of being diminished by the very means they took to increase it. They were in constant dread of giving each other pain or anxiety, so that there were perpetual little mysteries and concealments. As an instance of this, she told us that Mr Stewart once having made an appointment with Mrs Stewart to meet him at a bookeller's shop, she, arriving a little before the time, was asked to remain in the back shop, to which there was a glass door.[53] Presently Mr Stewart entered; and giving a glance through the glass door, he seemed in a low voice to enter earnestly into conversation with the bookseller, till suddenly they were interrupted by a scream from the inner shop. They flew in, and found Mrs Stewart sinking on the ground. She fancied that their little daughter Maria had fallen into the fire. It was not however of a burning little girl they had been talking, but of a new publication.[54]

Habitual overprotectiveness can give rise to unnecessary anxiety. But the evidence suggests that most of their friends would have agreed with the judgment of Archibald Constable's son Thomas when he wrote, "There never surely was a more perfect union than that of Dugald Stewart with his second wife."[55] By their friends they were perceived very much as a partnership. Before the breach over Lord Melville, Walter Scott wrote to Anna Seward, the Swan of Litchfield, "My friends Mr and Mrs Dugald Stewart are well acquainted with them [the Ladies of Llangollen referred to in chapter 10] and great admirers of their accomplishments and manners – a eulogium which conveys a great deal to all who know Mr and Mrs S———."[56]

"Mr S. promised to me to mention an earnest request of the Llangollen ladies to you," Mrs Stewart once wrote to Archibald Constable, "but forgot it as usual."[57] Perhaps wives are apt to make such observations about their husbands, but it may be that a little absent-mindedness was one of Stewart's failings. According to Henry Mackenzie, his forgetfulness extended to returning books which he had borrowed to read. "On its being said that, eminent as he was in many branches of knowledge, he confessed himself deficient in Arithmetic, a punster said, 'That, tho' very improbable, might be true: but he certainly excelled in book-keeping.'"[58] He was also, according to Veitch, "averse from letter-writing",[59] and occasional comments by his wife cofirm this, though by modern standards he did pretty well. At worst, in any case, these are fairly venal faults.

Although he considered excessive sensibility to be a sign of deficiency of taste, Stewart was not immune from sentiment. Tom Moore, the Irish poet, remarked, "I never saw any *man* that seemed to feel my singing more deeply."[60] Mrs Stewart told Lady Minto, "There is nobody in the world who feels so much pleasure as he does, in reading poetry, when it really touches his heart . . . "[61] His own sole surviving attempt at poetry, an epitaph *On an unfortunate lady*, is in rhyming couplets and rather in the manner of Gray's *Elegy*.[62] Gray, indeed, is one of those to whom he turns in his writings to illustrate or confirm his points; apart from Shakespeare, they are nearly all in the Augustan tradition – Milton, Pope, James Thomson, Akenside, Collins. Veitch remarked that Stewart's "catholicity enabled him to see and prize excellence in whatever form it appeared. There were indeed few aspects of truth, beauty, or virtue, which he was not capable of appreciating."[63] But he never alludes to the works of Blake or Burns, Wordsworth or Coleridge, Scott or Southey. The only contemporary poets whose books even had a place in his extensive library[64] were his friends Scott, Campbell and Moore, plus some works of Byron's which their author had presented to him.[65] ("Lord Byron's success may well make poor philosophers envious," Mrs Stewart observed to Archibald Constable.[66]) Nor has anything survived in the library which could be described as fiction. We know that in his later years Stewart enjoyed reading the Waverley novels, but in his philosophical writing he makes no reference to Scott, Fielding, Fanny Burney, Jane Austen or, with the exception of his friend Henry Mackenzie,[67] any other novelist whose work might lend itself to moral illustration. He may have felt that fiction and romantic poetry fell below the level of seriousness appropriate to philosophy; but it seems likely that his personal taste, which must have been significantly moulded by his early immersion in classical literature, remained conservative.

Probably many of these aspects of Stewart's character failed to come across to most of his students. Recounting the incident when Thomas Brown "summoned courage" to speak to the professor after one his lectures, his biographer remarks: "Those who remember the dignified demeanour of Mr Stewart in his class, which was calculated to convey the idea of one of those great and gifted men who were seen among the groves of the Academy, will duly appreciate the boldness of our young philosopher."[68] Henry Brougham compared Stewart unfavourably with the accessible and helpful Playfair, as the former, either, he thought, from exhaustion, or because of "aversion to disputation, which such conferences were apt to occasion, . . . very often declined to see his pupils after the class rose".[69] Indeed there is evidence that many, if not a majority, of Stewart's students must have been quite unknown to him personally. Mention has already been made of the attendance of James Mill at Stewart's lectures when he studied at Edinburgh University in the early 1790s, and of his admiration for them; but in 1805 Stewart wrote to Francis Horner in London about the *Literary Journal*, describing it as a publication "conducted as I am told by a Scotchman of the name of *Mill* or *Milne*". As the editors of *The Horner Papers* remark, "Evidently Stewart had no recollection of Mill as his pupil."[70]

Another instance emerged when the Royal Commission on the Scottish Universities was taking evidence in 1827. The Rev. John Lee, then minister of Lady Yester's Church in Edinburgh, told the Commissioners that he had attended Stewart's moral philosophy class for three complete sessions – and his name indeed appears on the matriculation roll for 1796, '97 and '98. Some years later he asked Stewart for his support in connection with an appointment which he was seeking. Stewart replied in encouraging terms, but stated firmly: "I cannot presume to transmit a written testimonial in favour of one with whom I am not personally acquainted."[71] Mr Lee's point in recounting this episode was that if students had been required to submit written work and to take examinations he might have become known to the professor; it irked him that the most assiduous students emerged only with the Certificate of Attendance which could "be obtained by one who has been as negligent as possible, or who has not even been personally present five or six times, if at all, during the whole session".[72] But even allowing for this aspect of the system, and for the large numbers who attended Stewart's lectures, Lee's experience suggests that his personal interest in his students was somewhat haphazard.

Indeed the question might suggest itself whether Stewart was a bit of a snob. There is no doubt that an account of his close friends and associates includes a remarkable number of people of titled or aristocratic background. But some of these connections came from his wife, and there is no evidence of Stewart deliberately cultivating such people; it seems more often to have been they who sought out him. Robert Burns had a keen nose for humbug, so some weight must be given to his description of Stewart as the only man he knew "who only values these players [in life], the Dramatis Personae, who build cities, or who rear hedges; who govern provinces, or superintend flocks, merely as they *act their parts*".[73] Lord Cockburn recorded how James Laing, one of the clerks to Edinburgh Town Council, "had an incomprehensible reverence for Dugald Stewart".[74] We also have the testimony of the minister of the parish which included Catrine that many years after Stewart's death "individuals still speak with delight of his unwearied benevolence, of his kindness and condescension [a word which then carried no patronizing overtone] to all who came within the sphere of his influence, particularly to those who he knew had been the objects of his father's regard".[75] So there are no grounds for supposing that Stewart was any less affable to those of humble background than to the great of the land with whom he came in contact.

A more fundamental criticism of Stewart's stance as a moralist arises from the conditions which were growing aound him during his tenure of the chair of moral philosophy – the results of the industrial revolution in terms of poverty, squalour and immorality among the growing urban working class. Apart from sharing with Adam Smith a perception that lives could be stunted by industrialization, Stewart had little to say about these matters, though he did maintain that in relation to the practice of moving children from urban workhouses to distant factories "the protecting interference of the Legislature is loudly called for",[76] and he offered education, "even to the lowest classes", as the only radical cure for the evils of crime. [77] The pleasures of imagination he considered to "be in a great measure necessarily denied" to "the laborious orders of society".[78] His kind of moral and philosophical outlook was that of a leisured and educated class – of those who possessed, in his own phrase, "a well informed and cultivated mind".[79] In this he was no different from his contemporaries in the Scottish Enlightenment,[80] and it would be anachronistic to accuse him of failing in forms of social analysis which had yet to be developed; but it is not unfair to find in his confidence and optimism a degree of complacency and selective oversight. He overestimated the power of unsupported reason to ensure the continuance of universal progress.

A difficulty in assessing his impact as a teacher is that some of those who knew him best are inconsistent in their judgments. A damning phrase sometimes used against him comes from his ardent admirer, Lord Cockburn, who described him as "without genius, or even originality"; but the sentence continues as a balanced assessment: "Stewart's intellectual character was marked by calm thought and great soundness".[81] We also find Francis Horner, whose doubts have been quoted about the compatibility of Stewart's oratorical style with rigorous argument, contradicting both Cockburn and himself in writing that Stewart's views on metaphysics, literature and political economy were all "original and profound".[82] What in any case, one might ask, counts as original in philosophy?

Horner was in truth one of Stewart's most devoted disciples, and was certainly ready to defend him against criticism from any other quarter. Lord Holland recorded a story told by Samuel Rogers, the poet and society host: "Rogers diverted us the other day with telling, before Horner and [Dr John] Allen, [Richard Payne] Knight's opinion of Dugald Stewart: how he had done nothing to merit his reputation, how his *Lives* were lifeless, and his philosophy sometimes trite and shallow and sometimes obscure. At all this the two Scotchmen fired; and Rogers sat enjoying the effects of his reported satire, and, when Allen stopped for breath, added, 'But I haven't done yet – there's more.'"[83]

Nor did all his students regard his teaching style as unstimulating. Thirty years after Stewart's death the advocate John Murray wrote of him as one –

> to whom Scotland has perhaps been more indebted than to any individual of his time ... No person more deeply felt the high importance of the duties which he had to perform as a teacher of moral philosophy. The object nearest his heart was to elevate the character of the Scottish youth; to make them, whatever might be their calling in life, aspire to something higher than had been done before. It was not his object to form any sect or to teach any peculiar doctrines, but to enlarge the mind and to cultivate the moral feelings of his students. This is shown in every part of his works, and is most deeply impressed upon all who attended his lectures. He presented all the different views of the subject which he brought before his students with great force and eloquence, but always with the aim of making them inquire and think for themselves, and form their own conclusions ...[84]

Stewart was explicit about this aim when he told his political economy students that he had quoted some passages "because I am always much more anxious to suggest a variety of ideas for your examination, than to establish any particular system".[85] The object of a public teacher, he observed elsewhere, is – perhaps he meant ought to be – not "to inculcate a particular system of dogmas, but to prepare his pupils for exercising their own judgments".[86]

Sir James Mackintosh, writing in 1830, seems to have been in no doubt that in his aim of enlarging his students' minds and cultivating their moral feelings Stewart triumphantly succeeded:

> The lectures of Mr Stewart, for a quarter of a century rendered [the profes-

sorship of moral philosophy] famous through every country where the light of reason was allowed to penetrate. Perhaps few men ever lived, who poured into the breasts of youth a more fervid and yet reasonable love of liberty, of truth, and of virtue. How many are still alive, in different countries, and in every rank to which education reaches, who, if they accurately examined their own minds and lives, would ascribe much of whatever goodness and happiness they possess, to the early impressions of his gentle and persuasive eloquence! He lived to see his disciples distinguished among the lights and ornaments of the council and the senate. He had the consolation to be sure that no words of his promoted the growth of an impure taste, of an exclusive prejudice, of a malevolent passion. Without derogation from his writings, it may be said that his disciples were among his best works.[87]

As Lord Cockburn put it, "No intelligent pupil of [Stewart's] ever ceased to respect philosophy, or was ever false to his principles, without feeling the crime aggravated by the recollection of the morality that Stewart had taught him."[88]

Whatever notes of qualification need to be attached to Stewart's reputation as a teacher, the evidence of his impact on these disciples is therefore striking. It was summed up by Veitch in these words:

The period of attendance on the prelections [lectures] of Stewart remained sacred in the mind of many a pupil, long after the quiet of the University had been exchanged for the bustle of the world, as a time of elevated converse with great themes, and the source of a refining and ennobling influence then first amalgamated with the current of life. The man – the purity and elevation of his personal character – the enlarged, liberal, and tolerant spirit which he carried into speculation – his unwavering confidence in the steady progress of humanity towards a fuller realisation of truth and virtue – his chastened eloquence and ample stores of illustrative imagery and classical reference – the thorough mastery he shewed of his powers of intellect and imagination, springing from assiduous culture – his grace of speech and manner – the repose and dignity of his academic demeanour, not unrelieved by a vein of quiet and kindly humour – long remained in the memory of numerous pupils, scattered abroad over many lands, whom his impressive teaching first awoke to a full sense of the duty and the dignity of man, and whose higher feelings and nobler impulses he called forth and animated. In the case, indeed, of the finer minds among his pupils who most thoroughly imbibed their master's spirit, and profited most fully by his teaching, the lapse of time, as they gradually receded in the journey of life, from the era of their attendance on Stewart's prelections, served but to enhance the feeling of sacredness with which they regarded the pure spring whence, in early youth, they had drawn supplies for the needs of their opening moral and intellectual life.[89]

CHAPTER FIFTEEN

The Early Years of Retirement 1810–1815

"We passed a very happy week with my old and excellent friend Dugald Stewart, whom we had the satisfaction to see in the full vigour of his great talents, and in the lively enjoyment of everything about him, of the charming country in which he lives, of the society of his very sensible and amiable wife and daughter, of his books, of his leisure, of his philosophical retirement, and, above all, of the delight he experiences in the pursuit of his metaphysical researches, and in continuing and completing his own admirable writings." Sir Samuel Romilly

Stewart's resolution to devote his retirement at Kinneil House to writing got off to a good start as so much of the *Philosophical Essays* had been written in Edinburgh before and after George's death. By May 1810 he was telling Archibald Constable that he had nearly finished the introduction, or *Preliminary Dissertation*, though he was a little worried about its length.[1] He dated the prefatory *Advertisement* 15 June, and dedicated the work to Prévost of Geneva[2] who had translated the first volume of his *Elements of the Philosophy of the Human Mind* into French. Before the end of the month he was sending instructions to the printer about who was to receive complimentary copies.[3] When he received his own, however, he had to write in haste to defer distribution because he found that in the Dedication 'Geneva' had been printed as 'Berlin'![4]

At the end of June he wrote to Sir Samuel Romilly to say how much he agreed with everything in the latter's reformist *Observations on the Criminal Law of England*; he added, "[Mrs Stewart and I] have both gained much in point of health since we settled in the country."[5] Soon after this he made a short trip to Hamilton and neighbourhood;[6] he later relaxed with "some excursions through the neighbouring counties", and intended to "be moving a good deal about, while the good weather continues".[7] His new book was being read by his friends. Francis Jeffrey wrote to Francis Horner:

> Have you seen Stewart's volume, and what do you think of it? I find it rather languid from its great diffusiveness, and want of doctrinal precision. The tone excellent, and the taste on the whole good. But this excessive length is the sin of all modern writers. Shall we never again see anything like Hume's Essays?[8]

Sydney Smith, however, told his daughter that as Stewart repeatedly stated that the philosophy of mind was still in its infancy he himself preferred to wait till it came to years of discretion.[9] Stewart was anxious to know how the book was selling.[10] Towards the end of August he was told from London:

> On the subject of the *Philosophical Essays* – Owing to the volume being published here so very late in the season, I have a much more favourable report to make to you of the manner in which it has been received by our most eminent literary friends, than of the extent of the sale – yet we cannot doubt that when it is again advertised, on the return of winter, its circulation will be equal to our wishes.[11]

At the end of the following year Stewart wrote to his former student, the Edinburgh lawyer Macvey Napier, to thank him for a particularly favourable review in the *Quarterly*.[12]

In August 1810, however, he was obliged to make another excursion. Maria Stewart had gone to stay with a friend in Glasgow, and during her visit had contracted scarlet fever. Stewart went through to look after her for ten days and bring her back to Kinneil, "tho' still in a state of great weakness".[13]

In the meantime Maria's half-brother, Matthew, was still in India. Early in 1809 Lord Minto had written to Stewart to explain the difficulty that arose from the young man's commission being with the Engineers. His post as agent at Allahabad was the only one that Minto had been able to find for him, and when he ceased to be his aide-de-camp he would be recalled, even if the army permitted him to retain that position for the time being. Minto felt that the best plan would be for him to transfer to a regiment of the line.[14] This advice was followed, and Matthew became a captain in the 22nd Foot.[15] Lord Minto continued to support him, and in September 1810 wrote a warm recommendation to Major-General Abercromby expressing the hope that if his regimental duties allowed "Captain Stewart may be permitted to return to my family".[16] Later Matthew was able to give his patron news of his sons in Calcutta when the Governor-General was absent on duty.[17] Stewart was deeply grateful for Lord Minto's protective interest in his son.[18]

During 1810 he had publications by his friends to interest him. Francis Horner, who had great affection and veneration for Stewart,[19] had become a Member of Parliament in 1808. He had been made chairman of a select committee whose task was to inquire into the high price of gold bullion, and his *Bullion Report*, though rejected by the Commons at the time, became an influential document for some years to come.[20] Robert Eden Scott, professor of moral philosophy at King's College, Aberdeen, dedicated a book to Stewart with the words, "I shall always be proud to acknowledge myself your disciple; and I shall ever reflect with delight upon the mingled instruction and pleasure which I have derived both from your writings and your lectures."[21] And another dedication came from Stewart's old friend the Rev. Archibald Alison; he brought out a second edition of his *Essays on the Nature and Principles of Taste*, and prefaced it (perhaps aware that the date was Stewart's birthday) "To Dugald Stewart, Esq. in whose friendship the author has found the honour and the happiness of his life; these essays are most respectfully and affectionately inscribed. Edinburgh, November 22, 1810."[22]

An older friend in point of years, Henry Mackenzie, came to life with an account of a strange dream occasioned, he thought, by hearing of the illness of George III.[23] In his reply on 10 December Stewart renewed an invitation to Kinneil.

> You will see our residence to great disadvantage, but I can promise you a hearty welcome, – plenty of Boness coals, – a dry walk in all states of the weather, and (if you bring no fog with you from Edinburgh) a magnificent prospect of the snowy tops of the Grampians. I have heard of no woodcocking this season [Mackenzie had asked about this], but without quitting the threshold of the door you may amuse yourself from morning to night with shooting crows which have been assembling here unmolested for many years past, after being scared away from every other corner of the country. At first we were much pleased with their society, but their incessant noise

The Early Years of Retirement (1810–1815)

is at last getting the better even of Mrs Stewart's patience and forbearance.

Our winter weather has been delightful, and we have been so fortunate as to enjoy perfect health. For myself I have not been so free of coughs in the months of November and December for the last twenty years. I only regret that we did not think sooner of betaking ourselves to a country life.[24]

A few weeks later Mrs Stewart's patience was to be further tried by the dentist's removing a tooth "with roots so extremely ragged," her husband reported to Lord Minto's daughter-in-law, "as to make it wonderful that her nerves have not been much more affected in consequence of the constant irritation".[25]

Henry Mackenzie had ascribed his dream to the madness of George III, and in the early part of 1811 the Stewarts were much exercised by the political situation. The prospect of a Regency (which actually began on 6 February) gave rise to the expectation that the Prince of Wales would dismiss the administration of Spencer Perceval and bring in his friends the Whigs. If there were to be an election, Lord Minto's eldest son and Stewart's former student, Gilbert Elliot, who was already an MP representing Ashburton in Devon, was going to stand for a local county constituency, and the Stewarts were annoyed by the tactics of his prospective opponent in representing himself as a friend of the Prince.[26] Mrs Stewart wrote to Gilbert to remind him of the annual dinner to be held in Edinburgh on 24 January to commemorate Fox's birthday; she suggested it would be a good idea for him to be there;[27] on the 25th Jeffrey wrote to Francis Horner that Stewart himself had come "from the country" to attend Fox's dinner.[28] In the event the Prince behaved circumspectly and retained Perceval in office.

In March Mrs Stewart told Lady Minto, "I could not but smile to see with what new eagerness Mr S. began . . . to a new volume of his work."[29] This was the second volume of *Elements of the Philosophy of the Human Mind*, to which he had referred the previous year in the *Advertisement* to *Philosophical Essays*, when he said he felt himself "sufficiently warned, by the approaching infirmities of age, not to delay any longer my best exertions for the accomplishment of an undertaking, which I have hitherto prosecuted only at accidental and often distant intervals; but which I have often fondly imagined (whether justly or not others must determine) might, if carried into complete effect, be of some utility to the public".[30]

This was a long-term project. A publication which appeared under Stewart's name in 1811 was a volume collecting his three biographical essays – those concerning Adam Smith, William Robertson and Thomas

The Early Years of Retirement (1810–1815)

Reid respectively.[31] He received from Archibald Constable a payment of £500 – more than a year's income, and equivalent to nearly £20,000 – for the copyright of the memoirs on Smith and Reid.[32]

The approaching infirmities of age did not dampen his enjoyment of travel. In May Mrs Stewart acknowledged a letter from Gilbert Elliot which "followed us to the kingdom of Fife, where we are paying a long promised visit".[33] Less than three weeks later they were in Durham – "on our way to Yorkshire," Stewart wrote, "where we propose to ramble about for a week or two, and then return home by way of the Lakes".[34] Their rambles took them to stay for three or four days with Sydney Smith, then living in what his daughter described as "a small but cheerful house" in Heslington near York while a new parsonage was being built at Foston.[35] They also spent a few days in Harrogate, from where they planned "to proceed slowly to Scotland by way of Carlyle". The weather, Stewart told Constable on 24 June, "has been remarkably cold and rainy since our arrival and as yet there is not the slightest symptom of its amendment".[36]

A matter which interested Stewart at this period arose from a letter he had received in October 1810 from a surgeon in London about a boy named James Mitchell, the son of a Church of Scotland minister in Moray, who had been born blind and deaf.[37] What first struck Stewart on hearing about this case was the opportunity which it presented for investigating the condition of someone (James became fifteen in November 1810) who had derived all his knowledge of the external world from the senses of touch, taste and smell. The conception of the visible world that could be acquired by anyone born blind had been a matter of interest to both David Hume and Thomas Reid. Stewart gathered such information as he could from those who knew or had examined the boy, and read a paper on the subject to the RSE in February 1812. Subsequently this was enlarged by additional information and published in book form.

But Stewart became increasingly concerned with the human side of this story. The Rev. Donald Mitchell died in 1811, and responsibility for looking after James lay solely with his mother and his sister. Stewart privately conveyed "a small sum" to the Mitchell family during 1812.[38] When the surgeon, Dr Wardrop, wrote to him at the end of the year to report on a partially successful operation which he had carried out on James's eyes, he referred to "the great interest you have taken, and the exertions you continue to make for the welfare of the unfortunate youth". On Boxing Day the RSE agreed to a motion proposed by Stewart to apply to the Prince Regent for a pension to be settled on James, and a small committee including John Playfair and Henry

The Early Years of Retirement (1810–1815)

Mackenzie, who had initiated the idea, was appointed to draft the petition.[39] Two days later another meeting was held to approve the draft and its transmission to London.[40] When the petition appeared to have failed, the Council of the RSE decided as individuals to open a fund to purchase an annuity on the lives of James and his eldest sister, but Stewart was still involved in drafting a letter of explanation to Lord Liverpool, the Prime Minister,[41] who apparently was unsympathetic.[42] Members of the RSE interested themselves in methods by which James might receive some education.[43]

Meanwhile in 1812 the Stewarts had received a succession of visitors at Kinneil House. In the spring Lord John Russell called to see them at the end of his three years at Edinburgh University, and wrote the lines of verse which were quoted in the preceding chapter.[44] (In the summer Lord John was active in a scheme to have a bust of Stewart done by Chantrey. In this he had the support of the former Lord Henry Petty, who had succeeded his half-brother as Marquess of Landowne, but it seems to have come to nothing.[45]) Sir James and Lady Mackintosh accepted a warm invitation to visit Kinneil in August.[46] Lady Catherine Mackintosh was a sister of the wives of John and Josiah Wedgwood. Early in September Francis Horner told his sister that the greatest pleasure of a recent visit to Edinburgh had –

> been in the society of Mr Stewart and Mr Playfair, who have been growing younger all the while that their pupils had been turning grey, and are in such good health, and such ardour of study, that the world will probably have the benefit of many years of their labour . . .They both have many projects; Mr Stewart has already a great deal of manuscript quite ready for the press . . . We went to Kinneil, four of us in a landau . . . [John] Murray, [Thomas] Thomson, Mr Playfair and myself. The day being very bright and beautiful, we drove through Lord Rosebery's grounds [Dalmeny Park], which are equal to any that I know anywhere for prospect and scenery. The Romillys came to Kinneil the same day; next morning all went away but Mr Playfair, with whom and Mr Stewart I passed an entire day. We went a mile beyond Falkirk to see Mrs Dalzell [Andrew's widow, who died in 1819].[47]

Sir Samuel Romilly left his own account of his visit, which apparently lasted for a week. Confirming that Stewart was at this time in good health and good heart, he wrote in his journal of "my old and excellent friend Dugald Stewart, whom we had the satisfaction to see in the full vigour of his great talents, and in the lively enjoyment of everything about him, of the charming country in which he lives, of the society of his very sensible and amiable wife and daughter, of his books, of his leisure, of his philosophical retirement, and, above all, of the delight he experiences in the pursuit of his metaphysical researches, and in continuing and completing his own admirable writings".[48]

At the beginning of October Stewart was in Dumbarton, writing to Archibald Constable that he was on his way home "after a short tour into the Highlands on which I found myself obliged to accompany a friend from England"; he expected to spend a day or two in Glasgow.[49] After that John Playfair brought his friends the eminent English chemist Sir Humphry Davy and his wealthy Scottish wife for a visit to Kinneil.[50] Later that month Stewart was in Ayrshire to vote in the general election, as his property at Catrine entitled him to the franchise there[51] – "though I fear to little good purpose", Mrs Stewart told Constable.[52] She added: "Mr S. has been sadly disturbed this autumn with visitors, and yet they were those we were so happy to see it was impossible to regret them. I trust a quiet winter will enable him to make up for all his late idleness."[53]

In November he was in bed with a bad cold.[54] But a few days later he was discussing with Constable a new edition of the *Encyclopaedia Britannica*. This characteristically Enlightenment enterprise had first been published in Edinburgh between 1768 and 1771, and had subsequently gone through three further and expanding editions. Archibald Constable had just taken it over. They spoke of possible authors, and the idea was floated that if health and time permitted, Stewart himself should contribute a major article on the history of philosophy. This, however, would not be begun until the second volume of *Philosophy of the Human Mind* was finished.[55] During November he sent the text of the latter to the press, but he told Francis Horner, "I propose to print very slowly, and to delay the publication till the beginning of next winter".[56]

Towards the end of November, he explained in the same letter to Horner, "Mrs Stewart and I had to set out to pay a visit at Donington, for a purpose which you will easily conjecture". With Maria they had travelled through Lancashire and Derbyshire in cold but fine weather, and spent some "very agreeable days" at Donington, which was the seat of the Prince Regent's friend, the Irish peer Lord Moira. His wife was Countess of Loudoun in her own right, and may have known Stewart through the Ayshire connection. The purpose of the visit to which Stewart alluded was probably connected with Matthew's career in the army. Moira had been widely expected to be be made a new Whig prime minister at the beginning of the Regency. This had not happened, but he had just been appointed Governor-General of Bengal and Commander-in-Chief of the forces in India, and Lady Holland had recommended Matthew Stewart to his attention.[57] When Moira reached India, Matthew was

1 (a) *Stewart*, aged about 55, by Sir Henry Raeburn.
  (b) Bronze bust of Stewart at the end of his life, by Samuel Joseph.

2 The older generation: (i) *Adam Smith*. (ii) *Thomas Reid*, by James Tassie.
(iii) *Professor Adam Ferguson*, after Raeburn.

3 The older generation: (iv) *Principal William Robertson*, by Raeburn.

4 (a) The Earl of Ancram, later 6th Marquess of Lothian. This portrait was apparently commissioned by Stewart from Sir Henry Raeburn a few years after Ancram and Stewart toured the Low Countries together in 1783.
 (b) Stewart and his family by Alexander Nasmyth. Stewart, aged about 32, is shown here with his first wife, Helen Bannatyne, and the infant Matthew, still 'unbreeched'.

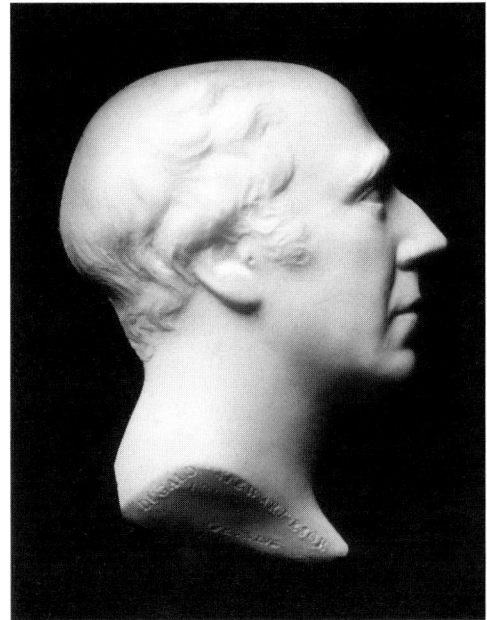

5 (a) Stewart, aged about 43.
(c) Mrs Helen D'Arcy Stewart, née Cranstoun.

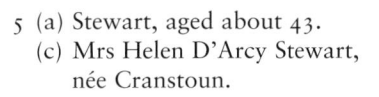

(b) Stewart, aged about 57.
(d) George Cranstoun, later Lord Corehouse, Mrs Stewart's brother.

The Successful Candidate

6 Stewart's intimate friends at Edinburgh University:
(i) Professor Andrew Dalzel. The legend refers to Dalzel's narrow victory in 1789 in becoming Clerk to the General Assembly of the Church of Scotland.
(ii) Professor John Playfair.

7 Stewart's two children by his second marriage: George and Maria, by Raeburn.

8 (a) Helen D'Arcy Stewart, aged about 39.
  (b) Matthew Stewart in the uniform of a 2nd Lieutenant, aged 20.

9 (a) Harry Temple, Lord Palmerston, during the period when he was resident with the Stewarts.
(b) The Rev. Sydney Smith.

10 (a) James Boswell and his family. The future Sir Alexander Boswell, killed in a duel, is missing from this group.
(b) The Rev. Archibald Alison, probably Stewart's closest friend. Bust by Samuel Joseph.

11 Kinneil House, Bo'ness, Stewart's home for nearly 20 years.

12 Stewart's devoted admirers:
   (i) Francis Horner, MP and economist.
   (ii) Charles Babbage, mathematician.

13 (a) Stewart, aged about 57.
(b) John Wilson ("Christopher North"), his unlikely successor in the chair of moral philosophy.

Kinneil House
Tuesday

My dear Sir

Your note makes me very happy, and I shall expect you by the steam boat on Thursday. As Doctor Parr is now with me, I have time only to subscribe myself
Yours most truly
Dugald Stewart

Kinneil House
Sunday 14th
Sept 1823

My dear Sir

We have been wandering — It was only last night yours came into my hand and I cannot lose a post in telling you how happy it will make Mr Stewart & me to see you here — I intreat you to come, and to persuade Mrs Babbage to do us the honour of coming with you. Mr Stewart is not alarmed with the idea of seeing kind friends and such we must ever consider you & Mrs Babbage — We intreat you to come this week as we may be absent afterwards. Our Children are absent but of that when we meet. In haste & with much esteem yours obliged H D Stewart

14 Letters to Charles Babbage:
(i) from Stewart.
(ii) from Mrs Stewart.

15 (a) Archibald Constable, Stewart's publisher and friend, by Andrew Geddes.
(b) Mrs Helen D'Arcy Stewart, aged about 65, by William Nicholson.

16 Stewart, aged 70, by Sir David Wilkie. This was considered to be the best likeness.

retained in his position as one of the Governor-General's aides-de-camp.[58] It was probably during this visit to Donington that Thomas Moore, the Irish poet, sang to the company (see chapter 16). The Stewart family returned to Kinneil at the end of December.[59]

In spite of his travels Stewart did sometimes feel rather isolated at Kinneil House. Early in the new year he told Lord Holland's librarian, steward and close friend, Dr John Allen, "I live here during the winter in a state of complete solitude and know nearly as little of what is going on at Edinburgh as in London." He asked for occasional letters to give him "a little of the political gossip of the day", for he was always curious about the procedings of Parliament (he mentioned the East India Charter and the state of the currency).[60] Throughout 1813 Stewart was working hard on the second volume of *Philosophy of the Human Mind*, calling on Macvey Napier, who was librarian to the Writers of the Signet, to send him books which he needed.[61] But interruptions were always liable to occur. On 24 March Mrs Stewart told Constable that her husband had been going to write on the previous day, but "first Mr Cadell [Robert Cadell had become Constable's partner] and then Lord Webb Seymour arrived and put a stop to all work. This day is so fine that Mr Cadell has taken them away to see divers wonders, and I dare say they won't be home for many hours."[62]

During the spring Stewart received an extract from the Register of the Royal Academy of Berlin informing him that he had been elected a member. There was no covering letter with this document, so he "was at a loss to know," as he told Baron de Gerando, "through what channel my thanks should be conveyed".[63] Two years later de Gerando established a new Philosophical Society in France and made Stewart a Corresponding Member.[64] By the end of his life Stewart was also an Honorary Member of the Imperial Academy of Sciences at St Petersburg, a Member of the Royal Academy of Naples and of the American Societies of Philadelphia and of Boston, and an Honorary Member of the Philosophical Society of Cambridge.[65]

Meanwhile, in 1813, travel does not seem to have been extensive, though Mrs Stewart wrote of "a short excursion to the North of England" in the summer,[66] and in August Stewart had to go to Ayrshire on business, and planned going on to Glasgow and St Mary's Isle[67] – presumably to visit the Earl of Selkirk. Towards the end of October Francis Horner spent the best part of two days at Kinneil with his two sisters and, as in the previous autumn, Playfair, Murray and Thomson. He told Lord Webb Seymour: "You will understand that I was highly gratified; with nothing more, however, than to see them both so well, particulay Mr Stewart, whose robust and tranquillised health makes me hope to see him live to the age of Plato, and continue writing to the last."[68]

The Stewarts may have left Maria at St Mary's Isle, for at the beginning of November, in one of his "letters to Ivy", John Ward told Mrs Stewart of meeting her at Bowood, the Lansdowne estate. She had just arrived from Bath with "Lady K.", the Earl of Selkirk's youngest sister, Katherine, who was then thirty-five.

> She is really a fine girl [Ward told her mother]. Her countenance and manners are most engaging, and she has an understanding that strikes me even more than her attainments, though they are evidently very considerable. But without the slightest ostentation or effort, quite naturally, and almost in spite of herself, her conversation is full of knowledge and talent. You have every reason to be proud of her. I might justly suspect myself of partiality to the child of the two persons both of whom she so much resembles, but everybody here is of the same opinion.[69]

Maria met Necker's daughter, the famous writer Madame de Staël, who, as she told her mother, "made heaps of speeches about Mr Dugald Stewart and my *clever mother*".[70] It seems that Maria was on an extended visit to the south of England – one which encompassed her twenty-first birthday. In February she was in Sandwich with her West Lothian neighbour, Lady Hope;[71] and she spent most of March and April 1814 in London,[72] where she was grateful for the attentiveness both of Lord Palmerston and (after a little awkwardness at Bowood) of John Ward.[73] One evening at Lady Lansdowne's she saw Lord Byron; she thought "his countenance milder and more ordinary than I expected from all I had heard, but I persuaded myself it was as fine as it ought to be, full of spirit and gloominess and all pretty things".[74] From Ward's house she saw the great procession of the Prince Regent accompanying Louis XVIII into London[75] – Louis's younger brother, the Comte d'Artois, had probably been a relatively familiar figure to her when he resided at Holyrood Palace as a refugee.[76]

Back at Kinneil, it must have been a matter of quiet satisfaction to Stewart that he was able to date his prefatory *Advertisement* to the second volume of *Elements of the Philosophy of the Human Mind* from Kinneil House on 22 November 1813.[77] On the same day, to relieve his guilt as a poor correspondent, Mrs Stewart was writing to Dr Will Drennan in Belfast:

> We are always planning a visit to Ireland too, and I do really think it is now likely to happen ere long, for Mr S. works so constantly and laboriously that he will soon, if God grant us health and quiet, finish the works he

considers himself as pledged to. With a grateful heart I can say, that he is stouter and better than he was fifteen years ago – the country life has removed all his complaints, and his winter cough is now nothing. I must tell you a secrret, *to-day* he is *sixty*, and there is no birthday gift I can contrive for him so acceptable, as allowing him to think of you without remorse, and consequently with the liveliest pleasure. All that you did and said and thought at Glasgow together will serve us for this evenings chat – and that I could see you meet – I will still hope to have that joy. Adieu my dear sir.[78]

A stir was caused in Edinburgh at the end of the year by the appearance of an American boy named Zerah Colburn, then only nine years old, whose father was taking him on a tour of the British Isles to demonstrate his remarkable ability to perform complex arithmetical calculations in his head with phenomenal rapidity. Stewart and Playfair were among those who interested themselves in this prodigy; and the former must have shown sympathy as well as fascination, for when the Colburns visited Scotland again six years later they made a detour on their journey from Edinburgh to Glasgow to make an hour's visit at Kinneil House, where Stewart "entertained them with hospitality and kindness".[79]

The winter of 1813-4 was very severe. In London the Thames was frozen over, and on 10 January 1814 Stewart, who had been in Ayrshire on business, wrote that he was snowed up in Kilmarnock: "it is impossible for me to move till the roads are open".[80] At the beginning of February he stayed in Portobello to check the proofs of the new book,[81] and shortly afterwards was able to send copies to a select few.[82] There seem to have been no errors on this occasion, and he presented a handsome silver cup to John Stark, the printer, inscribed for "his friendly attention and intelligent accuracy".[83] By 25 February Francis Horner was writing to John Murray, "I have read Mr Stewart's new volume with great satisfaction and instruction".[84] But as usual there were hitches. By that date the Stewarts were at Langley Park, near Montrose,[85] and Mrs Stewart wrote to Constable:

> Mr Stewart begins to be very uneasy at not seeing his Volume advertised in the London press, and at the astonishment expressed by his friends on its not appearing. He almost fears the copies must be lost at sea. Will you be good enough to relieve his mind if you can . . . It begins to look like snow again. I hope we shall not have another winter . . . I grudge making you pay postage for this scrap, but Mr S. begins to be quite terrified so that he insisted on my begging you to tell us if all was right.[86]

Presumably Constable was able to provide the necessary reassurance. The Stewarts returned to Kinneil House on 3 April.[87]

The Early Years of Retirement (1810–1815)

These were momentous days on the international stage, as the long war with Napoleon appeared at last to have come to an end. Stewart heard from de Gerando, and wrote in reply of his concern after the "late great events at Paris". He was anxious to hear of his many friends there. He had a thousand questions to ask. "In the meantime I shall only say, that if France had been my native country, I could not take a warmer interest than I do, in her freedom and prosperity."[88]

There was sad news too. Lord Moira's appointment in India had brought to an end that of Lord Minto, and the latter was at the same time created Viscount Melgund and Earl of Minto. He left India after the arrival of his successor in October 1813, and reached England in the following May. His health had suffered as a result of his journeys in the east, and while he was still in London he became seriously ill. He set out for his home in Scotland, but died on the way, at Stevenage, on 21 June. He was buried in Westminster Abbey. And so Stewart's former student, Gilbert Elliot, became 2nd Earl of Minto, and took his seat as a Whig in the House of Lords. A year or so earlier Matthew Stewart had written to Gilbert's brother John, who served as his father's secretary in India, to say –

> how truly and how deeply I am sensible of your father's kindness in *every way* but more particularly in his arduous and laborious situation. I should be insensible and unworthy of his goodness if I did not feel his devoting any portion of his time and his thoughts to my prospects as the greatest obligation he could bestow. I am fully aware that no merit of mine either deserved or obtained the protection he has afforded me but that it arose from the kindness and the friendship he is pleased to entertain for my father. However while I can give him the fullest assurances of my father's gratitude I hope he will not deny me the satisfatction of receiving my own.[89]

It seems certain that John Elliot would have shown this letter to Lord Minto, but it must have been a great sorrow to Dugald Stewart and his wife that they never had the opportunity to thank him in person for his many kindnesses to their son.

As at other times in his life, Stewart may have assuaged his grief by hard work. "He is very, very busy," Mrs Stewart wrote to Constable, of whom they saw much at this period, "and often in this fine weather does not move from his writing table till evening."[90] Although in the course of writing the second volume of *Philosophy of the Human Mind* he had accumulated a good deal of material towards a third volume,[91] he set this aside in order to devote himself to the lengthy article he was to produce for the *Encyclopaedia Britannica*. Its full title was to be *Dissertation exhibiting*

The Early Years of Retirement (1810–1815)

the progress of Metaphysical, Ethical, and Political Philosophy, since the revival of letters in Europe, and it became known as Stewart's *Dissertation*. He had never done anything of the kind before, but Constable had persuaded Macvey Napier to edit the new edition of the *Encyclopaedia*, and Napier knew that if he could secure Stewart's name and that of Sir Humphry Davy as prominent contributors he "could ask all the literary men of the day to unite in my undertaking"; and he agreed to pay Stewart's demand for the enormous sum of £1,000 (about £37,000 today) without specifying the length expected.[92] Stewart supplied him with letters to Francis Horner and Sir James Mackintosh in London asking for their help in finding suitable contributors. To Horner he added a plea fo any news from Paris: "What an anxious moment in the history of the world!"[93]

The latter part of 1814 seems to have been relatively undisturbed, and in October Constable was glad to hear that Stewart was making good progress.[94] His working methods were described thus:

> Mr Stewart continued during his life the practice of thinking out what he was about to write on any subject, while walking. When preparing his works for the press, during his residence at Kinneil, he usually walked backwards and forwards in the large dining-room of the mansion, or in the avenue, under the shade of its stately trees, meditating what he was about to write. He then retired to his study, and committed to writing, without break, what he had thus previously arranged in his mind. He spoke as well as composed with great ease, accuracy, and finish . . . [although] he was an assiduous corrector of the press.[95]

In addition to the help he received from his wife and daughter (and later, as we shall see, from Thomas Jackson), Stewart employed a succession of 'transcribers', whose job, presumably, was to make fair copies of his drafts.[96]

When Horner was in Edinburgh at the end of the year Stewart gave him the job of studying a manuscript he had received from Samuel Parr, 'the Whig Johnson', commenting at great length on Stewart's essay on the sublime.[97] Two days before Christmas Stewart wrote in a letter to a solicitor, "For the last five years I have been so completely out of the world . . ."[98] He continued doggedly with his assignment. Early in February he told Dr Parr how busily employed he had been on the *Encyclopaedia* article, adding "I have often repented of my rashness, as the task has turned out infinitely more difficult than I had at first apprehended, besides its interference with other plans, the execution of which I have much at heart."[99]

While Stewart was thus employed, his wife spent a good deal of time reading, and relied on Constable to keep her supplied with the latest publications. "I hope . . . you have brought down plenty of new and good books," she had written to him on his return from London a year previously; "I have been sadly starved of late, and only reading old magazines."[100] Now she renewed her plea: "If you have any curious new book, I need not say how glad I should be of a peep."[101] A few months later she acknowledged a copy of *Waverley* (in three volumes), adding, "They have gone near to turn all our heads, and certainly interested both Maria and me more than any prose ever did before: the third volume is quite overwhelming. Whoever the author may be, he must be allowed to draw characters more forcibly than any of his predecessors."[102]

In March 1815 she was no less entranced by the second of the Waverley novels. "I have tried to return *Guy Mannering*, but it will not do; it is impossible to part with such a treasure. I shall therefore keep it, and when I come to Edinburgh next week, will send its price, for it is my purchase, not Mr S.'s. I read it all day, and dream of it all night."[103] Interestingly, by the time she got to *The Antiquary* (which she claimed, somewhat incredibly, that Mr S. read all aloud "at one sitting"), she commented to Constable: "I am always too partial to old friends to be instantly smitten with new, so that I cannot say I prefer it to its elder brothers; but Mr Scott can only be compared to himself . . . Still, *Waverley* is my favourite."[104] Constable may have dropped a hint as to the authorship of this new sequel of novels, or Mrs Stewart may have been shrewd enough to work it out for herself; but her confident ascription shows how thin a veneer Scott's anonymity actually was from a very early stage.

Real events as well as fictional ones impinged upon the Stewarts' lives. In April 1815 their niece Margaret Miller, Janet's third child, married a Major James Miller. The Major, fighting under the Duke of Wellington, had been seriously wounded at the battle of Toulouse, the last of the Peninsular war. In the knowledge, perhaps, that he might not live for long, the banns were called three times on the same Sunday in Margaret's father's church in Old Cumnock, and she and the Major were married on the following day. Less than two months later James Miller died of his wounds.[105]

Early in May, Thomas Campbell visited Kinneil and spent a few days "with my beloved friends, Dugald Stewart and his family. His wife is most amiable – his daughter full of sense and spirit; and I am as happy as it is possible to be, from home. My time is spent in walking about with these good angels." He noted that Mrs Stewart "addresses me by the endearing name of 'son'."[106]

The Early Years of Retirement (1810–1815)

At the end of June Stewart received an anonymous letter which Veitch considered to be of sufficient interest to include in his *Memoir*.[107] It described an apparently dull and uneducated servant girl in Stirlingshire named Agnes Drummond who would often speak clearly and intelligently in her sleep about a variety of topics, sometimes in apparent conversation, having no recollection of it when she woke up. Stewart was sufficiently interested by this account to pass it to Sir Henry Moncrieff, who owned an estate at Tulliebole not far from the home of the ladies with whom Agnes lived. Sir Harry went to see them and reported back in a letter to Mrs Stewart in September.[108] He was able to confirm and indeed enlarge on the contents of the original letter. However, Stewart made no reference to this curious case in his published works.

Hard as he was working on his *Dissertation* throughout this period, he was not unmindful of the need for exercise, as appears from a letter which Mrs Stewart wrote to Gilbert, 2nd Earl of Minto, in October.

> Your letter has made Mr S. quite happy, for he now thinks himself certain of what he had set his heart upon, but began to think it impossible to attain. Ever since we came here, he has been buying Poney's and was always forced to part with them again. Your perfect knowledge of what he wants, and your experience of all the faults and failings to be feared, gives him very different hopes of success now. In truth his health depends on it, for since his last sprain he cannot take exercise sufficient for sleep and appetite. And his fame is no less interested, for unless his horse is so well broken, as to allow him to *think* his own thoughts, riding is out of the question. I need scarcely add that that the price is of no consequence if *you* are satisfied of the merits of the steed . . . Mr S. is convinced it is to lengthen his life and increase his Books – so you see how happy we all are . . .[109]

Later that month Stewart was writing from Marshall's Lodgings in Portobello to his old friend Ancram, who had recently succeeded on the death of his father. "You are now Marquis of Lothian, while I am only 'Gazette Writer to the King's most Excellent Majesty'", Stewart had written to him in August.[110] He had come to Portobello, he told him now, "for at least a fortnight, in order to print more conveniently and with greater dispatch" his piece for the *Encyclopaedia*.[111] He was still in Portobello in the middle of November, as were his wife and daughter and the new mare, which their servant Robert had ridden through Edinburgh. Mrs Stewart told Lord Minto: "Had you but seen Robert describing all the progress (after they left Princes St., where we were viewing them) and Mr S. listening, you would have wished for Wilkie the Painter to make the scene immortal . . . whether Mr S., Maria or Robert are most elated I cannot presume to say."[112] By the 22nd of the month they were all back at Kinneil ("We fled home, the moment Mr S. was free"), and Mrs Stewart told Minto, "Every day discovers new charms in Mr S.'s beloved mare."[113] Soon after this, however, Stewart fell ill, and early in December he wrote to the Marquess of Lothian to say that, though better, he was "still occasionally plagued with slight threatenings of my former disorder", and consequently to decline an invitation to visit Newbattle Abbey for Christmas.[114] Though it cannot have been evident at the time, this illness marked the end of the period of renewed good health which had followed from the move to Kinneil House.

CHAPTER SIXTEEN

Deaths of Friends and the Final Break
1815–1820

"This moment Mrs Dugald Stewart, who was out walking, has come in – the same dear woman! I have seen Mr Stewart – very, very weak – he cannot walk without an arm to lean on." Maria Edgeworth

The *Dissertation*, or what became the first part of it, had been published before the end of 1815. It had proved to be a difficult and laborious task. A year later Stewart told James Mackintosh (who had been knighted in 1803 and who had noticed the *Dissertation* favourably in the *Edinburgh Review*): "I wrote it much more hastily than I could have wished, and was forced to omit various important topics on which I would willingly have touched, by the scantiness of the library which I brought with me to Kinneil, and by the inconveniency I have experienced in sending to Ed. for by far the greater part of the books I have had occasion to consult."[1]

On publication he gave "a very large parcel of copies" to Constable to take to his friends in London. On his return, Mrs Stewart wrote, he was to bring London news "and I can promise you a dish of as good beef and greens (if London epicures can eat such simple fare) as ever you saw in your life time".[2] By 15 December 1815 Stewart's most devoted disciple, Francis Horner, was writing to his sister Nancy (who proceeded to read it for herself):

Deaths of Friends and the Final Break (1815–1820)

For the last week I have been reading, over and over again, Mr Stewart's new *Dissertation*, which refreshes me like a delicious repast, in having one's attention called to it from dull law and gloomy politics. It is, perhaps, the most pleasing of all his compositions; and, from what I have heard, is likely to become the most popular. It has the greatest of all charms, in common with all his writings, an uniform tone of high and pure sentiment; and as they all tend to inspire a confidence that, in spite of bad governments and of the mistakes committed by those who oppose them, knowledge and justice at last make their way . . .[3]

He added that he had just heard from Constable that he had sold the whole 7,000 copies of the first volume of the Supplement to the *Encyclopaedia*. Constable himself wrote to Mrs Stewart on Boxing Day that he had been longer in London than expected, but had done good business; long residence there had not spoiled his taste for good *beef and greens*, as he hoped to show before long "by a proof better than mere assertion".[4] Early in the new year John Ward told 'Ivy' that everybody in London was pleased with Mr Stewart's *Dissertation*, and admired it.[5] Shortly afterwards Francis Horner wrote to his sister: "I told Mrs Stewart you had ventured into the *Dissertation*, and I mentioned to her the particular delight you found in the moral impressions you received from it. She told me, Mr Stewart was flattered by your remark; he said, that these are the invaluable praises, from a simple heart and unspoiled taste; and that an author is sure he is right, when such readers are satisfied."[6]

Such tributes must have given pleasure not only to Stewart but to his wife and daughter. Nearly thirty years later Maria recalled "how welcome any praise of a book from a really good judge is to an author's *family*, however well satsfied they may themselves be, that the book needs no praise to prove its merits. And the praise used always to be more welcome to my mother and me when it came to us *indirectly*, not originally intended to reach us."[7] Stewart wished to be assured that a copy had been sent to Dr Parr, and asked Constable to "take the trouble to write him a few lines at the same time, *in your best and most flattering manner,* as such testimonials add more to the happiness of the good old man than might be expected from his real talents and learning".[8]

Towards the end of January 1816 the Stewarts went to Ayrshire to see their Miller relatives in Cumnock. Constable had written to Stewart a year previously to ask if it was true that Dr Miller, already nearly seventy-five, was looking for an assistant, as he had a suitable young man to recommend for "our good old friend".[9] Stewart's brother-in-law had a large library, some of it probably inherited from his bookseller father, and it may have been in this connection that he was known to Constable. Now

Deaths of Friends and the Final Break (1815–1820)

the Stewarts had heard that he was ill, but they found him better than they had feared, and his unfortunate daughter, so briefly married, "not worse – though very weak and low".[10] They got back from Cumnock to Kinneil on the evening of 7 February, "safely . . . tho' almost frozen to death".[11] But almost at once they were off again, this time to visit Minto.[12] At the end of the month they received news of Stewart's old predecessor, Adam Ferguson; having retired thirty years earlier of grounds of ill health, he had now died in St Andrews aged ninety-two.[13]

They had something to look forward to, however, for Matthew, whom they had not seen for nine years, had come back to Britain, and was expected at Kinneil as soon as he could get away from London. As Mrs Stewart explained to Constable, "uncertainty about my son's movements, and *when* he may pop in upon us, makes Mr S. more anxious to pass the time, for he cannot settle to work just now".[14] Matthew, who had recently purchased the rank of Lieutenant-Colonel,[15] arrived at Kinneil in late February or early March. Francis Horner's brother Leonard understood that he had left London sooner than he intended because of an accident sustained by Mrs Stewart; apparently she fell from a chair and either broke or severely dislocated an arm.[16]

Among the first of the summer visitors, brought by Constable from Edinburgh in April, was William Godwin, author of *Political Justice*, widower of Mary Wollstonecraft and soon-to-be father-in-law of Shelley. Dr Miller had evidently recovered well, and Mrs Stewart had some helpful advice for Constable's journey, as well as providing another little insight into life at Kinneil.

> May I suggest a trifle – If good Dr Miller is of the party he takes up a great deal of room in a carriage. Now a coach and pair takes only half an hour more time than a chaise and pair – as we know, having repeatedly brought out a coach instead of a chaise from Mr Smith's stables. In this way you would all be comfortable, and not crowded. How I regret my daughter's absence, she would have been so happy to see Mr Godwin. If you would not think me very troublesome I would request you to cater for me, for our markets here are very bad. A bit of fish and a few vegetables would really be a blessing to us who never see fish. To an Englishman a dinner with[out] fish is a misery.[17]

For those not staying overnight, the journey to Kinneil must have been fairly arduous. With reference to other visitors Mrs Stewart advised soon after this: "If they set out at seven, and take their horses from Mrs Smith, they will be here about half past 10; and the same horses will easily carry them back to Town in the evening . . . I will write to Mrs Smith, and desire

Deaths of Friends and the Final Break (1815–1820)

her to have a chaise, or a pair of good horses at the head of the Fish Market Close at whatever hour Mr Stark may appoint."[18]

A little later in the summer the Marquess of Lothian's third son, Henry, came to stay, and at the beginning of July Stewart told his father that they were sorry to part with him.[19] Henry Ker was fifteen, and the Marquess envisaged his going into the church, though Matthew Stewart had gained the impression that he might prefer the army. But Stewart thought that "from his quiet and amicable dispositions I should think him more likely to make a most respectable and useful clergyman" – which is what he eventually did, following his widowed stepmother into the Catholic Church in the early 1850s.[20]

In spite of these distractions Stewart was now engaged in a sequel to his *Dissertation* for the *Encyclopaedia*. In August he told Dr Parr:

> Since I had last the pleasure of writing to you, I have devoted every spare moment in my power to the second part of my Dissertation, which I am extremely anxious, *in case of accidents*, to bring to as speedy a conclusion as possible. The task of composition is become from long habit comparatively easy to me, but I find my progress retarded at every step by the numerous volumes which I am forced not only to turn over but to read with some attention; a labour which is peculiarly irksome in my present situation, where the smallness of my own library obliges me to send to Edinburgh (a distance of twenty miles) for by far the greater part of the books I have to consult.[21]

Matthew Stewart remained with his parents until the end of November, when he returned to London. He had just received a three months' extension of his leave, and promised to come back to Kinneil before setting off for his next posting. Writing to Constable, his mother referred to him as at home again at the end of January 1817,[22] and to his setting off in the mail for London on 21 February.[23] He carried with him a letter from his father to Lord Holland in which Stewart wrote: "He leaves me at present, not altogether with my consent or approbation, to join his regiment in the West Indies."[24]

When Stewart had seen Francis Horner in the middle of September he told Lady Holland that "his complaints, and still more his looks, and his air of feebleness are truly alarming".[25] Horner tried to make light of his poor health, but he accepted the advice that he should go abroad for the winter. He set out for Naples with Leonard early in October,[26] and wrote affectionate letters to Mrs Stewart from Lyons and from Pisa,[27] but in Pisa he died on 8 February. It was one thing for Adam Ferguson to pass away, full of years, but Horner, for whom everyone predicted a brilliant career,

Deaths of Friends and the Final Break (1815–1820)

had lived to be only thirty-eight. Stewart included a warm tribute to his young friend as a note in his *Dissertation*.[28]

But more gratifying news was on the way. At the end of March, referring to time broken by a succession of visitors from Edinburgh, Stewart acknowledged a letter from the Earl of Selkirk's sister, Lady Katherine Douglas.[29] In 1815 "Lady K." had married, as his second wife, John Halkett, her senior by some ten years and a former Governor of the Bahamas; now she had produced a son in London whom Stewart was to consider as his grandson. After this there must have been another scare about Stewart's health, for when Mrs Stewart wrote to Lady K., from Langley Park in May, she referred to being "just freed from sad alarm about Mr S. Dr Gregory terrified us, but I thought even at first, and still more so *now*, that he was needlessly apprehensive. At all events Mr S. is really well now, and the only effect Dr G.'s fears have had on him, is making him live lower than even before."[30]

But the occasion of Mrs Stewart's letter was the news that Lady K. and her husband had decided to give their little boy the second name of Stewart. "I cannot and will not attempt to tell you," his namesake wrote, "with what feelings I have read your letter. In the whole course of my life I never met with any mark of kindness which so deeply affected me. May God Almighty bless and protect you and yours."[31] At this point Mrs Stewart took over.

> My dearest, my beloved – What can I add to these few words written with eyes too full to allow him to go on. He truly says he never was as much affected or gratified. It was a compliment more valuable than any the fancy of man or woman could have devised. And that you should think of it at such a moment. O might it be but the will of God that the dearest infant might be spared to be our pride and glory.[32]

It seems that Master Dunbar Stewart Halkett did survive, and attained the age of sixty-nine years.[33]

By the third week in May, still at Langley Park, Stewart felt able to tell Macvey Napier, "I have been gaining strength daily since I came here, and am now going on, tho' but slowly, with the Dissertation." He planned to be at Blair-Adam, the home of Lord Chief Commissioner William Adam, on the way back to Kinneil.[34] The artist David Wilkie, who had just returned from a visit to the Low Countries, visited there during the summer. On the last day of July Mrs Stewart reported to Constable that they were all in love with him, especially Mr Stewart. Wilkie had agreed to stay for another day, and was off "immortalising a cottage" nearby.[35] The knowledge of Stewart which he gleaned during this visit, while his host was still in reasonably good health, was to be useful to the artist seven years later.

Shortly afterwards the American writer Washington Irving made his only visit to Scotland. On 27 August he wrote to his brother: "Jeffrey has just called on me. I am to dine with him to-day *en famille*, and also to-morrow when I shall meet Dugald Stewart . . . Jeffrey tells me I am lucky in meeting with Dugald Stewart as he does not come to Edinburgh above once in a month."[36] However, a few days later he had to add: "I was disappointed in my expectation of meeting with Dugald Stewart at Mr Jeffrey's; some circumstance prevented his coming; though we had Mrs and Miss Stewart."[37] Irving was by then at Abbotsford enjoying the hospitality of Walter Scott. He subsequently made a tour of the Highlands, and was back in Edinburgh before 22 September, when he wrote, "I dined yesterday with Jeffrey, and found a very agreeable party of Edinburgh gentlemen there."[38] The gentlemen were not specified, so it is not clear whether Washington Irving ever met Stewart himself, as he would evidently have liked to do; the assumption must be that he did not.[39]

During the autumn the Stewarts did a little travelling. At the end of September they were at Lord Selkirk's home near Kirkcudbright, from where Stewart told Dr Parr, "I shall be moving about, if the weather be at all tolerable, for the greater part of next month, but I hope to be established at Kinneil before the 20th of October . . . "[40] They must have spent the winter at home, for in March, writing to Constable to congratulate him on his remarriage, Mrs Stewart observed, "We have been such complete hermits . . . Mr Stewart has not been in Edinburgh since the first week of November . . . "[41] In this she may not have been strictly accurate, for the minutes of the RSE indicate that on 1 December 1817 Stewart proposed his nephew, described as Dr Patrick Miller, physician at Exeter, for membership; and at a meeting a fortnight later, evidently still anxious that the RSE should be international in outlook, he nominated the self-taught navigator and mathematician, Nathaniel Bowditch of Salem, Massachusetts, who, he told Thomas Thomson, "is very highly recommended by some of the first names in America".[42] For both motions he had the support of John Playfair and Thomson.[43]

There was some alarm about Matthew. Mrs Stewart added to a letter of her husband's to Thomson in December: "Our poor fellow has had the fever which has devastated Trinidad. *He says* he is better again, and to sail the end of October, but till we see him, days are like months."[44]

However, Stewart must have been pleased at Christmas 1817 by a letter from Constable in London reporting good sales for *Philosophical Essays*, which had got off to a slow start in 1810; an eighth printing, of a thou-

Deaths of Friends and the Final Break (1815–1820)

sand copies, was nearly exhausted, and Constable proposed that the next one should be of two thousand. Nevertheless, philosophy was still not at the top of the best-seller list: Constable added, "The shops are beset hourly for *Rob Roy*."[45] But towards the end of 1818 Stewart's textbook, *Outlines of Moral Philosophy*, which had reprinted twice while he was still teaching, went into a fourth edition.[46]

Another pleasing event occurred in 1818. Andrew Dalzel's third son John was called to the bar, and dedicated his thesis to his father's old friend in polished Latin. Stewart was clearly touched.

> My dear John, – Accept of my best thanks for the honour you have done me in the dedication of your Thesis. Nothing, I can with great truth assure you, ever gave me more pleasure than to see my name conjoined in so flattering a manner with that of my dear and never-to-be-forgotten friend, and to receive this record of our friendship from the hand of his son.[47]

But health problems recurred. Early in May Mrs Stewart told Constable, "I am sorry to say Mr Stewart is very unwell, and we fear a severe influenza – he had scarcely recovered his Edinburgh cough when the bad weather these last days have laid him up and he has been in bed all day."[48] Yet on the 21st Leonard Horner wrote that "he is now past all danger, and is indeed recovering fast".[49] By the end of June Mrs Stewart was able to tell Constable from Dunglass Castle near Dumbarton: "Mr Stewart has gained strength daily by change of air. His chief complaint is now the hardship of being kept idle. As he is very bad at reading common novels, we look forward with impatience to the new Vols of *My Landlord* [ie, the latest from Walter Scott]. May I beg you to send us them as soon as possible."[50] This cure seems to have worked, for early in August, back at Kinneil: "I am thankful to say that Mr Stewart tho' not yet strong is gaining ground steadily – the weather is favourable to invalids . . . PS. I was much indebted to the kind orders you had given for so quickly receiving the valuable volumes. Mr S. read every word of them, and is in love with Jeanie Deans."[51]

During the autumn of 1818 a piece of unexpected good fortune occurred to Mrs Stewart's brother, George Cranstoun. Miss Edmondstoune, an elderly lady with no immediate heirs who possessed a beautiful estate by the Falls of Clyde, gave George possession of it for life on the grounds that they were distantly related by marriage. According to George's friend Walter Scott it was "highly improvable"[52] and "a superb place";[53] the Stewarts became occasional visitors. When George Cranstoun, a very able lawyer, was appointed to the bench in 1826 [54] he took the title of Lord Corehouse after his Lanarkshire estate.

Deaths of Friends and the Final Break (1815–1820)

For the present, however, it was decided that it would be good for Stewart's health to have a break from study and spend the winter in a warmer climate than that of West Lothian,[55] and in October the Stewarts set out via Edinburgh for the south of England. At the beginning of November Maria Edgeworth encountered them at the Marquess of Lansdowne's home at Bowood. Stewart evidently struck her as much changed. "This moment Mrs Dugald Stewart, who was out walking, has come in – the same dear woman! I have seen Mr Stewart – very, very weak – he cannot walk without an arm to lean on."[56]

The next day the newspapers brought them shocking news. In grief at the death of his wife on 29 October, Sir Samuel Romilly shut himself up in his house in Russell Square and four days later cut his throat with a razor, surviving for little more than an hour. He might have become a great reforming Lord Chancellor, and his death was regarded as a calamity by all shades of political opinion. Miss Edgeworth recorded its effect at Bowood.

> There is no telling how it has been felt in this house. I did not know till now that Mr Dugald Stewart had been so very intimate with Sir Samuel, and so very much attached to him – forty years his friend: he has been dreadfully shocked. He was just getting better, enjoyed seeing us, conversed quite happily with me the first evening, and I felt reassured about him; but what may be the consequence of this stroke none can tell. I rejoice that we came to meet him here: they say that I am of use conversing with him. Lord Lansdowne looks wretchedly, and can hardly speak on the subject without tears, notwithstanding all his efforts.[57]

Three weeks later she wrote of "the gloom which the terrible and most unexpected loss of Sir Samuel Romilly cast over the whole society at Bowood during the last few days we spent there"; yet there had been some moments of pleasure.

> When I was consulting Mrs Dugald Stewart about my father's MS, I mentioned Captain Beaufort's opinion on some point; the moment his name had passed my lips, Mr Stewart's grave countenance lighted up, and he exclaimed, "Captain Beaufort! I have the very highest opinion of Captain Beaufort . . ." Mr Stewart has not yet recovered his health; he is more alarmed I think than he need be by the difficulty he finds in recollecting names and circumstances that passed immediately before and after his fever. This hesitation of memory, I believe, everybody has felt more or less afer any painful event. In every other respect Mr Stewart's mind appears to me to be exactly what it ever was, and his kindness of heart even greater than we have for so many years known it to be.[58]

Deaths of Friends and the Final Break (1815–1820)

It must also have been during this visit that Lady Lansdowne (the former Louisa Emma Fox-Strangeways) made a silhouette profile of Stewart which Maria Edgeworth took away with her; it is now in the Scottish National Portrait Gallery.

On Sunday 8 November, the Stewarts' last full day at Bowood, Lansdowne arranged for his temporary neighbour Tom Moore, the songwriter, to join them for dinner. In the evening Moore sang for the company and was pleased to see that Stewart as well as Miss Edgeworth was much affected. He noted in his journal, "When I met him some years ago at Lord Moira's, I watched him while I sang, and saw him, when I had finished, give a sort of decisive blow to the sofa, which he was reclining against. This gesticulation puzzled me, as I could not tell whether it was approbation or condemnation; but I am satisfied now."[59]

The flight from the West Lothian climate seems to have had the desired effect. On 20 January Stewart wrote to a correspondent: "Mrs Stewart and my Daughter, as well as myself, have derived great benefit from our migration to the South. We have now been upwards of two months in Devonshire, and have fixed our residence for the Winter in the village of Heavytreee near Exeter."[60] They were presumably drawn to Exeter – for Heavitree is now a central district – by the presence there of their nephew Dr Patrick Miller and his family. They seem still to have been there towards the end of February, when Maria sent a book of old Scottish psalm tunes to a Wiltshire clergyman whom she had met at Bowood, assuring him that "they can only be heard to advantage when sung by a country congregation in Scotland. It would make Mr & Mrs and Miss Stewart extremely happy if Mr & Mrs Bowles would give them an opportunity of taking them to the Parish Church of Kinneil to judge for themselves."[61]

A little later in the spring they were staying near Endsleigh House, the Devon home of Lord John Russell's father, the Duke of Bedford. Here they received a visit from John Grant of Rothiemurchus, father of the 'Highland lady' autobiographer. Grant was accompanied by his eleven-year-old son John, whom he was about to place at Eton. According to Elizabeth Grant:

> on their way [they] spent a day or two with Dugald Stewart, who lived then near the Duke of Bedford's cottage at Endsleigh. The old philosopher predicted the boy's future eminence, although we at home had not seen through his reserve. He was idle, slow, quiet, passing as almost stupid beside his brilliant brother. "Take care of that boy, Grant," said Dugald Stewart at their parting; "he will make a great name for himself, or I am much mistaken."[62]

Deaths of Friends and the Final Break (1815–1820)

This episode shows Stewart either tactful or perceptive – perhaps both: in the fulness of time John Grant became Lieutenant Governor of Bengal and Governor of Jamaica.

The year 1819 saw several deaths in the Stewarts' circle. Their landlord at Kinneil House, the 9th Duke of Hamilton, died on 16 February. But Stewart's closer relationship appears to have been with his Whig heir, who for the past twenty years had been styled Marquess of Douglas and Clydesdale and who was about to become Grand Master of Freemasons in Scotland, so there was no question of the Stewarts' tenancy at Kinneil being disturbed. The 10th Duke devoted his energies to the improvement of his estates. On 19 April the Stewarts lost their friend Lord Webb Seymour, aged forty-two; he had been in poor health for some time. And on 1 June Stewart's brother-in-law, the Rev. Thomas Miller, passed away at the age of seventy-nine. His death was a further blow for his daughter Margaret, whose marriage four years previously had proved so brief. She had the responsibility of disposing of her father's substantial library, and in her nervous state she declined an invitation to stay a night or two with the Stewarts in case the house would be broken into and the books taken in her absence.[63] Mrs Stewart did her best to solicit the help and understanding of Archibald Constable.[64]

Lastly, on 20 July, Professor John Playfair died. He had attended Lord Webb Seymour's funeral on a day of bad weather three months before; he was ill then, and people were shocked by his appearance. When Stewart had announced his intention to retire, Francis Horner wrote to Mrs Stewart: "I shall regret only Mr Playfair's solitude among the ignorant and illiberal priests with whom he will be left alone."[65] Now, after the passing of both Andrew Dalzel and Playfair, Stewart must have been very conscious that of the Whig triumvirate who had contrived to maintain a liberal outlook at Edinburgh University through the difficult days of the 1790s and beyond, he had become the only survivor. Tommy Thomson was at Kinneil on the 23rd, and told Lord Minto that he "found that Mr Stewart was determined to be present [at the funeral] – much against the remonstrances of his family."[66] It was a notable occasion, attended by the Town Council and University Senatus along with members of the RSE and the Astronomical Institution – one of the last gatherings of the Edinburgh literati.[67]

The family to whom Thomson referred may have included Matthew, who was certainly at home during the following month. He had been given a new appointment as Military Secretary at the headquarters in Malta of Lieutenant- General Sir Thomas Maitland,[68] who was commander of British forces in the Mediterranean. Maitland, a rather

Deaths of Friends and the Final Break (1815–1820)

eccentric and unpopular man, though politically shrewd, was known in the army as "King Tom". He was a brother of Stewart's friend the 8th Earl of Lauderdale, so it is quite probable that family connections again played a part in Matthew's career. It seems unlikely that he ever commanded troops; essentially he was a staff officer, and his various regimental moves (he was now with the 10th Foot) appear to have been designed to enable him to continue in that line of service.

While he was home the stream of visitors to Kinneil House continued. Dr Parr was there in August[69] and, if his biographer is to be believed, "was received as one great man must be received by another; and how he was estimated we may learn from Mrs Dugald Stewart's declaration, that she had never seen anyone there before who was equal to her husband, but she was proud to have Parr under her roof, who was his superior".[70] Stewart himself had considerable regard for Parr, of whom he remarked to Henry Mackenzie, "I have certainly nowhere met with an English man of letters so completely free from all national prejudice against Scotland."[71]

During Parr's visit Stewart received a letter from an admirer of *The Philosophy of the Human Mind* who wished to come and pay his respects.[72] This was Charles Babbage, a brilliant young English mathematician who was just beginning work on the production of a calculating machine to which he devoted most of the rest of his life and which is now seen as a forerunner of the computer. Babbage was on a visit to Scotland, and he arrived at Kinneil from Edinburgh by the steamboat. The meeting was a great success: "I never saw Mr S. enjoy a visit so much as he did yours," Mrs Stewart told him nearly two years later,[73] and a friendship developed which was to last for many years. On his departure Mrs Stewart presented him with some feathers from a Kinneil peacock for his little boy. In due course Babbage described the child as highly delighted with this gift, though Mrs Babbage had insisted "on two of them being put by untill the young philosopher could apprecate the value which the donor's name conferred upon them".[74]

In the middle of November Leonard Horner reported to Dr Parr that Mrs Stewart had been very unwell, but was better. "They propose," he added, "spending a few weeks in Edinburgh this winter, which will be very agreeable to us."[75] But they were still at Kinneil a fortnight later, when Mrs Stewart told Constable that Stewart was "truly happy with Mr Wallace's success".[76] This referred to the appointment of William Wallace, who had been his student in 1793–4, as professor of mathematics. Constable was to bring him for a day at Kinneil.

Early in December Mrs Stewart, still at Kinneil, told Babbage:

Deaths of Friends and the Final Break (1815–1820)

> I was confined to bed with a fever, and what was worse, was fifty miles from home, in a friend's house, where we had gone to pay a marriage visit. Having from my own impatience set out too soon, I was very ill for weeks after my return, and even when free from illness languor and blindness long remained, and it is only within these ten days I have begun to write letters at all.[77]

She went on to thank Babbage for something he had sent to Matthew. Though it had missed him, they had sent it on and had just heard from their son, who had got as far as Gibraltar "after a delightful passage of nine days". Stewart, she reported, was "really well – he is busy printing". A couple of days after this, Stewart proposed Babbage for membership of the RSE, so the proposed visit to Edinburgh had begun. At the same meeting two of his friends proposed Matthew. This was the last occasion on which Stewart's name appears in the RSE minutes.[78]

Early in January 1820 Stewart wrote to tell Samuel Parr: "I have heard from my son since his arrival in Malta. He assures me that he has not forgotten his promise to send Dr Parr some Lyrian tobacco."[79] There was also news from Babbage: his wife had been delivered of another son, and Stewart was to be godfather to the little boy, Edward Stewart Babbage. Rather oddly, perhaps, Mrs Stewart reported that her husband "laments that his little Godson should not receive a prettier name from him", but she expressed due appreciation and interest. She had "only rheumatism and toothache to complain of".[80] In February she told Babbage that his election to the RSE had been confirmed. Stewart's visit to Edinburgh had brought on a severe cough and cold, but a recent move to the Marquess of Lothian's seat at Newbattle Abbey had brought about an improvement, though they intended going back to Edinburgh on 1 March.[81]

The early part of 1820 had brought two deaths, apart from that of George III, whose long reign ended on 29 January. A week after that Stewart's old friend from his Glasgow days, Dr Will Drennan, died in Belfast. True to the last to his radical principles, he had requested that his coffin should pass by the Academical Institution, an interdenominational school which he had helped to establish, "and let six poor Protestants and six poor Catholics get a guinea piece for carriage of me, and a priest and a dissenting clergyman with any other friends that chuse".[82]

More momentous in its consequences was the death of Stewart's successor in the chair of moral philosophy, Thomas Brown. Though normally an active man who was still in his early forties, Brown had become ill a few days before Christmas 1819, and in January had been able to give only the first lecture of the new term. The Stewarts had seen him when they were in Edinburgh, and found him, as Mrs Stewart told Babbage, "*very* ill . . . [he] has no cough, or pain in his side, but his pulse is constantly about a hundred, and he is a shadow; he can neither eat nor sleep – it is heart breaking to see him".[83] Dr Gregory advised him to go to Lisbon. He got as far as London, but there he died on 2 April.[84] Stewart had not been as happy with Brown's teaching as he expected when Brown was first appointed, for he had come to regard him as deficient in the "capacity of *patient thinking*".[85] Nevertheless, he must have been shocked by the premature death of his *protégé*, and his special place in the situation was pointed up by Brown's obituary in the recently founded *Scotsman*.

> To the University of Edinburgh his loss is irreparable, unless indeed the Emeritus Professor of Moral Philosophy would, for the sake of his country, re-commence his course. But if that is too much to expect, as it certainly is, there is nothing unreasonable in looking to him for the exercise of all that influence in favour of a properly qualified candidate, which it is in his power to exert.[86]

Two days later, having heard of various candidates already putting themselves forward, Stewart wrote to the Lord Provost, John Manderton:

> In consequence of the death of my friend and colleague Dr Brown, I have the misfortune to find myself once more sole Professor of Moral Philosophy in the University of Edinburgh; and although my advanced age and delicate state of health leave me but little prospect of being able again to resume the duties of that office, I cannot help still feeling so deep an interest in a situation to which many of the best years of my life were devoted . . .

– that he took the liberty of recommending Macvey Napier,[87] the editor of the *Encyclopaedia Britannica*, to whom in his capacity as librarian he had been turning for the books he needed.[88]

Manderton acknowledged this letter a week later, declaring himself perfectly aware that there was no vacancy, and equally that in providing Stewart with a colleague, or in making an appointment should Stewart resign, the Council carried a great responsibility. He promised that Macvey Napier would be considered, and added "with perfect candour" that the candidates so far were Sir William Hamilton, Dr Macknight (the loser in the Leslie affair), Mr Wilson "and a Mr Esdale from Perth". He also understood that Sir James Mackintosh would assume the chair if assured that he would be acceptable.[89] In the meantime, however, Napier, though much gratified by Stewart's support, knew that as a Whig he stood no chance of success, and

Deaths of Friends and the Final Break (1815–1820)

declined to become a candidate.[90] (Four years later he became the University's first professor of conveyancing.)

Stewart acknowledged the Lord Provost's reply, and expressed himself truly happy that the candidates mentioned included some gentlemen "of so high respectability". He added:

> I have been strongly urged by some of my friends to resume again the duties of my office. As soon as I have formed my final resoluton on this point I shall have the honour of communicating my intentions to your Lordship. In the meantime it is fortunate that the season of the year [the letter was dated 20 April 1820] does not lay me under the necessity of coming to any immediate decision.[91]

However, the Lord Provost, not unreasonably, seems to have put a little pressure on Stewart to clarify his own position, for the incumbent professor wrote again.

> I had the honour of receiving your Lordship's letter yesterday; and am sorry that I cannot yet reply to it so explicitly as I would wish. Your Lordship I am sure will feel, that however eagerly disposed some of the Candidates for the Professorship of Moral Philosophy may be to obtain immediate possession of an Office to which I have still an undoubted right, it can scarcely be expected that I should consent, when there is an interval of nearly six months till the opening of the Winter Session of the College, to put it absolutely out of my power, by a hasty step, to resume the duties of the Professorship myself; if I should see a probability of my being able to do so.
>
> Independently of the state of my health and of various other circumstances, my plans for the next winter depend partly on those of my son, who is at present at Malta with his Regiment. If there should be any prospect of his speedy return to this country it would have a material influence on my determinations.
>
> At all events your Lordship may be assured, that if I am not to do the business of the Office myself, I shall afford ample time to the new Professor to prepare himself for his duties. I take it for granted that no candidate will think of undertaking them, who has not begun the study of Moral Philosophy. For my own part, I can only say, that when I gave my first Course of Lectures on that subject in 1778–9 I began the course with less than a week's notice; although at that time I was daily employed three hours beside doing my duties as Mathematical Professor. A very few weeks however will I flatter myself enable me to return a more satisfactory answer to your Lordship's letter than I can do at present.[92]

Whether or not after receipt of this somewhat ambivalent letter, the Town Council, by a majority, offered the post to Sir James Mackintosh,

Deaths of Friends and the Final Break (1815–1820)

who had taken over Sir Samuel Romilly's role in the House of Commons as promoter of liberal reform of the criminal system, and who had recently become professor of law and general politics at the East India College at Haileybury. However, his political friends in London persuaded him to decline it, rather to his later regret. Before his final decision was known Stewart wrote to the solicitor, James Gibson (later Sir James Gibson Craig, the acknowledged leader of the Scottish Whigs):

> I am truly sorry to learn that there is now so very little probability that Mackintosh will accept of the vacant professorship. For this, however, I was in some measure prepared ... I must own that I was not equally prepared for the sequel to your letter, having always flattered myself with the idea, that in the event of his retiring from the field, the choice of the Patrons of the University [the Town Council] would, in the next instance, have fallen on Sir William Hamilton ...[93]

The development for which Stewart was not prepared, causing considerable dismay to him and his Whig friends, was the growing strength of the application of "Mr Wilson". John Wilson was a polemical writer who contributed to the Tory *Blackwood's Magazine* under the name of Christopher North. A physically imposing man of thirty-five, Wilson was an unsuccessful advocate, a sportsman, a hard drinker, a poet and a vehement controversialist. Although he had studied at Glasgow and Oxford Universities, and had distinguished himself at the latter, he had no obvious qualifications for the post of professor of philosophy, and he had made himself specially obnoxious to Stewart's circle by co-operating with John Gibson Lockhart in an attack on John Playfair a year before the latter's death. James Mill, hearing of Wilson's candidacy from Macvey Napier, replied, "The one to whom you allude makes me sick to think of him."[94] But Wilson needed the money, and he had began to campaign vigorously. He secured the support of Walter Scott, who thought his appointment would be good for his character, and of many respectable men outside Scotland.

Although his candidature appeared scandalous to many in Edinburgh, Stewart ruled out any further attempt to influence the Council, telling Gibson: "As to my coming to Edinburgh at present, and waiting on any of the magistrates, it is a step which nothing can induce me to submit to. If my opinion and advice be wanted, the Patrons of the University know where I am to be found; and, everything considered, I cannot help thinking, that the application should rather come from them to me than from me to them." He added that he was determined not to be involved again in a joint appointment ("the painful anxiety I have felt since the present vacancy took place is more than sufficient to warn me against a repetition of the same error").

> If the accounts that have reached me, of the very high influence which has been already employed in support of a particular candidate be not incorrect, I am fully persuaded of the necessity of yielding calmly to what we cannot prevent. Let the responsibility rest with those who have taken an active share in the business. As for myself, it cannot reasonably be expected that, at my time of life, I should engage in a fruitless struggle with our political rulers in both parts of the island. While I remained in the University, I spared no pains to support, to the best of my abilities, the reputation of the Chair which I filled for so many years; and since I left it, I cannot help thinking, that I have given abundant proof of the deep interest which I take in its honour and prosperity.[95]

Sir William Hamilton, who had told Stewart in April of his intention to stand once Macvey Napier had made it clear he was not a candidate,[96] was now the principal standard-bearer for the anti-Wilson camp, and much the most distinguished candidate in the field. He was an erudite man who had studied at Glasgow, Edinburgh and Oxford, where, like Wilson, with whom he was on friendly terms, he had had an outstanding academic career. He had switched from medicine to law, and was now practising as an advocate in Edinburgh. Stewart, Jeffrey and others threw their weight behind him, and *The Scotsman* waged an anti-Wilson campaign in a series of opinion columns through May and June.[97] On the 19th of the latter month Stewart wrote to James Wedderburn, the Solicitor-General for Scotland:

> I have read with the greatest pleasure the testimonials in favour of Sir William Hamilton. Those from his friends of the University of Oxford are more flattering than anything of the kind I remember to have seen; and when added to the warm testimonies to his learning, talents, and character from some of the most respectable names in Scotland, cannot fail to make a strong impression on the public mind . . . I look forward with peculiar satisfaction to my future connection with him, if, fortunately for the University, he should succeed in obtaining the object of his present ambition.[98]

George Cranstoun, on being shown Hamilton's testimonials, exclaimed, "I would rather have failed with such credentials than have gained with any others."[99]

It is not clear whether news that Matthew would be coming home for the winter would have made Stewart more or less inclined to resume lecturing, but towards the end of June he received a packet from Malta which did nothing to resolve the uncertainty about his son's movements. It is hard to believe that the idea of his returning to the classroom as he approached his sixty-seventh birthday had ever really been a starter, and on 24 June he wrote a formal letter of resignation to the Council which was read at its meeting four days later.[100] A letter from Mrs Stewart to Macvey Napier on 19 July shows that Stewart, whose resignation at that stage had not even been acknowledged, was still in a state of anxious uncertainty as to the outcome, and whether an attempt might yet be made to re-elect him as joint professor.[101] But on that very day the Council was meeting. It made its decision on a straightforward party political basis: Wilson received twenty-one votes, and Hamilton, who had refused to declare that he was not a Whig, nine.[102]

On the day after the meeting the Lord Provost wrote to Stewart to tell him his resignation had been accepted, and John Wilson appointed. He added: "I am directed by the Magistrates and Council to express their unfeigned regret that circumstances should have prevented you from again resuming your academical labours, on the death of your late colleague, the Patrons being convinced that nothing could have contributed so much to the fame of the University, which your name has so long and so conspicuously upheld."[103] Mrs Stewart wrote to Macvey Napier with a copy of "the letter which has taken three weeks to compose it would appear. It is truly amusing to see their cowardice. Mr S. is quite delighted to be saved the touble of writing . . . I hope Sir William won't let the profligacy and hypocrisy of his enemies vex and disquiet him too much." She added, "Mr S. wonders if this last letter will be known. Of course he would not chuse it to become public through him or his friends – but should not be sorry if the history came out through the Town Council."[104]

In its report of the Council's decision, *The Scotsman* placed the blame not so much on the councillors as on those behind them – "the very tag-rag and bobtail of the Melville faction". It scathingly continued: "Their conduct on this occasion has been eminently calculated to prejudice the best interests of the University, to tarnish the literary fame of the country, and to make it be believed that ribaldry and obscenity are the only indispensable qualifications for a Professor."[105]

For the victor the struggle was not over. Wilson had little more than three months in which to find out what he was supposed to be teaching and to prepare a whole winter course of lectures. In the event he became popular with his students, but not as a result of any systematic presentation of his subject; he relied on his knowledge of the classics and of English literature to deliver sentimental and oratorical performances which were received as such. In this respect his tenure of the chair, which he occupied until 1851, was a product of the romantic movement. His appointment must have been a galling outcome for the scholarly and meticulous Stewart.[106] He could not rid himself of the deep interest of which he had spoken, and wrote to Macvey Napier in November, "You will oblige me greatly by writing a few lines to say how the Moral Philosophy Class promises to go on under the new Professor".[107] But Dugald Stewart must have been keenly aware that his long and intimate association with the University of Edinburgh was now finally at an end.

CHAPTER SEVENTEEN

The Last Years
1820–1828

"I am sorry to say that I have received very uncomfortable accounts of the Dugald Stewarts. Mathew has fixed himself at Kinneil merely for the purpose of tormenting them and it is impossible that his sister and Mrs Stewart can hold out long under such continual agitation and anxiety of mind. I have endeavoured to prevail upon them to come to Minto, where he cannot follow them, for a few weeks; which is the only chance that remains of saving their lives." Earl of Minto

In spite of all the brouhaha resulting from Brown's death, Stewart was still working on the second part of his *Dissertation* – "much longer than I could have wished", he told Lord Lansdowne.[1] At the end of August 1820 he wrote to Stark the printer about corrections to the text. However, he was not ready to finalize it, for he needed a little more time to obtain comments from his friends and to take account of them. Besides, that very morning Matthew had arrived from Malta. He had been granted a short leave, as a liver disorder made it necessary for him to be away during the three hot months.[2] Macvey Napier was one of those who offered some observations on the draft *Dissertation*, and he drew Stewart's attention to Brown's views on the philosophy of Reid which had become evident in his now posthumously published textbook, in press at the time of his death . Stewart replied in mid-November:

> I am more particularly puzzled with what you say about our late most excellent friend Dr Brown; but after revolving the subject long in my mind, I am nearly resolved (according to my *first* impressions) to pass over in silence any differences between our opinions concerning Dr Reid; more especially, as it is a subject on which I cannot help thinking that our friend has laid himself open to a most triumphant reply. But on this point it would be *most* painful to me to enter so soon after Dr Brown's death and the late dispute about his successor.[3]

In the end Stewart inserted only a brief note in the first edition of the *Dissertation*, indicating that he might have commented on his differences from Brown concerning Bacon and Reid "if the circumstances of his recent and much lamented death had not imposed silence on me, upon all questions of controversy between us".[4] He reserved a fuller response to Brown until the third volume of his *Philosophy of the Human Mind*, published several years later, and then he confined it to another note.[5]

During the autumn Stewart found himself involved in the posthumous affairs of two old friends. John Whishaw, whom Sir Samuel Romilly had appointed as his literary executor, visited Kinneil to consult him about the publication of Romilly's papers. He came away, as he told Leonard Horner, with his mind quite made up as to the parts he should publish, having had the sanction of one on whose judgment and caution in a matter of this sort he placed more reliance than on that of any other person he knew. Horner himself had reluctantly undertaken to produce a biographical memoir of his brother Francis, and in November he too went to Kinneil to seek Stewart's advice about the project. Stewart, he told a correspondent, "is remarkably well just now, and I have not seen him for a long time looking more healthy or so robust".[6]

Matthew was still at Kinneil at the end of the year, "and I entertain hopes," his father wrote, "that he will not be obliged to return again to the Mediterranean, as his Regiment, it is thought, is about to come home. For many reasons I wish most anxiously that this may be the case."[7] It seems likely, therefore, that Matthew was still with his family when, on 6 January 1821 – in spite of Horner's optimistic assessment of his health – Stewart suffered a severe stroke.[8] This, his son wrote later –

> which nearly deprived him of the power of utterance, in a great measure incapacitated him for the enjoyment of any other society than that of a few intimate friends, in whose company he felt no constraint. This great

calamity, which bereaved him of the faculty of speech, of the power of exercise, of the use of his right hand, – which reduced him to a state of almost infantine dependence on those around him, and subjected him ever after to a most abstemious regimen, he bore with the most dignified fortitude and tranquillity. The malady which broke his health and constitution for the rest of his existence, happily impaired neither any of the faculties of his mind, nor the characteristic vigour and activity of his understanding, which enabled him to rise superior to the misfortune.[9]

Yet contemporary references do not make Stewart's condition sound quite so dire. Archibald Constable wrote to Mrs Stewart in the middle of February, hoping she had received *Kenilworth*, and saying "how glad I was to hear that Mr Stewart was quite well again". He asked for authority to print the second part of the *Dissertation*.[10] Printing must have proceeded, for Mrs Stewart wrote of her husband to Charles Babbage towards the end of March:

He is now thank God, well in all essential respects, but the severity of the disorder, and the strong remedies used, reduced him to a state of weakness from which we cannot expect him to recover till the season allows of air and exercise. You would be delighted however to see how chearful he is, and how much alive to his own pursuits. Fortunately he has the amusement of printing the 2nd part of his Dissertation at present, which is just the sort of easy work suit to him. It is only lately his medical friends allowed him even that degree of employment.[11]

Lady Holland had sent some light reading material to amuse the invalid, and Mrs Stewart thanked her profusely on her husband's behalf.[12] "Mr S. doing really well," she wrote at the beginning of May at the top of a letter to Babbage in which she told him, "His disorder was a slight shock of Palsy – his mind never was the least affected, but his right side, and slight thickness of articulation, which every day is lessening. Only the right arm is weaker still but they assure us it will improve. Mr S. is correcting the Dissertation ... We have infinite cause for thankfulness."[13] Later in May, he "continues to recover, and it is wonderful, considering the extreme coldness of the weather, how well he has been. He is chearful and active in mind, and walks two miles every day."[14]

At a fairly early stage a young man named Thomas Jackson was called in to help. Some years later Mrs Stewart told Lord Lansdowne:

Mr Jackson, Nephew to Mr Thomas Thomson, and educated from infancy in his Uncle's house, had become a favourite of Mr Stewart's, and of course of mine, from his obliging attention and quiet modesty. When neither my

The Last Years (1820–1828)

Daughter's strength nor mine were sufficient for the walks and for the support required, he gladly gave up everything, and came to Kinneil where he watched over Mr Stewart, and in fact did all the most affect. Son could have done.[15]

Jackson had studied for the ministry, though he never held a charge; fifteen years later he became professor of divinity at St Andrews, and subsequently professor of church history at Glasgow University. Matthew Stewart had had to return to London; Babbage met him at Greenwich Observatory in July, and spent a pleasant day with him.[16]

At the end of that month Archibald Constable was becoming even more anxious to get the latest volume of the *Supplement to the 4th and 5th Editions of the Encyclopaedia Britannica* published; delay was now causing financial losses.[17] But he did not have much longer to wait: the *Advertisement* to the second part of the *Dissertation* was dated from Kinneil House on 7 August. Stewart apologized for its length, but made no reference to his health other than his "advanced years".[18] Mrs Stewart told Macvey Napier that everything had now been sent to the printer, adding: "It is a great relief to my mind in some respects that the task is finished, and in another view, we cannot but regret the loss of so pleasant an occupation."[19] Soon arrangements were being made for copies to be sent to such friends as the Marquess of Lansdowne and Lord Palmerston.[20] At the beginning of September Constable sent Stewart £600,[21] a sum which, since prices had fallen after the end of the war, was worth not far short in purchasing power of what he received for the first part of the *Dissertation*. Sir James Mackintosh did not like the second part so well as the first,[22] and John Ward found it "pleasing, full of learning on his subject, but surely over-cautious, and I think a little *senile*".[23] However, the comments which reached Stewart himself, as his wife told Macvey Napier, conveyed "approbation even from those whose opinion Mr S. most values . . . beyond his utmost wishes".[24]

Mrs Stewart was still reporting favourably on her husband's recovery. She told Napier at the beginning of December that she would be returning some books he had borrowed, but –

> truth to say, it is hard work to get them out of Mr S.'s grasp – he casts such tender looks on them and says, "not just yet – there is a curious thing I mean to look at again." Thankfully, I can say he is very well. He seizes every possible hour of fair weather to go out, and when that is impossible walks his 2 hours and 1/2 in the large room. But the open air makes a difference very great, from what walking in the home does, as to sleep. His spirits on the whole are wonderfully good. He now allows my reading aloud, or

Maria, and if we could only fall on amusing books, our evenings would be too short. His provoking memory makes old books familiar to him. O that we could find new ones to his taste.[25]

Sad news came later in the month. Mrs Stewart had made several enquiries after the Babbages' baby, and in April his father had reported, "Although he is fifteen months old he does not walk yet, not from any want of ability but from having formed a decided opinion that locomotion is much more safely performed by crawling on the carpet at which he is very expert."[26] But now Stewart's little godson had died, and Mrs Stewart wrote to say how distressed they were at the loss of one who had been "a pleasing memorial of your regard". Of her husband she reported:

> Mr Stewart is now obliged to be so careful, and to study so little at a time. Yet even he is assured that he may expect complete recovery. He is I am thankful to say really well, and never had the slightest return of the disorder. The mind never was more active, and his memory as astonishing as ever, so that to keep him idle is very difficult. He has been amusing himself with reading the Latin poets again, and that has done him much good.[27]

Shortly before Christmas, Constable wrote from London to Thomas Thomson that it gave him "infinite pleasure to hear lately such excellent accounts of Mr Stewart's health".[28] Thomson replied on the first day of 1822, "Mr Stewart is certainly improving in general health, but does not venture to work much."[29] Writing in January to Lady Holland (to acknowledge some more books), Mrs Stewart conceded that "Mr S. has not used his pen for a year past"; she added, "He is a very obedient Patient, and keeps strictly to the regimen ordered."[30] Five months later a rather gloomy impression was gained by the twenty-year-old Henry Fox, later to be the last Lord Holland, who visited Kinneil and recorded in his journal:

> Mr Stewart is a melancholy instance of the mind outliving the body. He is terribly feeble and at times very inarticulate, and quite aware of his own situation. His spirits are very low, and his consciousness of the distressing state he is in very evident. Mrs Stewart . . . is a sensible woman, as is also the daughter. Both are (and I fear not unjustly) very much alarmed at Mr Stewart's illness. His manner is still calm and pleasant, but to see the breaking up of a superior understanding is a painful sight . . . The evening was pleasant; we had ghost stories . . .[31]

Stewart may have appeared more ill to a young man than to his own contemporaries, or it may have been, as often happens, that the course of recovery had setbacks as well as advances.

The Last Years (1820-1828)

He and his wife were still liable to be much excited by happenings in the world outside. "If ever there was a blessed and glorious event on earth," Mrs Stewart wrote to Macvey Napier in June, "this triumph of Mr J. S.'s is one of the noblest. To think the man they had slandered and tormented should come out so pure, so noble, so adored a character what a glory to his friends, and what humiliation to the despicable gang of his enemies. Will none of them have soul enough to hang themselves."[32] The reference was to a sensational trial which had just taken place in Edinburgh. The accused, "Mr J. S.", was a landed gentleman and Writer to the Signet, James Stuart the younger of Dunearn. He had been libelled as a coward by Sir Alexander Boswell, the eldest son of James Boswell (who had died in 1795). Alexander Boswell was an MP of extreme Tory persuasion, regarding all Whigs (of whom Stuart was one) as dangerous and irresponsible. Although a man of some culture, he was also imperious and unforgiving, and when Stuart demanded an apology he refused all attempts at mediation. The result was a duel, which took place in Fife. In the encounter Stuart was unharmed, but to his own astonishment (for he was not an experienced shot) he inflicted a wound on his opponent from which Boswell almost immediately died.

Stuart was of course tried on a capital charge, and the trial became a party political confrontation. The jury, according to *The Scotsman,* were all Stuart's political opponents, but he was represented in court by a group of eminent Whig advocates, including Francis Jeffrey, Henry Cockburn and John Murray. They made a spirited case in mitigation of Stuart's action, and the Lord Justice Clerk, while stressing that homicide in the course of a duel was still murder in law, delivered a summing-up which gave due weight to the mitigating circumstances. The jury did not even leave the box, but after a brief consultation among themselves delivered a unanimous verdict of "Not Guilty". The Stewarts apparently kept watch all night: "twice at least every hour did I trim the rush light, and look how the hours went", until a note from Napier brought them the news for which they were waiting.[33] *The Scotsman* regarded the outcome, against the political probabilities, as a triumph for Scottish justice.[34] But Mrs Stewart's prejudices, or convictions, were not easily appeased. "Query," she wrote at the end of her letter, "how was the Justice Clerk so good and so wise – was it Nature or Art?"[35]

Stewart was well enough for "a gay and happy dinner party" at Kinneil a week later,[36] and soon he was able to travel, for John Ward met him in Buxton in July. He found him "a good deal shattered in body", but his mind remained "quite entire. The paralytic seizure by which he suffered about a year and a half ago has affected his speech a little – but only a little, and occasionally. In general he is quite articulate."[37] Though Ward often puzzled and upset Mrs Stewart by his strangely worded letters, he was on this occasion particularly attentive and affectionate towards her.[38]

The Stewarts may still have been away from Edinburgh during the second half of August when there occurred the tartan extravaganza of the visit of King George IV, though in due course they no doubt heard all about it from the Marquess of Lothian who, in his capacity as Lord Lieutenant of Midlothian, welcomed the King at Leith and on the afternoon of his last full day in Scotland entertained him at Newbattle Abbey. At a levee at Holyrood Palace Sir Walter Scott presented the professor of moral philosophy, John Wilson, to the King. Mrs Stewart wrote afterwards to the Marquess of Lansdowne, "The good people of this Country are beginning to wonder at their own enthusiasm while the King was here, and it is remarked nobody talks of his Majesty, but every body sighs for the heavy bills they have to pay."[39]

She must herself have been unwell around this period, for early in September Ward was glad to hear that she was better again "after so severe an attack".[40] It seemed that the Stewarts might be going to Lord Selkirk's place at "the Isle", and this may have been on their way back from England. Later in the autumn they received a visit from Lord Holland's sister Miss Fox and her cousin Miss Vernon, who were making a tour of the Highlands. "Mr Stewart was really the better for it," his wife told Lord Lansdowne, "it made him so happy and they were so good to Maria."[41] In January the Stewarts spent a fortnight at Howard Place in Edinburgh with their widowed niece, Margaret Miller.[42] Margaret was now nearly thirty, but three years later she contracted a second marriage which made her very comfortably off.

In September Robert Cadell had asked Stewart if he could manage to pay his book account, which now stood at £143.19s.3d (over £8,000 today), the last payment having been made in 1817; Archibald Constable & Co. had their own bills to settle, including, as he pointed out, the £600 paid to Dugald Stewart![43] In January 1823 the publishers had discouraging news, which Constable conveyed to Mrs Stewart. He had earlier suggested bringing out a new edition of the volume containing Stewart's three biographical memoirs, and Stewart, as his wife said, "felt it would be a pleasant and useful employment. Indeed it was precisely what we all thought would be of the utmost importance to him as restoring his former habits of study gently, and without too much fatigue of mind."[44]

Now, however, Constable had to report that Cadell and Strachan, who had the greater interest in the book, did not wish to reprint it at present.[45] Mrs Stewart was badly disappointed by this information, and wrote

The Last Years (1820–1828)

secretly to Macvey Napier to see if he might intervene with Constable.[46] Before long, however, Stewart's own enquiries obliged her to reveal the situation to him. But, she added, writing to Constable at the end of March, "Mr Stewart is really well, considering the variable and severe weather."[47]

In the spring they must have left home again, for on 8 May Mrs Stewart wrote to her brother George from Langley Park at Montrose.[48] On 1 June, back at Kinneil, they received a visit from Maria Edgeworth and two of her sisters on their way to see Sir Walter Scott in Edinburgh and stay with him at Abbotsford. In a letter written on the following day Miss Edgeworth described their arrival from the shore road, late in the evening, at the back of the "old but white-washed castle-mansion".

> A short-faced old butler in black [Robert?] came out of a sort of sentry-box back door to receive us, and through odd passages and staircases we reached the drawing-room, where we found fire and candles, and Mrs Stewart and a tall young man; Mrs Stewart, just as you saw her at Bowood, received Harriet and Sophy in her arms, spoke of their dear mother and of Honora [to whom this letter was written], and seated us on the sofa, and told Sophy to open a letter from Fanny, which she put into her hand, and "feel herself at home", which indeed we did. The tall young man was no hindrance to this feeling; an intimate friend, a Mr Jackson, who has been staying with Mr Stewart as his companion ever since his illness.[49]

Miss Edgeworth left no record of her impression of Stewart at this reunion (he may already have gone to bed on the evening when she arrived); but when the Edgeworth party left Kinneil for Edinburgh a few days later, he and Maria Stewart accompanied them for some miles on their road in order to show them Linlithgow Palace.[50]

In September the Stewarts received another visit from Charles Babbage, this time accompanied by his wife. To assist Babbage in his life's work, Stewart gave him a plan for the construction of a machine for calculating multiplication which Lord Daer had drawn up nearly thirty-five years before.[51] At the beginning of November, George Cranstoun told Thomas Thomson that he was expecting a visit from the Stewarts, adding, "Their situation at present is truly afflicting."[52] Later that month Stewart became seventy. The Stewarts went to Newbattle Abbey at Dalkeith to spend Christmas with the Marquess of Lothian and his family, and from there Mrs Stewart wrote to the Countess of Minto, who was a daughter of Principal Robertson's daughter, Mary Brydone, to acknowledge the news that she and her husband wished Stewart to be godfather to their fourth son, George Francis Stewart Elliot, who had been born in October.

The Last Years (1820–1828)

> It is impossible for me to express the gratification your kind letter has given us. Mr Stewart charges me to say, that joyfully and gratefully he accepts the honour done him – his most affectionate blessing and prayers will ever rest on his dear little Godson, and although it is not easy to devise a stronger claim on his anxious good wishes than what every child of Lord Minto and of yours must possess yet this is indeed a delightful claim added, and a most flattering testimony of your friendship . . . if Lord Minto and you wished to give happiness you have truly done so.[53]

It perhaps showed particular sensitivity on the part of the Mintos that they should have asked Stewart to stand in this relationship to a child to whom they had given the name of the Stewarts' own son, who, had he lived, would by now have been thirty-two, and might have had children of his own. In April 1827 Mrs Stewart told Lord Minto: "*Our* boy's witticisms amuse God-Papa more than any flowers of wit. Mr S. often wonders what he will turn out – certainly an Original."[54] Little George (Doddy) Elliot was only four when his godfather died; in due course he became a barrister and remained unmarried. He survived into the twentieth century.

As so often happened, happy events alternated with sad ones. On 27 April 1824 the 6th Marquess of Lothian – the young Ancram with whom Stewart had made his first journey abroad in 1783, and with whom he had been on the most intimate terms ever since – died at the age of sixty. The closeness of the family ties is illustrated by a note of condolence sent to the thirty-year-old new Marquess by Mrs Stewart's brother George, who had recently become Dean of the Faculty of Advocates and acted as a legal adviser to the Lothian family.

> No one can sympathize with you on this occasion more than myself. He was the benefactor of my youth, and thro' life he has been my steadiest and warmest friend. For thirty-two years his confidence and esteem have been to me a source of unspeakable satisfaction, and it will now be my duty and great pleasure to shew my gratitude and attachment by being of use, if ever I can be of use, to you, or to any of his children or family, or connections.[55]

Mrs Stewart's own emotions found expression in a letter to the 7th Marquess's younger brother Henry, who had stayed with the Stewarts as a boy eight years before. Lord Henry had hastened to Newbattle Abbey only to find that the new head of the family had gone to England to console his stepmother.

> Now my dear Child [Lord Henry was now twenty-three!], let me intreat you to come to us, if you can . . . Here you will have perfect quiet, and the truest, tenderest sympathy. I can offer you nothing else – but you may be

The Last Years (1820–1828)

> assured that if you find it convenient to come here, it will give us the most unfeigned satisfaction. Alas to me it looks like a moment when I brought you home in my arms, after you met with a loss you cannot remember [an allusion, perhaps, to the death of Lord Henry's mother when he was not quite five]. Many thanks for your excellent letter. It gave Mr Stewart much comfort. I am thankful to say his health has not suffered, but his spirits have been deeply affected. No loss out of his own family could have been so felt by him.

She added on the cover: "A steam-boat to Stirling passes Bo-ness twice every day, so that you can land within a short walk of Kinneil."[56]

About this time Mrs Stewart gave a more general account of her husband in replying on his behalf to a letter from Professor Prévost.

> I am thankful to say, Mr Stewart's health is as good as, after the severe attack he had more than three years ago, we could possibly hope. He suffers no pain, his spirits are uniformly cheerful, and his mind as acute as ever. He walks between two and three hours every day; and, in fact, except a difficulty of speech, and a tremor in his hand when he attempts writing, no symptoms of paralytic affection remain. He is forbidden severe study by his medical friends; but he amuses himself with reading on his favourite pursuits, and with the classics.[57]

In May 1824 Stewart was one of a small group which tried to help a blind man named Alexander Davidson.[58] After a successful career at Edinburgh University, Davidson had supported himself for thirty years by touring Britain and Ireland as a free-lance lecturer in physics and chemistry. But now he had begun to be afflicted by epileptic fits when lecturing, and he and his wife were facing destitution. Stewart made an application on his behalf to the Royal Society in London, but when this failed (because the Society could assist only people who had published), and other possible sources of help had also proved fruitless, Stewart together with James Pillans, the professor of humanity, and Leonard Horner, who agreed to be treasurer, acted as trustees of a fund which they hoped to establish by persuading sympathizers to make donations or annual contributions. In the spring of the following year Mrs Stewart was asking Charles Babbage to suggest people in London who might be prepared to subscribe.[59]

Meantime in the summer of 1824 Stewart received an emissary from his old Paris acquaintance, Thomas Jefferson, who had served two terms as President of the United States during the first decade of the century and was now engaged in establishing the University of Virginia. He sent a young attorney named Francis Walker Gilmer to Europe to recruit the first professors, and furnished him with a letter of introduction to Stewart which began:

> It is now 35 years since I had the great pleasure of becoming acquainted with you in Paris, and since we saw together Louis XVI led in triumph by his people thro' the streets of his capital; these years too have been like ages in the events they have engendered without seeming at all to have bettered the condition of suffering man ... At a subsequent period you were so kind as to recall me to your recollection on the publication of your invaluable book on the Philosophy of the Human Mind, a copy of which you sent me, and I have been happy to see it become the text book of most of our colleges and academies, and pass thro' several impressions in the US ... .[60]

Jefferson asked Stewart "to lead Mr Gilmer by the hand in his researches". However, Gilmer's visit to Edinburgh proved fruitless; no one knew anything about this embryonic university in the wilds of North America, and the salary offered was not attractive.[61]

In September David Wilkie came back to Kinneil. He wrote to his sister: "I have made ... at the earnest request of his friends, a drawing in chalk of Dugald Stewart for Mrs Stewart, as there is, it is said, no satisfactory likeness of him known. He suffers much from paralysis, and his friends suppose that no person could make the drawing but one acquainted with him in his better days."[62] This drawing naturally shows Stewart as an older man than the Raeburn portrait, but he looks both alert and benign. It eventually found its way to his nephew Dr Peter Miller in Exeter, and is now held by the Scottish National Portrait Gallery [Plate 16].[63]

There is evidence that before the end of the year Stewart had resumed work with a view to producing a third volume of *Elements of the Philosophy of the Human Mind*, for a notebook exists with writing in Mrs Stewart's hand on 'Conjectures concerning the Origin of the Sanscrit', which in due course formed a section in that book. She noted on it, "Written in the end of 1824 and beginning of 1825."[64] (Stewart advanced the mistaken conjecture that Sanskrit had developed from Greek.)

During this period Matthew was at home. He had recently retired from active army service on grounds of ill health.[65] The problem may have been the liver disorder which had troubled him four years previously, or it may primarily have been one indicated by Lord Minto in writing to his old friend the Marquess of Lansdowne on 25 December. Minto touched on various topics of mutual interest (making no reference to the fact that it was Christmas Day), and the letter included this paragraph.

> I am sorry to say that I have received very uncomfortable accounts of the Dugald Stewarts. Mathew has fixed himself at Kinneil merely for the purpose of tormenting them and it is impossible that his sister and Mrs Stewart can hold out long under such continual agitation and anxiety of mind. I have endeavoured to prevail upon them to come to Minto, where he cannot follow them, for a few weeks; which is the only chance that remains of saving their lives. Stewart is quite aware of Mathew's state of mind; but does not speak of it.[66]

These "accounts" must have come from the Stewarts themselves, but it seems less likely that Matthew's behaviour was motivated by malice, as Minto seems to have believed, than that he was showing symptoms of an illness for which there was to be more evidence in the years ahead. The Stewarts must have yielded to their friend's persuasion, for they spent several weeks at Minto. After Matthew had at last departed Mrs Stewart wrote, from "Loretto by Musselburgh", to the Earl:

> The seperation was to a wish, calm and tranquil. He saw only Maria and he is now I hope, *really* gone south. I am satisfied that it is to your Brother alone we owe this blessing, and that it was Captain Elliot's delicacy and firmness, that persuaded him to leave Scotland so pleasantly. The happy effect of this on Maria, is beyond expression and gives a prospect of future peace. The interview *before* he saw your Brother [Matthew had of course known Captain Elliot well in India] was dreadful – she was almost gone she was so exhausted by his violence. Judge of what we owe to Captain Elliot. Yet except that one delusion of our Servants every one who has seen him says he is to appearance quite well.[67]

A week later she wrote again, saying that they would be in Edinburgh for another fortnight "for want of coals to heat Kinneil". They would be staying with Margaret Miller. She referred to "Mr Stewart's *Tutor*, Mr Broster", who treated speech difficulties, and reverted to the subject of Matthew.

> What do we not owe your Brother for it was he assuredly who led poor M. to go, calmly and kindly. Maria saw him, owing to accident, the day before he sailed [perhaps to London], and their parting was to a wish – so that no anguish rests on her mind. She is very weak, but already there is rest and peace in her looks and she sleeps sweetly. Mr S. is really well too – the load seems off his mind, and both in spirits and health he is again like himself – and to what is his life owing, but the seven weeks of safety and repose at Minto – had he been within reach of home misery, he could not have survived.[68]

The Last Years (1820–1828)

Mrs Stewart told Babbage about the same time that Stewart was "fully better than when you saw him; he had a severe cold lately, but has now recovered from it".[69]

Stewart's spirits may also have been lifted from the nightmarish situation by further evidence of the esteem in which he was held. Dr Samuel Parr had died on 6 March, and his will included the clause: "I leave a ring to Professor Dugald Stewart, a friend who is endeared to my Soul from the simplicity of his manners, the candour of his spirit and the purity of his principle . . . occasionally by the glowing and sublime eloquence which adorns his style."[70]

By the middle of April 1825 the Stewarts were back at Kinneil, having just missed the Minto family on their way through Edinburgh to Fife. Mrs Stewart told the Countess: "Maria is better – she walks well and we are now satisfied that she has no ailment but what rest of mind and body would cure . . . being the only person in the house allowed to use a pen, it is to me now a sad labour. Why am I then bestowing so much on you my dear Lady Minto – the question is not easily answered . . . "[71]

Reading was still a solace, and early in June, inviting Constable to visit, she told him, "We are starving for want of books."[72] Constable declined the invitation because of a current heatwave, but responded by sending the *Tales of the Crusaders* – the latest two novels by Sir Walter Scott. Before long Mrs Stewart replied:

> You fell on an excellent device to reconcile us to the absence of all visitors. In fact, I fear no mortal would have been welcome from the moment the brown parcel arrived. Mr Stewart at first said he would give his daughter and me the start for a day, but he was glad to retract; and he has read every word with more attention and eagerness than any of us. It is quite delightful his deep interest and his speculations on every character and incident. Indeed, all *your* novels have been a source of great pleasure to him. He had just finished *Ivanhoe* for the second time when the Crusaders came. I suspect *The Talisman* is to rival any of them.[73]

Such accounts of his old teacher's enjoyment may well have found their way back to the author.

Stewart was "really well" through the summer and autumn, his wife told Lord Lansdowne. He was still at work on the third volume of his *Philosophy of the Human Mind* – pleasant occupation, she added, "especially as *Miss* Dugald Stewart (she is very vain of the name) can now assist him with pen and eyes – which his old clerk, *Mrs* D.S. can no longer do".[74] In November he dined at the house of Lady Keith along with Jeffrey and John Murray, when he was able to renew his acquaintance with Tom

The Last Years (1820–1828)

Moore, who was on a visit to Edinburgh.[75] An amusing aspect of his research emerges from a letter which his wife wrote to Lord Minto in January 1826. A section of the book was to deal with "the power of imitation", and Stewart planned an appendix to illustrate "how very much the effects of all the imitative arts are aided by the imagination of the spectator or of the hearer".

One such illustration was ventriloquism, and at this time the well known comic actor, Charles Mathews, who included ventriloquism in his "At Home" entertainments, was performing at an Edinburgh theatre.

> I am going to tell you a *little secret* [Mrs Stewart wrote], and it must be a secret, or people would think us crazy. Mr Stewart means to be in Edinburgh on Thursday next – for what purpose? to see Matthews. Do you recollect a chapter on the powers of *Imitation* and *Mimicry* [Minto had been shown a draft] he thinks he will gain infinite information on these subjects and he is just within a few pages of them in printing his Vol. You will guess what I am going to say *Could you go with us*. I have only heard we have got places in the 2d box from the Stage this moment – and I cannot resist the earnest desire to tell you my dear Lord Minto. Alas I fear Lady Minto will not dare to venture. We shall get an early dinner and sleep at Sir David Wedderburn's, and we must go early. O if you are not engaged what it would be to have you. We must let it pass that Mr S. has come in on business, and goes by chance. We come home on Friday for my sister Mrs Cunninghame is here . . . .[76]

Whether or not the Earl of Minto was able to join in this surreptitious adventure undertaken in the cause of philosophy, it appears that Stewart's wish was accomplished, for Mathews is duly named in a footnote to the Appendix.[77]

In February they were from home, as Mrs Stewart told Minto: "We have been worse, but now better, and soon I hope we shall get out of this vile little cage. The idea of large clean rooms in delightful and old Kinneil will seem a Paradise."[78] There is evidence that in the summer of this year Thomas Jackson was still, at least on occasion, assisting Stewart, for on the latter's behalf he declined an offer from Constable of Scott's *Woodstock* on the grounds that he had got it from a neighbour. Stewart hoped Constable could come to see him soon "as the weather is fair and Kinneil in beauty".[79]

Around this time Mrs Stewart must have been unwell, for Maria, writing to Stark the bookseller in the middle of August, reported: "My mother is still very feeble – not stronger I think than when you saw her but not positively ill. My father pretty well but we have had so much company for the last fortnight he was obliged to put off his work. Now I hope nothing will interrupt him."[80]

Macvey Napier and Thomas Thomson were now acting on Stewart's behalf in relation to some of his business affairs,[81] and following the bankruptcy of Constable and Co. they had to make alternative arrangements for the publication of the forthcoming final volume of *Philosophy of the Human Mind*. Constable had been going to pay £735 for the copyright, but in approaching the London publisher John Murray, Napier conceded that "the altered state of the times may perhaps operate somewhat to diminish it pecuniary value". After negotiation Stewart accepted an offer from Murray of 200 guineas (nearly £10,000 today) for the copyright of the first edition.[82]

Stewart dated the *Preface* to his third volume from Kinneil on 24 November 1826.[83] It included as an appendix the papers relating to James Mitchell, the boy born blind and deaf. In preparing these for the press it had occurred to Stewart to wonder how James was getting on, and he made enquiries through Macvey Napier. These elicited a long letter from James's sister, which was included in the book. In spite of some accidents, James had now lived to be thirty, derived much satisfaction from smoking a pipe, and had adapted to his very restricted existence in a manner which seemed to Stewart evidence of even greater "intellectual capacity" than he had first detected.[84]

The volume was printed just before Christmas. In his November *Preface* Stewart gave notice that even then he had not come to the end of his plans for publication.

> If such a measure of health shall be continued to me as shall enable me to devote occasionally a few hours to the revision of my Papers, it is my present intention to begin, in the course of the ensuing winter, to print my *Inquiries into the Active and Moral Powers of Man*. They who are aware of my very advanced age [he wrote two days after his seventy-third birthday], and are acquainted with the infirmities under which I have laboured for a course of years, will not suppose that I look forward with undue confidence to the completion of my design; but, besides that some employment is necessary to beguile the passing hours, I will satisfy my own mind, if, by giving a beginning to the undertaking, I shall render it more easy for others to put into form that part of my task that may be left unfinished.[85]

His name and reputation were still potent, and two instances occurred of its use in the context of adult education. At a public meeting in London in November 1823 to launch the Mechanics' Institutes, Stewart's former student George Birkbeck had chosen his inspiring words to quote: "When theoretical knowledge and practical skill are happily combined in one person, the intellectual power of man appears in its full perfection."[86] Three years later a letter passed from another former student of Stewart's to a third. Henry Brougham wrote from London to his old College friend Henry Duncan on behalf of a private committee "for promoting popular education, by the propagation and diffusion of cheap and elementary works on all branches of science". He sought Duncan's help, either dircetly or by suggesting people who might contribute. "Do you know any one," he asked, "either as a volunteer or for reward who will give a popular view of the philosophy of mind, abridged from D. Stewart for example?"[87]

In the spring of 1827 the Stewarts were much concerned about political developments in London resulting from a breakdown in the health of the Earl of Liverpool which brought his long premiership to an end. After a good deal of manoeuvring, the King had asked George Canning to try to form a government. "What would I give for a talk with Lord Minto, was Mr S.'s first reflection to-day," wrote Mrs Stewart to the Earl in London, seeking more information about what was going on. "It is impossible now to think of anything but Politics, and we are so ignorant . . . "[88] The government which Canning gradually put together included several of their friends. Lord Palmerston was brought into the cabinet for the first time, and John W. Ward, who had succeeded to his father's title in 1823 and become Viscount Dudley and Ward, was made Foreign Secretary; he had moved from being a moderate Whig to being a follower of Canning. Canning was obliged to seek the aid of the moderate Whigs themselves, and the Marquess of Lansdowne, who had become in effect their leader, eventually agreed to enter the cabinet without portfolio, and in July became Home Secretary. Mrs Stewart was enormously grateful to Lansdowne for having written to keep Stewart informed: "it was so glorious a proof of affection for Mr S."[89] With regard to Lord Dudley, she wrote to Minto:

> It is rather too vain to expect you to remember anything but what is important, but if ever it should occur at a spare moment with Lord Dudley, I wish you would tell him how happy Mr S. has been made by seeing him *forced* to use his talents, and for so noble a purpose. Mr S. often said what a misfortune to Mr Ward to have such a fortune – had he been a poor man, he would have employed his talents and gloried in them. As it was, indolence could always get the better of ambition, but *now* he is fairly committed. Perhaps it may be better not to say this to him however. I leave it to you my dear Lord. With all [his] little peculiarities I do love him tenderly and Mr S. does so most sincerely.[90]

The Last Years (1820–1828)

As one friend prospered, the Stewarts must have been saddened by another's death. Archibald Constable was so demoralized by the bankruptcy of his great publishing house and by a breach with his partner, Robert Cadell, that he lacked the will to fight an illness which he suffered early in 1827; his bulky frame wasted away, and he died on 21 July aged fifty-three.

Mrs Stewart, though always with profuse apologies, did not scruple to use her influential connections on behalf of her family circle. In March 1821 she had sought advice from Charles Babbage on behalf of Lady Wedderburn, whom she described as "one of my most intimate friends", about getting her mathematically talented son into Cambridge.[91] (Babbage responded most helpfully.) In October 1825 she had approached the young Lord Lothian at the request of her nephew William Miller "who lived with us many years". William, who was the third of Janet's four surviving children, had been serving in the army in Ireland, but promotion from captain to major had resulted in his being posted to Woolwich and having to leave his wife and four children. There was then a vacancy for Brigade Major in Dublin, and a word from Lord Lothian to the Duke of Wellington's secretary would be of great help.[92] Later she had asked for the help of the Marquess of Lansdowne in support of an application by Thomas Jackson for the professorship of rhetoric at Edinburgh (another candidate, she told him, was "a man of the name of Carlyle, every way disreputable").[93]

Now, in May 1827, she wrote to Lothian again about plans being made by Sir Walter Scott and his creditors (for of course Scott had also been caught up in the Constable collapse) to turn their oil gas works into coal gas with work near the new Botanic Gardens, "and for a certainty mining *my nephew* Mr Henderson's property around it" and thus, she thought, halving the value of his house.[94] (Margaret Miller's second husband was a banker named Alexander Henderson.) She wrote in similar terms to Lord Minto – "All this to serve Sir Walter Scott who is at the head of the whole".[95] A few months later she asked Minto to apply to Lord Dudley for a consulship at Bahia for a brother-in-law of Matthew Miller, the last of the nephews.[96]

But the Stewarts had now an even more personal reason for looking to their influential friends for help. The twenty-one years for which Stewart had been awarded his sinecure by the Whig government in 1806 was due to expire at the end of the year. During the intervening period, especially under Lord Liverpool's premiership, it had become accepted on all sides that the granting of sinecures to political friends was a practice that ought to cease. There was therefore some doubt as to whether Stewart's could or would be renewed. It was probably to this that Mrs Stewart was alluding in March 1826 when she wrote to Minto:

> I threatened you with a letter, for I hoped to have something to tell you about ourselves, that I know would have given Lady Minto and you pleasure as it would make us so comfortable – but it has not happened yet, though I will not despair, great people have been all occupied. If we are blest with it, you will learn the news in London from the best and kindest of friends Lord Palmerston, to whom we owe what words cannot tell.[97]

Stewart himself prepared a memorandum in which he pointed out that "the reduction of my income by three hundred a year would be attended with very serious inconveniences".[98] (Since he resigned from his joint professorship in 1820 he had not, of course, received any salary or pension from Edinburgh University.) Mrs Stewart made contact with Lord Palmerston on the subject.[99] She was now sixty-two, and the uncertainty which persisted for some considerable time may have contributed to a state of agitation which was described in a letter from Maria to Lady Minto. The family had been staying at Minto, and had moved on to Eildon Hall, from where, after a September day spent at Dryburgh, Maria wrote:

> You bade me write to-day and therefore I do so, tho' in fact I am quite as much in the dark with respect to our plans as I was when we left Minto. Only that I am more and more convinced of the great wisdom as well as kindness of the proposal that we should return to Minto when we leave this. My Mother is in a most painful state of mind and yesterday when the English newspaper announced the probability of Lord Lansdowne immediately resigning [Lansdowne, as Home Secretary, would have had a strong influence on Stewart's behalf] she was even alarmingly agitated. My Father was present and was so much shocked and terrified by the state in which he saw her that every other evil was forgotten, and he said that as soon as she recovered the power of speaking he was happy. I am quite sure that she would hear whatever is to be borne better at Minto than anywhere else, but there are some difficulties I did not foresee and I am almost afraid she will herself object to our return for she expessed yesterday a strong wish to be at home. My Father and I are however so anxious to accept of your kindness that I think we shall make it out . . .[100]

The next day Maria reported to their would-be hostess:

> I walked to the top of the Hill to-day and down on t'other side to Melrose. Papa and Mama went there in the Carriage to bring me home . . . Mama is on the whole better to-day – but she is still a poor silly body. And a party

of *ten* strangers has confused our brains completely. I have stolen away to recover my senses and write this. I had a letter from Matt to-day and *I think* we shall certainly come to you but it will probably be without a maid, and till Mama makes up her mind how far that is practicable I cannot say *quite* certainly.[101]

But good news was at hand. An arrangement had been agreed whereby Stewart would resign from his current appointment and would then be offered a further heritable Patent as Gazette Writer at the same annual salary. Sending the formal statement of this to Lord Minto, Maria wrote:

You and Lady Minto who have so kindly soothed and assisted us in all our anxieties will easily believe how very happy and grateful we are for the enclosed. My Father is much happier than I could have believed from the apparent calmness with which he took every delay. He bids me say that we shall *certainly* return to Minto. We would have been thankful to go and be miserable there it is still better to go and be happy.

My Father sends off by this day's post a blank signature to my Uncle Lord Corehouse that it may be filled up by form of immediate resignation, so that not a moment may be lost. We have indeed had kind friends.

Pray have the goodness to return the enclosed, for we should like to send it to Matt.[102]

By the middle of October Mrs Stewart was able to write to Minto herself to express her almost incoherent gratitude to him and Lord Lansdowne (though it seems likely that the influence of Palmerston, then still a Tory, was no less crucial).

Important kindness that saves from want is much much but when added to that, there is tenderest, most delicate attentions, unwearied pains to give happiness in every shape – what must we not feel to you both, it gives a sweetness to gratitude that none but the happy few who have experienced such blessings, can ever imagine . . . I must lay down my pen – my heart gets so full. One thing I regret, I am sure Mr S. proposed to himself trying to write a few words to Lord Lansdowne – but it would not do – the more he felt he was the less capable of holding the pen, and I saw by his countenance it would not do. You know him too well to wonder at the agitation, yet I regret the impossibility. Perhaps it may yet be in his power for he is greatly better the last week. I hope to have my Brother here and to get all business matters settled soon.[103]

George Corehouse came to Kinneil on 6 November, and a week later his sister wrote to Lord Minto in more like her usual form:

when [my Brother] did come, it was found a more difficult matter to settle the Patent so as to secure every thing, and name lives *likely* to outlast the period of twenty-one years, than he had forseen. It is settled however, and he hopes, in a way to be satisfactory to Lord Lansdowne... What a blessing that brother of mine is – a very sage remark you will say – yet he had nearly got his bones broken coming here, for his carriage broke down, and they lost 3 hours on the road mending and creeping. And our own old tub has followed the example and smashed, past mending, but 12 years hard work, and not new when we got it may be its excuse. Luckily the servants warned us in time and nobody was in it...

I am sure you will be pleased to know that I have had two very kind notes from Lord Dudley – a few sharp scolds, but kind ones too – and now I hope all shall be well. It makes me happy, for I cannot help loving him.

Saturday. This was begun on Tuesday but rheumatism and business writing kept it in the Drawer... there is no end to my trash. Ever Ever Your gratefully affect.[104]

Another characteristic letter followed in January, when Mrs Stewart felt she might have seemed less than grateful to Minto and Lansdowne for some church appointments about which she had intervened. "You I dare say know not what it is to *remorse*. Alas I often do, and the misery of lying awake *remorsing* for hours, is so terrible. Anything to make amends seems a relief."[105] At the end of January Stewart made his last will.[106]

In spite of all these distractions he had been persevering with the preparation of his final book. Stark the printer had spent a couple of days at Kinneil in June 1827 at Mrs Stewart's urgent request;[107] and in the following spring the job was done. The publisher this time was Adam Black, from whom Macvey Napier obtained the same terms as for Stewart's previous work – namely, 200 guineas.[108] Stewart dated the *Preface* to the two volumes of *The Philosophy of the Active and Moral Powers of Man* from Kinneil House on 16 April 1828. He justified the amount of space devoted to natural religion by reference to the circumstances in which his lectures had been delivered in 1792–3 and thereafter, when "at the dawn of the French Revolution" there had been "a supposed connexion between an enlightened zeal for Political Liberty and the reckless boldness of the uncompromising free-thinker".[109] He expressed his satisfaction at observing a reviving taste for the philosophy of the human mind in France, and the pleasure he had lately derived from an elegant translation by Théodore-Simon Jouffroy of his *Outlines of Moral Philosophy*.[110] (Jouffroy subsequently translated other Stewart texts into French.)

Shortly after the completion of this project, the Stewarts went to

The Last Years (1820–1828)

Newbattle Abbey to stay with the young Marquess of Lothian and his family.[111] They seem to have stopped on the way at 5 Ainslie Place in Edinburgh, for it was from there on 24 April that Mrs Stewart sent a copy of *The Active and Moral Powers* to Lord Palmerston,[112] who soon acknowledged it in terms that gave Stewart great pleasure.[113] "Mr Stewart has a heavy cold but is getting better," she told him. "I have been *very* ill, but am now doing well."[114] They certainly stopped at 5 Ainslie Place on their way back from Newbattle. It was the home of "their friend Mrs Lindsay",[115] and seven doors along the crescent from the house which George Corehouse had recently bought to stay in when in town.[116] There is some mystery about Mrs Lindsay. During the previous year she had become the first owner of this house in the latest phase of Edinburgh's New Town. She is described in the title deeds as "Amy Cruickshank, relict of Alexander Lindsay, Captain, East India Company Marine Service".[117] The records show that Alexander Lindsay had been born near Forfar in 1788, had joined the sevice as a midshipman in 1802, and had made rapid progress up the ranks until in 1818 he had become captain of the new ship *Kellie Castle*. He had made one voyage to China in this capacity, presumably engaged in the tea trade, but failed to complete his second, dying at sea on 25 July 1822, aged thirty-four.[118]

It is possible that his path had crossed that of Matthew in India, and that this was the origin of his widow's friendship with the Stewarts. A more likely explanation is that Mrs Lindsay, *née* Cruickshank, was related to the Cruickshank family with whom they had apparently stayed on at least three occasions at Langley Park. Her own father was Alexander Cruickshank of nearby Stracathro. A Victorian history of County Angus records that members of the Cruickshank family which acquired Langley Park towards the end of the eighteenth century purchased other properties in the area, including Stracathro, so the Stewarts may have known Amy as a relative of the Cruickshanks of Langley Park.[119] Before Captain Lindsay's untimely death, the Lindsays had a son, another Alexander, who would have been six at this time.[120] But the mystery of the Stewarts' connection with Mrs Lindsay is compounded by the fact that in no surviving letter from Mrs Stewart or Maria while they remained at Ainslie Place is any mention made of her and her small son, as if they might not actually have been present. And writing to Lord Lothian after she and her husband had been there for some time, Mrs Stewart said, "You may well be astonished, and were it any mortal but yourself I might add *shocked*, at the liberty we have taken in remaining so long here"[121] – which seems to imply that she felt they were in some way encroaching on *his* tolerance. So the circumstances of their stay at 5 Ainslie Place are unclear.

The Last Years (1820–1828)

But there is no doubt about what happened there, as Mrs Stewart first wrote to Lord Lothian to explain on or about 9 May:[122]

> not a moment of comfort have we had since [we left Newbattle Abbey]. On Monday Mr S. was seized with violent shivering succeeded by high fever – but thank God the fever is lowered and we are *assured danger is over*, though still he is constantly in bed. But I can rely on our Physicians and we ourselves feel he is better tonight . . . One line from you would be a blessing for I am sadly unhappy – address here alas there is no chance of our removing soon.[123]

Three or four weeks later she wrote again to report that they were still at 5 Ainslie Place. The cold wind had brought back Stewart's cough, and she herself had had severe rheumatism in her knee. "Today a west wind gives hopes of better health and soon I trust we shall move."[124] But it was not to be. According to Macvey Napier, Stewart had "been sinking for some weeks",[125] and on 10 June he had a second stroke. Soon afterwards Maria told Palmerston's sister that "for the last twenty-four hours Matthew would not quit my Father's bed but did every thing for him with his own hand".[126] However, love and care could not save him; on the morning of Wednesday the 11th he died, aged seventy-four.

On the following day Maria wrote on black-edged paper to Lord Minto:

> You must before this have heard of our loss. But we know that you and all yours will wish to hear from ourselves that all is calm and tranquil. There was little apparent suffering and what there was thank heaven my Mother did not see, and she now knows that a recovery from *this* stroke would have been the greatest of all misfortunes. It never could have been an existence of any comfort to him – and indeed Dr Thomson says that even before the stroke (which was on Tuesday afternoon) he thought him so much reduced by the fever that there was nothing to be looked for but a protracted struggle between the disease and his constitution. We ought therefore to feel only gratitude that all was so easily and so quickly over.
>
> Mother is too calm as yet but not alarmingly so. I hope she will soon be in a perfectly natural state. She has resolved to return to Kinneil as soon as all is over and says she looks forward to that place as her greatest enjoyment.[127]

A fortnight later Mrs Stewart gave Lord Minto her own account of her husband's end. "Surely none ever had so many mercies – no pain or suffering, the blessed mind tranquil and perfect to the last – all those we could most rely on, watching over him not only as medical men, but with the fondest care and all of them saying, never was Death so worthy of such a life." She added as a postscript, referring to Lady Minto's mother, Principal Robertson's daughter, "Well do I know what Mrs Brydone will feel for her early friend."[128] On Saturday 14 June *The Scotsman* carried a long obituary. It conceded "a want of adventurousness" on Stewart's part in failing to deal with contemporary philosophy, but concluded: "He was a lover of liberty and letters, a scholar, a gentleman, a philosopher, and, beyond all, he was, in the truest sense of the word, a philanthropist."[129] (*The Times* reprinted the opening sentences a few days later.[130]) The Edinburgh evening paper followed suit on Monday the 16th, paying tribute to his "companionable disposition" and total freedom from jealousy or envy.[131]

The funeral took place on Tuesday 17 June. A private procession left Ainslie Place at three o'clock. When it reached the junction of the Bridges with the High Street it was joined by the professors of the University in their gowns, walking in twos with their mace-bearer in front and the Principal at the rear; then came the officers and regalia of the Town Council, the Magistrates and Councillors, and the Lord Provost walking behind. After them came two mutes and the hearse drawn by six horses, with three baton-men on each side of it, and then the mourning coaches and private carriages with Stewart's relations and friends. The procession moved down the High Street to the Canongate Churchyard, where Stewart was laid to rest.[132] Lord Cockburn recorded, "I could not resist going to the Calton Hill and contemplating a ceremony which awakened so many associations."[133]

In London Stewart's death was announced at a large dinner-party at which Sydney Smith was present. His daughter remembered: "The news was received with so much levity by a lady who sat by him, that he turned round and said, 'Madam, when we are told of the death of so great a man, it is usual in civilized society to look grave for at least the space of five seconds.'"[134]

CHAPTER EIGHTEEN

Epilogue

"God knows it is in vain to attempt to suggest to you any grounds of consolation because those who have known you and him as I have done must be fully sensible that greater deprivation never was or could be sustained." Lord Palmerston

Mrs Stewart returned to Kinneil immediately after her husband's funeral. Her brother George, who arrived in Edinburgh on the following day, reported Thomas Thomson as saying "she is exactly in that state which one would wish, calm and composed in her grief, and not only able to support herself but Maria in very trying circumstances". Shortly afterwards she went to stay with George at his Corehouse estate.[1]

The meeting held on 9 July 1828 to consider some means of commemorating Stewart's life was described in chapter 1. Mrs Stewart was naturally gratified by this evidence of the respect in which her husband had been held, but by the beginning of August she was voicing disquiet to Lord Minto.

> I have just learned what grieves me much – that Lord Lansdowne strongly recommends a full-length statue instead of anything architectural – and that it is to be in the College Library. I cannot express my sorrow at the C. Library being fixed on, instead of something to be seen by all – there it is locked up and confined to stupid Professors and ignorant Students – whereas any memorial however simple would have done good to all Scotland.[2]

Epilogue

Thomson, rather to his dismay (he had just been made one of the principal clerks of the Court of Session), had become 'prime mover' in the business, and had been trying to raise more money from Stewart's friends in London.[3] Early in December he told Lord Minto, who had attended the first meeting, that opinion was divided between sculpture and architecture; the latter probably had a majority, and if that view prevailed "it is expected that a very magnificent point at the Calton Hill would be obtained for its site".[4] A further meeting ("not numerous") was held on 8 December. Lord Lauderdale spoke for sculpture and Henry Cockburn for architecture; but on the sculptural side no headway was made when a small-scale model submitted by Samuel Joseph, who offered to do the work for 1500 guineas, was received with "a mortifying silence". In the end a small committee was appointed to ascertain the preference of the subscribers generally for the nature of the monument.[5]

Five months later the question seems still to have been unresolved, for Mrs Stewart had heard of a proposal for "a statue in a small building" to cost £2000;[6] and in the middle of June 1829 a circular was sent to all the subscribers asking for a reply before a meeting on 7 July whether a statue or a building was their choice, and enclosing letters in support of each.[7] The decision – possibly made at this meeting – was in favour of an architectural construction, but a letter from Mrs Stewart to Lord Lothian on 1 January 1830 shows that she was still unhappy. Her original objection, it seems, had not been to the memorial taking the form of a statue but to the suggestion that it should be sited within the University. She now understood that supporters of a public statue had proposed having it done by Bertel Thorvaldsen, of which she would have approved, but the idea had been outvoted. Referring to the monument erected on Calton Hill in 1826 in memory of her husband's friend John Playfair, she wrote that "knowledge of *his* [Stewart's] own opinion as to Mr Playfair's monument, and how much more suitable to the *merits* and *situation* of literary men a statue was, than any building, made *us* of course very anxious".[8] She hoped, therefore, that if the matter was still open, it might yet be reconsidered.

But she and George Corehouse felt that they could not press their own views too hard,[9] and the majority among the subscribers may have been mindful of the difficulty of obtaining a satisfactory representation posthumously. At all events a decision had been made, and the commission was given to the distinguished architect William Playfair, Professor John's nephew. He designed a monument in the form of a small circular Grecian temple based loosely on the Choragic Monument of Lysikrates in Athens[10] which was built in 334 BC in honour of the winner of the annual choral

Epilogue

and dramatic festival, though as *The Scotsman* pointed out at the time it also bears some resemblance to the rather larger St Bernard's Well in Edinburgh's Stockbridge,[11] substituting a cinerary urn for a statue. Foundation work began about the beginning of April 1831 [12] and the monument was completed by the end of the year. *The Scotsman* reported on 21 December: "This structure being now finished in all its parts, the eye can judge of its proportions, design, and effect. It is simple, pure, and classical in taste, yet spirited and striking. The situation it ocupies is extremely fine."[13] And there it still stands, a prominent landmark on Calton Hill, thus perhaps at least fulfilling Mrs Stewart's desire that it should do good to all Scotland.

For some years, however, it carried no writing.[14] At the end of 1853 Lord Palmerston, who never ceased to feel involved with Stewart and all that related to him, wrote to the judge and former Lord Advocate Lord Rutherfurd, a close friend of Playfair the architect, reminding him –

> of the Inscriptionless Stewart Monument the purpose of which is now made known only by tradition, and is learnt by a stranger only by Inquiry of the first ragged urchin he meets with on the Calton.
> Would not a short Inscription in English be better than a long Eulogium in Latin[?] would it not be enough to say something like this. To the memory of Dugald Stewart Professor of Moral Philosophy at the University of Edinburgh who was born – and who died – this monument was erected by his admiring Fellow Countrymen.[15]

In the event the inscription around the base of the monument records only Stewart's name and the dates of his birth and death. Even in the middle of the nineteenth century this may have seemed sufficient, although a hundred and fifty years later it may be little less baffling to "a stranger" than complete inscriptionlessness.

Apart from the monument, a recurrent theme in Mrs Stewart's correspondence in the months following her husband's death was anxiety about the mental state of Matthew. "It is like a miracle how well *M.* is now," she wrote to Lord Minto a fortnight after Stewart's death. "If it but lasts – he was very grateful, and how much so poor Mia is, for your kind letter to him."[16] A few weeks later Matthew was corresponding sensibly with Macvey Napier about his father's papers – chiefly amendments to the *Dissertation*.[17] He must also have lost little time in organising the erection of a monumental tomb for his father in Canongate Kirkyard, for it bears the date 1828. Above the door words are inscribed in Latin which translate roughly (for they are now very worn) as "His son and daughter, his surviving children, have in mourning dedicated here a tomb to a most beloved father of the highest character."[18]

But at the beginning of 1829 Mrs Stewart told Lady Minto that she dared not name a day for a visit; "O that we were out of this purgatory, but dependent as we are on M. – poor fellow nothing is so uncertain."[19] From her letter to Lord Lothian on new year's day 1830 it would appear that Matthew's peculiarities took the form of unreasonable resentment or suspicion towards others. Almost incoherently she wrote:

> O that I could see you and say what cannot be written, one thing I may venture, that if the strongest most anxious remonstrances *can* open eyes blinded but in one instance they are not and shall not be spared. All that is painful proceeds from distracted affection on the one hand, the gratitude and love where they are so deservedly due, is all that can be wished, and I hope and trust that time, and hearing *truth*, will obliterate every mistake.[20]

In his will Stewart had left to Matthew all his books and manuscripts. The sole exception was the copyright of his final publication, *The Philosophy of the Active and Moral Powers of Man*, which he left to Maria, probably in acknowledgement of her work on this book as amanuensis.[21] Perhaps partly because of his role as his father's literary executor, Matthew at once published a memoir of his father, extending to some 4,000 words, which he dated 1828.[22] He must from the outset have intended to produce a more extensive account of his father's life. In May 1829 his mother told Lord Minto of letters between Stewart and Francis Horner which Matthew meant to publish, adding "M. has a strong feeling of horror for improper disclosures and anecdotes".[23]

Stewart also left to Matthew his land and estate at Catrine, and it was there that Matthew made his home – not in the original house which had belonged to his great-grandfather, but in an extensive, two-storey dwelling with a large library[24] which he built "on a very commanding position"[25] some distance upstream from the village. It no longer exists, and the grounds which Matthew laid out around it are now occupied by a garden centre and caravan site. Between 1826 and 1831 he wrote a number of pamphlets about Indian affairs, and he became a Fellow of the RSE,[26] but his state of mind still caused anxiety to his mother and sister. In March 1832 Mrs Stewart wrote to Lady Minto referring to Maria's "vexation about the endless cause – her B.[;] he writes that he has been very ill and *privately* complains of neglect of servants I see. She would fain go to him but I *cannot* consent."[27] Yet as so often happens in cases of mental instability his condition was variable. Five months later Mrs Stewart was able to report, "*He* is wonderfully well just now and esteemed by all his neighbours – but to her [she had been speaking of Maria] his very love makes him a tyrant."[28] Maria's close relationship with her brother made the situation especially trying for her. In July 1833 Mrs Stewart wrote that Mia's heart was broken with distress. "He (M) went to London hoping some employment and is of course disappointed and cannot, poor fellow, guess the reason why. *She* is the victim."[29]

In a letter of 1834 Matthew was sufficiently lucid to express a cogent criticism of Maria Edgeworth's last novel, *Helen*.[30] In June of that year Leonard Horner visited him, and reported: "He was very hospitable, and is a clever and agreeable man, with a vast fund of information on many subjects. He seems to lead a very active life, both as a country gentleman, and in literary occupations."[31] With his father's papers around him he succeeded in putting together what he described as *An Account of the Life and Writings of Dugald Stewart, together with all his Correspondence. Among others with Madame de Staël, La Fayette, Jefferson, and many other literary and well-known characters, French and English; with Anecdotes from his Journals kept during his residence in Paris, before and at the commencement of the Revolution, and during his visits to that city with Lord Lauderdale, during the Fox Administration*.[32] But in March 1837 – during which year he became a full colonel through seniority – he wrote to a publisher who had undertaken to make the existence of this work known within the publishing world:

> You need not, however, farther trouble yourself on this head; because, finding myself getting on in life, and despairing of finding a sale for it at its real value, I have destroyed the whole of it. To this step I was much induced by finding my locks repeatedly picked during my absence from home, some of my papers carried off, and some of the others evidently read, if not copied from, by persons of whom I could procure no trace, and in the pursuit or conviction of whom, I never could obtain any efficient assistance from the judicial functionaries.[33]

He proceeded to list the works in question, and against the decription just quoted of his *Account of the Life and Writings of Dugald Stewart* he added emphatically: "*All of which I burnt.*"[34] When the recipient of this letter published it after Matthew Stewart's death he observed, "I believe there was no foundation for Colonel Stewart's suspicions respecting his locks having been picked";[35] and this belief was endorsed by Sir William Hamilton when he edited Stewart's *Collected Works*.[36]

Hamilton offered as a possible explanation for what he called so rash a proceeding that "when on professional sevice in India, he had suffered from an attack of coup-de-soleil; a malady which, I believe, often mani-

Epilogue

fests its influence in the most capricious manner, and long after an apparent disappearance of the affection".[37] In Sir Walter Scott's late novel *The Surgeon's Daughter* it is said of his character General Witherington that "he had a coup de soleil in India, and is capable of anything in his fits", and that "even his reason became occasionally shaken by anything which violently agitated his feelings".[38] Scott, of course, may have heard about Matthew Stewart, but at this time various illnesses, especially those affecting the mind, were attributed to the effects on the brain of the tropical sun. Medically this no longer makes sense. During his years as a young man in India, before British women went out there, army men consorted freely with local women, and a possible and indeed not unlikely explanation of the irrational delusions apparent in Matthew is syphilis.[39] At all events his destructive action is attested by his own words, and the loss of the insights into his father's character and opinions which these papers might have provided is irreparable.

An inventory of Stewart's estate was appended to his will after his death. The total valuation – mostly in bank accounts, and exclusive of his property at Catrine – was £5,762 11s 8d, a sum approaching £300,000 in modern terms. (The inventory included "20 dozen of Madeira wine".) With the exception of the bequests already mentioned, and a few portraits left to Matthew, everything went to Mrs Stewart. Stewart left to his spouse and daughter jointly, and then to the survivor, the income from his Gazette sinecure.[40] He could not leave them Kinneil House, for they were there as tenants of the Duke of Hamilton; but Mrs Stewart and Maria continued to live at Kinneil for about six further years.

At first, of course, there was a period of mourning, though it was allayed by family and friends. Mrs Stewart wrote from Corehouse to Lord Palmerston at the end of July 1828:

> I am better in health, and Maria as usual, only thinking of me and her Brother tried to forget her own grief. She is beginning to get stronger too ... We (Maria and I) are with my kind Brother, and my Sister – so that all that can be done for our comfort is attended to. But why should I talk of comfort. Our grief is so purely selfish, we are happy. Never was a Death so suitable to so virtuous and exemplary a life – and then the esteem and love that have followed him and the devoted attachment of some who knew him best, and whom he loved tenderly – it is all so sweet, it would be a crime not to be thankful.[41]

But this philosophical mood must have been hard to maintain, as Palmerston perhaps realized. "God knows," he replied, "it is in vain to attempt to suggest to you any grounds of consolation because those who have known you and him as I have done must be fully sensible that a greater deprivation never was or could be sustained."[42] Shortly afterwards Mrs Stewart confessed to Lord Minto, "I pray to be grateful, and hope I shall in a little time – but grief is selfish – and the days are so long, and the nights longer."[43] She and Maria were at Minto after Christmas,[44] and from there she wrote to Charles Babbage, who had recently suffered the loss of his wife and had sent his condolences:

> As for me I should be the most ungrateful of creatures if I were not conscious that for 38 years none ever enjoyed such perfect happiness. Yet selfish human nature shudders at present misery and dwells on the past. But I hope I am resigned. O that I may be worthy to join him. Soon the appointed years of my life must pass. For the sake of my Daughter who was her Father's delight, his companion, and support, life is in some respects valuable to me, – and we try mutually to console each other.[45]

Later in January the Stewart ladies were with the Hendersons at Warriston.[46] In the summer of 1829 they went to Glasgow to the Bannatynes,[47] and from there to Rothesay, where Maria's health benefitted greatly by sea bathing.[48] They spent the winter of 1829–30 in the south of England – certainly at Brighton[49] and at Southampton, where they spent some time until Peter Miller's wife, who had been seriously ill, was able to receive them in Exeter.[50] Christmas 1830 found them at Bowood House, where the Marquess of Lansdowne invited Tom Moore to have dinner with them;[51] after that they spent some weeks in Bath.[52] At the end of the year they were in Glasgow, probably with the Bannatynes, and about to go again to Corehouse.[53] One August Mrs Stewart was in London for a few days, and made contact with Charles Babbage.[54]

Remembering her Christmas at Bowood six years later, Maria observed to Lady Mary Elliot, who had just made a similar visit, "It would not be like a Minto Christmas. I have been at Bowood at this season and even then when all was health and youth and happiness there was none of the bright merry young faces that it gladdens one's heart to remember dancing with the servants, romping, acting, giving and taking enjoyment in all possible ways at dear dear Minto."[55] Lord Minto and his wife seem to have been especially kind and considerate to Stewart's widow and daughter. All ten Elliot children, the youngest set of whom were known collectively as "the Bairns", regarded them as virtually part of the family, and Mrs Stewart became an honorary grandmother.[56] While she was in Bute a year after Stewart's death she received a long letter dictated by Charlotte (Lotty), the second youngest of the five girls, to her older sister Fanny which began:

Epilogue

My dear sweet Mrs Stewart
   Is Aunt Maria well? Maria used to give us coffee and sugar, my lovely, sweet, dear darling Mrs Stewart . . .[57]

Mrs Stewart acknowledged to Lady Minto "my *dear sweet lovely letter*", saying "It is long since I laughed, or saw Maria laugh, with such heartfelt glee, as on reading it."[58] To Lotty she wrote, "Maria bathes in the sea every day. A whale sometimes comes to look at her, but she says she likes them."[59] When in England in February 1831 Mrs Stewart was much stimulated by the opportunity to please William, the eldest of the family, who held the courtesy title of Lord Melgund and was then at Eton with his brother Henry.

My dear William
   Granny Stewart was a very happy Granny when she heard from Sister Mary [the eldest daughter] that the dear Eton boys wished for a mutton ham. The first plan was to get it from Scotland, for there is no denying that everything from that part of the world is better than elsewhere – but then if it came by a coach the carriage would be terribly high and if by sea, the ship might sink, or the rats might eat the Ham. So I enquired here, and a Lady Duncan (a Scotch Lady) assured me she had got mutton ham at Bath *almost* as nice as in Edinburgh and I went myself to the Shop and bespoke it and gave the direction and sent a man with it who booked it and I was promised it should go safe, and the price of Carriage be reasonable. It went last night the 16th by the Company's Coach addressed to Lord Melgund at Mrs Hallancey's, Eton, Windsor. Glad shall I be if it is good – but as writing a letter even to Granny S. would be a dull job, I only ask that the first time either of you write to Paris, you will say it was a good ham, for if it is not, woe to the fine Shopkeeper who vouched for its merits . . . Adieu my dear boys – Maria sends her best love to you both. Your affect. Granny Stewart.[60]

The ham duly arrived, "a capital present", and was duly acknowledged by the future 3rd Earl of Minto – "quite as good as if it had come from Scotland".[61] He still remembered the incident nearly six years later.[62]

But the Stewart ladies' intimacy with the Minto family was about to be interrupted. When Gilbert Elliot had succeeded to his father's title he allied himself with the Whig party in the House of Lords, and in August 1832, after Lord Grey had become Prime Minister, he was appointed British ambassador in Berlin, and took his family with him. They were there for two years, and soon after that posting ended the Earl was appointed First Lord of the Admiralty and they lived at the Admiralty in London. Lady Mary Elliot wrote to "Granny Stewart" after their first Christmas away from Scotland to assure her that she had not been forgotten at that season. "It is impossible that the time of our play and our many follies should go by without bringing again before us all that we have done at home and all those who were with us. It is a very long time since Maria and Father Time acted together but it is all so distinct still sometimes I can fancy it has but just happened."[63]

She gave news of all her brothers and sisters, including "your own Doddy", and Mrs Stewart did her best to keep in close touch through correspondence. "You are so very good in answering all our letters to you when we really do not expect or deserve it," Mary Elliot wrote in November 1833;[64] but of course the children were growing older and changing. Mary wrote to Maria at the beginning of 1835: "much of our Minto life must always bring you and your dear Mother before us, and tho' the bairns you left us are now old and much less agreeable, we are still the same at the bottom of our hearts, and we seem to have grown up loving you and feeling you belong to us, so as to prevent the years that pass making you more strangers to us."[65]

Fanny Elliot tried to persuade Mrs Stewart and Maria to visit them in Berlin ("you both like travelling very much, and it is quite an easy journey with excellent inns all the way");[66] but Mrs Stewart was now in her late sixties and her health was not good. "Maria and I have both had a sickly season," she told Palmerston in January 1833, referring to bad colds.[67] Yet when she learned two months later of the death in Liverpool at the age of forty-six of Matthew Miller, the youngest of Janet's family, leaving a widow and three small children, she invited them all to come to Kinneil for some months so that they could let out their house for a while. Perhaps she hardly knew what she was letting herself in for. "I am rather enfeebled with the fears and sorrows of past months," she wrote to the Mintos in July, "and at present what an old neighbour used to call *damnified* by the noise of 3 noisy spoild children . . .".[68] The eldest of these, however, may have touched her heart, for he had been given the name of Dugald Stewart Miller. (He became Captain Dugald Miller of the North Yorkshire Rifles, living until 1914, and his son and grandson both bore the same name.[69])

During the first part of 1833, also, two old family servants had died at Kinneil – the housekeeper, and Robert, the servant who had ridden Stewart's pony to Portobello for him nearly twenty years before: "his last day," Mrs Stewart wrote to the Mintos, "he expressed pleasure that *I* happened to be from home, for it would have vexed me to know he suffered pain."[70] No doubt all these things were in Maria's mind when she wrote to Lady Minto saying that her mother had "been sorely worried and wearied of late with many things". Maria felt that what would

Epilogue

comfort her most would be if she could go and rest at Minto if Lady Minto, in Berlin, would allow this.[71] It seems very likely that she did, but in the following year Mrs Stewart was reporting "constant severe pain", and worried about the effect on Maria of the constant need to look after her.[72]

It must have been just before or during 1834 that the ladies decided the time had come to leave Kinneil House.[73] They moved to No. 9 Brighton Crescent, Portobello – still a seaside town outside Edinburgh, as it had been when Stewart, on at least two occasions while living at Kinneil, had used it as a base for conducting business in the city. The houses in Brighton Crescent – now East Brighton Crescent – are solid two-storey stone-built double villas which were put up in the 1820s facing, at the east end, a little grassy park. There are small gardens at front and rear. No. 9 is half of one such dwelling, with three astragalled windows in the upper floor and two beside the front door at ground level. It is a quiet area, but only five minutes' walk from Portobello High Street, with the beach a further short distance beyond that. However much smaller in scale than Kinneil House, their new accommodation must have been considerably more convenient for Mrs Stewart and her daughter.

The elderly lady was beginning to fail. In August 1836 Thomas Campbell, on a visit to Edinburgh, recorded calling, on a Saturday evening after dinner, on Dr William Alison, the elder son of Stewart's old friend, and finding him –

> waiting for me with an open barouche, to accompany me to Mrs Dugald Stewart's at Portobello, two miles out of town. It was a great trial to see Mrs Stewart. I sat with her some twenty minutes, with my hand between her's, and her daughter on one side, and Margaret Alison on the other. Her mind is not gone, but depressed, since her husband's death . . . She looked and spoke to me with her ancient motherly smile; but she had not strength to say much.[74]

However, she and Maria continued to benefit from the watchful care of their friends. In 1836 the income from the Gazette sinecure temporarily fell off, and Lord Palmerston was able to arrange a new civil list pension of £200 a year for Mrs Stewart.[75] But during that year Maria, now in her early forties, had a fright. She became seriously ill, and for the first time it struck her as possible that she might die before her mother; what would become of Mrs Stewart then? As soon as she recovered she asked their solicitor, one of the Glasgow Bannatynes, to draw up a will; but when she suggested that he might be an executor and Lord Corehouse another, he advised her that she should look for someone younger than her uncle and

Epilogue

closer at hand than himself who could, if necessary, establish a trust for her mother's care.[76] Although George Corehouse actually lived until 1850, Maria saw that the advice was sound.

With the Earl of Minto now spending most of the year in London, her thoughts turned to her distant relative Lord Lothian. The 7th Marquess had been much preoccupied in recent years with his own family affairs. In July 1831 he had married a daughter of the Earl of Talbot, and their first son had been born in 1832; his stepmother had died in the following year, and a second son had come along after that. As a result, personal contact with Mrs Stewart and her daughter seems to have been relatively slight. When Mrs Stewart wrote to congratulate Lord Lothian on the birth of his son, of which he had written to tell her, she admitted to some frustration that she, "to whom your happiness was more deeply interesting than it would be to any one in Scotland", had not yet – though only through "accidental circumstances" – met the Marchioness.[77] "We had a kind call from Lady Lothian yesterday," she told the Marquess in March 1835, "but I did not see her for she would not light – indeed she stopt but a minute."[78] However, Maria now wrote and explained the situation to him.

> I have looked round me in vain and can find no one who lives at all near this to whose care I could trust my mother with confidence if I were taken away but *yourself* and Dr Alison. Will you permit me then to name you as one of my Executors if my mother survives me? If she does not everything goes of course to my brother and there is no will needed. I *hope* you may never therefore be called on to act if you do consent to be named. It would be dreadful to think she was left without me – but the only consolation if it is to happen, would be that she was left to the care of those she loves and trusts.[79]

Lord Lothian replied promptly and generously.

> Pray make me an Executor. Tho' I say this without hesitation do not think I accept the office without feeling all its responsibility. You grant I may not be called upon [to] act but if contrary to the course of nature your mother should lose you, I will if I live fulfil to the best of my ability the duty I should owe to the survivor of the two truest and best loved friends of my parents.[80]

Early in 1837 Maria told Lady Mary Elliot that she was "threatened with the loss of sight";[81] but "the course of nature" was not upset – or if it was, it was only through the Marquess himself dying in 1841, aged forty-seven. By that time, however, Mrs Stewart was no longer alive.

The Stewart ladies were not able to see the Minto family when they

Epilogue

came to Scotland in the summer of 1837, and in all probability this was due to Mrs Stewart's declining health. Fanny Elliot wrote to Maria in March 1838: "We had looked forward to seeing you and dear Granny Stewart at Minto last summer and then how glad we should have been to make you re-acquainted with the children whom you can now only know by name, altho' they fancy that they know you quite well."[82]

On 28 July 1838 Mrs Stewart died at Warriston House, the home of her husband's niece, Margaret Henderson. She was seventy-three years of age, and had survived her husband by ten years. Her funeral took place on 3 August, when she was buried beside Dugald in Canongate Churchyard. Maria stayed in Ann Street for a day or two afterwards with Andrew Dalzel's daughter Mary,[83] described by Mrs Stewart a few years before as "the best of little things".[84] Shortly afterwards a tribute appeared in the Edinburgh newspapers which had been written by her old admirer, Thomas Campbell.

> The friends of Mrs Stewart who lament her loss are very numerous; perhaps no individual has departed from life, within the memory of those who knew her, more deeply regretted... She was favoured in her power of doing good by her situation in society. The wife of Dugald Stewart, a Philosopher in the highest rank of literary reputation, she was looked up to with a respect inferior to none that was paid to intellect, rank, or power. When she was in the zenith of her life, it may be doubted, if a person departing from Scotland could have carried a stronger recommendation into the intellectual world of England or America, than a letter of introduction from Mrs Dugald Stewart. She was the habitual and confidential companion of Dugald Stewart during his studies, and he never considered a piece of his composition to be finished until she had reviewed it...
>
> In her youth, she was stately and handsome, – in her latter life, a certain benignant expression in her eyes continued to retain her peculiar image in the memory of her friends. To the last, she was remarkable for a winning gentleness of manner, – a meekness more impressive than austerity, by which during her whole life, she had exercised greater influence on those around her than others could do by an assumption of dignity. Her last hours, nay, her last days and months, were serene, and free from suffering.
>
> This slight tribute of affectionate respect for her memory... has been prompted by a strong desire, that one so rare, one so remarkable for every feminine grace, should not pass away from among us, without a word to tell the rising generation of what her influence was, in the very remarkable society of which Edinburgh could at one time boast.[85]

Lord Minto wrote an affectionate letter of condolence to Maria, and said she must now think of Minto as *her* home.[86] Lord Lothian suggested

Epilogue

she might like to walk in the peace of Newbattle Park,[87] which it was now possible to reach from Edinburgh by train. (Portobello Sation was just round the corner from Brighton Crescent.) Maria replied saying "how sweet it is to me to receive kindness from your Father's family and to feel that they whom my Father and Mother so truly loved continue to be my friends".[88] When she replied to Lady Minto, who had written in similar terms to her husband's, she said:

> I will add all I have as yet fixed with my Uncle L[ord] Corehouse, that I shall have a small home somewhere near Edinburgh where my furniture books &c can be easily removed and where my old servants will be, and where I myself can at all times find *perfect quiet*. My first occupation after the painful arrangements for sorting and burning papers &c will be to look for such a spot. And this is perhaps the best occupation I can have . . .[89]

But in fact 9 (East) Brighton Crescent, Portobello continued to be Maria's home for the rest of her life. Her parents had left her comfortably off, and she inherited the income from the Gazette. She may have travelled a little. Certainly in the spring and early summer of 1844 she was in London, staying for at least part of the time with her old friend Lady Katherine Halkett.[90] From Lady K.'s home in Wimpole Street she wrote one day in May to the Countess of Minto:

> We were in town on Thursday forenoon and returning through the Park I caught a glimpse of one bright face as your coach drove past my sober fly. But I could not say *which* it was – ?Lotty's I think. But it was a happy face that I saw. Long long may your present health and true heartfelt happiness be yours dearest Lady Minto. How sweet it is to see those we love aware of all the blessings they enjoy and feeling them as you do.[91]

Her words carry a hint of loneliness, as by implication she thinks of times that had been so very different. Maria Stewart died in Harrogate on 10 August 1846,[92] aged fifty-three.

Matthew, also unmarried, was still living at Catrine. His will had left everything to his sister, but if she and his stepmother predeceased him his property was to be divided among his cousins.[93] However, a codicil in June 1836 emphatically deleted Andrew and Dugald Bannatyne, the sons of Dugald Bannatyne, now postmaster. Evidently Matthew had become seriously disaffected from this branch of his family; the Bannatyne brothers were both solicitors, and Matthew may have suffered from delusions about their conduct of his affairs. In a further codicil, made shortly after Maria's death, he certified "that my father's manuscripts are destroyed and that I destroyed all my own written manuscripts and threw

Epilogue

into the fire (with the intention to destroy) all my own memoranda . . . " Yet he continued to take a proprietary interest in his father's published writings; in 1846 he brought an action for breach of copyright against A. & C. Black for publishing the *Dissertation* as a separate work.[94] Veitch observed that "even during the clouded years of the latter portion of his life" he cherished his father's memory "with a feeling akin to idolatry".[95] He gave his father's library, and his own, to the United Service Club in Pall Mall, London, "to be preserved entire".[96]

He also prescribed in his will that when his sister and he had been buried in the tomb in the Canongate Kirkyard which he had built for his father, "the door of the said tomb shall be strongly built up with stone and lime so that no other person may ever be buried there . . . after my death and interment there thenceforward for ever". His wishes were evidently carried out, and it remains the only sealed tomb in Canongate Churchyard. Col. Matthew Stewart died in 1851, but not before completing the census return at the end of March of that year. He appears there as a bachelor of sixty-six years of age and a half-pay Colonel in the British Army living in Catrine House in the parish of Sorn. There were four female servants in the house.[97] To the end of her life Mrs Stewart had loved Matthew dearly, but one is tempted to hear her voice adding, "poor fellow".

The day of her own death was exactly a month after the coronation of Queen Victoria. A new age was beginning, and the ideas which Dugald Stewart and his contemporaries had developed and expounded were being overtaken by new science, new methodologies and new ways of thinking. Yet this did not happen suddenly. Stewart remained an influential figure in philosophy for three or four decades after his death. Most of his works were translated into French, and in France and Spain he was widely influential.[98] For almost a century the Scottish school of common sense philosophy as represented by Reid, Stewart, Brown and Hamilton was dominant in American academic thought.[99] Thomas Jefferson rated Stewart among "the ablest metaphysicians living". Ralph Waldo Emerson, who in 1821 graduated from Harvard where Stewart's work was used as a text until 1837, wrote an undergraduate prize essay on the subject.[100] Nathaniel Hawthorne read the *Philosophical Essays* in 1827; and William James, born in 1842, reported himself as having been, at an early stage in his interest in philosophy, "immersed in Dugald Stewart".[101]

In this country Thomas Carlyle told his brother John in August 1828, "Dugald Stuart is dead, and British philosophy with him."[102] John Stuart Mill records in his *Autobiography* how, in the 1830s, an idea of Stewart's which he came on when reading his chapters on reasoning for the second

Epilogue

or third time with the closest attention proved the key to solving a point of logic which had long perplexed him.[103] In the summer of 1847 Lord John Russell and his wife (the former Lady Frances Elliot), who usually had a book on hand which they read together, occupied themselves with some of the writings of their old friend Dugald Stewart.[104] "There were four men," Lord Cockburn wrote in his journal in 1850, " who in my time have made Scotland illustrious – Dugald Stewart, Walter Scott, Thomas Chalmers, and Francis Jeffrey."[105]

At this time Stewart was still a sufficiently prominent figure for a collected edition of his works to be mooted.[106] The task of editing them was given by Maria Stewart's trustees to Sir William Hamilton, the unsuccessful candidate for Stewart's old chair after the death of Thomas Brown. He had been Maria's own first choice for the job.[107] Hamilton was now professor of logic and metaphysics at Edinburgh University. He died in 1856 before completing the task, which was taken over by his young assistant, John Veitch, who later became professor of logic, rhetoric and metaphysics at St Andrews and subsequently professor of logic and rhetoric at Glasgow.

In the *Collected Works* were included all of Stewart's writings that were published during his lifetime with the exception of his pamphlet on the Leslie affair. Hamilton decided also to reconstitute as accurately as he could Stewart's course on political economy. It was known that "during the latter years of his life, he had revised, corrected, amplified and rearranged its constituent parts" with a view to publication. In accordance with the terms of his will, Maria had handed over to her brother seven manuscript books in which the corrected version of the lectures was written out. Before doing so, she took a copy of the table of contents, but by the time Hamilton undertook his task this copy was almost all that remained, for the manuscripts were among the papers that Matthew destroyed. Hamilton was therefore obliged to work from Stewart's original lecturing papers, most of which were still extant, supplemented by notes taken by a few of his surviving students. The most helpful of these were the work of two men who had both become Writers to the Signet, James Bridges and John Dow; they were taken in shorthand and written out afterwards. At the time, Stewart told them "he would take it for granted we would not publish our notes", but Bridges now felt that by giving them to Hamilton he was "discharging a duty to his memory and to the public". Hamilton was also given a copy of Francis Jeffrey's notes from 1802, but found them impossible to decipher! However, he became satisfied that what he was able to reconstruct, in two volumes, was "eminently worthy of publication".[108]

Epilogue

Veitch incorporated in the eleven volumes of the *Collected Works*, which were published by Thomas Constable and Co. between 1854 and 1860, the short life of Stewart which has been occasionally referred to in this book. Born in the year after that of Stewart's death, he did not find the biographical task easy, or, perhaps, entirely congenial, "but," he told a friend, "I have sought to do justice to his general merits, which I believe to be very great."[109] Veitch expressed thanks for their help to Dr Peter Miller of Exeter, Dr W. P. Alison, the family of Dugald Bannatyne of Glasgow, and to Mrs Romilly of Liverpool, "the intimate friend of Miss Stewart".[110] Mrs Romilly was probably Elizabeth, the third daughter of the Earl of Minto, who married a Lt.-Col. Romilly.

Stewart's reputation as a teacher also survived for many years. As late as 1872 a writer in the *Edinburgh Review* observed that "as a public lecturer he was, and has remained, without a rival".[111] The *Collected Works* were reprinted in 1877. But by then Stewart's heyday had passed. The concept of a "philosophy of the human mind" had become outdated, and more specialist studies were replacing the broad sweep of his kind of literary writing. In the nature of things the prominence in public life of men whom he had taught and influenced – the disciples whom Sir James Mackintosh considered to be among his best works[112] – was also passing; but the record was impressive. As was noted in its place, all four founders of the *Edinburgh Review* had attended Stewart's lectures, and in varying degrees acknowledged the inspiration he had given them. One of them, Henry Brougham, was prominent along with Thomas Campbell and others in establishing the University of London, and its foundation council included six of Stewart's one-time students.[113] Another former student, John Ramsay McCulloch, was London's first professor of political economy, and yet another, John Hoppus, was its first professor of the philosophy of mind and logic.

The administration formed by Lord Grey in 1830 which introduced the Reform Act included Brougham as Lord Chancellor, Palmerston as Foreign Secretary, and the Marquess of Lansdowne, who had special responsibility for drafting the Bill, as Lord President of the Council. All three continued to serve under Lord Melbourne, and so in due course did Lord John Russell as Home Secretary. Russell's own first cabinet in 1846 included the Earl of Minto as Lord Privy Seal as well as Lansdowne and Palmerston, while Russell and Palmerston successively led the Liberal Party in the House of Commons for more than thirty years and were both Prime Minister in the 1860s. As Professor Haakonssen has recently suggested, these men "clearly demonstrated the point that politics was now for men of intellect as well as for men of property".[114] They retained a lively sense of Stewart's principled moderation, love of freedom and zeal for improvement as a formative influence on their political outlook and the causes they advocated throughout their careers. Veitch was hardly exaggerating when he wrote in the late 1850s:

> From the class-room of Stewart there have gone forth almost all the men whose names are now, after half a century, familiar to this generation as having helped forward the cause of liberal politics, some by their personal influence merely, others by their writings as well, and not a few by their splendid exertions on the field of practical statesmanship. The internal history of Britain, during the past half century, is in great measure the record of the slow but secure prevalence of the political principles of Smith and Stewart . . .[115]

When that generation passed on, the name of Dugald Stewart meant little for a hundred years. The later Victorian perception of him as a kind of bland belle-lettrist persisted. His works, in the words of F. D. Maurice, "it behoved all who were completing a liberal education to read, and all who were forming a library to buy. They were written in a graceful style; they excited no prejudices in any school, political or religious. All critics commended them . . . They were unsatisfactory only to the man who wished to know what he was, whence he had come, whither he was going. They were *about* philosophy; they were not inquiries after wisdom in one direction or another."[116]

But since the early nineteen-seventies there has been an upsurge of interest in the Scottish Enlightenment – an interest which is not confined to Britain, but extends to North America, Australia and Japan. With it has come a revival of interest in Dugald Stewart. He was, as Dr George Davie said to the writer in conversation, "a very cautious chap"; you have to read him carefully to see what he is getting at. If you do, as Dr Michael Brown and others have recently been arguing,[117] you find a considerably more radical and interesting figure than Maurice believed. It has also come to be recognized that in a significant sense it was Stewart, in his biographical essays and in his seminal passage in the *Dissertation,* who invented the notion of a Scottish school of philosophy, and thus determined the terms of a debate about it which has continued ever since. Professor Paul Wood, Director of the Humanities Centre at the University of Victoria in Canada, has declared that the impact of these works "on subsequent scholarship has been enormous". At the end of a literature survey, written in the year 2000, he concluded:

> even though William Robert Scott can be credited with coining the term

Epilogue

"the Scottish Enlightenment", the core element of our conception of the central actors, the formation of their leading ideas, and the social and institutional frameworks that promoted the thought of the Scottish "school" are effectively the creation of Dugald Stewart.[118]

In 1994 the Thoemmes Press of Bristol brought out a reproduction edition of Stewart's *Collected Works* with an introduction by Professor Haakonssen, then of the Australian National University, in which he declared that Stewart "had become a European cultural institution by the time of his retirement in 1810".[119] Professor Broadie's 1997 *Anthology* includes two extracts from Stewart's writings.[120] More recently still the American Arthur Herman, in his book on *The Scottish Enlightenment – the Scots' Invention of the Modern World*, remarked that "We are still waiting for a single definitive study or biography of Stewart . . . Dugald Stewart languishes in a scholarly limbo."[121] It is hoped that this book does something to repair that gap. The story of Stewart's active and useful life, imperfectly though we can now know it, is a significant part of the cultural history of Scotland, and indeed of Britain and the western world.

Supplement A
THE WRITINGS

Chapter 14 surveyed the evidence about the impact of Stewart's lectures on his students. Although this book is concerned primarily with his life, it seems appropriate to include some survey of the content of his work as reflected in his writings. He himself rather pointedly remarked: "the few incidents which diversify a philosopher's life derive their whole interest from the light they throw on the history of his studies, and on the progress of his mind."[1]

Although Stewart's publications are referred to individually in the preceding chapters, it may be useful to provide a comprehensive list with a brief indication of their contents where this is not obvious from the title. Many of his works had several subsequent editions, but they are given here in the order in which they originally appeared, or, in the case of the biographical memoirs, were first read. (The compilation of all but one of them as *Collected Works* is described in the chapter 18.)

1792 *Elements of the Philosophy of Human Mind, Vol. I* is an analysis of man's intellectual faculties. It is divided into seven chapters, which deal respectively with how the mind perceives external objects; attention, including a variety of mental processes; conception (the power to form a notion without perception); abstraction (classification on the basis of common qualities); the association of ideas; memory; and imagination.

1793 *An Account of the Life and Writings of Adam Smith*

1793 *Outlines of Moral Philosophy* is essentially a textbook. Its aim was to provide students with the framework of Stewart's philosophy lectures so that in delivering his course he might have more time for illustrative material. Set out in relatively short numbered paragraphs, the book tackles its theme in three parts: the intellectual powers of man (covering ground similar to the first of his published works); the active and moral powers of man (see below); and man considered as a member of a political body. The final part was later replaced by a brief table of contents, since its substance had been subsumed in Stewart's lectures on political economy.

1796 *An Account of the Life and Writings of William Robertson*
1802 *An Account of the Life and Writings of Thomas Reid*
1805 *A Short Statement of Facts relative to the late Election of a Mathematical Professor in the University of Edinburgh* (see chapter 12). This work was not included in the *Collected Works*.

1810 *Philosophical Essays* comprises ten essays, the first of which is a general attempt to counter prevalent errors in the philosophy of the human mind. The next four deal respectively with the work and influence of Locke, with Berkeley's idealism, and with the theories of Hartley, Priestley and Erasmus Darwin. The sixth is concerned with philology. The last four, constituting the second part of the volume, are on aesthetics, dealing with the nature of the beautiful and the sublime, and with the acquisition of taste.

1812 *Some Account of a Boy born Blind and Deaf* (see chapter 15).

1814 *Elements of the Philosophy of the Human Mind, Vol. II*, "particularly intended for the use of Academical Students",[2] is essentially about logic. It discusses at length the nature of mathematical axioms; laws of belief; intuition; reasoning and language; mathematical proofs; probable or contingent truths; the evidence respectively of experience, of analogy and of testimony; the use and abuse of hypotheses; and the place of final causes in science and in the philosophy of the human mind.

1815 *Dissertation on the Progress of Philosophy and the Revival of Letters*. This lengthy work was originally written in two parts for inclusion respectively in the 1815 and 1821 editions of the *Encyclopaedia Britannica*; it was later printed as a single volume. In the preface Stewart explains his intention to confine himself to the philosophy of mind, ethics and political philosophy, though in practice the emphasis is heavily on the first of these fields. The critical survey which follows is concerned almost entirely with the seventeenth and eighteenth centuries in Europe, and includes a detailed section on "the Metaphysical Philosophy of Scotland".

1827 *Elements of the Philosophy of the Human Mind, Vol. III*. The first section of this volume concerns language – the natural language of bodily gesture, communication through non-linguistic signals, and the origins of speech. The second deals with how we learn from the appearance and conduct of others. The third considers the varieties of character associated with different intellectual pursuits, and the fourth discusses instinct and reason in man and in animals. (The volume also reproduces the papers concerning the boy born blind and deaf.)

1828 *Philosophy of the Active and Moral Powers of Man*. This two-volume work presents an expanded version of the second section of the *Outlines of Moral Philosophy*. It deals with the instinctive principles of action (appetites, desires, affections); the moral faculty, and principles which cooperate with our moral powers; free will; proofs for the existence of God and his moral attributes; arguments for immortality; and man's duties to God, to his fellow-ceatures and to himself, with particular reference to happiness and virtue. Of this and the preceding publication Lord Cockburn wrote, "they are so tinged with his lectures, that I cannot read them without thinking I hear his pleasing voice".[3]

Lectures on Political Economy (published pothumously – see chapter 18). The two volumes which comprise this work cover the relationship between population and the economy; national wealth, including freedom of trade; principles of taxation; the maintenance of the poor; the education of the lower orders; and theory of government.

Although even this brief summary indicates that the range of subject matter is wide, the synopsis still conveys an inadequate impression of the scope of Stewart's interests. With the exception of the *Outlines of Moral Philosophy*, his philosophical writings are leisurely and discursive. They include digressions and illustrations drawn from classical and 'modern' literature, science, medicine, aesthetics, philology, political theory and several other fields. Sir James Mackintosh felt that Stewart's writings could not be summaized because they were so much distinguished by illustrations and the expression of delicate feelings: "such beauties are crushed in the attempt to compress them."[4] Clearly no shadow was cast over the writer's shoulder by any publisher or editor concerned about a word-count. Stewart was enormously well read (the Library of Edinburgh University now holds his personal library, and it extends to some 4,000 books),[5] and on every topic to which he turns he refers to the views of several earlier and sometimes now rather obscure writers in the field, often quoting from them at length. (Not infrequently the quotations are in French or Latin, and occasionally in classical Greek; only very rarely, in the original publications, does Stewart provide a translation.)

The practice of philosophical writers expounding their views by arguing against or developing those of other thinkers is of course a familiar one. Indeed it cannot be avoided, for philosophers do not work in isolation, and much of what they say can be understood only in historical context. Stewart's writing is notable for the calm and confident manner in which he expresses his qualifications or dissent. The writer whom he cites most frequently is his old friend and mentor Thomas Reid. Often he does so with approval, and even when he expresses some disagreement, or points to the need for a more precise formulation of the view propounded, he does so with evident diffidence. He also makes many and respectful references to David Hume. Other writers, however, can be dealt with quite sharply. Thus, for example: "It is difficult to suppose, that a person of mature years, who had read and studied Locke and Berkeley with as much care and attention as Condillac appears to have bestowed on them, should have reverted to this ancient and vulgar prejudice [that perception is natural and not acquired], without suspecting that his metaphysical depth has been somewhat overrated by the world."[6] And even: "Aristotle's demonstrations amount to nothing more than a specious and imposing parade of words."[7] D'Alembert, Cudworth, Erasmus Darwin,

Supplement A – The Writings

Hartley, Priestley, Price and Horne Tooke are all dealt with – at least in respect of some of their writings – in similarly magisterial fashion.

Yet his contemporaries were not blind to certain weaknesses. Sydney Smith wrote of the *Dissertation* when he had just read it:

> it is totally clear of all his defects. No insane dread of misrepresentation; no discussion put off till another time, just at the moment it was expected, and would have been interesting; no unmanly timidity; less formality of style and cathedral pomp of sentence. The good, it would be trite to enumerate: – the love of human happiness and virtue, the ardour for the extension of knowledge, the command of fine language, happiness of allusion, varied and pleasing literature, tact, wisdom, and moderation! Without these high qualities, we all know Stewart cannot write.[8]

A few years earlier a writer in the *Quarterly Review* had listed faults in Stewart's writing very similar to those noted by Smith:

> we still feel ourselves bound in duty to state, that Mr Stewart is often faulty in not sufficiently developing and connecting his ideas; that he often contents himself with hints and loose general remarks, when the subject required full and continuous elucidation; and that he rarely condescends to assist his reader by concisely stating the sum of what he proposes to prove, and the grounds and limits of his argument. His style is remarkable for its purity and elegance; for its harmonious flow and uniform majesty; but it is somewhat too diffuse and oratorical for pure metaphysical discussion; though it must at the same time be admitted, that it has lent graces and attractions to metaphysical inquiry which few writers have ever been able to communicate.[9]

To the list of demerits might be added an aspect of the "diffuseness" noted by a commentator on Stewart's political economy at the end of the nineteenth century (quoted here in spite of its admonitory message): "he is too much given to quotation, even when there is nothing in the passage cited which might not as fitly have proceeded from his own pen".[10] An anonymous reviewer of the *Philosophical Essays* suggested that Stewart's "tendency to diffuseness, and to an unnecessary copiousness of illustration" may have been a habit produced by lecturing to immature students; but it was still seen as a flaw.[11] When Thomas Carlyle told a friend that he had been reading the second volume of *Philosophy of the Human Mind*, he observed: "The greater part of the book is taken up with statements of the opinions of others; and it often required all my penetration to discover what the Author's own views of the subject were."[12]

This is a feeling which many readers of Stewart must share, though if one considers what Stewart's own response might have been, an indication perhaps lies in a quotation from Cicero that he included in one of his writings and that translates thus:

They who inquire of what opinion I myself am upon every point, are actuated by a principle of needless curiosity. For in discussion, the grounds of determination are to be sought for not so much in authority as in reason. But, besides, the authority of those who profess to teach, commonly proves a hindrance in the way of those who seek to learn; for these cease to exercise their own judgment, holding as established what they see already determined by him of whom they approve.[13]

However, Stewart may occasionally have sensed that he was open to criticism on this score. One question which he raised with his students of political economy he described as "a subject of extreme difficulty, and I am much afraid that what I have to state will tend more to invalidate the reasoning of others, than to establish any satisfactory conclusions of my own".[14]

Carlyle suggested in the *Edinburgh Review* that "his writings are not a Philosophy, but a making ready for one".[15] But in fact judgments do fall fairly readily from Stewart's pen, though often, as has been noted, in the form of comment on the writings of others. It is true that a favourite phrase is to speak of his throwing out "hints" about his subject-matter. This may seem like a form of self-defence ("I could have stated my position more fully, and would then have met the objections that may occur to you"); but the implication usually is that the hints, if not wholly comprehensive, may be taken as pretty authoritative. Common phrases are, "It is scarcely necessary for me to observe . . . ", and "A moment's reflection (or consideration) will show . . . ": few, one feels, would be so crass as to offer any disagreement from the pronouncement which follows. His English contemporary Dr Samuel Parr referred to Stewart as "one whom I am proud to call my friend, because he has explored the deepest recesses, the most complex qualities, and the remotest tendencies of human action; because, to the researches of philosophy he adds the grace of taste; because with powers commensurate to the amplitude and dignity of his subject, he *can*, and he also will state without obscurity, reason without perplexiy, assert without dogmatism, instruct without pedantry, counsel without austerity, and even refute without acrimony."[16]

Stewart's style is never clumsy, though it can be somewhat stilted. He seems to have had a standing joke with his friend Ancram about the avoidance of Scotticisms. "I was very anxious you should have seen it before it was sent to the press," he wrote to him about the *Dissertation*, "as I was ambitious to give the London Authors a faultless model of pure *English*."[17] In his *Life of Robertson* he discussed at some length the disadvantage in achieving good style of "the provincial residence of a Scotsman".[18] But in reviewing that book, the *Edinburgh* detected in his prose style the tendency to "lull into reverie" which Francis Horner discovered in his lectures. "The stream of his diction rolls on with admirable smoothness, sometimes with considerable rapidity, and with great variety of windings, though unbroken in its course. Its sound changes from time to time in loudness. The music is always grateful, often charming; but sometimes its effect is to lull, rather than to raise attention."[19]

Indeed it is hard not to feel that there is some justice in the remark attributed to the connoisseur of ancient art, Richard Payne Knight, that all Stewart's lives are somewhat *lifeless*.[20] As the *Edinburgh Review* justly remarked of the *Life of Robertson*, "We meet neither with striking anecdotes, nor discriminative touches, nor fine descriptive sketches."[21] Stewart might of course have responded that he was not attempting that kind of biography; he wrote that he sought "to avoid . . . those frivolous or degrading details which, in the present times, are so frequently presented to the public by the indiscretion of editors".[22] He made similar comments in his *Life of Reid* about the potentially misleading nature of anecdotes in biography.[23] It has indeed been argued that his biographical essays are essentially an extension of his total philosophical design.[24]

The "excessive timidity" which Horner noted in Stewart's lectures concerning the issues of the day also had a parallel in his writing, as Sydney Smith implied. Samuel Romilly told a friend that Stewart excluded some letters from his *Life of Robertson* "because he thought they might scandalize his pious and loyal countrymen".[25] He seemed to many of his contemporaries to have retained an eighteenth-century illusion that philosophers and political economists could remain above and detached from everyday politics and controversy. Though he lived through Pitt's introduction of an income tax, he disavowed any intention of examining this fiscal innovation "as I am always unwilling to touch upon any questions which are connected with the political discussions of our times".[26] He showed little interest in contemporary German philosophy, and did "not not pretend to be an adept in the philosophy of Kant",[27] ascribing his reputation largely "to the imposing aspect of his enigmatical oracles",[28] and confessing his own "utter inability to unriddle the author's meaning".[29] (Though as Stewart did not read German he was obliged to struggle with Kant in a Latin translation and in what Kant himself wrote in Latin,[30] which cannot have made comprehension any easier.)

Had Stewart himself been asked what he regarded as the most distinctive feature of his philosophy, he might well have replied in terms of its method and approach. He was anxious to dissociate philosophy from what he termed "the vain and unprofitable disquistions"[31] of mediaeval metaphysicians. For him, "it shall ever be my study and my pride to follow the footsteps of those faithful interpreters of nature, who, disclaiming all pretensions to conjectural sagacity, aspire to nothing higher than to rise slowly from particular facts to general laws."[32]

This is the method of induction, and Stewart ascribes to it "the rapid progress which physical knowledge has made since the time of Lord Bacon".[33] Francis Bacon and Isaac Newton may indeed be seen as the principal founders of the 'modern' way of thinking, and to their writing and example Stewart frequently recurs. "Bacon's philosophy . . . was constantly present to my thoughts," he writes, "when I have dwelt in any of my publications on the

Supplement A – The Writings

importance of the Philosophy of the Human Mind."[34] Newton's discovery of the law of gravity, which unified men's perception of the physical universe through a coherent, experimentally supported theory, provided a model for a similar transformation of the philosophy of the mind.

> the first step in the study of Philosophy is to ascertain the simple and general laws on which the complicated phenomena of the universe depend. Having obtained these laws, we may proceed safely to reason concerning the effect resulting from any given combination of them.[35]

This approach led Stewart to a belief in the essential unity of the various branches into which philosophy might be divided – logic, ethics, aesthetics, political science, and so on. Indeed, "all the pursuits of life, whether they terminate in speculation or action, are connected with that general science which has the human mind for its object".[36] Reid and Stewart were both firm in their belief that matter and mind are totally different: a mental action cannot be explained in physical terms. But in specifying how the philosophy of the human mind is to be pursued, he makes the analogy with the physical sciences very clear.

> As all our knowledge of the material world rests ultimately on facts ascertained by observation, so all our knowledge of the human mind rests ultimately on facts for which we have the evidence of our own consciousness. An attentive examination of such facts will lead in time to the general principles of the human constitution, and will gradually form a science of mind not inferior in certainty to the science of body.[37]

Stewart credits his old teacher Thomas Reid with being the first to apply this method of observation and reflection in analysing our various mental powers[38] – what Reid once referred to as "the constitution of the mind".[39]

Stewart's disciple Francis Jeffrey respectfully questioned the comparison of Reid's method with that of Bacon. Observation, he contended, may lead to knowledge becoming more systematic, but most of the advances in knowledge deriving from Bacon's approach were due principally to experiment, where phenomena are within man's power to control. Yet observation is the only way in which we can study the phenomena of the human mind, and therefore he doubted whether much advance in our knowledge of them can be achieved.[40] Stewart responded robustly to this criticism. He denied that there is any intrinsic difference between observation and experiment, and he also disputed the assertion that the philosophy of the human mind depends solely on observation: experimental work had in fact been conducted on aspects of vision and perception, and it could also be applied to attention, association, habit, memory, imagination and above all the use of language.[41] "The whole of a philosopher's life, indeed," he writes in one of his works, "if he spends it to any purpose, is one continued *series of experiments* on his own faculties and powers."[42] Moreover, human life naturally presents a boundless variety of intellectual and moral phenomena which may be studied in place of contrived experiments.

From the last point it is not difficult to understand the nature of Stewart's interest in history, which was also that of David Hume: it presents a kind of case study of human nature at work. A revealing comment occurs in his *Life of Robertson* when he refers to that historian's handling of the character of Mary Queen of Scots and the degree of guilt which may be imputed to her, adding that this "is a subject which I have never examined with attention, and which, I must confess, never excited my curiosity. Whatever judgment we form concerning the points in dispute, it leads to no general conclusion concerning human affairs, nor throws any new light on human character."[43]

In other words, the mere facts of history are of little interest unless they attest to what Hume called "the constant and universal principles of human nature".[44] The search for general principles had led writers such as David Hume and Adam Smith to a form of hypothesis for which Stewart suggests the term 'theoretical or conjectural history': for "when we cannot trace the process by which an event *has been* produced, it is often of importance to show how it *may have been* produced by natural causes".[45] The role of conjectural history is to explain how the transition from rude to advanced societies took place.

Stewart cites as an example of this method of proceding the speculations of Adam Smith about the development of speech from "the first simple efforts of uncultivated nature" to "that systematical beauty which we admire in the structure of a cultivated language".[46] Stewart himself included philology among the wide range of his intellectual interests, and his search for a natural history of language was characteristic of the Enlightenment. He anticipates more recent semiology by distinguishing "between the sign and the thing signified".[47] Very little, he believes, is to be gained by tracing a word's historical progress through successive meanings:

> We speak of *communicating*, by means of words, our ideas and our feelings to others; and we seldom reflect sufficiently on the latitude with which this metaphorical phrase ought to be understood. Even in conversing on the plainest and most familiar subjects, however full and circumstantial our statements may be, the words which we employ, if examined with accuracy, will be found to do nothing more than to suggest *hints* to our hearers, leaving by far the principal part of the process of interpretation to be performed by the Mind itself . . . our words, when examined separately, are often as completely insignificant as the letters of which they are composed; deriving their meaning solely from the connexion, or relation, in which they stand to others.[48]

Prompted perhaps in part by the writing of his friend Archibald Alison on the subject of 'taste', Stewart was also interested in what we should now call aesthetics. He writes at length about theories of beauty and the sublime. His own view is that beauty is not a quality that resides *in* objects, but that they appeal to our senses as the result of a process of association.[49] Sound taste he believes to be closely connected with love of truth and nature, and with good sense: indeed "The intellectual efforts by which such a taste is formed are, in reality, much more nearly allied than is commonly suspected, to those which are employed in prosecuting the most important and difficult branches of the Philosophy of the Human Mind."[50]

Taste does not consist in sensibility alone, for it is "susceptible of improvement from culture, in a higher degree, perhaps, than any other power of the mind".[51] A higher level of taste is achieved by study of approved models of excellence, and powers of discrimination are acquired through habits of observation and comparison. Taste should be modified by reason, so "a susceptibility to Beauty does not necessarily imply the power of Taste"[52] – indeed extreme sensibility may make correct taste impossible. Cultivation of the imagination in childhood through fiction and poetry is the best way of making it subject to reason in later life.[53] Those with cultivated taste are the most likely to recognize the worth of a new work and to produce good work themselves.[54]

Any modern reference to Stewart as a philosopher is likely to describe him principally as a member of the Scottish "common sense" school. Apart from its failure to do justice to the breadth of his intellectual interests, this is somewhat ironic, for one respect in which Stewart dissented from his mentor Thomas Reid was in pointing out that Reid's use of the term "common sense" was misleading. Reid's concern had been to mount a defence against the 'scepticism' of David Hume, who argued persuasively that while we cannot do without our natural beliefs, they are essentially a construct of our imagination and cannot be supported rationally. Not only is this an uncomfortable philospical position, it appeared to undermine the basis of natural religion and morality, and Reid, as a Christian minister, could not find this acceptable.

Reid's counter-argument is that there are certain beliefs which are the foundation of all reasoning and science: they serve the philosopher as self-evident axioms do the mathematican – in Stewart's words, "their truth is supposed or implied in all our reasonings".[55] Because all men share these beliefs, they can be called our "common sense". Stewart endorses this view, which may have appealed to him particularly in view of his background – similar, in fact, to Reid's own – as a mathematician; but he feels that since "common sense" is used in everyday speech to mean something like "mother wit", it would be more appropriate to refer to the philosophic axioms as "fundamental laws of human belief". Neither Reid nor Stewart attempts to set out a comprehensive list of these; but the examples Stewart gives are belief in our own existence and continuing identity ("I am the same person today that I was yesterday"), in the existence of other intelligent beings besides ourselves, in the independent existence of the material world, in the evidence of memory and in belief that the general laws of nature will continue in future to operate uniformly as in time past. These are not principles from which our reasoning takes off, he argues, but essential elements of reason itself.[56] Reid and Stewart also felt compelled to dissent from Hume's ethical views. Hume regarded moral rules as merely conventional, virtuous because of their general usefulness. Although Adam Smith had rejected this picture of morality and criticized Hume's utilitarianism, he argued that the formation of our morality arises from social approval and disapproval. For Reid and Stewart these positions placed morals on too relative a basis to sustain sound standards of behaviour. Stewart in particular is very strong on the absolute nature of morality:

> the power of distinguishing *right* from *wrong* is one of the most remarkable circumstances which raise man above the brutes . . . the constitution of our nature determines us to conceive the distinction between Right and Wrong as Eternal and Immutable; not as arising from an arbitrary accommodation of our frame to the qualities of external objects, like the distinction between agreeable and disagreeable tastes or smells, but as a distinction necessary and essential, and independent of the will of any being whatever, – analogous in this respect to that between mathematical truth and falsehood.[57]

How we perceive right and wrong is analogous to our perception of primary qualities such as shape and size, which we are convinced are separate and independent.[58] If there appears to be a conflict of duty, we must use our reason to resolve it.[59] And having made this judgment about what is right, why should we do it? "It is absurd . . . to ask *why* we are bound practice virtue. The very notion of virtue implies the notion of obligation."[60] Thus Stewart is no utilitarian (as Madame de Staël let out a "scream of joy" to be told):[61] it is intention that counts.

Stewart was well aware of another argument which appeared to support a more relativist view of morality. This was the evidence which had plentifully emerged in the eighteenth century of differing customs in other lands and other periods. William Robertson had written a history of the early inhabitants of America; Stewart had a number of travel books in his library; he refers to the observations of Captain Cook;[62] he knew Mungo Park; and at one point he mentions conversing with Captain Bligh of *The Bounty*, whom he describes as "one of the most intelligent travellers of the present age".[63] But he denies that evidence of diverse practices proves the subjectivity of morals – that man is "entirely a factitious being, that may be moulded into any form by education and fashion": proper allowance must be made, he claims, for the different circumstances of mankind in different periods of society, their different beliefs, and "the different moral import of the same action, under different systems of external behaviour".[64] All his arguments about morality are based on the firm assumption of free will: man can choose between good and evil. This belief, as he points out, is (like the fundamental laws of human belief) "agreeable to the common apprehensions of mankind".[65]

He also identifies "certain principles which co-operate with our moral powers in their influence on the conduct".[66] These include a regard for the good opinion of others, our desire to avoid appearing ridiculous, and the cultivation of our moral taste. They also include the sympathy we feel for other people's joys and sorrows. This results from the power of our imagination, and it ought therefore to be a prime aim of education to stimulate the imagination; providing children with well selected works of fiction is a good way to do this.[67]

Stewart holds, in the natural law tradition, that there are three divisions of duty – to the Deity, to our fellow-creatures and to ourselves.[68] He follows Thomas Reid in expressing an Enlightenment belief that virtue reflects our true humanity – a denial of Hobbes's "state of nature". Among our duties is "a steady regard, in the conduct of life, to the happiness and perfection of our own nature, and a diligent study of the means by which these ends may be obtained".[69] The happiness in question is not, of course, selfish pleasure pursued for its own sake, but that which rewards the person "whose ruling principle of action is a sense of duty" and who "conducts himself in the business of life with boldness, consistency and dignity".[70]

Reference was made in the preceding paragraph to "the Deity", and Stewart devotes a good deal of space to discussing the arguments for the existence of such a being. It does not seem to him to be an intuitive truth: it requires the use of reason, but the process is really a fairly simple one. Everything which begins to exist must have a cause, and a combination of means conspiring to a particular end implies intelligence.[71] He finds the argument from design to be convincing,[72] and evidence that the design is a benevolent one attests to the moral attributes of God.[73] Nor does he see creation as a single act: "the divine power is constantly exerted to produce the phenomena of the material world".[74] It is noticeable, however, that in his writings Stewart seldom uses the word "God"; when he does not speak of "the Deity" he employs expressions such as "the Supreme Being", "the Creator", "the Author of Nature". These sound more like a metaphysical concept than the personal, loving God of orthodox Christianity: it is the Enlightenment God of rational religion. Also interesting to observe is that in the tradition of classical humanism Stewart is as likely when he wishes to illustrate a moral point to cite Cicero as any Christian writer.

In his course on political economy Stewart discussed the merits and demerits of various forms of government. He argues elsewhere that the principles of jurisprudence lie midway between ethics and law. The rules of justice can be expressed in two ways – as a system of duties, the province of the moralist, or as a system of rights, the province of the lawyer. The rights and the obligations correspond to each other. But jurisprudence should not be regarded merely as a system of natural justice. Political considerations cannot be excluded, and so the subject really comes into the area of man as a member of society, and is concerned with general principles of justice and expediency.[75]

The final aspect of Stewart's thinking which deserves some notice is his attitude to education. Again, this was an Enlightenment preoccupation, for it was thought to be through education that men are enabled to see clearly where their duty lies and so achieve true happiness. Although Stewart did not address education as a major theme, his writings are sprinkled with ideas about it. Education was, after all, the business in which he was engaged throughout his professional life, and he had brought up three children of his own. He describes with some pride the Scottish system of parochial schools, as a result of which –

> the means of a literary education, and of religious instruction, were in Scotland placed within the reach of the lowest orders of the people, in a greater degree than in any other country of Europe; and the consequences have been everywhere favourable to their morals and industry; while the opportunity which has thus been afforded to gentlemen of moderate fortune, and to the clergy, to give an education to their children, at so easy a rate, in the elements of literary knowledge, has bestowed on this part of the United Kingdom a political importance, to which it was neither entitled from the fertility of its soil, nor by the number of its inhabitants.[76]

In the late 1790s Stewart was a visitor to New Lanark,[77] where David Dale's progressive theories of schooling were put into practice, and he became interested in the pioneering work of Joseph Lancaster, to which Francis Horner drew his attention.[78] He considered the most important part of the philosophy of the human mind to be the light which it throws on intellectual and moral education.[79] He makes the following general statement on the subject:

> The most essential objects of education are the two following: First, to cultivate all the various principles of our nature, both speculative and active, in such a manner as to bring them to the greatest perfection of which they are susceptible; and, secondly, by watching over the impressions and associations which the mind receives in early life, to secure it against the influence of prevailing errors, and, as far as possible, to engage its prepossessions on the side of truth.[80]

The second of these aims is one that seems to have loomed large in Stewart's mind: "the correction of one single prejudice," he writes, "has often been attended with consequences more important and extensive than could be produced by any possible accession to the stock of our scientific information".[81] The first of his objectives is what we might now call self-realization, and advocates of adult education may be cheered by his observation that "it is never too late to think of the improvement of our faculties".[82] Children's education, he says elsewhere, should be accommodated to those turns of mind to which they have a natural tendency;[83] and again, "the great aim of education is not to thwart and disturb, but to study the aim, and to facilitate the accomplishment of her beneficial arrangements".[84] In another context, reflecting perhaps the influence of such contemporaries as Maria Edgeworth and her father:

> I only wish to impress on all those who have any connexion with the education of youth, the great importance of stimulating the curiosity, and to directing it to proper objects, as the most effectual of all means for securing the improvement of the mind: I may add, as one of the most effectual provisions that can be made for the happiness of the individual, in consequence of the resources it furnishes when we are left to depend on ourselves for enjoyment . . .[85]

Nothing is of greater importance than "to keep the curiosity always awake".[86] Some of his practical prescriptions for achieving this have a remarkably modern ring:

> I cannot help, therefore, disapproving greatly of a very common practice in this country, that of communicating to children general and superficial views of science and history by means of popular introductions. In this way we rob their future studies of all that interest which can render study agreeable, and reduce the mind, in the pursuits of science, to [a] state of listlessness and languor . . . It would contribute greatly to the culture and the guidance of this principle of curiosity, if the different sciences were taught as much as possible [by] accustoming the student to the proper method of investigation; and thereby preparing him in due time to enter on the career of invention and discovery. Nor is this all. It would impress the knowledge he thus acquired, in some measure by his own ingenuity, much more deeply on his *memory*, than if it were passively imbibed from books or teachers.[87]

It is a broad-based education which Stewart advocates. Without this, as Josiah Walker recorded Stewart as saying as early in his career as 1779, the man who is *only* a mathematician, a metaphysician or a chemist "is but an intellectual tradesman".[88] Just as the body needs a variety of exercises, "a variety of those occupations which literature and science afford, added to a promiscuous intercourse with the world, in the habits of conversation and business, is no less necessary for the improvement of the understanding".[89] He considers that there are two opposite extremes in which men may err "in preparing themselves for the duties of active life".

> The one arises from habits of abstraction and generalization carried to an excess; the other from a minute, an exclusive, and an unenlightened attention to the objects and events which happen to fall under their actual experience. In a perfect system of education, care should be taken to guard against both extremes, and to unite habits of abstraction with habits of business, in such a manner as to enable men to consider things, either in general or in detail, as the occasion may require . . . When theoretical knowledge and practical skill are happily combined in the same person, the intellectual power of man appears in its full perfection . . .[90]

Thus "a perfect system of education" should produce that Enlightenment ideal – the rational man who is also a man of the world.

Supplement B
Stewart's Written Words

The short extracts from Stewart's writings which comprise this section have not been selected to demonstrate salient aspects of his philosophy. Rather they have been chosen from a biographical point of view to illustrate his style, the range of his interests, and his opinions on a wide variety of topics. For that purpose their number could easily have been increased.

To avoid unnecessary irritation for the reader no indications have been included to show, in the few cases where this has happened, that a quotation begins part-way through a sentence, that words have been omitted, or that in order to make a passage intelligible a pronoun has been replaced by words from a previous sentence. By definition these extracts are taken out of context, but there has been no distortion of meaning.

National prejudice and the advantages of travel

* A person who has never extended his views beyond that society of which he himself is a member, is apt to consider many peculiarities in the manners and customs of his countrymen as founded on the universal principles of the human constitution; and when he hears of other nations whose practices in similar cases are different, he is apt to censure them as unnatural, and to despise them as absurd. There are two classes of men who have more particularly been charged with this weakness, – those who are placed at the bottom, and those who have reached the summit of the scale of refinement; the former from ignorance, and the latter from national vanity.[1]

* Much may be expected from a change of scene, and a change of pursuits; but above all, much may be expected from foreign travel. The objects which we meet with excite our surprise by their novelty; and in this manner we not only gradually acquire the power of observing and examining them with attention, but, from the effects of contrast, the curiosity comes to be aroused with respect to the corresponding objects in our own country, which, from our early familiarity with them, we had formerly been accustomed to overlook. In this respect the effect of foreign travel, in directing the attention to familiar objects and occurences, is somewhat analogous to that which the study of a dead or of a foreign language produces, in leading the curiosity to examine the grammatical structure of our own.[2]

The ready talker

* It is but rarely we find a man of very splendid and various conversation to be possessed of a profound judgment, or of great originality of genius.[3]

Medicine

* It is seldom, if ever, possible that the description of any medical case can include all the circumstances with which the result was connected; and therefore, how true soever the facts described may be, yet when the concluson to which they lead comes to be applied as a general rule in practice, it is not only a rule rashly drawn from one single experiment, but a rule transferred from a case imperfectly known, to another of which we are equally ignorant.[4]

* Let us suppose that a savage, who, in a particular instance, has found himself relieved of some bodily indisposition by a draught of cold water, is a second time afflicted with a similar disorder, and is desirous to repeat the same remedy. With the limited degree of experience which we have here supposed him to possess, it would be impossible for the acutest philosopher, in his situation, to determine whether the cure was owing to the water which was drunk, to the cup in which it was contained, to the fountain from which it was taken, to the particular day of the month, or the particular age of the moon. In order, therefore, to repeat the success of the remedy, he will very naturally and very wisely copy, as far as he can recollect, every circumstance which accompanied the first application of it. He will make use of the same cup, draw the water from the same fountain, hold his body in the same posture, and turn his face in the same direction; and thus all the accidental circumstances in which the first experiment was made, will come to be associated equally in his mind with the effect produced. The fountain from which the water was drawn will be considered as possessed of particular virtues; the cup from which it was drunk will be set apart from vulgar uses, for the sake of those who may afterwards have occasion to apply the remedy. It is the enlargement of experience alone, and not any progress in the art of reasoning, which can cure the mind of these associations, and free the practice of medicine from those superstitious observances with which we always find it encumbered among rude nations.[5]

The Scotch accent

* In the same manner in which an article of dress acquired an appearance of elegance or of vulgarity from the persons by whom it is habitually worn,

so a particular mode of pronunciation acquires an air of fashion or of rusticity, from the persons by whom it is habitually employed. The Scotch accent is surely in itself as good as the English, and, with few exceptions, is as agreeable to the ear; and yet how offensive does it appear, even to us who have been accustomed to hear it from our infancy, when compared with that which is used by our southern neighbours! No reason can be given for this, but that the capital of Scotland is now become a provincial town, and London is the seat of our court.[6]

* If Scotland, at this period [the latter part of the seventeenth century], produced no eminent authors, it was not from want of erudition or of talents; nor yet from the narrowness of mind incident to the inhabitants of remote and insulated regions; but from the almost insuperable difficulty of writing in a dialect, which imposed upon an author the double task of at once acquiring a new language, and of unlearning his own.[7]

The attributes of God

* It must be granted that there is something peculiarly wonderful and overwhelming in those conceptions of immensity and eternity, which it is not less impossible to banish from our thoughts, than the consciousness of our own existence. Nay, further, I think that these conceptions are very intimately connected with the fundamental principles of Natural Religion. For when once we have established, from the evidence of design everywhere manifested around us, the existence of an intelligent and powerful *cause*, we are unavoidably led to apply to this *cause* our conceptions of *immensity* and *eternity*, and to conceive Him as filling the infinite extent of both with his presence and with his power. Hence we associate with the idea of God those awful impressions which are naturally produced by the idea of infinite space, and perhaps still more by the idea of endless duration.[8]

The case for internationalism

* The more we can unite mankind together by their common interest, the more effectual is the security we provide for the prosperity of the human race. If it is a necessary and inevitable law imposed on all political societies, that they shall have their vicissitudes of good and bad fortune, we may, at least, by a mutual communication of light, of spirit, and of virtue, prevent the extremity of ignorance, of slavery, and corruption. Genius will be always *somewhere* inventive and active for the benfit of the human race; and there will be always some happy corner where the sacred sparks of liberty will be kept alive, ready to rekindle its expiring flame in other nations. In the present state of the *commercial* world, we no longer dread the miseries of famine, because we find that where nature holds her bounty from one quarter, she lavishes it on another. When a more perfect intercourse among nations is established, may we not hope for a similar remedy to those melancholy vicissitudes of fortune to which human affairs have always hitherto been subject?[9]

John Milton

* No poet in our language has shewn so strikingly as Milton, the wonderful elevation which style may derive from an arrangement of words, which, while it is perfectly intelligible, departs widely from that to which we are in general accustomed. Many of his sublime periods, when the order of the words is altered, are reduced nearly to the level of prose.[10]

Rivalry

* Human life has often been likened to a race, and the parallel holds, not only in the general resemblance, but in many of the minuter circumstances. When the horses first start from the barrier how easy and sportive are their sallies, – sometimes one taking the lead, sometimes another! If they happen to run abreast, their contiguity seems only the effect of the social instinct. In proportion, however, as they advance in their career, the spirit of emulation becomes gradually more apparent, till at length, as they draw near to their goal, every sinew and every nerve is strained to the utmost, and it is well if the competition closes without some suspicion of jostling and foul play on the part of the winner.

How exact and melancholy a picture of the race of ambition; of the insensible and almost inevitable effect of political rivalship in extinguishing early friendships; and of the increasing eagerness with which men continue to grasp at the palm of victory, till the fatal moment arrives when it is to drop from their hands for ever![11]

Establishing an academic discipline

* In the infancy of every science, the grand and fundamental *desideratum* is a bold and comprehensive Outline; – somewhat for the same reason, that, in the cultivation of an extensive country, forests must be cleared, and wildernesses reclaimed, before the limits of private property are fixed with accuracy; and long before the period, when the divisions and subdivisions of separate possessions give rise to the details of a curious and refined husbandry.[12]

Philosophy

* When our views are limited to one particular science, to which we have been led to devote ourselves by taste or by accident, the course of our studies resembles the progress of a traveller through an unexplored country; whose wanderings from place to place are determined merely by the impulse of occasional curiosity, and whose opportunities of information must necessarily be limited by the objects which accidentally present themselves to his notice. It is the philosophy of the mind alone which, by furnishing us with a general map of the field of human knowledge, can enable us to proceed with steadiness, and in a useful direction; and while it gratifies our curiosity and animates our exertions, by exhibiting to us all the various bearings of our journey, can

conduct us to those eminences from whence the eye may wander over the vast and unexplored regions of science.[13]

* How small is the number of individuals who are qualified to think justly on metaphysical, moral or political subjects, in comparison of those who may be trained by practice to follow the longest proceses of mathematical reasoning.[14]

* The truth is, that one of the most valuable effects of genuine philosophy, is to remind us of the limited powers of the human understanding; and to revive those natural feelings of wonder and admiration at the spectacle of the universe, which are apt to languish in consequence of long familiarity. The most profound discoveries which are placed within the reach of our researches, lead to a confession of human ignorance; for while they flatter the pride of man, and increase his power, by enabling him to trace the simple and beautiful laws by which physical events are regulated, they call his attention at the same time to those general and ultimate facts which bound the narrow circle of his knowledge, and which by evincing to him the operation of powers, whose nature must for ever remain unknown, serve to remind him of the insufficiency of his faculties to penetrate the secrets of the universe.[15]

Ploughed fields

* I recollect the period when serpentine ridges, in ploughed land, were pretty generally considered in Scotland as beautiful; and if they were equally consistent with good husbandry, I have no doubt that they would be more pleasing to the eye than straight ones. The association, however, which is now universally established between the former, and the ideas of carelessness, sloth, and poverty; – between the latter and the ideas of industry, skill, and prosperity, has completely altered our notions concerning both.[16]

The French

* A person, although totally ignorant of the French language, could scarcely see a company of Frenchmen together, without catching somewhat of their disposition to briskness and vivacity. He would unintentionally, and probably unconsciously, display a propensity to copy in his own movements the most expressive peculiarities in theirs; and in doing so, would experience a state of spirits very different from what is inspired by the sight of a Dutch coffee-house.[17]

* The peculiar richness of the French tongue in appropriate expressions, (a circumstance, by the way, which not unfrequently leads foreigners to over-rate the depth of a talkative Frenchman) is itself a proof of the degree of attention which the ideas they are meant to convey have attracted in that country among the higher and more cultivated classes.[18]

* Nothing is more difficult than for a person who has received his education in one country, to enter into all the asociations which influence the mind of a subject of a different government, or to ascertain, especially on political

subjects, all the combinations of ideas he annexes to his words. One striking proof of this is the imperfect and erroneous notions which the ablest and best instructed French writers have formed of the constitution of England.[19]

Female Beauty

* – the complicated assemblage of charms, physical and moral, which enter into the composition of Female Beauty. What philosopher can presume to analyze the different ingredients; or to assign to *matter* and to *mind* their respective shares in exciting the emotion which he feels? I believe, for my own part, that the effect depends chiefly on the Mind; and that the loveliest features, if divested of their expression, would be beheld with indifference. But no person thus philosophizes when the object is before him, or dreams of any source of his pleasure, but that beauty which fixed his gaze.[20]

The power of language

* In a cultivated society, one of the first acquisitions which children make is the use of language; by which means they are familiarized, from their earliest years, to the consideration of classes of objects, and of general truths; and before that time of life at which the savage is possessed of the knowledge necessary for his own preservation, are enabled to appropriate to themselves the accumulated discoveries of ages.[21]

The power of reflection

* The power of Reflection, it is well known, is the last of our intellectual faculties that unfolds itself; and, in by far the greater number of individuals, it never unfolds itself in any considerable degree.[22]

Weakness of mathematicians

* Of the various mathematicians whom I have happened to be acquainted with, (some of them, certainly, of the first eminence,) I cannot recollect one who was at all distinguished as a player of whist. Many of them, at the same time, were fond of the game, and devoted to it regularly a portion of their leisure hours. But all of them, without exception, were mere novices when compared, not only with professional gamesters, but with such men and women as may be selected to form a card-party from any large promiscuous assembly.[23]

Weakness of lawyers

* The habits of thought which the long exercise of the profesion of law has a tendency to form, on its appropriate topics, seem unfavourable to the qualities connected with what is properly called *judgment*; or, in other words, to the qualities on which the justness or correctness of our *opinions* depends; they accustom the mind to those partial views of things which are suggested by the separate interests of litigants; *not* to a calm, comprehensive and discriminating survey of details, in all their bearings and relations. Hence the apparent inconsistencies which sometimes astonish us in the intellectual character of the most distinguished practitioners, – a talent for acute and refined distinctions; powers of subtle, ingenious, and close argumentation; inexhaustible resources of invention, of wit, and of eloquence; – combined, not only with an infantile imbecility in the affairs of life, but with an incapacity of forming a sound decision, even on those problematical questions which are the subject of their daily discussion.[24]

Joseph Addison and Benjamin Franklin

* Franklin, whose fugitive publications on political topics have had so extraordinary an influence on public opinion, both in the Old and New Worlds, tells us that his style in writing was formed upon the model of Addison: Nor do I know anything in the history of his life which does more honour to his shrewdness and sagacity.[25]

Experience of the past

* I have always thought, not only that a religious veneration is due to such fundamental maxims as the united experience of past ages has proved to be essential to the existence of the social order, but that even prejudices which involve a mixture of sound and useful principles, should seldom or ever be attacked directly; and that the philosopher should content himself with exhibiting the truth pure and unadulterated, leaving it to the operation of time and of reflection to secure its future triumph. In this manner the errors which prevail in the world, whether on political or moral subjects, will gradually decay, without ever unsettling the opinions of the multitude, or weakening the influence of those truths that are essential to human happiness; and the scaffolding will appear to vulgar eyes to add to the stability of the fabric, till, the frail materials mouldering into dust, the arch exhibit its simple and majestic form.[26]

Gender differences

* The intellectual and moral differences between the sexes seem to me to be entirely the result of *education*; using that word in its most extreme sense, to comprehend not merely the instruction received from teachers, but the habits of mind imposed by situation, or by the physical organization of the animal frame.[27]

* In the present state of the civilized world, the scientific or the profesional pursuits of young men, establish very early in their understandings the influence of the stricter and more philosophical principles of association; while the minds of young women, like those of well educated *men* of independent fortune, are left much more open to the effects of casual impressions, and of such associations as regulate the train of thought in a mind which has no particular object in view. To these early habits I think it is owing, that, in general,

women are inferior to well educated men in a power of steady and concentrated attention; or in what Newton called a capacity for *patient thought*.[28]

* It is impossible to name a branch of knowledge in which there have not been female authors of the first eminence. But that these examples are comparatively rare, may be inferred from this, that good sense and good taste invariably dispose women who have made exraordinary attainments in any of the abstract sciences, to draw a veil over them to common observers, as not according well wih the more appropriate accomplishments of their sex.[29]

* Women in general possess a greater *docility* or aptitude to learn than men; a docility much aided by that easy faith in the infallibility of their instructors, which they are led to repose by the deference they are early taught to pay to superior knowledge, and which, it must be owned, too often serves to mislead their confidence.[30]

Avarice

* It is on account of the enjoyments which it enables us to purchase that money is originally desired; and yet, in process of time, by means of the agreeable impressions which are associated with it, it comes to be desired for its own sake, and even continues to be an object of our pursuit, long after we have lost all relish for those enjoyments which it enables us to command.[31]

Perception of evil

* For my own part, I can as easily conceive a rational being so formed as to believe the three angles of a triangle to be equal to *one* right angle, as to believe that if he had it in his power it would be *right* to sacrifice the happiness of other men to the gratification of his own animal appetites, or that there would be no *injustice* in depriving an industrious old man of the fruits of his own laborious acquisitions. The exercise of our reason in the two cases is very different; but in both cases we have a perception of *truth,* and are impressed with an irresistible conviction that the truth is immutable and independent of the will of any being whatever.[32]

Distinction between virtue and judgment of others

* One great cause of the perversion of our nature, is a very common and fatal prejudice, which leads men to believe that the degree of their own virtue is proportioned by the justness and the liveliness of their moral feelings; whereas in truth virtue consists neither in liveliness of feeling, nor in rectitude of judgment, but in an habitual regard to our sense of duty in the conduct of life. To exercise our powers of moral judgment and moral feeling on the character and conduct of our neighbours, is so far from being necessarily connected with our moral improvement that it has frequently a tendency to withdraw our attention from the real state of our own character; and to flatter us with a belief, that the degree in which we possess the different virtues, is proportioned to the indignation excited in our minds by the want of them in others.[33]

Literacy in Scotland and the need for government action

* In England, there cannot be a doubt, that the mass of the community enjoy the comforts of animal life much more amply than in Scotland; and yet, in the latter country, in consequence of the footing on which our parochial schools are established, there is scarcely a person of either sex to be met with who is not able to read, and very few who do not possess, to a certain degree, the accomplishments of writing and of cyphering; whereas, in the southern part of the island, there are many parishes where the number of those who can read, bears a very inconsiderable proportion to the whole body of inhabitants.[34]

* That the influence of education has been great, may be presumed from this circumstance, that although England had obtained the benefits of a regular government at a much earlier period than Scotland, the progress of national improvement was, by no means, so rapid there, or universal. This is particularly striking when we attend to the comparative attainments of the lower orders in the two countries; and it demonstrates, that in the present state of society, the diffusion of knowledge, even when assisted by the art of printing, will not be sufficient to assure the instruction of the lower orders, unless proper arrangements for that purpose are made on the part of Government.[35]

The perversion of idealism

* I have quoted this passage at length, because it illustrates strongly, when considered in connexion with the events which have since taken place in France, the extreme danger of exhibiting such Utopian pictures of human affairs, as may be supposed, by the most remote tendency, to inflame the passions of the multitude. Engrossed with the magnitude of the beneficent ends which they believe themselves forwarding, men lose gradually all moral discrimination in the selection of means; and are hurried by passions, originally grafted on the love of their country and of mankind, into enormities which would appal those ordinary profligates who act from the avowed motives of interest and ambition.[36]

The human face

* It has frequently been observed by writers on physiognomy, and also by those who have treated of the principles of painting, that every emotion, and every operation of the mind, has a corresponding expression of the countenance; and hence it is, that the passions which we habitually indulge, and also the intellectual pursuits which most frequently occupy our thoughts, by strengthening particular sets of muscles, leave traces of their workings behind them, which may be perceived by an attentive observer. Hence, too, it is that a person's countenance becomes more expressive and characteristic as he advances in life; and that the appearance of a young man or woman, though more *beautiful*, is not so *interesting*, nor, in general, so good a subject for a

painter, as that of a person whose character has been longer confirmed by habit.[37]

A girl who used her foot like a hand

* I myself remember to have seen, more than twenty years ago, an Anglo-American girl who was exhibited in Edinburgh, and who supplied, in great measure, the want of a *hand* by means of a *foot*. I recollect, in particular, to have seen her cut watch-papers, of a great variety of patterns, with a pair of scissors, – an operation which she executed with great neatness, and with astonishing rapidity. It may be worth while to add, that in order to preserve entire the sensibility and the pliability of her foot, (which approached very nearly to those of the hand in other individuals,) she had been obliged to give up almost entirely the practice of walking. This might be owing partly to her anxious care of the white leather gloves she wore on her feet, about the cleanness of which she seemed to be finically nice.[38]

True happiness

* If the desire of happiness were the sole, or even the ruling principle of action in a good man, it could scarcely fail to frustrate its own object, by filling his mind with anxious conjectures about futurity, and with perplexing calculations of the various chances of good and evil; whereas he, whose ruling principle of action is a sense of duty, conducts himself in the business of life with boldness, consistency, and dignity; and finds himself rewarded by that happiness which so often eludes the pursuit of those who exert every faculty of the mind in order to attain it.[39]

Happiness and prosperity

* Has *no* change taken place in the aspect of human affairs since the revival of letters; since the invention of printing; since the discovery of the New World; and since the Reformation of Luther? Has not the happiness of our species kept pace, in every country where despotism has not dried up or poisoned the springs of human improvement, with the diffusion of knowledge, and with the triumphs of reason and morality over the superstition and profligacy of the dark ages? What else is wanting, at this moment, to the repose and prosperity of Europe, but the extension to the oppressed and benighted nations around us, of the same intellectual and moral liberty which are enjoyed in this island? Is it possible, in the nature of things, that this extension should not, sooner or later, be effected? Nay, is it possible, (*now* when all the regions of the globe are united together by commercial relations,) that it should not gradually reach to the most remote and obscure hordes of barbarians? The prospect may be distant, but nothing *can* prevent it from being one day realized, but some physical convulsion which shall renovate or destroy the surface of our planet.[40]

Notes and Further Reading

The following references and abbreviations have been employed in the chapter notes.

DS	Dugald Stewart
Mrs S.	Helen D'Arcy Stewart (DS's second wife)
Matthew S.	Matthew Stewart (DS's elder son)
Maria S.	Maria D'Arcy Stewart (DS's daughter)
BA	Broadlands Archive at University of Southampton
BL	British Library
ECA	Edinburgh City Archives
EUL	Edinburgh University Library
NAS	National Archives of Scotland
NLS	National Library of Scotland
RSE	Royal Society of Edinburgh

DS's Writings:

CW	Collected Works, ed. Sir William Hamilton
Diss	Dissertation
EPMH	Elements of the Philosophy of the Human Mind
Life of Reid	{ Account of the Life and Writings of
Life of Robertson	{ Thomas Reid, William Robertson, DD,
Life of Smith	{ Adam Smith, respectively
OMP	Outlines of Moral Philosophy
PAMP	Philosophy of the Active and Moral Powers
PE	Philosophical Essays
Pol Econ	Lectures on Political Economy

Works frequently referred to:
Cockburn, *Memorials*
   Lord Cockburn, *Memorials of his Time*, Edinburgh, 1856.

MRUE
A. Morgan (transcriber), *Matriculation Roll of the University of Edinburgh – Arts – Law – Divinity*, Edinburgh, 1862.

M. Stewart, *Memoir*
M. Stewart, *Memoir of the late Dugald Stewart, Esq.*, Edinburgh, 1828.

Veitch, *Life*
J. Veitch, *Life of Dugald Stewart* , 1858, in *Collected Works of Dugald Stewart, Vol. X.*

DNB – Dictionary of National Biography (The DNB is the source for numerous biographical details about people mentioned in the text; to avoid a proliferation of references the DNB has not usually been specifically cited except where there is a direct quotation.)

Preface

1 M. Stewart, *Memoir of the late Dugald Stewart, Esq.* (Edinburgh, 1828). Hereafter: M. Stewart, *Memoir*.
2 J. Veitch, *Life of Dugald Stewart*, 1858, in Sir W. Hamilton (ed.), *Collected Works of Dugald Stewart, Vol. X* (Edinburgh, 1854–8). Hereafter: Veitch, *Life*.
3 Lord Cockburn, *Memorials of his Time* (Edinburgh, 1856). Hereafter: Cockburn, *Memorials*.
4 *Dictionary of National Biography, Vol. 54* (London, 1898).
5 Veitch, *Life, Preface*; CW X, p. iii.
6 See *Preface* to B. Connell, *Portrait of a Whig Peer* (London: André Deutsch, 1957).
7 DS: *Life of Reid, Section I*; CW X, p. 245.
8 William Robertson junior, Rev. Archibald Alison, William Drennan, Andrew Dalzel, Lord Ancram (the 6th Marquess of Lothian).

I Who Was Dugald Stewart?

1 *Edinburgh Evening Courant*, 10 July 1828.
2 This term appears to have been first used in 1900 in W. R. Scott, *Francis Hutcheson: His Life, Teaching and Position in the History of Philosophy* (Cambridge: Cambridge University Press). It gained general currency during the last third of the twentieth century.
3 Prof. Broadie (*The Scottish Enlightenment*, Edinburgh: Canongate, 2001) suggests that it was "a period of a few decades on either side of 1760"; *The Scottish Enlightenment* (Edinburgh: Saltire Society, 1986), edited by D. Daiches, P. Jones and J. Jones actually carries the dates *1730–1790* in its title. Some would extend it forward by a decade or two.

4 DS: Diss, Part Second, note 5; CW I, p. 551.
5 DS: Diss, Part Second, DectionI; CW I, p. 216.
6 D. J. Withrington, *What was Distinctive about the Scottish Enlightenment?* in J. J. Carter and J. H. Pittock, *Aberdeen and the Enlightenment* (Aberdeen: Aberdeen University Press, 1987).
7 "Edinburgh is a hot-bed of genius." – T. Smollett, *The Expedition of Humphry Clinker* (1771); Matthew Bramble to Dr Lewis, Edinburgh, August 8. Other often quoted testimony comes from the Englishman, Amyat, King's Chemist, who declared that at Edinburgh Cross he could, "in a few minutes, take fifty men of genius and learning by the hand". – W. Smellie, *Literary and Characteristic Lives of Gregory, Kames, Hume, and Smith* (Edinburgh, 1800).
8 Glasgow may plausibly claim to have been the focus of the first phase of the Scottish Enlightenment through the presence there, for varying periods, of Robert Simson, Francis Hutcheson, Thomas Reid, Adam Smith, Joseph Black and John Millar. There was also a centre of enlightenment in Aberdeen.
9 B. Silliman, *A Journal of Travels in England, Holland and Scotland in 1805–6*, no. lxxxv (1810).

2 Family Background and Infancy

1 P. Gordon, *The Scholarly Stewarts* in *Descent (Journal of the Society of Australian Genealogists) Vol. 26, No. 2* (June 1996).
2 This statement is made in a MS note of fairly modern appearance which has been inserted with letters from DS and Mrs S. to the Rev. Mr MacLea of Rothesay, who succeeded as minister in the Rev. Dugald Stewart's church (Ref. 1/456/30 in the NAS). If the letters were given to the NAS by a descendant of Archibald MacLea, he or she may have been the writer of the note. The information is attributed to "a descendant [of the Rev. DS's] in Nova Scotia". Since a son and grandson of the Rev DS emigrated to North America, the attribution is plausible.
3 This information, presumably supplied by DS, is in the statement granting him arms held by the Court of the Lord Lyon, King at Arms, Edinburgh.
4 Glasgow University Library, MS General 465.
5 See note 2.
6 H. Scott, *Fasti Ecclesiae Scoticanae; Presbytery of Dunoon* (Edinburgh: Oliver and Boyd, 1915–26).
7 Blain: *History of Bute*, quoted in Gordon, *The Scholarly Stewarts*.
8 R. Craig, *Parish of Rothesay* in *New Statistical Account of Scotland* (Edinburgh, 1845).
9 A. I. B. Stewart, *Some Kintyre Stewarts* in *The Scottish Genealogist* (September 1994).
10 W. Johnston, *Commissioned Officers in the Medical Services of the British Army 1660–1960, Vol. I* (London: The Wellcome Historical Medical Library, 1968).
11 Scott, *Fasti*.

12 J. Playfair, *Biographical Account of Matthew Stewart, DD* in *Transactions of the Royal Society of Edinburgh, Vol. I*, 1788.
13 DS: Diss, Part Second, Sect. 8; CW I, p. 428.
14 A. L. Drummond and D. Bulloch, *The Scottish Church 1688–1843* (Edinburgh: St Andrews Press, 1973).
15 J. H. Burton (ed.), *The Autobiography of Dr Alexander Carlyle of Inveresk 1722–1805* (London and Edinburgh, Foulis, 1910).
16 DS: Life of Smith, Note B; CW X, p. 81.
17 I. S. Ross, *The Life of Adam Smith* (Oxford: Clarendon Press, 1995).
18 R. L. Emerson and P. Wood, *Science and Enlightenment in Glasgow, 1690–1802* in C. W. J Withers and P. Wood (eds), *Science and Medicine in the Scottish Enlightenment* (East Linton: Tuckwell Press, 2002).
19 Burton, *Alexander Carlyle*.
20 Playfair, *Matthew Stewart*.
21 Ibid.
22 C. Maclaurin, *An Account of Sir Isaac Newton's Philosophical Discoveries* (London, 1750).
23 Playfair, *Matthew Stewart*.
24 Sir W. Scott, *The Heart of Midlothian*, Chs. XLII ff. (1818).
25 *Scots Magazine* (1741).
26 Matthew Stewart to John McLea, 4 September 1746; NAS GD1/456/163.
27 According to A. Bower, *The History of the University of Edinburgh* (Edinburgh, 1830) to a Mr Stirling who was in charge of the lead-mines at Leadhill.
28 ECA, Council Record Vol. 66, Minute of 2 September 1747.
29 ECA, Council Record Vol. 66, Minute of 4 September 1747.
30 ECA, Council Record Vol. 67, Minute of 9 March 1748.
31 A. G. Frazer, *The Building of Old College* (Edinburgh: Edinburgh University Press, 1989).
32 ECA, Council Record Vol. 67, Minute of 6 March 1752.
33 W. R. Scott, *Adam Smith as Student and Professor* (Glasgow: Jackson, 1937). Scott cites the *Caledonian Mercury* of October and November 1748.
34 See note 2.
35 Scott, *Fasti*.
36 Of two letters to the Rev. Dugald Stewart in Edinburgh which survive in NAS, one (GD1/456/96), dated 26 October 1748, was addressed to him "to the care of Mr Matthew Stewart, Professor of Mathematics in the University of Edinburgh", and one (GD1/456/164), dated 30 August 1751, "to the care of Mr John [sic] Sands Bookseller in the Parliament Close, Edinburgh".
37 Edinburgh Marriage Register. Matthew Stewart, in his *Memoir*, refers to his great-grandfather as "one of the Writers to the Signet of Scotland", but no Archibald Stewart appears in the *Register of the Society of Writers to Her Majesty's Signet*.
38 Information supplied by Mrs Pat Gordon.
39 Scott, *Fasti*.

40 Will of Janet Bannatyne, "widow of Mr Dougal [sic] Stewart, minister at Rothesay" in NAS.
41 M. Stewart, *Memoir*.
42 The description occurs in a letter of 14 June 1834 from Leonard Horner to his daughter. Horner was visiting Col. Matthew Stewart in Catrine at that time, so presumably the information came from him.
43 J. McCosh, *Scottish Philosophy* (London, 1875).
44 R. Steven, *Village of Catrine* (1797) in *Statistical Account of Scotland, Vol. 20* (Edinburgh, 1791–9).
45 Information supplied by Mrs Pat Gordon.
46 Veitch, *Life, Chapter I*; CW X, p. ix.
47 M. Stewart, *Memoir*.
48 DNB: Matthew Stewart.
49 Playfair, *Matthew Stewart*.
50 A. Smith, *The Theory of Moral Sentiments, Part III, Chapter II, paragraph 20* (1759).
51 Playfair, *Matthew Stewart*.
52 T. Somerville, *My Own Life and Times 1741–1814* (Edinburgh, 1861).
53 Burton, *Alexander Carlyle*.
54 Playfair, *Matthew Stewart*.

3 At School and University (1761–1772)

1 M. Stewart, *Memoir*.
2 Information about the High School of Edinburgh during the relevant years is drawn principally from the following sources: W. Steven, *The History of the High School of Edinburgh* (Edinburgh, 1849); W. C. A. Ross, *The Royal High School* (Edinburgh: Oliver and Boyd, 1934); A. Law, *Education in Edinburgh in the Eighteenth Century* (London: Scottish Council for Research in Education, 1965).
3 M. Stewart, *Memoir*.
4 Sir W. Scott, *General Preface to the Waverley Novels, Appendix III* (1829). The High Scool of which Scott was a pupil was in a building which replaced, on the same site, that attended by DS.
5 Sir W. Scott, *Redgauntlet, Letters I and II* (1824).
6 William Robertson to Hugh Cleghorn, c.1800; Cleghorn Papers, Envelope B, *6, quoted in A. Clark, *An Enlightened Scot – Hugh Cleghorn, 1752–1837* (Duns: Black Ace, 1992).
7 William Steven, an early historian of the High School, states in a footnote that he obtained most of his information about Matheson from two men, one of whom was DS.
8 Cockburn, *Memorials*.
9 Lord Brougham, *The Life and Times of Henry, Lord Brougham and Vaux, written by Himself* (Edinburgh and London, 1871).
10 DNB: Alexander Adam.
11 Veitch, *Life, Chapter I*; CW X, p. x.
12 A. L. Drummond and D. Bulloch, *The Scottish Church 1688–1843*, (Edinburgh: St Andrews Press, 1973).
13 For a full account of William Robertson's appointment as Principal, see J. J.

Cater, *The Making of Principal Robertson in 1762* in *Scottish Historical Review*, Vol. xliv (1970).
14 A. G. Frazer, *The Building of Old College* (Edinburgh: Edinburgh University Press, 1989).
15 DS: EPHM II, Part Second, Chapter II, Section 3; CW III, pp. 147–8, fn.
16 Information about the University of Edinburgh during the relevant years is drawn principally from the following sources: H. Arnot, *The History of Edinburgh* (Edinburgh, 1779); A. Bower, *The History of the University of Edinburgh* (Edinburgh, 1830); A. Chitnis, *The Scottish Enlightenment – a Social History* (London: Croom Helm, 1976); A. Dalzel, *History of the University of Edinburgh* (Edinburgh, 1862); MRUE.
17 Mrs S. to Thomas Thomson, 8 December 1817; J. T. Gibson Craig and C. Innes, *Memoir of Thomas Thomson* (Edinburgh, 1854).
18 Veitch, *Life, Chapter I*; CW X, p. xiii.
19 J. H. Burton (ed.), *The Autobiography of Dr Alexander Carlyle of Inveresk 1722–1805* (London and Edinburgh: Foulis, 1910).
20 R. Chambers, *Scottish Biographical Dictionary: Dr William Cullen* (Glasgow, 1833).
21 DS: Diss, Part First, Chapter II, Section 3; CW I, p. 195.
22 Here I am consciously parting from Veitch and from Leslie Stephen in the DNB who follows him in saying that DS spent only four years at Edinburgh University. This would leave the years 1769–71 unaccounted for, and provides no time when DS was a student of Ferguson, whom he himself refers to as one of his teachers. The conclusive evidence for the version I give in the text is that DS's name appears in MRUE in the classes of Blair and Ferguson for both 1769–70 and 1770–71.
23 According to the DNB, following Sir Walter Scott, Ferguson's commanding officer was astonished to see the chaplain at the head of the column with a drawn broadsword in his hand. However, Professor Broadie (*The Scottish Enlightenment* [Edinburgh: Canongate, 2001]) begs leave to doubt this story.
24 Veitch, *Life, Chapter I*; CW X, pp. xvi–xvii.
25 DS: Life of Reid, Section I; CW X, p. 261.
26 M. Stewart, *Memoir*.
27 DS: Life of Reid, Section I; CW X, p. 261.
28 Veitch, *Life, Chapter I*; CW X, p. xviii.
29 Ibid. Veitch attributes this piece of information to DS's future brother-in-law, Dugald Bannatyne.
30 Ibid.
31 DNB: Dugald Stewart.
32 Mrs S. to William Drennan, 22 November 1813; EUL Dc.1.100 (2), ff. 1–2
33 Veitch, *Life, Chapter I*; CW X, p. xxvii fn.
34 DS: Life of Reid, Section I; CW X, p. 264.
35 Veitch, *Life, Chapter I*; CW X, p. xxvii fn.
36 Ibid. According to S. W. Brown, *William Smellie and Natural History: Dissent and Dissemination* in C. W. J. Withers and P. Wood, *Science and Medicine in the Scottish Enlightenment* (East Linton: Tuckwell Press, 2002),

DS's views were influenced by the Edinburgh printer and writer, William Smellie.
37 DS: EPHM I, Part First, Chapter V, Part I, Section 5; CW II, pp. 289–305. DS refers to its almost unaltered state in Note O, p. 494.
38 DS: EPHM I, Part First, Chapter I, Section 1; CW II, p. 91.
39 *The Scotsman*, 12 July 1828.

4   The Young Stewart, Mathematician (1772–1780)

1 J. Playfair, *Biographical Account of Matthew Stewart, DD* in *Transactions of the Royal Society of Edinburgh*, Vol. I (1788). DS wrote in later life: "When I first ventured to appear before the public as an author, I resolved that nothing should ever induce me to enter into any controversy in defence of my conclusions, but to leave them to stand or fall by their own evidence." – PE, Preliminary Dissertation, Ch. II; CW V, p. 23.
2 Montesquieu's son, the Baron de Secondat, wrote to Clerk of Penicuik of "les beaux traites de Mr Matthieu Stewart, je les admire beaucoup". – NAS, GD/18/5120 (Clerk of Penicuik papers).
3 A. Bower, *History of the University of Edinburgh* (Edinburgh, 1830).
4 Playfair, *Matthew Stewart*.
5 Bower, *History of the University of Edinburgh*.
6 Anecdote "which we believe to be quite authentic" recounted in *The Scotsman* (12 July 1828).
7 Cockburn, *Memorials*.
8 A. G. Frazer, *The Building of Old College* (Edinburgh: Edinburgh University Press, 1989).
9 H. Arnot, *The History of Edinburgh* (Edinburgh, 1779).
10 Veitch, *Life, Chapter I*; CW X, p. xxvii.
11 M. Stewart, *Memoir*.
12 Bower, *History of the University of Edinburgh*.
13 ECA, Council Record Vol. 92, Minute of 14 June 1775.
14 A. Dalzel, *History of the University of Edinburgh* (Edinburgh, 1862).
15 DS to William Robertson, 14 September 1775; NLS MS 3942, f. 208.
16 ECA, Council Record Vol. 93, Minute of 8 May 1776.
17 Frazer, *Building of Old College*.
18 ECA, Council Record Vol. 95, Minute of 11 June 1777.
19 Now in the Public Record Office of Northern Ireland, Belfast; edited by J. Agnew, *The Drennan–McTier letters 1776–1793* (Dublin: Women's History Project, 1998).
20 Ibid.: William Drennan to Martha McTier, 30 November 1777.
21 Ibid.: William Drennan to Martha McTier, 13 December 1777.
22 See G. Wills, *Inventing America – Jefferson's Declaration of Independence* (New York: Vintage Books, 1979).
23 William Drennan to Martha McTier, 13 December 1777; Agnew, *Drennan–McTier Letters*.
24 William Drennan to Martha McTier, 20 January 1778; ibid.
25 *Catalogue of Graduates* (Edinburgh: Edinburgh University, 1858).

26 Andrew Dalzel to Robert Liston, 4 May 1778; C. Innes, *Memoir of Professor Dalzel* in A. Dalzel, *History of the University of Edinburgh*.
27 D. D. McElroy, *Scotland's Age of Improvement* (Washington: Washington State University Press, 1969).
28 Lord Monboddo to DS, 2 April 1778; W. Knight, *Lord Monboddo and some of his Contemporaries* (London: John Murray, 1900).
29 In EPHM II, Chapter III, Section I, fn. DS referred to Monboddo as one "whom I knew well, and for whose memory I entertain a sincere respect" – CW III, p. 198.
30 DS to Lord Monboddo, 1778; Knight, *Lord Monboddo*.
31 Arnot, *History of Edinburgh*.
32 M. Stewart, *Memoir*. Dr Charles Burney had written an essay about planets in 1769, and Adam Smith's *History of Astronomy* was published posthumously in 1795.
33 C. W. J. Withers, *Situating Practical Reason: Geography, Geometry and Mapping in the Scottish Enlightenment* in C. W. J. Withers and P. Wood, *Science and Medicine in the Scottish Enlightenment* (East Linton: Tuckwell Press, 2002).
34 DS to Lord Monboddo, 1778; Knight, *Lord Monbodo*.
35 Lord Monboddo to Samuel Horsley, 24 July 1780; ibid.
36 ECA, Council Record Vol. 97, Minute of 4 November 1778.
37 Veitch, *Life, Chapter I*; CW X, p. xxx.
38 ECA, Council Record Vol. 97, Minute of 4 November 1778.
39 M. Stewart, *Memoir*.
40 Andrew Dalzel to Robert Liston, 16 February 1779; Innes, *Professor Dalzel*.
41 EUL Gen.2023.
42 DS to Archibald Alison; NLS MS 9819, f. 249. This letter is undated, but its contents are consistent with its having been written earlier in 1779.
43 DS to Archibald MacLea, undated; NAS GD 1/456/30.
44 DS to Archibald Alison, 13 April 1780 or 81; Veitch, *Life, Appendix A, I*; CW X, pp. cxviii–cxix.
44 Information supplied by Mrs Pat Gordon.

5 Boarders, Travels, Marriage and Change (1780–1785)

1 M. Stewart, *Memoir*.
2 2nd Viscount Palmerston: *Journal*; B. Connell, *Portrait of a Whig Peer* (London: André Deutsch, 1957).
3 MRUE.
4 Minutes of Literary Class of RSE, 17 December 1792; NLS Acc 10000, 3.
5 T. Smollet, *The Expedition of Humphry Clinker* (1771); Matthew Bramble to Dr Lewis, 28 August.
6 T. M. Devine, *The Tobacco Lords* (Edinburgh: John Donald, 1975).
7 J. A. Mackay, *A Biography of Robert Burns* (London, 1992).
8 William Drennan to Samuel McTier, September 1782; J. Agnew, *The Drennan–McTier Letters 1776–1793* (Dublin: Women's History Project, 1998).

Notes to pp. 39–46

9 First published in 1773.
10 DS to William Robertson, 4 June 1783; NLS MS 3943, f. 149.
11 Ibid.
12 *Lord Ancram's Journal*, 1783; NAS, Lothian Muniments.
13 Franklin had visited Scotland in 1759, when DS was a small child, and in 1771; it is possible that DS saw him on one or both of these occasions.
14 Benjamin Vaughan to John Jay, 8 August 1783; see chapter 6, note 26.
15 In June 1784 the Edinburgh bookseller Charles Elliot wrote to his counterpart in Paris, Pierre-Théophile Barrois, referring to a conversation which the Frenchman had had with "my friend Mr Stewart" during the preceding autumn (quoted by W. McDougall, *Charles Elliot's Medical Publications and the International Book Trade* in C. W. J. Withers and P. Wood (eds), *Science and Medicine in the Scottish Enlightenment* [East Linton: Tuckwell Press, 2002]).
16 L. Sterne, *A Sentimental Journey through France and Italy* (1762).
17 DS to Archibald Alison, 6 October 1783 (assumed year); St Andrews University Library msdep 7, Autograph collection 24 (Box 13). There is a slight inconsistency in dates between DS's letter and Ancram's jornal, but those given in the text are the most likely.
18 Old Parish Register, Midlothian; NLS.
19 Veitch, *Life, Chapter I*; CW X, p. xxxii.
20 Edinburgh Directory, June 1784–June 1785.
21 MRUE: 1783.
22 B. Constant, *Ma Vie (Le Cahier Rouge)*, ed. C. P. Courtney (Cambridge: Daemon Press, 1991).
23 Transactions of the RSE, Vol. I.
24 *ad promovendas Literas et Scientiam utilem.*
25 Minutes of the RSE, NLS Acc. 10000.
26 I. S. Ross, *Life of Adam Smith* (Oxford: Clarendon Press, 1995).
27 Andrew Dalzel to Robert Liston, 20 April 1784; C. Innes, *Memoir of Professor Dalzel* in A. Dalzel, *History of the University of Edinburgh* (Edinburgh, 1862).
28 EUL Doc.6.111, ff. 17–21.
29 A. Broadie (ed.), *The Scottish Enlightenment – an Anthology* (Edinburgh: Canongate, 1997): *Appendix – Biographical Sketches of Authors.*
30 I. S. Lusty and F. A. Pottle, *Boswell: the Applause of the Jury 1782–85* (London: Heinemann, 1982).
31 Veitch, *Life, Chapter I*; CW X, p. xii.
32 Ibid; p. xxxiii, fn. 1784–5 would have been DS's 13th year of teaching mathematics.
33 DS to William Robertson; NLS MS 3943, f. 200. A note on this undated letter suggests that it was written in 1785, but the text indicates that DS's father was still alive, and he died on 23 January of that year. The year 1784 is therefore a more likely date.
34 Ibid.
35 ECA Council Record Vol. 106, Minute of 18 May 1785.

36 This point is made by Bryan Magee in *Confessions of a Philosopher* (London: Weidenfeld & Nicolson, 1997).
37 Adam Smith to James Menteath, 22 February 1785; E. Mossner and I. S. Ross (eds), *The Correspondence of Adam Smith* (Oxford: Clarendon Press, 1977).
38 A. Herman, *The Scottish Enlightenment – the Scots' Invention of the Modern World* (London: Fourth Estate, 2002).

6 The Young Stewart, Philosopher (1785–1787)

1 See A. Chitnis, *The Scottish Enlghtenment – a Social History* (London: Croom Helm, 1976).
2 J. G. Lockhart, *Peter's Letters to his Kinsfolk*, Letter 7 (Edinburgh, 1819).
3 In 1801 the Senatus authorized the Faculty of Divinity to refuse admittance to any student who had not attended (among others) the class in moral philosophy (Minute of 7 December 1801).
4 Note made by Mrs S. as supplement to DS's memorandum about his sinecure, 1827; NLS Ms 12135, f. 114.
5 G. E. Davie, *The Democratic Intellect* (Edinburgh: Edinburgh University Press, 1982).
6 R. J. Mackintosh (ed.), *Memoir of the Life of the Rt. Honourable Sir James Mackintosh* (Boston, 1853).
7 Veitch, *Life, Chapter II*; CW X, p. xxxiv fn.
8 J. Wilson, Evidence to Scottish Universities Commission, 10 October 1826.
9 "The present Professor gives a course of lectures on moral philosophy, following chiefly the arrangement of Dr Ferguson's institutes of that science." – H. Arnot, *The History of Edinburgh* (Edinburgh, 1788). Also, A. Bower, *The History of the University of Edinburgh* (Edinburgh, 1830).
10 DS: OMP. DS was anxious to be seen no longer as a mere follower of Ferguson: "I have been guided almost entirely by the train of my own speculations." – Preface; CW II, p. 4.
11 Edinburgh Directories, 1786–8 and 1788–90.
12 ECA, Council Records Vol. 155, Minute for 1 May 1810.
13 DS to James Currie; Currie's *Life of Burns* – see chapter 7.
14 DS to Lady Jane Home, September 1785 (assumed month); Douglas-Home Archive.
15 DS to James Boswell, autumn 1785 (assumed date); Beinecke Rare Book and Manuscript Library, Yale University. Boswell's *Book of Company* shows that DS and Thomas Miller dined at Auchinleck on 21 October 1784, and DS called there on 10 October 1785.
16 DS: EPHM III, Part Third, Ch. I, Sect. iv fn.; CW IV, p. 230.
17 S. Johnson, *Journey to the Western Isles of Scotland* (London, 1775).
18 J. Boswell, *Journal of a Tour to the Hebrides with Samuel Johnson, LL.D.* (London, 1785).
19 DS to James Boswell, autumn 1785; Beinecke Manuscript Library.
20 See correspondence held in Beinecke Rare Book and Manuscript Library, Yale University.
21 MRUE

22 B. and H. Wedgwood, *The Wedgwood Circle 1730–1897* (London: Cassell, 1980). This and the following reference were given to me by Miss Helen Burton of the Special Collections and Archives Department at Keele University. I am also indebted to Mr Arthur Tough, formerly of Keele University, for his help in this connection.
23 R. B. Litchfield, *Tom Wedgwood* (London: Duckworth, 1903).
24 Minutes of the Physical Class of the RSE, 7 February 1786 and 3 April 1786 respectively; NLS Acc. Ms 10000, 2.
25 Northamptonshire is stated as their destination in DS to Bernard Vaughan, 19 May 1786 (assumed year); NLS Ms 2521, f. 171.
26 Benjamin Vaughan to John Jay, 8 August 1783; H. P. Johnston (ed.), *The Correspondence and Public Papers of John Jay* (New York and London, 1891).
27 DS to Benjamin Vaughan, 19 May 1786.
28 DS to Archibald MacLea, July 1786; NAS GD1/456/30.
29 T. Smollett, *The Expedition of Humphrey Clinker* (1771); Matthew Bramble to Dr Lewis, 8 August.
30 Portrait in private hands.
31 M. Stewart, *Memoir*.

7 Stewart and Robert Burns

1 Facts about the life of Robert Burns referred to in this chapter may be found in any standard biography.
2 Thomas Blacklock to George Lawrie, 4 September 1786; R. Chambers, *The Life and Works of Robert Burns*, revised by W. Wallace (Edinburgh and London, 1896).
3 Robert Burns to John Moore, 2 August 1787; J. A. Mackay, *The Complete Letters of Robert Burns, no. 125* (Ayrshire: Alloway Publishing, 1987).
4 R. Burns, *The Vision*, 1786, ll. 121–6.
5 J. Kinsley, *The Poems and Songs of Robert Burns, Vol. III: Commentary* (Oxford: Oxford University Press, 1968).
6 R. Burns, *The Brigs of Ayr*, 1787, ll. 229–30.
7 DS to James Currie, incorporated in Currie's *Life of Burns* (1800).
8 D. Wright, *Robert Burns and Freemasonry* (Paisley, undated).
9 DS to James Currie, *Life of Burns*.
10 Ibid.
11 R. Burns, *Lines on Meeting with Lord Daer*, 1786, ll. 25, 28–30, 40–8.
12 Robert Burns to John Mackenzie, 25 October 1786; Mackay, *Complete Letters, no. 53A*.
13 DS to James Currie, *Life of Burns*.
14 W. Creech, *Edinburgh Fugitive Pieces* (Edinburgh, 1793).
15 H. Mackenzie, *The Lounger* (9 December 1786).
16 Robert Burns to John Mackenzie, 6 December 1786; Mackay, *Complete Letters, no. 61A*.
17 Robert Burns to John Ballantine, 13 December 1786; Mackay, *Complete Letters, no. 63*.

18 H. W. Thompson (ed.), *The Anecdotes and Egotisms of Henry Mackenzie, 1745–1831* (Oxford: Oxford University Press, 1927).
19 Robert Burns to John Ballantine, 14 January 1787; Mackay, *Complete Letters*, no. 77.
20 Wright, *Burns and Freemasonry*.
21 Robert Burns to Gavin Hamilton, 7 December 1786; Mackay, *Complete Letters*, no. 63.
22 The question is discussed in J. Weir (ed.), *Robert Burns the Freemason* (Surrey: Ian Allan Regalia, 1996).
23 Sir Walter Scott to John Lockhart, 1827: *Life of Scott* (1837–8).
24 DS to James Currie, *Life of Burns*.
25 R. Burns, *Burlesque Lament for the Absence of William Creech, Publisher*, 1787, ll. 39–40.
26 W. Harvey, *Robert Burns as a Freemason* (Dundee: Masonic Publications, 1921).
27 DS to James Currie, *Life of Burns*.
28 Ibid.
29 Robert Burns to Frances Dunlop of Dunlop, 24 November 1787; Mackay, *Complete Letters*, no. 152A.
30 Robert Burns to DS, 3 May 1788; ibid., no. 239.
31 Robert Burns to DS, 20 January 1789; ibid., no. 297.
32 DS to James Currie, *Life of Burns*. Thomas Carlyle refers to this observation in his 1828 essay on Burns and in *On Heroes and Hero Worship – The Hero as Man of Letters* (1841).
33 Ibid.
34 Robert Burns to DS, July 1790; Mackay, *Complete Letters*, no. 409.
35 Robert Burns to Francis Grose, July 1790; NLS MS 23150, f. 12 (no. 410 in *Complete Letters*).
36 Robert Burns to DS, 30 July 1790; Mackay, *Complete Letters*, no. 410.
37 J. Johnson, *Scots Musical Museum* (Edinburgh, 1792).
38 Robert Burns to William Creech, 16 April 1792; Mackay, *Complete Letters*, no. 502.
39 Robert Burns to William Creech, late 1792 (assumed date); ibid.
40 This was certainly the case twelve years later, when DS asked for money to be sent "to the House of Sir Wm Forbes, to be placed to my credit"; NLS MS 581, f. 426.
41 Alexander Cunningham to John Syme, 9 August 1796; I. McIntyre, *Dirt and Deity – a Life of Robert Burns* (London: Flamingo, 1996).
42 H. Mackenzie, *Anecdotes and Egotisms*.
43 DS to James Currie, *Life of Burns*.
44 DS to James Currie, 6 September 1800; W. C. Currie (ed.), *Memoir of the Life, Writings and Correspondence of James Currie, MD, of Liverpool* (London, 1831).

8 Revolutionary France and Remarriage (1787–1790)

1 Veitch, *Life, Chapter III*; CW X, p. lvi fn.

2. J. S. Gibson, *Deacon Brodie* (Edinburgh: Saltire Society, 1993).
3. DS to Archibald Alison, 1788; Veitch, *Life, Chapter III*; CW X, p. lvi fn.
4. DS to Archibald MacLea, 5 April 1788; NAS GD 1/456/30.
5. T. C. Smout, *A History of the Scottish People 1560–1830* (London: William Collins, 1969).
6. DS to Lady Jane Home, 17 March (1785); Douglas-Home Archive.
7. This may be inferred from DS to Dugald Bannatyne, 4 August 1788; Veitch, *Life, Appendix A, III*; CW X, pp. cxxi–cxxii.
8. Information supplied by Mrs Pat Gordon.
9. M. Cant, *Villages of Edinburgh: an Illustrated Guide, Vol. I* (Edinburgh: Malcolm Cant Publications, 1997).
10. S. G. Checkland, *Scottish Banking – A History 1695–1973* (Glasgow and London: Collins, 1975). In 1790 Thomas Coutts of London described Ramsay as "one of the richest men of business in the UK".
11. Josiah Walker to James Finlayson, 25 June 1788; Glasgow University Library, MS Gen. 1103/2(g).
12. Ibid.
13. DS to Archibald Alison, 18 June 1788; Veitch, *Life, Appendix A, II*; CW X, p. cxx.
14. R. J. Mackintosh, *Memoirs of the Life of Sir James Mackintosh*, (Boston, 1853). DS's letter was dated 4 June 1789.
15. Walker to Finlayson, 25 June 1788.
16. Benjamin Vaughan to Thomas Jefferson, 6 June 1788; J. P. Boyd et al., *The Papers of Thomas Jefferson* (Princeton: Princeton University Press, 1958).
17. DS to Archibald Alison, 18 June 1788.
18. DS to Archibald Alison, 23 June 1788 (assumed year); NLS MS 9819, f. 247.
19. MRUE. Cleghorn's uncle, William Cleghorn, had been professor of moral philosophy at Edinburgh, 1745–54.
20. A. Clark, *An Enlightened Scot: Hugh Cleghorn* (Duns: Black Ace Books, 1992).
21. DS to Dugald Bannatyne, 4 August 1788; Veitch, *Life, Appendix A, III*; CW X, pp. cxxi–cxxii.
22. DS: Pol Econ, Book Second, Chapter III, Section i, Subject 1; CW X, p. 12.
23. DS to Archibald Alison, 27 August 1788; Veitch, *Life, Appendix A, IV*; CW X, p. cxxii.
24. DS to Robert Liston, 11 October 1788; NLS MS 5552, f. 13.
25. Minutes of the Physical Class of the RSE, 1 December 1788; NLS MS Acc. 10000, 2.
26. MRUE. Benjamin and Stephen de Lessert both attended the mathematics class in 1784–5.
27. Information supplied by Mrs Pat Gordon.
28. Mrs S. to 2nd Earl of Minto, 27 September 1827; NLS MS 13169, f. 130.
29. DS to Archibald Alison, 30 May 1789: Veitch, *Life, Appendix A, VI*; p. cxxvi.
30. DS to Archibald Alison, 17 September 1789; Veitch, *Life, Appendix A, VIII*; CW X, p. cxxxii.
31. Richard Price to Thomas Jefferson, 4 May 1789; Boyd, *Papers of Thomas Jefferson*.

32 DS to Adam Smith, 6 May 1789; Glasgow University Library MS Gen 1097/9.
33 DS to Archibald Alison, 10 May 1789; Veitch, *Life, Appendix A, V*; CW X, pp. cxxii–cxxvi.
34 Ibid.
35 DS to Archibald Alison, 18 June 1789; NLS MS 3112, f. 32.
36 DS to Archibald Alison, 10 May 1789.
37 DS to Archibald Alison, 17 September 1789.
38 DS to Archibald Alison, 10 May 1789.
39 Ibid.
40 DS to Archibald Alison, 30 May 1789.
41 DS must have regarded the Duke's invitation as something to keep. It has survived in EUL as Dc.6.111, f. 97.
42 DS: Life of Smith, Section III, fn.; CW X, p. 46.
43 DS: PAMP II, Book Second, Chapter IV; CW VI, p. 256.
44 DS to Archibld Alison, 18 June 1789.
45 Thomas Jefferson to John Adams, 14 March 1820; J. Cappon (ed.), *The Adams-Jefferson Letters* (Chapel Hill: University of North Carolina Press, 1959).
46 Thomas Jefferson to DS, 26 April 1824; M. D. Peterson, *Thomas Jefferson – Writings* (New York: Oxford University Press, 1984).
47 This is stated by DS in the letter of 1794 to Lord Craig quoted in chapter 9. At this time DS covered the topic "Man considered as the member of a political body" as the final part of his general course on moral philosophy. He dealt with the various forms of government. See DS: Chapter heads to OMP III in CW VIII, p. xxv.
48 DS to Archibald Alison, 17 September 1789.
49 The account which follows is drawn from A. G. Fraser, *The Building of Old College* (Edinburgh: Edinburgh University Press, 1989).
50 T. Somerville, *My Own Life and Times 1741–1814* (Edinburgh, 1861).
51 Minutes of Literary Class of RSE; NLS Acc 10000, 3.
52 William H. Playfair.
53 Sir W. Scott, autobiographical passage (1808) which appears at the beginning of J. G. Lockhart, *The Life of Sir Walter Scott* (Edinburgh, 1837–38).
54 Lockhart's *Life of Scott* and E. Johnson, *Sir Walter Scott – The Great Unknown* (London, Hamish Hamilton, 1970).
55 The influence of DS on Scott as a novelist is discussed in D. Forbes, *The Rationalism of Sir Walter Scott*, Cambridge Journal 7 (1953– 4).
56 Andrew Dalzel to John Young, 7 December 1794; C. Innes, *Memoir of the Author* in A. Dalzel, *History of the University of Edinburgh* (Edinburgh, 1862).
57 *Quarterly Review, Vol. LXVII* (December 1840); footnote to review of *Letters of the Earl of Dudley to the Bishop of Llandaff*.
58 Apart from the evidence of their lifelong friendship, we know that DS heard frequently from Ancram during a tour of the continent made by the latter two years after his trip with DS; DS to Lady Jane Home, September 1785 (assumed month); Douglas-Home Archive.

59 J. Johnson, *The Scots Musical Museum* (Edinburgh, 1787–1803). The lines added by Burns were as follows:

> No cold approach, no alter'd mien,
> Just what would make suspicion start;
> No pause the dire extremes between,
> He made me blest – and broke my heart.

He inserted these before the final four lines of the original, thus making it possible to treat the poem as five eight-line stanzas. The eight-line format suited the music to which the poem was set, an old English air by John Barret called *Ianthe the lovely*; but it seems unlikely that Helen Cranstoun wrote a poem in the form of four and a half stanzas, and I have therefore set her poem out in the text as nine stanzas of four lines each, which works well in terms of the sense.

60 Old Parish Registers, Midlothian; NLS.
61 On 30 December 1788.
62 T. M. Devine, *The Tobacco Lords* (Edinburgh: John Donald, 1975).
63 See letters from Scott to the Countess Purgstall (1821), to his son Walter (9 March 1824) and to Walter's wife Jane (23 March 1825) in Sir H. Grierson (ed.), *The Letters of Sir Walter Scott* (London: Constable, 1932). Scott regarded Henry Cranstoun as a terrible bore.
64 *The Scotsman*, quoted in M. Stewart, *Memoir*.
65 Ibid.
66 Thomas Campbell to a friend, 28 January 1808; W. Beattie, *Life and Letters of Thomas Campbell* (London, 1850).
67 M. Stewart, *Memoir*.
68 Mrs S. to Archibald Constable, 4 May 1818; NLS MS 575, f. 208.

9 *Liberal Philosopher in a Harsh Climate (1790–1796)*

1 Frances Dunlop of Dunlop to Robert Burns, 5 August 1790; W. Wallace (ed.), *Robert Burns and Mrs Dunlop – Correspondence now published in full for the first time* (London, 1898).
2 Ibid., 18 August 1790.
3 Frances Dunlop to Mrs S., August 1790; EUL Dc.6.111, ff. 13–14.
4 A. L. Drummond and J. Bullough, *The Scottish Church 1688–1843* (Edinburgh: St Andrews Press, 1973).
5 Claud Alexander of Ballochmyle – see R. H. Campbell, *Scotland since 1707 – the Rise of an Industrial Society* (Edinburgh: John Donald, 1985).
6 A cotton mill was built in 1788 in John Galt's fictional parish of Dalmailing, and his Rev. Mr Balwhidder records that "Some of the ancient families in their turreted houses were not pleased with this innovation, especially when they saw the handsome dwellings that were built for the weavers." (*The Annals of the Parish*.)
7 R. Steven, *Village of Catrine* (1797) in *Statistical Account of Scotland*, Vol. 20 (Edinburgh, 1791–9).
8 Campbell, *Scotland since 1707*.

9 See chapter 7.
10 H. M. Milne (ed.), *Boswell's Edinburgh Journals* (Edinburgh: Mercat Press, 2001) – Note for June 1781 and entry for 24 June.
11 *Edinburgh Directories* for June 1790–June 1792, July 1793–July 1794, July 1794–July 1795 and July 1795–July 1796.
12 Veitch, *Life Chapter III*; CW X, p. lx fn.
13 From Lord Craig quoted later in the chapter.
14 J. Grant, *Old and New Edinburgh* (Edinburgh, 1882).
15 DS to Robert Liston, undated; NLS MS 5647, f. 185.
16 Veitch gives an average attendance (26) at DS's summer class for 1791–6 – *Life, Chapter II*; CW X, p. xxxiv fn.
17 DS to 1st Marquess of Lansdowne, 13 March 1796; NLS MS Acc. 11140.
18 On 26 June 1807 Mrs S. wrote to 3rd Viscount Palmerston: "This is G's birthday – only think he is sixteen, is not that terrible"; BA – BR22a/7.
19 DS to Mr Duncan, Bookseller, 10 October 1791; NLS MS 582, f. 683.
20 T. Miller, *Old Cumnock* in *Statistical Account of Scotland, Vol. 6* (Edinburgh, 1791–9).
21 M. H. B. Sanderson, *Robert Adam and Scotland* (Edinburgh: HMSO, 1992).
22 A. G. Fraser, *The Building of Old College* (Edinburgh: Edinburgh University Press, 1989).
23 Mrs S. to Archibald MacLea, 18 January 1792; NAS GD 1/456/30.
24 Thomas Reid to DS, 1791 (assumed year); P. Wood (ed.), *Correspondence of Thomas Reid* (Edinburgh: Edinburgh University Press, 2002).
25 DS: EPHM I, Dedication and Advertisement: CW II pp. 41 and 43.
26 Thomas Cadell to Edward Gibbon, 8 January 1792: C. R. Fay, *Adam Smith and the Scotland of his Day* (Cambridge: Cambridge University Press, 1956).
27 DS to Thomas Cadell, 17 August 1792; NLS MS 5319, f. 34.
28 DS to Archibald Alison, 29 October 1792; Veitch, *Life, Appendix A, X*; CW X, p. cxxxiv.
29 Minutes of the Literary Class of the RSE for 21 January 1793; NLS MS Acc. 10000, 3.
30 DS to Thomas Cadell, 13 March 1793; NLS MS 5319, f. 35.
31 Minutes of the Literary Class of the RSE for 18 March 1793; NLS MS Acc. 10000, 3.
32 Sir R. Romilly, *Life, written by Himself* (London, 1842).
33 I. S. Ross, *The Life of Adam Smith* (Oxford: Clarendon Press, 1995).
34 D. Thomson, *Raeburn Exhibition Catalogue* (Edinburgh, National Galleries of Scotland, 1997). Dalzel, in a letter to Principal Robertson of 4 March 1792, says it was DS's idea – C. Innes, *Memoir of the Author* in A. Dalzel, *History of Edinburgh University* (Edinburgh, 1862).
35 Thomson, *Raeburn Exhibition Catalogue*.
36 Ibid.
37 Dalzel, *History of the University of Edinburgh*.
38 Ibid.
39 Information supplied by Mrs Pat Gordon.
40 DS to Thomas Cadell, 25 August 1793; NLS MS 3648, f. 176.
41 Sir Samuel Romilly to M. Dumont, 14 September 1793; Romilly, *Life*.

Notes to pp. 84–93

42 DS: OMP, Preface; CW II, p. 4.
43 A. Ferguson, *Institutes of Moral Philosophy* (1772).
44 DS to Archibald Alison, 27 November 1791; Veitch, *Life, Appendix A, IX*; CW X, p. cxxxii.
45 DS to Archibald Alison, 29 October 1792, ibid., *Appendix A, X*; CW X, p. cxxxiv.
46 DS to Archibald Alison, (early) January 1793, ibid., *Appendix A, XI*; CW X, p. cxxxv.
47 Wordsworth: "Bliss was it in that dawn to be alive, / But to be young was very heaven!" Fox (of the fall of the Bastille): "How much the greatest event it is that ever happened in the world! and how much the best!"
48 J. Clive, *Scotch Reviewers – The Edinburgh Review 1802–1815* (Cambridge, Mass. and London: Harvard University Press, 1957).
49 DS to Archibald Alison, (early) January 1793; Veitch, *Life, Appendix A, XI*; CW X, p.cxxxvi.
50 DS: Life of Smith, Section 4; CW X, pp. 55–6.
51 Ibid., pp. 54–5.
52 DS: EPHM I, Chapter IV, Sec. 8; CW II pp. 228–9.
53 Ibid. pp. 236–7.
54 Lord Cockburn, *Life of Francis Jeffrey* (Edinburgh, 1852).
55 William Drennan to Martha McTier, 1785; Agnew, J.: *The Drennan – McTier Letters 1776–1793* (Dublin: Women's History Project, 1998).
56 William Drennan to Martha McTier, 28 January 1786; ibid.
57 Lord Cockburn, *An Examination of the Trials for Sedition in Scotland, Vol. I* (Edinburgh, 1888).
58 Lord Craig to DS, 15 February 1794; EUL Dc.6.111, ff. 113–15.
59 DS to Lord Craig, 20 February 1794; ibid.
60 Note in Mrs S.'s writing; ibid.
61 Cockburn, *Memorials*.
62 J. A. Mackay, *Collected Letters of Robert Burns* (Ayrshire: Alloway Publishing, 1987).
63 Sir W. Scott, *The Antiquary*, Chapter VI (1816).
64 Dalzel, *History of the University of Edinburgh*.
65 DS to Macvey Napier, 18 May 1817; BL Add MS 34612, f. 101.
66 MRUE
67 James Mill to Macvey Napier, 10 July 1831; M. Napier (ed.), *Selection from the Correspondence of the late Macvey Napier, Esq.* (London, 1879).
68 S. Hall, *Dr Duncan of Ruthwell, founder of Savings Banks* (Edinburgh: Oliphant, Anderson and Ferrier, 1910).
69 This story is told by D. Welsh, professor of church history in the University of Edinburgh, in the biographical memoir prefacing his edition of Brown's *Lectures on the Philosophy of the Human Mind* (1836).
70 M. Stewart, *Memoir*.
71 Veitch, *Life*; CW X, p. lix.
73 The story is told in Lockhart's *Life of Scott, Chapter II*, supplemented by Scott's letter of 15 November 1796 to William Taylor in Sir H. Grierson (ed.), *Collected Letters of Sir Walter Scott* (London: Constable, 1932). Scott enti-

tled his version of the poem *William and Helen*. The detail of the printing being done by Robert Miller is in Capt. B. Hall, *Schloss Hainfeld* (Paris, 1836).

73 Jane Cranstoun to Walter Scott, 18 April 1796, quoted in Sir H. Grierson, *Sir Walter Scott, Bart* (London: Constable, 1938).

74 Edinburgh Directories for July 1796–July 1797 and July 1797–July 1798. Lothian House continues to be given as DS's address in the Directories until the issue for July 1804–July 1805.

75 Information about Lothian House is drawn from J. Grant, *Old and New Edinburgh* (Edinburgh, 1882).

76 DS to Walter Scott, undated; NLS Ms 3874, f. 20.

77 Minutes of Literary Class of RSE for 21 March 1796, 20 May 1799 and 28 June 1799; NLS MS Acc 10000, 3.

78 Thomas Reid to DS, 1792; DS: Life of Reid, Section III; CW X, p. 312–13.

79 Thomas Reid to DS, 21 January 1793; Veitch, *Life*, Appendix B, I; CW X, p. cxlviii.

80 DS: Life of Reid, Section III; CW X, p. 313.

81 DS to Archibald Alison, 1797; Veitch, *Life*, Chapter III; CW X, p. lxxv.

82 DS to Samuel Parr, 30 May 1801; J. Johnstone (ed.), *The Works of Dr Samuel Parr, LLD, with Memoir of his Life and Writing* (London, 1828).

83 Minutes of Literary Class of RSE for 17 May 1802; NLS MS Acc. 10000, 3. These record the reading of the first part of the *Life of Reid*, the remainder being deferred; no subsequent reading was minuted.

84 Sir L. Stephen, in DNB: *Dugald Stewart*.

10 Students and Travels (1796–1800)

1 M. Stewart, *Memoir*.

2 This is implied by DS's reply.

3 DS to 1st Marquess of Lansdowne, 13 March 1796; NLS MS Acc 11140, f. 25.

4 These events are implied by DS's letter of 26 June.

5 DS to Lady Ashburton, 26 June 1796; NLS MS Acc 11140, f. 29.

6 Lady Ashburton to 1st Marquess of Lansdowne, 13 July 1796; NLS MS Acc 11140, f. 31.

7 1st Marquess of Lansdowne to DS, 25 September 1796; NLS MS Acc 11140, f. 32.

8 DS to 1st Marquess of Lansdowne, 1 October 1796; NLS MS Acc 11140, f. 34.

9 Matthew Stewart wrote of Petty in his *Memoir* that "for him he [DS] contracted the highest esteem"; and in writing to Petty in 1802 DS said, "Mrs Stewart sends her love and best wishes" – an unusually warm expression.

10 MRUE.

11 Ibid.

12 DS to 1st Marquess of Lansdowne, 11 February 1797; NLS MS Acc 11140, ff. 36–8.

Notes to pp. 98–107

13 S. H. Romilly (ed.), *Letters to "Ivy" from the First Earl of Dudley* (London: Longmans Green, 1905); Introduction.
14 MRUE.
15 Mrs S. to 3rd Viscount Palmerston, 17 August 1802; BA MS 62, BR22 (i)13.
16 DS: *Diary of Journeys in England and Scotland 1797–1803*; EUL Dc.8.178.
17 Rev. Sydney Smith to Michael Hicks Beach, 30 June 1798; N. C. Smith (ed.), *The Letters of Sydney Smith* (Oxford: Oxford University Press, 1953).
18 DS: *Diary of Journeys*.
19 Denbighshire Record Office, DD/LL/1.
20 I am indebted for this suggestion to David Castledean of the Denbighshire Record Office.
21 W. Beattie, *Life and Letters of Thomas Campbell* (London, 1850).
22 DS to Lord Henry Petty, 9 July (1799); NLS MS Acc 11140.
23 *The Journal of Elizabeth, Lady Holland*, 25 September 1799; BL MS 51929, ff. 27.
24 Ibid. (13 October 1799), f. 40. It cannot be regarded as certain that this dinner took place at Holland House, for I am told by Dr Wright of the BL that the Hollands usually kept a house in Mayfair to which they often migrated during the Parliamentary session.
25 M. Stewart, *Memoir*.
26 J. Small, *Biographical Sketch of Adam Ferguson, LLD, FRSE, Professor of Moral Philosophy in the University of Edinburgh* (Edinburgh, 1864).
27 M. Stewart, *Memoir*.
28 Ibid.
29 Lady S. Holland, *Memoir of the Reverend Sydney Smith* (London, 1854).

11 The Stewarts and the Palmerstons (1800–1803)

1 Much of the information about Harry Temple's residence with the Stewarts in this chapter is taken from B. Connell, *Portrait of a Whig Peer* (London: André Deutsch, 1957) and from K. Bourne, *Palmerston – the Early Years* (London: Allen Lane, 1982). Except where otherwise stated, quotations from letters are taken from these sources. Direct quotations from the Broadlands Papers, now held in the Hartley Library of the University of Southampton, are referenced accordingly.
2 2nd Viscount Palmerston to DS, (first half of) June 1800.
3 DS to 2nd Viscount Palmerston, 16 June 1800.
4 Mary Somerville, *née* Fairfax; D. McMillan, *Queen of Science – Personal Recollections of Mary Somerville* (Edinburgh: Canongate, 2001).
5 Published in 8 volumes in 1802. "Huttonian" of course refers to Professor James Hutton of Edinburgh University.
6 DS to Major Hutton 6 October 1800; NLS MS Adv 29.4.2 (VII), f. 120.
7 2nd Viscount Palmerston, *Tour of North of England, Lake District, Edinburgh and Highlands of Scotland and notebook for this journey, 1800*.
8 DS to 1st Marquis of Lansdowne, 13 March 1796; NLS MS Acc 11140.
9 Hon. Henry Temple to Hon. Elizabeth Temple, 15 November 1800.
10 Hon. Henry Temple to 2nd Viscount Palmerston, 28 November 1800.

11 2nd Viscount Palmerston to Hon. Henry Temple, undated.
12 Hon. Henry Temple to Lady Palmerston, 8 December 1800.
13 Hon. Henry Temple to 2nd Viscount Palmerston, 3 February 1801.
14 Ibid., 10 December 1800.
15 Ibid., 28 November 1800.
16 M. Edgeworth, *Moral Tales* (1801).
17 Hon. Henry Temple to 2nd Viscount Palmerston, 18 April 1801.
18 M. Butler, *Maria Edgeworth – a Literary Biography* (Oxford, Clarendon Press, 1972).
19 Cockburn, *Memorials*.
20 Ibid.
21 Ibid.
22 Veitch, *Life, Chapter II*; CW X, p. li.
23 Mrs S. [to Lady Palmerston], quoted in Lady Palmerston to Hon. Henry Temple, 3 December 1800.
24 DS to 2nd Viscount Palmerston, 23 January 1801.
25 DS to 2nd Viscount Palmerston, 20 May 1801.
26 *Hansard*, cxxxvii, 243–8, for 8 March 1855.
27 DS to Archibald Alison, January 1793; Veitch, *Life*, Appendix A, XI; CW X, p. cxxxv.
28 DS: *Diary of journeys in England and Scotland 1797–1803*; EUL Dc.8.178.
29 James Mackintosh to DS, 14 December 1802; R. J. Mackintosh, *Memoirs of the Life of Sir James Mackintosh* (Boston, 1853).
30 DS: OMP, postscript to Preface dated 2 November 1801.
31 MRUE.
32 Mrs S. to 1st Earl of Minto, 7 January 1802; NLS MS 11152, f. 90.
33 Lord Minto to Lady Palmerston, January 1802; Countess of Minto (ed.), *Life and Letters of Sir Gilbert Elliot, First Earl of Minto, 1751–1806* (London, 1874).
34 Hon. Henry Temple to 2nd Viscount Palmerston, 8 January 1802.
35 A. Ferguson, *The Hon. Henry Erskine, Lord Advocate of Scotland* (Edinburgh, 1882).
36 Countess of Minto, *Life of Sir Gilbert Elliot*.
37 W. Beattie, *Life and Letters of Thomas Campbell* (London, 1850).
38 Thomas Campbell to Mrs S., 27 February 1802; EUL Dc.6.111, f. 108.
39 Thomas Campbell to a friend, 14 July 1808; Beattie, *Life of Thomas Campbell*.
40 Mrs S. to Hon. Henry Temple, April 1802; BA – BR 22a/7.
41 Lady Palmerston to 1st Earl of Malmesbury, 29 April 1802.
42 Mrs S. to 3rd Viscount Palmerston, May 1802 (assumed date); BA – BR 22a/8.
43 3rd Viscount Palmerston to Lady Palmerston, June 1802.
44 DS to London printer, 8 June 1802; NLS MS 1003, f. 160.
45 DS to Lord Henry Petty, 19 April (1802); NLS MS Acc 11140.
46 Minutes of RSE Literary Class; NLS MS Acc 10000, 3.
47 Lady S. Holland, *Memoir of the Reverend Sydney Smith* (London, 1854).
48 A. Hook, *Scotland and America: a Study of Cultural Relations, 1750–1838* (Glasgow and London: Blackie and Sons, 1975).

49 Mrs S. to 3rd Viscount Palmerston, 17 August 1802; BA – BR22a/8.
50 DS to unnamed correspondent, 1 September 1802; NLS MS 5319, f. 37.
51 DS to Lord Henry Petty, 1 September 1802; NLS MS 2521, f. 169.
52 E. D. Berger, Memoirs of the late Mrs Elizabeth Hamilton (London, 1818).
53 Mrs S. to 3rd Viscount Palmerston, 5 October [1802]; BA – BR22a/8. Though this letter is marked "1803" in the archive, internal evidence suggests 1802.
54 Sir H. Lytton Bulwer, *The Life of Henry John Temple, Viscount Palmerston* (London, 1870).
55 1st Earl of Malmesbury to 3rd Viscount Palmerston, 23 November 1802.
56 1st Earl of Malmesbury to 3rd Viscount Palmerston, 5 March 1803.
57 Sir J. Mackintosh to DS, 2 November 1805; Mackintosh, *Life of Sir James Mackintosh*.
58 DS: Life of Reid, Section III; CW X, pp. 323–4.
59 Butler, *Maria Edgeworth*.
60 M. Edgeworth, *Memoirs of Richard Lovell Edgeworth, Esq., begun by himself and concluded by his daughter Maria Edgeworth* (London, 1820).
61 Maria Edgeworth to Mrs Ruxton, 30 March 1803; A. J. C. Hare, *Life and Letters of Maria Edgeworth* (London, 1894).
62 Information about Callander House is taken from *Short History of Whiteford House*, available from Whiteford House, Edinburgh.
63 Matthew S. to 3rd Viscount Palmerston, 30 May 1803; BA – BR22a/7.
64 Matthew S. to 3rd Viscount Palmerston, 26 June 1803; BA – BR22a/7.
65 DS: *Diary of journeys*.
66 Ibid.
67 Ibid.
68 Sidney Smith to Hon. Caroline Fox, 20 July 1803; N. C. Smith, *The Letters of Sydney Smith* (Oxford: Oxford University Press, 1953).
69 Mrs S. to 3rd Viscount Palmerston, 2 September [1803]; BA – BR22a/8.
70 Sydney Smith to Hon. Caroline Fox, October 1803; Smith, *Letters of Sydney Smith*.
71 Thomas Campbell to John Richardson, 3 November 1803; Beattie, *Life of Thomas Campbell*.
72 R. B. Litchfield, *Tom Wedgwood* (London: Duckworth, 1903). Wordsworth referred to Tom Wedgwood's "tall person and beautiful face".
73 Matthew S. to Hon. William Temple, 19 October 1803; BA – BR22a/7.
74 3rd Viscount Palmerston to Mrs S., October 1803; BA – BR22(i)13.

12 Social Life and the Leslie and Ashburton Affairs (1803–1805)

1 Minutes of Physical Class of RSE; NLS MS Acc. 10000.
2 D. D. McElroy, *Scotland's Age of Improvement* (Washington: Washington State University Press, 1969).
3 A source for information about both the Poker Club and the Friday Club is *An Account of the Friday Club written by Lord Cockburn, together with notes on certain other social clubs in Edinburgh* in Book of the Old Edinburgh Club, Vol. III.
4 Lord Cockburn, *The Life of Lord Jeffrey, with Selections from his Correspondence* (Edinburgh, 1852).

5   Mrs S. to 3rd Viscount Palmerston, 8 January 1804; BA – BR22a/8.
6   C. Nimmo, *Memoir of the Author* in A. Dalzel: *History of the University of Edinburgh* (Edinburgh, 1862).
7   M. Stewart, *Memoir*.
8   Mrs S.: supplementary note to DS memorandum re. his sinecure, 1827; NLS MS 12135, f. 114.
9   Mrs S. to 3rd Viscount Pamerston, 17 February 1804; BA – BR22a/8.
10 Mrs S. to 3rd Viscount Palmerston, 25 August 1804; BA – BR22a/8.
11 Francis Horner to John Murray, 1 December 1804; K. Bourne and W. Banks Taylor (eds.) *The Horner Papers* (Edinburgh: Edinburgh University Press, 1994).
12 Mrs S. to 3rd Viscount Palmerston, 1 January 1805; BA – BR22a/8.
13 Mrs S. to 3rd Viscount Palmerston, 26 January 1805; BA – BR22a/8.
14 Mrs S. to 3rd Viscount Palmerston, 19 February 1805; BA – BR22a/8.
15 Information supplied by Mrs Pat Gordon.
16 Mrs S. to Lord Henry Petty, early spring 1805 (assumed date); BL, Lansdowne Papers.
17 The primary source for information about the Leslie affair is DS's *A Short Statement of some important Facts relating to the Election of a Mathematical Professor in the University of Edinburgh,* first published in May 1805 and subsequntly reissued with the various supplements referred to in the text. Useful background information, used in the text, is to be found in A. L. Drummond and J. Bulloch, *The Scottish Church 1688–1843* (Edinburgh: St Andrews Press, 1973); T. C. Smout, *A History of the Scottish People 1560–1830* (London: William Collins, 1969); P. Flynn, *Enlightened Scotland* (Edinburgh: Scottish Academic Press, 1992); and L. Williams, 'Pulpit and Crown' – *Edinburgh University and the Church, 1760–1830* in J. J. Carter and D. J. Withrington, *Scottish Universities: Distinctiveness and Diversity* (Edinburgh: John Donald, 1992). Two journal articles have discussed the controversy, from a mainly theological and a mainly biographical point of view respectively – I. D. Clark, *The Leslie Controversy* in *Scottish Church History Society*, Vol. XIV (1962); and J. B. Morrell, *The Leslie Affair* in *Scottish Historical Review*, Vol. LIV (1975).
18 DS: Diss, Part First, Chapter II, Section 3; CW I, P. 179.
19 DS to Lord Provost, 12 February 1805; ECA, Council Record Vol. 142.
20 Ibid., March 1805.
21 Mrs S. to 3rd Viscount Palmerston, spring 1805 (assumed date); BA – BR22a/8.
22 DS: EPHM I, Chapter I, Section II; CW, Vol. II, p. 96.
23 Ibid., Note C, pp. 476ff.
24 In 1819. Some observations about Leslie appear in Mary Somerville's *Personal Recollections*.
25 DS: EPHM III, Part Third, Chapter I, Section iii; CW IV, p. 205.
26 Mrs S. to Lord Henry Petty, 7 June 1805; BL, Lansdowne Papers.
27 Lord Minto to DS, 3 January 1806; NLS MS 11153, f. 105.
28 Sydney Smith to Francis Jeffrey, 12 June 1805; N. C. Smith (ed.), *The Letters*

Notes to pp. 130–40

    of Sydney Smith (Oxford: Oxford University Press, 1953. By 'Darcy', Smith of course meant Mrs Helen D'Arcy Stewart.
29 Thomas Thomson to Francis Horner, 20 July 1805; L. Horner (ed.), *Memoirs and Correspondence of Francis Horner* (London, 1843).
30 Mrs S. to 3rd Viscount Palmerston, 5 August 1805; BA – BR22a/8.
31 Mrs S. to 3rd Viscount Palmerston, 25 August 1804; BA – BR22a/8.
32 Mrs S. to 3rd Viscount Palmerston, 16 September 1805; BA – BR22a/8.
33 Mrs S. to 3rd Viscount Palmerston, 26 October 1805; BA – BR22a/8.
34 E. Grant, *Memoirs of a Highland Lady, Vol. II* (Edinburgh: Canongate, 1988).
35 Mrs S. to 2nd Earl of Minto, January 1826; NLS MS 11798, f. 119. See chapter 17.
36 Mrs S. to Lady Minto, 6 March 1806; NLS MS 11079, f. 81.
37 Mrs S. to 3rd Marquess of Lansdowne, autumn 1822 (assumed date); BL, Lansdowne Papers.
38 Mrs S. to Countes of Minto, March 1826; NLS MS 11798, f. 124.
39 Mrs S. to 3rd Viscount Palmerston, 25 August 1804; BA – BR22a/8.

13   *Towards Retirement (1806–1810)*

1 K. Bourne, *Palmerston: The Early Years 1784–1841* (London: Allen Lane, 1982).
2 DS to Francis Horner, 12 February 1806; Veitch, *Life*, Appendix A, XIII; CW X, pp. cxxxviii–cxxxix.
3 W. J. Couper, *The Edinburgh Periodical Press* (Stirling: Eneas Mackay, 1908).
4 Veitch, *Life*, Chapter III; CW X, p. lxxix.
5 Walter Scott to Lady Abercorn, 20 July 1807; Sir H. Grierson (ed.), *The Letters of Sir Walter Scott* (London: Constable, 1932–37).
6 The debate was reported in *Cobbett's Political Register, Vol. XII, No. 3* (18 July 1807).
7 Mrs S. to Lord Henry Petty, 18 July 1807; BL, Lansdowne Papers.
8 B. Silliman, *A Journal of Travels in England, Holland, and Scotland in 1805–6, No. LXXXV* (1810).
9 R. P. Gillies, *Memoirs of a Literary Veteran* (London, 1851).
10 Mrs S. to Lord Henry Petty, 7 June 1805; Ibid.
11 DS to Francis Horner, 8 June 1805; K. Bourne and W. Banks Taylor, *The Horner Papers* (Edinburgh: Edinburgh University Press, 1994).
12 Sir W. Scott, *Health to Lord Melville*, 1806.
13 DS to Lady Minto, end of June 1807 (assumed month): Countess of Minto, *Life and Letters of Sir Gilbert Elliot, First Earl of Minto from 1751 to 1806* (London, 1874).
14 Lady Minto to DS; ibid.
15 Sir Walter Scott to John Wilson, 16 April 1820; Grierson, *Letters*.
16 The ensuing account of this diplomatic episode is taken from H. Butterfield, *Charles James Fox and Napoleon: the Peace Negotiations of 1806 (the Creighton Lecture in History, 1961)* (London: University of London, 1962).

Notes to pp. 140–6

17 Veitch, *Life*, Chapter II; CW X, p. liv fn.
18 J. W. Ward to Mrs S., July 1806 (assumed date); S. H. Romilly (ed.), *Letters to "Ivy" from the First Earl of Dudley* (London: Longmans Green, 1905).
19 Holland House Dinner Book; BL Add MS 5195. "Mrs Stewart" is recorded as having dined on 7, 21 and 31 August and on 22 October 1806.
20 M. Stewart, *Memoir*.
21 DS to John Allen, 8 September 1806; BL Add MS 52193, f. 70.
22 DS: Life of Smith, Note E; CW X, p. 86.
23 See NLS MS 5319, ff. 48, 50 and 57.
24 EUL Dc.3.104.
25 DS to William Drennan, 20 September 1808; EUL Dc.1.100(2), ff. 5–8.
26 Matthew S.'s army record; Public Record Office.
27 Mrs S. to 3rd Viscount Palmerston, 8 January 1804; BA – BR22a/8.
28 Scottish National Portrait Gallery.
29 Francis Horner to Mrs S., 30 June 1806: "There is scarcely any circumstance in Lord Lauderdale's resignation of India, that gives me regret, except Matthew's disappointment; and that, I hope to his friends at least, carries its consolation along with it." (Bourne and Banks Taylor, *Horner Papers*).
30 Mrs S. to 3rd Viscount Palmerston, January 1807; BA – BR22a/8.
31 Before Minto left for India he gave DS several letters between his father, Sir Gilbert Elliot, and David Hume to which DS refers in EPHM II Note C and Diss. Note CCC. T. Somerville, *My Own Life and Times, 1741–1814* (Edinburgh, 1861).
32 Mrs S. to Matthew S., 13 April 1808; NLS MS 11327, f. 1.
33 Mrs S. to 3rd Viscount Palmerston, 11 June 1807 (assumed month); BA – BR22a/8.
34 3rd Viscount Palmerston: *Autobiographical Fragment* (1830).
35 The story is told in R. Chambers, *Traditions of Edinburgh*, (Edinburgh, 1830); the old servant's words are in the Edinburgh Review, Vol. CXXXV (January–April 1872), No. 276: *Letters and Discoveries of the late Sir Charles Bell*.
36 Court of Lord Lyon, Edinburgh.
37 DS to Thomas Greenfield, 23 May (1807) and 2 April 1812; NLS MS 19770, ff. 39 & 35.
38 Robert P. Gillies wrote of Henry Mackenzie: "Like Dugald Stewart . . . he showed from youth to age a decided predilection for a country life"; H. W. Thompson, *A Scottish Man of Feeling – Some Account of Henry Mackenzie, Esq., of Edinburgh and the Golden Age of Burns and Scott* (Oxford: Oxford University Press, 1931).
39 I am indebted for this suggestion to Emeritus Professor Alex Garvie of Glasgow University.
40 Mrs S. to 3rd Viscount Palmerston, 26 June 1807; BA – BR22a/8.
41 Mrs S. to 3rd Viscount Palmerston, 2 October 1807; BA – BR22a/8.
42 Mrs S. to 3rd Viscount Palmerston, 30 October 1807; BA – BR22a/8.
43 Mrs S. to William Drennan, November 1807; EUL Dc.1.100(2), ff. 3–4.
44 Mrs S. to Dr Anderson, 1 January 1808; NLS Adv.22.4.17, f. 31.

45 He wrote to the Earl of Minto on 5 February; NLS MS 11147, f. 100.
46 He attended one on 1 April; NLS Acc. 10000, 4.
47 Mrs S. to 3rd Viscount Palmerston, April [1808]; BA – BR22a/8.
48 DS to William Drennan, 20 September 1808.
49 Matthew S. to John Elliot, 23 April 1809; NLS Ms 11327, ff. 9–16.
50 Lord Minto to Matthew S., 19 June, 1809; NLS Ms 11285, f. 279.
51 Matthew S. to Lord Minto, 6 July 1809; NLS Ms 11327, f. 35.
52 Francis Horner to Lord Webb Seymour, 7 January 1809; L. Horner (ed.), *Memoirs and Correspondence of Francis Horner* (London, 1853).
53 This is implied in Horner's reply.
54 Francis Horner to Mrs S., 25 January 1809; Bourne and Banks Taylor, *Horner Papers*.
55 Francis Horner to Lord Webb Seymour, 27 January 1809; ibid.
56 Archibald Alison to Thomas Telford, 2 March 1809; W. Beattie, *Life and Letters of Thomas Campbell* (London, 1850).
57 Thomas Campbell to his Sydenham friends, 7 March 1809; ibid.
58 D. Welsh, *Memoir of Thomas Brown* in *Lectures on the Philosophy of the Human Mind by the late Thomas Brown, MD* (Edinburgh, 1830).
59 DS: PE, Preliminary Dissertation, Chapter II; CW V, p. 54.
60 Mrs S. to Lady Minto, 3 August 1809; NLS Ms 11156, f. 82.
61 Information about Kinneil House is available from Historic Scotland and from Falkirk District Council.
62 D. D. McElroy, *Scotland's Age of Improvement* (Washington, Washington University State Press, 1969).
63 David Wilkie to Benjamin Haydon, 7 August 1817; F. W. Haydon, *Benjamin Robert Haydon: Correspondence and Table-Talk* (London, 1876).
64 DS to Earl of Buchan, 23 July 1792; BL Add MS 28104, f. 63. In 1810 DS told the Earl of Minto that he proposed "to pass, in future, the whole year in the country" – NLS MS 11148, f. 153.
65 DS: Pol Econ, Vol. I, Part First, Chapter II Section iii, Subsection 3; CW VIII, p. 205.
66 Mrs S. to Lady Minto, 3 August 1809; the last phrase has been partially obscured in the MS and is therefore slightly speculative.
67 Sir A. Alison (ed. Lady Alison): *Some Account of my Life and Writings – an Autobiography* (Edinburgh, 1883).
68 DS to Archibald Constable, 13 November 1809; NLS Ms 675, f. 77.
69 DS to William Trotter, December 1809; NLS Ms 9657, f. 61.
70 Welsh, *Memoir of Thomas Brown*.
71 Maria Edgeworth to Mrs Ruxton, January 1810; A. J. C. Hare, *The Life and Letters of Maria Edgeworth* (London, 1894). The date of the letter, in which Miss Edgeworth reports hearing from Mr Holland, suggests that this may have been the occasion described.
72 Welsh, *Memoir of Thomas Brown*. Holland claimed the chairmanship in his *Recollections of Past Life* (London: 1872).
73 ECA, Council Record Vol. 155, Minute of 1 May 1810.
74 Lord John Russell to Lady Holland, 4 February 1810; BL Add MS 51678, f. 17.

75 ECA, Council Record Vol. 155, Minute of 1 May 1810.
76 DS to Samuel Parr, 1810: J. Johnstone, *Samuel Parr with Memoirs of his Life and Writings and a Selection of his Correspondence* (London, 1828).
77 Thomas Campbell to a friend, 8 May 1815; Beattie, *Life of Thomas Campbell*.
78 Cockburn, *Memorials*.

14 The Teacher and the Man

1 EUL Dc.6.11, f.11.
2 R. P. Gillies, *Memoirs of a Literary Veteran* (Edinburgh, 1851).
3 Ibid.
4 Cockburn, *Memorials*.
5 Sir A. Alison (ed. Lady Alison), *Some Account of My Life and Writings – An Autobiography* (1883).
6 Veitch, *Life*, Chapter II; CW X, p. xxxviii, fn. Mrs Siddons made a triumphant visit to Edinburgh in 1784, and was there again in 1808, when Robert Gillies encountered DS trying to find a seat in the theatre to see her play Lady Macbeth.
7 M. Stewart, *Memoir*.
8 James Mill to Macvey Napier, 10 July 1831; M. Napier (ed.), *Selection from the Correspondence of the late Macvey Napier, Esq.* (London, 1879).
9 *The American Review of History and Politics*, I (1811).
10 *Scots Magazine* (September, 1810).
11 A. Bell, *Lectures on Moral Philosophy by Dugald Stewart 1793-4*, EUL Dc.4.97.
12 J. Bridges, *Notes from Dugald Stewart's Moral Philosophy Lectures, 1801-2*; EUL Dc.5.88.
13 Veitch, *Life*, Chapter II; CW X, p. xliv.
14 DS: Pol Econ, Book Fourth, Part Second, Chapter II, Section ii; CW IX, p. 453.
15 Alison, *Some Account of my Life*.
16 K. Bourne and W. Banks Taylor, *The Horner Papers*, (Edinburgh: Edinburgh University Press, 1994); Horner's *Journal* for 17 December 1800.
17 G. Strickland, *Notes of Dugald Stewart's lectures on Political Oeconomy, November 1803-13 April 1804*; NLS MS 3771.
18 DS: Pol Econ, Introduction, Chapter I; CW VIII, p. 10.
19 Veitch, *Life*, Chapter II; CW X, pp. xlii-xliii.
20 Bourne and Banks Taylor, *The Horner Papers*; Horner's *Journal* for 16 January 1801.
21 Alison, *Some Account of my Life*.
22 Sir W. Scott, *Journal* for 10-14 June 1828 (Edinburgh: Oliver and Boyd, 1950).
23 W. Hanna, *Memoirs of Dr Chalmers* (Edinburgh, 1849-52).
24 Cockburn, *Memorials*.
25 Ibid.
26 B. Silliman, *A Journal of Travels in England, Holland, and Scotland in 1805-06* (1810).

27 The information in this paragraph is mainly derived from the Library of the Scottish National Portrait Gallery, Edinburgh.
28 Mrs S. to Lady Minto, 1810 (assumed date); NLS MS 11156, f. 143.
29 A. Bower, *The History of the University of Edinburgh* (Edinburgh, 1830).
30 Cockburn, *Memorials*.
31 D. Welsh, *Memoir of the Author* in *Lectures on the Philosophy of the Human Mind by the late Thomas Brown* (Edinburgh, 1830). James Harris wonders whether Brown may have exaggerated the difficulty of DS's notes in order to explain why he developed his own rather different account of common sense philosophy.
32 K. Bourne, *Palmerston: The Early Years 1784–1841* (London: Allen Lane, London, 1982).
33 Bourne and Banks Talylor, *The Horner Papers*; Horner's *Journal* for 24 April 1801.
34 R. P. Gillies, *Memoirs of a Literary Veteran* (London, 1851).
35 David Wilkie to Benjamin Haydon, 7 August 1817; F. W. Haydon (ed.), *Benjamin Robert Haydon: Correspondence and Table-Talk* (London, 1876).
36 Countess of Minto, *Life and Letters of Sir Gilbert Elliot, First Earl of Minto from 1751 to 1806* (London, 1874).
37 Lady S. Holland, *A Memoir of the Reverend Sydney Smith* (London, 1854).
38 Matthew S. to Macvey Napier, 1833 (assumed date); BL Add MS 34616, f. 84.
39 Silliman, *Journal of Travels*.
40 Earl of Dudley to Bishop Copleston, 31 January 1818; E. Copleston, (ed.), *Letters of the Earl of Dudley to the Bishop of Llandaff* (London, 1840).
41 M. Stewart, *Memoir*.
42 Quoted in chapter 11, see note 60.
43 M. Stewart, *Memoir*.
44 Earl of Dudley to Bishop Copleston, 31 January 1818; Copleston (ed.), *Letters*.
45 R. Burns, *Second Common Place Book*; A. Bold, *A Burns Companion* (Basingstoke: Macmillan, 1991).
46 J. W. Burgon, *The Portrait of a Christian Gentleman – a Memoir of Patrick Fraser Tytler* (London, 1859).
47 *The Scotsman*, 14 June 1828.
48 Thomas Campbell to a friend, 8 May 1815; W. Beattie, *Life and Letters of Thomas Campbell* (London, 1850).
49 Sydney Smith to Lady Holland, 9 September 1808; Lady Holland, *Memoir*.
50 *The Quarterly Review*, Vol. LXVII (Dec. 1840 & March 1841), no. CXXXIII.
51 Gillies, *Memoirs of a Literary Veteran*.
52 J. W. Ward to Mrs S., 1 April 1809; S. H. Romilly (ed.), *Letters to "Ivy" from the first Earl of Dudley* (London: Longmans Green, London, 1907).
53 This may well have been William Creech's shop facing down the High Street at the east end of the Luckenbooths. James Boswell referred in his *Journal* (12 January 1786) to sitting "in the room behind Creech's shop". It was an established literary rendez-vous.

54 J. W. Burgon, *Portrait of a Christian Gentleman*.
55 T. Constable, *Archibald Constable and his Literary Correspondents* (Edinburgh, 1873).
56 Walter Scott to Anna Seward, October/November 1802; Sir H. Grierson (ed.), *The Letters of Sir Walter Scott* (London: Constable, 1932–37).
57 Mrs S. to Archibald Constable, November 1813 (assumed date); NLS MS 675, f. 149.
58 H. W. Thompson (ed.), *Anecdotes and Egotisms of Henry Mackenzie* (Oxford: Oxford University Press, 1927). This joke was included in *The Oxford Book of Literary Anecdotes* (1976).
59 Veitch, *Life, Appendix A*; CW X, p. cxvii.
60 T. Moore, *Journal*, 8 November 1818; Earl Russell, *Memoirs, Journal and Correspondence of Thomas Moore* (London, 1853–6).
61 Mrs S. to Lady Minto, 7 January 1802; NLS MS 11152, f. 90.
62 DS: *Epitaph*, not dated; NLS MS 3953, f. 46.
63 Veitch, *Life, Chapter III*; CW X, p. xliii.
64 DS's library; EUL.
65 J. R. Guild and A. Law (eds), *Edinburgh University Library 1580–1980* (Edinburgh: Edinburgh University Library, 1982).
66 Mrs S. to Archibald Constable, 15 February 1814; NLS MS 675, f. 157.
67 DS: PAMP I, Book Second, Chapter V; CW VI, p. 306.
68 D. Welsh, *Memoir of the Author*.
69 *The Life and Times of Henry Lord Brougham written by himself* (Edinburgh and London, 1871).
70 DS to Francis Horner, 8 June 1805; Bourne and Banks Taylor, *Horner Papers*.
71 DS to Dr John Lee, 23 September 1820; the letter has survived as NLS MS 3434, f. 328.
72 Scottish Universities Commission, Vol. I (Edinburgh); evidence taken on 8 November 1827.
73 Robert Burns to Mrs Dunlop of Dunlop, 24 November 1787; see chapter 7, note 29. Burns made a similar comment to Captain Grose in July 1790, quoted in chapter 7 – see note 35.
74 Cockburn, *Memorials*.
75 J. Stewart, *Parish of Sorn* in *New Statistical Account of Scotland, Vol. 5* (Edinburgh, 1845).
76 DS: Pol Econ, Part First, Book First, Chapter II, Section iii, Subsection 2, second, 1); CW VIII, p. 188.
77 DS: Pol Econ, Introduction, Chapter II, Section iv, CW VIII, p. 44.
78 DS: PE Part Second, Essay Fourth, Chapter I; CW V, p. 390.
79 DS: PE Part Second, Essay Third, Chapter I; CW V, p. 337.
80 This criticism of the Scottish Enlightenment was voiced by J. McCosh, *Scottish Philosophy* (London, 1875).
81 Cockburn, *Memorials*. De Quincey was another who complained that DS had "no originality".
82 Francis Horner to Thomas Thomson, 8 August 1805; Bourne and Banks Taylor, *Horner Papers*.

83 Earl of Ilchester, *The Home of the Hollands 1603–1820* (London: John Murray, 1937).
84 J. A. Murray in *The Scotsman*, 1858; NLS MS 11808, f. 389.
85 DS: Pol Ecom, Part First, Book First, Chapter II, Section iii, Subject 2, First–5; CW VIII, p. 151.
86 DS: Diss, Part First, Chapter I; CW I, p. 31.
87 Sir J. Mackintosh, *Dugald Stewart* in *On the Progress of Ethical Philosophy* (Edinburgh, 1872).
88 Cockburn, *Memorials*.
89 Veitch, *Life, Chapter II*; CW X, pp. xliv–xlv.

15 The Early Years of Retirement (1810–1820)

1 DS to Archibald Constable, 24 May 1810; NLS MS 675, f. 83.
2 DS: PE, CW V, pp. 1 and 3.
3 DS to John Stark, 30 June 1810 (NLS MS 675, f. 90) and to Archibald Constable, July 1810 (assumed date), (NLS MS 675, f. 92).
4 DS to Archibald Constable, June 1810 (asumed date); NLS MS 675, f. 88. Prévost had occupied the chair of philosophy at Berlin from 1780 until 1784.
5 DS to Sir Samuel Romilly, 28 June 1810; Romilly (ed.): *Memoirs of the Life of Sir Samuel Romilly, written by himself, with a selection from his correspondence* (London, 1842).
6 DS to Archibald Constable, 5 July 1810; NLS MS 675, f. 94.
7 DS to William Davies, 26 July 1810; NLS MS 675, f. 96.
8 Francis Jeffrey to Francis Horner, 20 July 1810; Lord Cockburn, *The Life of Lord Jeffrey* (Edinburgh, 1852).
9 Sydney Smith to his daughter, July 1810; N. C. Smith (ed.), *The Letters of Sydney Smith* (Oxford: Oxford University Press, 1953).
10 DS to Archibald Constable, 5 July 1810; NLS MS 675, f. 94.
11 William Davies to DS, 24 August 1810; NLS MS 675, f. 100.
12 DS to Macvey Napier, 18 December 1811; BL Add MS 34611, f. 19.
13 DS to Archibald Constable, 4 September 1810; NLS MS 675, f. 101.
14 Lord Minto to DS, 22 January 1809; NLS MS 11285, f. 200.
15 According to Matthew S.'s army records, he was promoted Captain on 4 May 1809 and transferred to the 22nd Foot on 11 May.
16 Lord Minto to Major-General Abercromby, 10 September 1810; NLS MS 11327, f. 40.
17 Matthew S. to Lord Minto, 29 April 1811 (NLS MS 11096, f. 33) and 16 May 1811 (NLS MS 11327, f. 44).
18 DS to Lord Minto, 27 June 1810 (NLS MS 11148, f. 153) and 3 June 1811 (NLS MS 11147, f. 100).
19 John Allen to Macvey Napier, 25 March 1843: "[Horner] had great affection and veneration for Mr Stewart"; M. Napier, *Selection from the Correspondence of the late Macvey Napier, Esq.* (London, 1879).
20 DS agreed that the increased issue of banknotes had caused the currency to depreciate, but attributed this more specifically to the sudden increase in credit causing increase in demand. See DS: Pol Econ, Appendix II; CW VIII, pp. 431–52.

21 R. E. Scott, Dedication of *Inquiry into the Limits and Peculiar Objects of Physical and Metaphysical Science* (Edinburgh, 1810).
22 Rev. A. Alison, Dedication of *Essays on the Nature and Principles of Taste* (2nd edn., 1810).
23 Henry Mackenzie to DS, 28 November 1810; NLS MS 676, f. 16.
24 DS to Henry Mackenzie, 10 December 1810; NLS MS 124, f. 25.
25 DS to Hon. Mrs Elliot, 1811; NLS MS 11906. f. 5. According to a letter from Mrs S. to Lady Minto dated 12 January 1812, the dentist visited Kinneil House on that day; NLS MS 11156, f. 144.
26 DS to Lady Minto, 15 January 1811; NLS MS 13339, f. 70.
27 Mrs S. to Hon. Gilbert Elliot, 20 January 1811; NLS MS 13336, f. 114.
28 Francis Jeffrey to Francis Horner, 25 January 1811; K. Bourne and W. Banks Taylor (eds.), *The Horner Papers* (Edinburgh: Edinburgh University Press, 1994). Cockburn wrote in his *Memorials*: "These Fox dinners did incalculable good. They animated, and instructed, and consolidated the Whig party wih less trouble and more effect than anything else that could have been devised."
29 Mrs S. to Lady Minto, 10 March 1811; NLS Ms 11081, f. 314.
30 DS: PE, Advertisement; CW V, p. 3.
31 DS: *Biographical Memoirs of Adam Smith, William Robertson, and of Thomas Reid, read before the Royal Society of Edinburgh* (Edinburgh, 1811).
32 DS to Archibald Constable & Co., 30 May 1811; NLS MS 21001, f. 102.
33 Mrs S. to Hon. Gilbert Elliot, 20 May 1811; NLS MS 11798, f. 80.
34 DS to Archibald Constable, 9 June 1811; NLS MS 675, f. 115.
35 Lady S. Holland, *A Memoir of the Reverend Sydney Smith, with a selection from his Letters* (London, 1855). Saba Smith married Sir Henry Holland.
36 DS to Archibald Constable, 24 June 1824; NLS MS 675, f. 118. DS was still in Harrogate on the 28th, when he wrote to the Rev. James Graham (NLS MS 3519, f. 45).
37 DS's account of the boy born blind and deaf, as read to the RSE and subsequently supplemented, first published in *Transactions of the RSE, Vol. VII*, appears as an Appendix to EPHM II, Part Third, Chapter Second; CW IV, pp. 300–70.
38 DS to Francis Horner, 4 January 1813; NLS MS 675 f. 43.
39 *Draft Minutes of Council of RSE and General Meetings 1795– 1826*, 26 December 1812; NLS Acc. 10000.
40 Ibid., 28 December 1812.
41 Ibid., February and 8 March 1814.
42 Mrs S. to Lord Melgund, 12 August 1813; NLS MS 11793, f. 93.
43 Transactions of the RSE, Vol. VIII.
44 S. Walpole, *Life of Lord John Russell* (London, 1889).
45 Lord John Russell to "Kennedy", 15 July 1812; NLS MS 11869.
46 DS: EPHM II, Part Third, Chap. II, Appendix; CW IV, p. 359.
47 Francis Horner to Frances Horner, 9 September 1812; Bourne and Banks Taylor, *Horner Papers*.
48 Sir Samuel Romilly, *Journal*, August or September 1812; Romilly, *Life of Sir Samuel Romilly*.

Notes to pp. 178–81

49 DS to Archibald Constable, 3 October 1812; NLS MS 675, f. 132.
50 DS to Macvey Napier, 18 October 1812; BL Add MS 34611, f. 25.
51 The Cess (tax) valuation for Catrine House in 1816 was £76.16s.8d.
52 Mrs S. was justified, from her point of view, in her forebodings, as the general election of 1812 resulted in the return of Lord Liverpool's government, with the Tories in power until 1830.
53 Mrs S. to Archibald Constable, 22 October 1812; T. Constable, *Archibald Constable and his Literary Correspondents* (Edinburgh, 1873).
54 Mrs S. to Archibald Constable, 11 November 1812; NLS MS 675, f. 138.
55 DS to Archibald Constable, 15 November 1812; Constable, *Constable and his Literary Correspondents*.
56 DS to Francis Horner, 4 January 1813; NLS MS 5319, f. 43.
57 DS to John Allen, 2 February 1813; BL Add MS 52194, f. 48.
58 Veitch, *Life*, Chapter I (CW X, p. xxxii fn) confirmed by Matthew S.'s army record.
59 This is implied by DS's letter to Horner of 4 January 1813, in which he writes of receiving his mail "a few days ago".
60 DS to John Allen, 2 February 1813; BL Add MS 52194, f. 48.
61 DS to Macvey Napier, 27 February 1827; BL Add MS 34611, f. 27.
62 Mrs S. to Archibald Constable, 24 March 1813; NLS MS 675, f. 142.
63 DS to Baron de Gerando, 5 March 1815; NLS MS 5319, f. 53. In this letter DS refers to receiving the communication from Berlin "not much less than two years" previously.
64 Ibid.
65 These honours are attached to DS's name in CW.
66 Mrs S. to William Drennan, 22 November 1813; EUL Dc.1.100 (2), ff. 1–2.
67 DS to Archibald Constable, 14 August 1813; NLS MS 675, f. 145.
68 Francis Horner to Lord Webb Seymour, 26 October 1813; Bourne and Banks Taylor, *Horner Papers*.
69 J.W. Ward to Mrs S., 3 November 1813; S. H. Romilly (ed.), *'Letters to "Ivy" from the First Earl of Dudley* (London: Longmans Green, 1905).
70 Maria S. to Mrs S., 2 November 1813; ibid.
71 Mrs S. to Archibald Constable, 25 February 1814; NLS MS 675, f. 159.
72 Romilly, *Letters to Ivy*.
73 Maria S. to Mrs S., 22 March 1814; Romilly, *Letters to Ivy*.
74 Ibid.
75 Maria S. to Mrs S., 7 April 1814; Romilly, *Letters to Ivy*.
76 The future King Charles X of France was given refuge at Holyrood Palace – virtually opposite Lothian House – from January 1796 until August 1799, and again from December 1801 until April 1803. See A. J. Mackenzie-Stuart, *A French King at Holyrood* (Edinburgh: John Donald, 1995).
77 DS: EPHM II, Advertisement; CW III, p. 4.
78 Mrs S. to William Drennan, 22 November 1813; EUL Dc.100 (2), ff. 1–2.
79 Z. Colburn, *Memoir of Zerah Colburn, written by himself* (Springfield, Mass., 1833). (Colburn described his travels in the third person.) Harriet Elliot mentioned DS when writing to her brother about Zerah: Lady Harriet Elliot to Viscount Melgund, 19 January 1814; NLS MS 11756, f. 39.

80 DS to Archibald Constable, 10 January 1814; NLS MS 675, f. 152.
81 Mrs S. to Archibald Constable, early February 1814 (assumed month); NLS MS 675, f. 154.
82 For example, he sent a copy to the Marquess of Douglas, son of the Duke of Hamilton, on 15 February; NAS, Hamilton Archive, Bundle No. 769.
83 T. Constable, *Constable and his Literary Correspondents*.
84 Francis Horner to John Murray, 25 February 1814; *Memoirs and Correspondence of Francis Horner* (1853).
85 This is the first of three known visits which the Stewarts made to Langley Park, the last being in May 1823. Langley Park was a mansion built about 1780 which at this period belonged to James Cruickshank, a Deputy Lieutenant for County Angus. The nature of the connection between DS and the Cruickshank family has not been established. See also chapter 17.
86 Mrs S. to Archibald Constable, 25 February 1814; NLS MS 675, f. 159.
87 Mrs S. to Archibald Constable, 4 April 1814; NLS MS 675, f. 163.
88 DS to Baron de Gerando, 27 May 1814; NLS MS 5319, f. 46.
89 Matthew S. to Hon. J. Elliot, undated; NLS MS 11334, f. 104.
90 Mrs S. to Archibald Constable, 1814; T. Constable, *Constable and his Literary Correspondents*.
91 He says so in DS: EPHM II, Advertisement; CW III, p. 2.
92 Account of the origin and progress of the *Encyclopaedia Britannica* and its Supplement by John Ogle Robinson in T. Constable, *Constable and his Literary Correspondents*.
93 DS to Francis Horner, 29 April 1814; BL Add MS 34611, f. 5.
94 Archibald Constable to DS, 8 October 1814; NLS MS 789, f. 134.
95 Veitch, *Life, Chapter I*; CW X, p. xxx fn.
96 In a letter of 31 January 1811 to Thomas Thomson, DS referred to one "Ainslie" as "by far the most correct transcriber I have ever employed"; and Mrs S. referred to a copyist employed around the same time.
97 Bourne and Banks Taylor, *Horner Papers*.
98 DS to George Wilson, 23 December 1814; NLS MS 849, f. 319.
99 DS to Samuel Parr, 4 February 1815; J. Johnstone, *Samuel Parr, with memoirs of his Life and Writings and a selecion from his Correspondence* (London, 1828).
100 Mrs S. to Archibald Constable, 24 March 1813; NLS MS 675, f. 142.
101 Mrs S. to Archibald Constable, (1814); NLS MS 675, f. 173.
102 Mrs S. to Archibald Constable, 19 July 1814; NLS MS 675, f. 167.
103 Mrs S. to Archibald Constable, 15 March 1815; NLS MS 675, f. 174.
104 Mrs S. to Archibald Constable, 1816 (*The Antiquary* was published early in May of that year); T. Constable, *Constable and his Literary Correspondents*.
105 Information supplied by Mrs Pat Gordon.
106 T. Campbell to a friend, 8 May 1815; W. Beattie, *Life and Letters of Thomas Campbell* (London 1850)
107 Anonymous letter to DS, 25 June 1815; Veitch, *Life, Appendix B, IV*; CW X, pp. cliii–clix.
108 Rev. Sir H. Moncrieff Wellwood to Mrs S., 22 September 1815; Veitch, *Life, Appendix B, V*; CW X, pp. clix–clxii.

Notes to pp. 185–90

109 Mrs S. to 2nd Earl of Minto, October 1815; NLS MS 11793, f. 95.
110 DS to 6th Marquess of Lothian, 10 August 1815; GRH, Lothian Muniments.
111 DS to 6th Marquess of Lothian, 23 October 1815; NAS, Lothian Muniments. On 10 November Leonard Horner told a correspondent of DS having been "for some days at a village within a mile of Edinburgh" to correct his proofs.
112 Mrs S. to 2nd Earl of Minto, (?) 18 November 1815; NLS MS 11793, f. 102.
113 Mrs S. to 2nd Earl of Minto, 22 November 1815; NLS MS 11793, f. 97.
114 DS to 6th Marquess of Lothian, 7 December 1815; NAS, Lothian Muniments.

16 Deaths of Friends and the Final Break (1815–1820)

1 DS to Sir James Mackintosh, 18 November 1816; BL Add MS 52452, f. 207.
2 Mrs S. to Archibald Constable, 14 December 1815; NLS MS 675, f. 179. Mrs S. seems to have prided herself on providing simple fare; in 1814 she made no apologies for offering to Lady Liston, who was about to visit Kinneil, "the plainest of Dinners and the most old fashioned of houses" – Mrs S. to Lady Liston, NLS MS 5671, f. 177.
3 Francis Horner to Anne Horner, 15 December 1815; *Memoirs and Correspondence of Francis Horner* (Edinburgh, 1843).
4 Archibald Constable to Mrs S., 26 December 1815; NLS MS 789, f. 465.
5 J. W. Ward to Mrs S., 7 January 1816; S. H. Romilly (ed.), *Letters to "Ivy" from the First Earl of Dudley* (London: Longmans Green, 1905).
6 Francis Horner to Anne Horner, 29 January 1816; *Memoirs of Francis Horner*.
7 Maria S. to Mrs Leonard Horner, 11 April 1843; K. M. Lyell, *Memoir of Leonard Horner* (London, 1890).
8 DS to Archibald Constable, 22 April 1816; NLS MS 675, f. 188.
9 Archibald Constable to DS, 14 February 1814; NLS MS 789, f. 219.
10 Mrs S. to Archibald Constable, 1 February 1816; NLS MS 675, f. 181.
11 Mrs S. to Archibald Constable, 8 February 1816; NLS MS 675, f. 182.
12 Mrs S. to Archibald Constable, 12 February 1816; NLS MS 675, f. 183.
13 DS to Rev. John Lee, 6 March 1816; NLS MS 3434, f. 29.
14 Mrs S. to Archibald Constable, 8 February 1816; NLS MS 675, f. 182.
15 Matthew S.'s army record shows that he obtained the rank of Major by purchase in 1814, and that of Lt.-Col. by brevet and subsequently by purchase in 1816.
16 Leonard Horner to Dr Marcet, 14 March 1816; Lyell, *Memoir of Leonard Horner*.
17 Mrs S. to Archibald Constable, 15 April 1816; NLS Ms 675, f. 185. Soon after the Stewarts' arrival at Kinneil, DS had told Constable, "we have no Fish here altho close by the sea".
18 Mrs S. to Archibald Constable, 3 May 1816; NLS Ms 675, f. 190.
19 DS to 6th Marquess of Lothian, 5 July 1816; NAS, Lothian Muniments.
20 M. Bence-Jones: *The Catholic Families* (London: Constable, 1992).
21 DS to Samuel Parr, 17 August 1816; J. Johnstone, *Samuel Parr with Memoirs of his Life and Writings and a Selection from his Correspondence* (London,

1828). A letter of 1816 from DS to Prévost in similar terms is quoted in Veitch, *Life*, Chapter III; CW X, p. lxxxiii fn.
22 Mrs S. to Archibald Constable, 29 January 1817; NLS MS 675, f. 201.
23 Mrs S. to Archibald Constable, 20 February 1817; NLS MS 675, f. 203.
24 DS to 3rd Lord Holland, 20 February 1817; BL Add MS 51828, f. 153.
25 DS to Lady Holland, 26 September 1816 (assumed year); BL Add MS 51847, f. 165.
26 Mrs S. to Sir James Mackintosh, 1 October 1816; BL Add MS 52452, f. 205.
27 Francis Horner to Mrs S., 6 November and 17 December 1816 respectively; *Memoirs of Francis Horner*.
28 DS: Diss, Note C; CW I, pp. 534–6.
29 DS to Lady Katherine Halkett, 30 March 1817; NLS MS 546, f. 24.
30 DS and Mrs S. to Lady Katherine Halkett, 11 May 1817; NLS MS 546, f. 26.
31 Ibid.
32 Ibid.
33 This information is written in pencil on the correspondence in NLS.
34 DS to Macvey Napier, 18 May 1817; BL Add MS 34612, f. 101.
35 Mrs S. to Archibald Constable, 31 July 1817; NLS MS 675, f. 205.
36 Washington Irving to Peter Irving, 27 August 1817; P. M. Irving, *The Life and Letters of Washington Irving* (London, 1862).
37 Washington Irving to Peter Irving, 1 September 1817; ibid.
38 Washington Irving to Peter Irving, 22 September 1817; ibid.
39 That Irving did meet DS is stated in S. J. Brown (ed.), *William Robertson and the Expansion of Empire* (Cambridge: Cambridge University Press, 1997); but I have found no confirmation of this, and it may be that by the time of Irving's return to Edinburgh the Stewarts had already set out on their autumn holiday.
40 DS to Samuel Parr, 30 September 1817; Johnstone, *Samuel Parr*.
41 Mrs S. to Archibald Constable, 10 March 1818; NLS MS 675, f. 206.
42 DS to Thomas Thomson, 8 December 1817; J. T. Gibson Craig and C. Innes, *Memoir of Thomas Thomson* (Edinburgh, 1854).
43 Minutes of the Physical and Literary Class of the RSE, 1 and 15 December 1817 respectively; NLS Acc. 10000, 4.
44 Mrs S. to Thomas Thomson, 8 December 1817; Gibson Craig and Innes, *Thomas Thomson*.
45 Archibald Constable to DS, 24 December 1817; NLS MS 790, f. 90.
46 Archibald Constable to DS, 6 October 1818; NLS MS 790, f. 273.
47 DS to John Dalzel, February 1818 (assumed month); C. Nimmo, *Memoir of the Author* in A. Dalzel, *History of the University of Edinburgh* (Edinburgh, 1862). John Dalzel died in 1823, aged 26.
48 Mrs S. to Archibald Constable, 4 May 1818; NLS MS 675, f. 208.
49 Leonard Horner to Dr Marcet, 10 November 1815; Lyell, *Memoir of Leonard Horner*.
50 Mrs S. to Archibald Constable, 30 June 1818; NLS MS 675, f. 211. The actual castle of Dunglass had long been a ruin, but there was a house within the castle walls which is presumably where the Stewarts were staying – with whom, or at whose invitation, is not clear.

51 Mrs S. to Archibald Constable, 7 August 1818; NLS MS 675, f. 214. Jeanie Deans is, of course, the heroine of Scott's *The Heart of Midlothian* (1818).
52 Sir Walter Scott to 4th Duke of Buccleuch, 14 November 1818; Sir H. Grierson (ed.), *The Letters of Sir Walter Scott* (London: Constable, 1932).
53 Sir W. Scott, *Journal* for 9 September 1827 (Edinburgh: Oliver and Boyd, 1950).
54 "Cranstoun – Lord Corehouse, took his seat on the bench to-day. This is the most important event for Scotland that has taken place for many years." – Thomas Thomson to 2nd Earl of Minto, 21 November 1826; Gibson Craig and Innes, *Thomas Thomson*.
55 Leonard Horner wrote on 16 October that DS was "going to spend the winter in the South of Devonshire – he had a severe illness early in the summer from which he has not entirely recovered, and it is thought prudent to take him away from his more severe studies". See also Mrs S. p.p. DS to Maxwell Gordon, 17 February 1819; NLS MS 581, f. 512.
56 Maria Edgeworth to Mrs Edgeworth, 3 November 1818; A. J. C. Hare (ed.), *Life and Letters of Maria Edgeworth* (London, 1894).
57 Maria Edgeworth to Mrs Edgeworth, 4 November 1818; ibid.
58 Maria Edgeworth to Miss Walker, 24 November 1818; ibid. Francis Beaufort was a brother of Maria Edgeworth's stepmother. He became a Rear-Admiral and hydrographer to the navy, and was knighted. He was the creator of the Beaufort wind scale.
59 T. Moore, *Journal* for 8 November 1818; Earl Russell, *Memoirs, Journal and Correspondence of Thomas Moore* (London, 1853– 6).
60 DS to William Hamilton, 11 January 1819 (assumed year); NLS MS 11000, f. 250.
61 Maria S. to Rev. Mr Bowles, 19 February 1819; NLS MS 14299, f. 83. William Bowles, Vicar of Bremhill, near Bowood House, was a poet.
62 E. Grant, *Memoirs of a Highland Lady, Vol. II (1818–19)* (Edinburgh: Canongate, 1988).
63 Mrs S. to Archibald Constable, 2 December 1819; NLS MS 675, f. 224.
64 Mrs S. to Archibald Constable, 17 November 1819; NLS MS 675, f. 228.
65 Francis Horner to Mrs S., 25 January 1809; K. Bourne and W. Banks Taylor (eds), *The Horner Papers* (Edinburgh: Edinburgh University Press, 1994).
66 Thomas Thomson to 2nd Earl of Minto, 24 July 1819; Gibson Craig and Innes, *Thomas Thomson*.
67 Lord Cockburn, *The Life of Lord Jeffrey with selections from his correspondence* (Edinburgh, 1852). Cockburn mentions, among others in attendance, Henry Mackenzie, Dr James Gregory, the Rev. Archibald Alison and Jeffrey himself.
68 Army record of Matthew Stewart, PRO WO25/775.
69 DS to Charles Babbage, August 1819; BL Add MS 37182, f. 165.
70 J. Johnstome (ed.), *The Works of Dr Samuel Parr, with Memoirs of his Life and Writing, Vol. I* (London, 1828).
71 DS to Henry Mackenzie, 30 August 1818 (assumed year); NLS MS 124, f. 31.
72 Charles Babbage to DS, August 1819; BL Add MS 37182, f. 164.

73 Mrs S. to Charles Babbage, 22 May 1821; BL Add MS 37182, f. 354.
74 Charles Babbage to Mrs S., 22 September 1819; BL Add MS 37182, f. 170.
75 Leonard Horner to Samuel Parr, 13 November 1819; Johnstone, *Samuel Parr*.
76 Mrs S. to Archibald Constable, 27 November 1819; NLS MS 675, f. 230.
77 Mrs S. to Charles Babbage, (4) December 1819; BL Add MS 37182, f. 182.
78 Minutes of the Physical and Literary Class of the RSE, 6 December 1819; NLS Acc.10000, 4.
79 DS to Samuel Parr, 11 January 1820; Johnstone, *Samuel Parr*.
80 Mrs S. to Charles Babbage, 6 January 1820; BL Add MS 37182; f. 197.
81 Mrs S. to Charles Babbage, 9 February 1820; BL Add MS 37182, f. 219.
82 K. Newman, *Dictionary of Ulster Biography* (Belfast: Institute of Irish Studies, the Queen's University of Belfast, 1993).
83 Mrs S. to Charles Babbage, 9 February 1820.
84 D. Welsh, *Memoir of the Author* in *Lectures on the Philosophy of the Human Mind by the late Thomas Brown, MD* (Edinburgh, 1830).
85 DS: EPHM III, Note C; CW IV, p. 375.
86 *The Scotsman*, 8 April 1820.
87 DS to Lord Provost of Edinburgh, 10 April 1820; NLS MS 675, f. 321 and BL Add MS 34612, f. 335.
88 DS to Macvey Napier, 28 October and 15 November 1819; BL Add MS 54612, ff. 301 and 306 respectively.
89 Lord Provost to DS, 18 April 1820; BL Add MS 34612, f. 339.
90 M. Napier (ed.), *Selection from the Correspondence of the late Macvey Napier, Esq.* (London, 1879).
91 DS to Lord Provost, 20 April 1820; BL Add MS 34612, f. 341.
92 DS to Lord Provost, May 1820; NLS MS 5319, f.59 and BL Add MS 34612, f. 361.
93 DS to James Gibson, 12 May 1820; Veitch, *Life*, Chapter III; CW X, p. lxxxv–lxxxvi.
94 James Mill to Macvey Napier, 11 May 1820; Napier, *Correspondence of Macvey Napier*.
95 DS to James Gibson, 12 May 1820.
96 J. Veitch, *Memoir of Sir William Hamilton, Bart* (Edinburgh, 1869).
97 These appeared in the issues of 13 May, 20 May, 27 May, 10 June and 24 June.
98 Veitch, *Sir William Hamilton*. See also BL Add MS 34612, ff. 368, 369 and 372.
99 Ibid.
100 ECA Council Records Vol. 181, Minute of 28 June 1820.
101 Mrs S. to Macvey Napier, 19 July 1820; BL Add MS 34612, f. 370.
102 ECA Council Records Vol. 181, Minute of 19 July 1820.
103 Lord Provost to DS, 20 July 1820; BL Add MS 34612, f. 314.
104 Mrs S. to Macvey Napier, 22 July 1820; BL Add MS 34612, f. 373.
105 *The Scotsman*, 22 July 1820.
106 Some degree of antipathy may have been reciprocated. Thomas Carlyle (*Reminiscences*) recalled an evening in 1827 spent in the company of John

Wilson when the latter engaged in some "caricature" of DS among others.
107 DS to Macvey Napier, 14 November 1820; Napier, *Correspondence of Macvey Napier*.

17 The Last Years (1820–1828)

1. DS to 3rd Marquess of Lansdowne, 30 December 1820; NLS MS Acc 11140.
2. DS to John Stark, 30 August 1820; EUL DF. 4.45–52.
3. DS to Macvey Napier, 14 November 1820; BL Add MS 34612, f. 399.
4. DS: Diss, Note appearing only in 1st Edition; CW I, pp. 613–14.
5. DS: EPHM III, Note C; CW IV, pp. 375–7.
6. Leonard Horner to Dr Marcet, 8 November 1820; K. M. Lyell, *Memoir of Leonard Horner* (London, 1890).
7. DS to 3rd Marques of Lansdowne, 30 December 1820.
8. Matthew Stewart (*Memoir*) wrote that his father's stroke occurred in January 1822, and he was followed in this by Veitch and by Leslie Stephen in the DNB. However, I have concluded that Matthew must have made a mistake. January 1821 fits the various references quoted subsequently in the text, in particular John Ward's reference in July 1822 to "the paralytic seizure by which he suffered about a year and a half ago". Cockburn gives the year of DS's "first attack of palsy" as 1821. The date 6 January occurs in a letter from Mrs S. to Charles Babbage (BL Add MS 37182, f. 325) dated only 27 March, but almost certainly written in 1821.
9. M. Stewart, *Memoir*.
10. Archibald Constable to Mrs S., 16 February 1821; NLS MS 790, f. 245.
11. Mrs S. to Charles Babbage, 27 March 1821 (assumed year).
12. Mrs S. to Lady Holland, 7 April (1821); BL Add MS 51849, f. 62a.
13. Mrs S. to Charles Babbage, 2 May 1821 (assumed year); BL Add MS 37182, f. 327.
14. Mrs S. to Charles Babbage, 22 May 1821 (assumed year); BL Add MS 37182, f. 354.
15. Mrs. S. to 3rd Marquess of Lansdowne, 26 February (no year given); BL, Lansdowne Papers. George Davie in *The Democratic Intellect* (Edinburgh: Edinburgh University Press, 1982) refers to Jackson as DS's nephew; this seems to have been a mistake.
16. Charles Babbage to Mrs S., 14 July 1821; BL Add MS 37182, f. 376.
17. Archibald Constable to Mrs S., 31 July 1821; NLS MS 790, f. 352.
18. DS: Diss, Advertisement to Part Second; CW I, pp. 201–2.
19. Mrs S. to Macvey Napier, 6 August 1821; BL Add MS 34612, f. 434.
20. Mrs S. to Macvey Napier, 14 August 1821; BL Add Ms 34612, f. 436.
21. Archibald Constable to DS, 4 September 1821; NLS MS 790. f. 371.
22. Sir James Mackintosh to Thomas Thomson, 6 September 1821; J. T. Gibson Craig and C. Innes, *Memoir of Thomas Thomson* (Edinburgh, 1854).
23. J. W. Ward to Bishop Copleston, 24 June 1822; *Letters of the Earl of Dudley to the Bishop of Llandaff* (London, 1840).
24. Mrs S. to Macvey Napier, 3 December 1821; BL Add MS 34612, f. 457.
25. Ibid.

26 Charles Babbage to Mrs S., April 1821 (assumed month); BL Add MS 37182, f. 327.
27 Mrs S. to Charles Babbage, 26 December 1821; BL Add MS 37182, f. 392.
28 Archibald Constable to Thomas Thomson, 21 December 1821; T. Constable, *Archibald Constable and his Literary Correspondents* (Edinburgh, 1873).
29 Thomas Constable to Archibald Constable, 1 January 1822; ibid.
30 Mrs S. to Lady Holland, 22 January 1822 (assumed year); BL Add MS 51848, f. 167.
31 Earl of Ilchester (ed.), *The Journal of Henry Edward Fox, afterwards fourth and last Lord Holland 1813–1830* (London, 1923); entry for 6 June 1822.
32 Mrs S. to Macvey Napier, 14 June 1822; BL Add MS 34613, f. 73.
33 Ibid.
34 *The Scotsman*, 15 June 1822.
35 Mrs S. to Macvey Napier, 14 June 1822.
36 Ibid.
37 J. W. Ward to Bishop Copleston, 23 July 1822; *Letters to the Bishop of Llandaff*.
38 Mrs S. said so five years later in writing to the 2nd Earl of Minto, 27 September 1827; NLS MS 13169, f. 132.
39 Mrs S. to 3rd Marquess of Lansdowne, autumn 1822 (assumed date); BL, Lansdowne Papers
40 J. W. Ward to Mrs S., 4 September 1822; S. H. Romilly (ed.), *Letters to "Ivy" from the First Earl of Dudley* (London: Longmans Green, 1905).
41 Mrs S. to 3rd Marquess of Lansdowne, autumn 1822.
42 Mrs S. to Macvey Napier, 27 January 1823; BL Add MS 34613, f. 289.
43 Robert Cadell to DS, 20 September 1822; NLS MS 791, f. 605.
44 Mrs S. to Archibald Constable, 28 March 1823; NLS MS 675, f. 234.
45 Archibald Constable to Mrs S., 24 January 1823; NLS MS 792, f. 24.
46 Mrs S. to Macvey Napier, 27 January 1823.
47 Mrs S. to Archibald Constable, 28 March 1823.
48 Mrs S. to George Cranstoun, 8 May 1823; NLS, MS 3494, f. 181.
49 Maria Edgeworth to Honora Edgeworth, 2 June 1823; A. J. C. Hare (ed.), *Life and Letters of Maria Edgeworth* (London, 1891).
50 Maria Edgeworth to Mrs Ruxton, 8 June 1823; ibid.
51 The visit was arranged in Charles Babbage to Mrs S., BL Add MS 37183, f. 72 and Mrs S. to Charles Babbage, ibid., f. 73; Lord Daer's paper (ibid., f. 72) bears the note "Given me by Mr Dugald Stewart when I was staying with him at Kinneil near Edinburgh Sep 1823."
52 George Cranstoun to Thomas Thomson, 6 November 1823; Gibson Craig and Innes, *Thomas Thomson*.
53 Mrs S. to Countess of Minto, January 1824; NLS MS 11798, f. 107. George Elliot was born on 9 October 1823.
54 Mrs S. to 2nd Earl of Minto, March 1826; NLS MS 11798, f. 124.
55 George Cranstoun to 7th Marquess of Lothian, 3 May 1824; NAS, Lothian Muniments GD 40/9 – 305.
56 Mrs S. to Lord Henry Elliot, 5 May 1824; NAS, Lothian Muniments GD 40/9 – 306.

Notes to pp. 214–19

57 Veitch, *Life, Chapter III*; CW X, pp. lxxxvii–lxxxviii.
58 BL Add MS 37183, ff. 124–5.
59 Mrs S. to Charles Babbage, 27 March 1825 (assumed year); BL Add MS 37183, f. 165.
60 Thomas Jefferson to DS, 26 April 1824; M. D. Peterson, *Thomas Jefferson – Writings* (Cambridge: Cambridge University Press, 1984).
61 M. D. Peterson, *Thomas Jefferson and the New Nation* (New York: Oxford University Press, 1970).
62 David Wilkie to Miss Wilkie, 26 September 1824; A. Cunninghame, *Life of Sir David Wilkie* (London, 1843).
63 It was engraved by Samuel Cousins, and a legend on the engraving refers to "the original Portrait in the possession of Mr Stewart's Nephew, Dr Miller of Exeter".
64 EUL Dc.8.177. The passage occurs in DS: EPHM III, Chapter I, Section vi; CW IV, pp. 78–115.
65 Matthew S.'s army record; PRO WO/225 775.
66 2nd Earl of Minto to 3rd Marquess of Lansdowne, 25 December 1824; BL, Lansdowne Papers.
67 Mrs S. to 2nd Earl of Minto, 21 March 1825; NLS MS 11798, f. 112.
68 Mrs S. to 2nd Earl of Minto, 28 March 1825; NLS MS 11798, f. 114.
69 Mrs S. to Charles Babbage, 27 March 1825.
70 EUL Dc.6.111, ff. 60–1.
71 Mrs S. to Countess of Minto, 14 April 1825; NLS MS 11798, f. 110.
72 Mrs S. to Archibald Constable, 7 June 1825; NLS MS 675, f. 236.
73 Mrs S. to Archibald Constable, 27 June 1825; NLS MS 675, f. 240.
74 Mrs S. to 3rd Marquess of Lansdowne, 10 December 1825; BL, Lansdowne Papers.
75 T. Moore, *Journal* for 9 November 1825; Earl Russell, *Memoirs, Journal and Correspondence of Thomas Moore* (London, 1853– 6). Lady Keith was Dr Johnson's "Queeney" Thrale.
76 Mrs S. to 2nd Earl of Minto, January 1826; NLS MS 11798, f. 119. Sir David Wedderburn, Bart. lived at 8 Albyn Place, the west end of Queen Street. He was Postmaster General for Scotland, and a relative of the Stewarts' West Lothian neighbour, Lady Hope of Hopetoun House.
77 DS: EPHM III, Appendix to Chapter 2, fn.; CW IV, p. 177. Another instance of DS's intellectual curiosity apparently occurred in November of 1826, when the American ornithologist and bird artist, J. J. Audubon, recorded meeting "Mr Stuart" at the Edinburgh home of George Combe, the phrenologist; Audubon's 1967 editor believed this to have been DS.
78 Mrs S. to 2nd Earl of Minto, 22–4 February 1826; NLS MS 11798, f. 121.
79 Thomas Jackson to Archibald Constable, 1826; NLS MS 675, f. 238.
80 Maria S. to John Stark, 14 August 1826; EUL, AAF 26.
81 As has been noted, Napier was DS's first choice for the chair of moral philosophy in 1820, and he had once referred to Thomson as "a friend of mine, who ranks very high at our bar, and on whose judgment I have great reliance" – DS to Lady Katherine Halkett, 30 March 1817; NLS MS 546, f. 24. Thomson reciprocated this respect.

82 Macvey Napier to John Murray, 9 November 1826 and fn.; M. Napier (ed.), *Selection from the Correspondence of the late Macvey Napier, Esq.* (London, 1879).
83 DS: EPHM III, Preface; CW IV, p. 3.
84 DS: EPHM III, Appendix to Part Third, Chapter Second; CW IV, pp. 300–70.
85 DS: EPHM III, Preface; CW IV, p. 3.
86 J. G. Godard, *George Birkbeck – the Pioneer of Popular Education* (London, 1884). DS's words occur in EPHM I, Chapter IV, Section 7; CW II, p. 219.
87 Henry Brougham to Henry Duncan, 18 November 1826; J. G. C. Duncan, *Memoir of the Rev. Henry Duncan, D.D., Minister of Ruthwell* (Edinburgh, 1848).
88 Mrs S. to 2nd Earl of Minto, 17 April 1827; NLS MS 11798, f. 130.
89 Mrs S. to 2nd Earl of Minto, 30 April 1827; NLS MS 11798, f. 134.
90 Mrs S. to 2nd Earl of Minto, May 1827 (assumed month); NLS MS 12135, f. 56.
91 Mrs S. to Charles Babbage, 27 March 1821 (assumed year); BL Add MS 37182, f. 325.
92 Mrs S. to 7th Marquess of Lothian, 22 October 1825; NAS, Lothian Muniments GD 40/9 – 321.
93 Mrs S. to 3rd Marquess of Lansdowne, 26 February (no year given); BL, Lansdowne Papers. Andrew Brown was professor of rhetoric and belles lettres at Edinburgh University from 1801 until 1835, but there may have been rumour of a change before that. "Carlyle" may have been Thomas, who at one stage in his early career was interested in obtaining an appointment in Edinburgh, and also in the putative chair of rhetoric in London, but this is not certain.
94 Mrs S. to 7th Marquess of Lothian, 15 May 1827; GRH, Lothian Muniments GD 40/9 – 321.
95 Mrs S. to 2nd Earl of Minto, 30 April 1827.
96 Mrs S. to 2nd Earl of Minto, 27 September 1827; NLS MS 12135, f. 130.
97 Mrs S. to 2nd Earl of Minto, March 1826; NLS MS 11798, f. 124.
98 DS: draft memorandum; NLS MS 12135, f. 110.
99 Mrs S. to 3rd Viscount Palmerston, 20 June 1827 (assumed year); BA – BR22(i)10.
100 Maria S. to Countess of Minto, September 1827; NLS MS 11798, f. 137.
101 Maria S. to Countess of Minto, September 1827; NLS MS 11798, f. 139.
102 Maria S. to 2nd Earl of Minto, September 1827; NLS MS 12135, f. 115.
103 Mrs S. to 2nd Earl of Minto, 18 October 1827; NLS MS 12135, f. 159.
104 Mrs S. to 2nd Earl of Minto, 13 November 1827; NLS MS 12135, f. 177.
105 Mrs S. to 2nd Earl of Minto, 25 January 1828; NLS MS 11798, f. 155.
106 Now in NAS.
107 Mrs S. to John Stark, June 1827; NLS MS 3713, f. 31. Stark noted on the letter, "I went to Kinneil on the 19th and returned with Mrs Stewart on the 21st."
108 Macvey Napier to John Murray, 9 November 1826, fn.
109 DS: PAMP, Preface; CW VI, pp. 111–16.
110 T. Jouffroy, *Esquisses de philosophie morale* (Paris, 1826).

111 This may be inferred from Mrs S. to 7th Marquess of Lothian, undated (June 1828); NAS, Lothian Muniments GD 40/9 – 321.
112 Mrs S. to 3rd Viscount Palmerston, 24 April 1828 (assumed year); BA – BR22(i)10.
113 Maria S. to Hon. Mrs Bowles, 23 June 1828; ibid.
114 Mrs S. to 3rd Viscount Palmerston, 24 April 1828.
115 Veitch, *Life*, Chapter III; CW X, p. lxxxviii.
116 A. Mitchell, *No More Corncraiks* (Edinburgh: Scottish Cultural Press, 1998). Lord Corehouse lived at 12 Ainslie Place from 1827 until 1840. Latterly he shared the house with his niece, Maria Cunninghame, to whom he left his Corehouse estate when he died in 1850.
117 NAS, Edinburgh Book of Sasines.
118 BL, Oriental and India Office Collections. A. J. Farrington, *Biographical Index of East India Company Maritime Service Officers*; and *Catalogue of EIC Maritime Journals*.
119 A. J. Warden, *Angus or Forfarshire – the Land and People, Vol. III* (Dundee, 1882). See also chapter 15, note 85.
120 Information supplied by Mrs Pat Gordon.
121 Mrs S. to 7th Marquess of Lothian, June 1828 (assumed date).
122 Mrs S.'s letter is dated only "Friday". She refers to leaving Newbattle Abbey "on Sat.y 2". The 2nd of May 1828 was a Friday, and Saturday was the 3rd, but the surrounding circumstances make it clear that it is in May she is writing: DS was at Kinneil on 16 April, and the Stewarts were too long at Ainslie Place for DS to have become ill only at the beginning of June. Friday 9 May therefore seems the most likely date for this letter; it is understandable that Mrs S. should have made a slip about the date a week previously.
123 Mrs S. to 7th Marquess of Lothian, undated (9 May 1828); NAS, Lothian Muniments GD 40/9 – 321.
124 Mrs S. to 7th Marquess of Lothian, undated (June 1828).
125 Macvey Napier to Sir James Mackintosh, 22 June 1828;
126 Maria S. to Hon. Mrs Bowles, 23 June 1828.
127 Maria S. to 2nd Earl of Minto, 12 June 1828; NLS MS 11798, f. 165.
128 Mrs S. to 2nd Earl of Minto (26 June 1828); NLS MS 11798, f. 171.
129 *The Scotsman*, 14 June 1828.
130 *The Times*, 17 June 1828.
131 *Edinburgh Evening Courant*, 16 June 1828.
132 *Edinburgh Evening Courant*, 17 June 1828.
133 Cockburn, *Memorials*.
134 Lady S. Holland, *Memoir of the Reverend Sydney Smith* (London, 1854).

18 Epilogue

1 Lord Corehouse to 2nd Earl of Minto, 18 June 1828; NLS MS 11798, f. 169. She was still there on 28 July when she wrote to Lord Palmerston; see (41) below.
2 Mrs S. to 2nd Earl of Minto, 3 August 1828; NLS MS 11798, f. 176.
3 Thomas Thomson to 2nd Earl of Minto, 19 July 1828; NLS MS 11811, f. 89.

Notes to pp. 229–32

4   Thomas Thomson to 2nd Earl of Minto, 5 December 1828; NLS MS 11811, f. 91.
5   Thomas Thomson to 2nd Earl of Minto, 9 December 1828; NLS MS 11811, f. 93.
6   Mrs S. to 2nd Earl of Minto, 3 May 1829; NLS MS 11798, f. 192.
7   Mrs S. to 2nd Earl of Minto, 15 June 1829; NLS MS 11798, f. 196.
8   Mrs S. to 7th Marquess of Lothian, 1 January 1830; NAS, Lothian Muniments GD 40/9 – 321.
9   "[My Brother] says with truth, it would not become him to take any lead, or even seem to wish to do so"; Mrs S. to 2nd Earl of Minto, 3 August 1828.
10 A. L. Youngson, *Edinburgh and the Border Country* (London: Harper-Collins, 1993).
11 *The Scotsman*, 26 March 1831: "Dugald Stewart's Monument".
12 Ibid.
13 *The Scotsman*, 21 December 1831: "Professor Stewart's Monument".
14 "Stewart's monument must now bear his name" – Lord Cockburn to James Gibson Craig, 4 October 1852; J. T. Gibson Craig and C. Innes, *Memoir of Thomas Thomson* (Edinburgh, 1854).
15 3rd Viscount Palmerston to Lord Rutherfurd, 12 December 1853; NLS MS 9717, f. 153.
16 Mrs S. to 2nd Earl of Minto, (end of) June 1828; NLS MS 11798, f. 171.
17 Matthew S. to Macvey Napier, 1 October 1828; BL Add MS 34613, f. 435.
18 Some of the letters are now very obscure, but the inscription can plausibly be deciphered as reading: FILIUS ET FILIA LIBERI SUPERSTITES PATRI CARISSIMO MORUM SUPREMUM MOERENTES HIC SEPULCRUM DEDICAVERUNT. I am indebted to Emeritus Professor Alex Garvie of Glasgow University and to Mrs Jane Garvie for assisting me with the translation.
19 Mrs S. to Countess of Minto, January 1829; NLS MS 11798, f. 187.
20 Mrs S. to 7th Marquess of Lothian, 1 January 1830.
21 DS: Will; NAS.
22 M. Stewart, *Memoir of the late Dugald Stewart, Esquire* (Edinburgh, 1828). [Elsewhere – M. Stewart, *Memoir*.]
23 Mrs S. to 2nd Earl of Minto, 3 May 1829.
24 Leonard Horner to his daughter, 14 June 1834; K. M. Lyell, *Memoir of Leonard Horner* (London, 1890).
25 J. Stewart, *Parish of Sorn* in *New Statistical Account of Scotland, Vol. 5* (Edinburgh, 1845).
26 Veitch, *Life*, Chapter I; CW X, p. xxxii fn.
27 Mrs S. to Countess of Minto, 29 March 1832; NLS MS 11798, f. 215.
28 Mrs S. to Countess of Minto, 18 August 1832; NLS MS 11798, f. 221.
29 Mrs S. to Countess of Minto, 15 July 1833; NLS MS 11798, f. 229.
30 M. Butler, *Maria Edgeworth – a Literary Biography* (Oxford: Clarendon Press, 1972).
31 Leonard Horner to his daughter, 14 June 1834.
32 Matthew S. to Henry Fox, 30 March 1837; *Advertisement by the Editor* to DS: Pol Econ; CW VIII, pp. ix–xi.

33 Ibid.
34 Ibid.
35 H. Fox, *Notes and Queries, Vol. XL, No. 284*, 7 April 1865; *Advertisement* to DS: Pol Econ.
36 Sir W. Hamilton, *Advertisement* to DS: Pol Econ.
37 Ibid.
38 Sir W. Scott, *The Surgeon's Daughter* (1827); Chapters VIII and IX.
39 I am indebted to my brother-in-law, Dr Robin Doherty of Canberra, Australia, for first making this suggestion, which subsequent enquiries have tended to confirm. In the days before penicillin, tertiary syphilis could appear after a latent period of many years, and could cause personality deterioration featuring delusions which evidence or reason could not overcome.
40 DS: Will; NAS.
41 Mrs S. to 3rd Viscount Palmerston, 28 July 1828; BA – BR22(i)10.
42 3rd Viscount Palmerston to Mrs S., 4 August 1828; BA – BR22(i)10.
43 Mrs S. to 2nd Earl of Minto, August 1828; NLS MS 11798, f. 174.
44 An impending visit to Minto was discussed in Maria S. to Countess of Minto, 24 September 1828 (NLS MS 11798, f. 180), and Mrs S. wrote to Charles Babbage from Minto on 3 January 1829 (BL Add MS 37184, f. 187).
45 Mrs S. to Charles Babbage, 3 January 1829.
46 Mrs S. wrote to Countess of Minto from Warriston, 10 January 1829; NLS MS 11798, f. 185. After her second marriage, in 1825, the former Margaret Miller appears to have moved from Howard Place to Warriston House, the nearby home of her husband, Alexander Henderson.
47 Mrs S. to 2nd Earl of Minto from Glasgow, 15 June 1829; NLS MS 11798, f. 196.
48 Mrs S. to Countess of Minto, 23 June 1829; NLS MS 11798, f. 200.
49 Lady Mary Elliot wrote to Mrs S. at Brighton on 29 December 1829 (NLS MS 11798, f. 205).
50 Mrs S. told 7th Marquess of Lothian from Southampton on 10 February 1830: "our friends at Exeter are not able to receive us, as my niece Mrs Miller has been dangerously ill. We have therefore taken a lodging here by the week, till better able to move." NAS, Lothian Muniments GD 40/9 – 321.
51 T. Moore, *Journal for 3 January 1831*; Earl Russell, *Memoirs, Journal and Correspondence of Thomas Moore* (London, 1853–6).
52 Lady Mary Elliot wrote to Maria S. at 3 River Street, Bath, 16 January 1831 (NLS MS 11798, f. 207); Mrs S. wrote to Lord Melgund from Bath, 17 February 1831 (NLS MS 21233, f. 1); J. W. Mackie wrote to Mrs S. at 3 River Street, Bath, 19 February 1831 (EUL Dc.6.111, f. 137).
53 Mrs S. to Minto family, 29 December 1831; NLS MS 11798, f. 212.
54 Mrs S. to Charles Babbage, 5 August (no year given); BL Add MS 37201, f. 536.
55 Maria S. to Lady Mary Elliot, 5 January 1837; NLS MS 13169, f. 44.
56 The earliest surviving reference to this status is in a letter from Lady Mary Elliot to Maria S. in April 1829, when she sent "best love to dear Granny Stewart"; NLS MS 11798, f. 190.
57 Lady Charlotte Elliot to Mrs S., 19 June 1829; NLS MS 11798, f. 198.

Notes to pp. 235–40

58 Mrs S. to Countess of Minto, 23 June 1829; NLS MS 11798, f. 200.
59 Mrs S. to Lady Charlotte Elliot, 23 June 1829; NLS MS 11778, f. 1.
60 Mrs S. to Lord Melgund, 17 February 1831.
61 Lord Melgund to Mrs S., 3 March 1831; NLS MS 11798, f. 209.
62 Lord Melgund to Mrs S. and Maria S., 24 December 1836; NLS MS 11798, f. 245. He told them: "You must never think of calling me anything but William which would be far too unlike old times."
63 Lady Mary Elliot to Mrs S., 22 January 1833; NLS MS 13169, ff. 23–7.
64 Lady Mary Elliot to Mrs S., November 1833; NLS MS 13169, f. 40.
65 Lady Mary Elliot to Maria S., 26 January 1835; NLS MS 11798, f. 240.
66 Lady Frances Elliot to Mrs S., 4 September 1833; NLS MS 13169, f. 28.
67 Mrs S. to 3rd Viscount Palmerston, 25 January 1833; BA – BR22(i) 10.
68 Mrs S. to Minto family, 15 July 1833; NLS MS 11798, f. 229. Mrs S. enjoyed a bizarre phrase. On another occasion she wrote to the Earl of Minto about "what the Taylor at Denholm used to call a *Critic Affair*" (NLS MS 11798, f. 102).
69 Information supplied by Mrs Pat Gordon.
70 Mrs S. to Minto family, 15 July 1833.
71 Maria S. to Countess of Minto, 22 July 1833; NLS MS 11798, f. 232.
72 Mrs S. to Countess of Minto, 1834; NLS MS 11798, f. 235.
73 Maria S.'s letter to the Countess of Minto of July 1833 was written from Kinneil; Lady Mary Elliot wrote to Maria S. at Portobello on 5 January 1835 (NLS MS 11798, f. 237).
74 Thomas Campbell to a friend, 8 August 1836; W. Beattie, *Life and Letters of Thomas Campbell* (London, 1850).
75 K. Bourne, *Palmerston: The Early Years 1784–1841* (London: Allen Lane, 1982).
76 Maria S. to 7th Marquess of Lothian, 10 October 1836; NAS, Lothian Muniments GD 40/9 – 321.
77 Mrs S. to 7th Marquess of Lothian, 14 August 1832; ibid.
78 Mrs S. to 7th Marquess of Lothian, 1 March 1835; ibid.
79 Maria S. to 7th Marquess of Lothian, 10 October 1836.
80 7th Marquess of Lothian to Maria S., October 1836 (assumed month); ibid.
81 Maria S. to Lady Mary Elliot, 5 January 1837; NLS MS 13169, f. 44.
82 Lady Frances Elliot to Maria S., 9 March 1838; NLS MS 11798, f. 256.
83 2nd Earl of Minto wrote on 4 August 1838 to Maria S. "c/o Miss Dalzel, 48 Anne Street"; NLS MS 111798, f. 264. Maria was back in Portobello by the 6th, when she wrote to the Marquess of Lothian.
84 Mrs S. to Countess of Minto, 29 March 1832; NLS MS 11798, f. 215.
85 M. Stewart, *Memoir*, addendum, attributed to T. Campbell, *Memoir of Mrs Dugald Stewart*.
86 2nd Earl of Minto to Maria S., 4 August 1838; NLS MS 11798, f. 264.
87 This is implied in Maria S.'s reply dated 6 August.
88 Maria S. to 7th Marquess of Lothian, 6 August 1838; NAS, Lothian Muniments GD 40/9 – 321.
89 Maria S. to Countess of Minto, 8 August 1838; NLS MS 11798, f. 267.
90 Writing to the Countess of Minto on 28 January 1844, Maria said, "I have

promised Lady Katherine Halkett to go to her *if possible* in March" (NLS MS 11798, f. 286); as the following note shows, she was in London in May.
91 Maria S. to Countess of Minto, 26 May 1844; NLS MS 11798, f. 291.
92 NAS: Inventory and will of Maria Stewart.
93 NAS: Will of Matthew Stewart and codicils.
94 NLS MS 9834, f. 64A.
95 Veitch, *Life, Chapter I*; CW X, p. xxxii.
96 NAS: Will of Matthew Stewart.
97 1851 Census return for parish of Sorn; Ayrshire Archives.
98 See, for example, N. Philipson, *In Pursuit of Virtue in Scottish University Education: Dugald Stewart and Scottish Moral Philosophy in the Enlightenment* in N. Philpson (ed.), *Universities, Society and the Future* (Edinburgh: Edinburgh University Press, 1983); K. Haakonssen, *Dugald Stewart* in J. W. Yolton, J. V. Price and J. Stephens (eds.), *Dictionary of Eighteenth Century British Philosophy* (Bristol: Thoemmes Press, 1999).
99 Thomas Jefferson has been quoted on the subject in Chapter 17. See also, for example, J. D. Hoeveler, *James McCosh and the Scottish Intellectual Tradition* (Princeton: Princeton University Press, 1981); and E. Flower, *Some interesting connections between common sense realists and the pragmatists, especially James* in P. Caws, *Two Centuries of Philosophy in America* (Oxford: Blackwell, 1980).
100 A. Hook, *Carlyle and America* cited in W. C. Lehmann, *Scottish and Scotch-Irish Contributions to Early American Life and Culture* (New York, Kennikat Press Corporation, 1978).
101 W. James, *Varieties of Religious Experience (Gifford Lectures), Lecture I* (London: Longmans Green, 1902). Prof. Flower suggests that DS's thinking contains some of the seeds of pragmatism.
102 Thomas Carlyle to John Carlyle, 25 August 1828; C. R. Sanders (ed.), *Collected Letters of Thomas and Jane Welsh Carlyle* (Durham, N. Carolina: Duke University Press, 1970).
103 J. S. Mill, *Autobiography* (1873).
104 S. Walpole, *The Life of Lord John Russell* (London, 1891).
105 Lord Cockburn, *Journal, 8 February 1850* (Edinburgh, 1874).
106 A correspondent named Howden suggested a new edition of the works of DS in a letter dated 30 August 1853; NLS MS 4102, f. 159.
107 J. Veitch, *Memoir of Sir William Hamilton, Bart.* (Edinburgh, 1869).
108 Sir W. Hamilton, *Advertisement by the Editor* to DS: Pol Econ; CW VIII, pp. vi–xxiii.
109 M. R. L. Bryce, *Memoir of John Veitch, LLD, Professor of Logic and Rhetoric, University of Glasgow* (Edinburgh and London, 1896).
110 Veitch: *Life, Preface*; CW X, p. v.
111 *Edinburgh Review*, Vol. CXXXV (Edinburgh, January 1872–April 1872).
112 Sir J. Mackintosh, *Dugald Stewart* in *On the Progress of Ethical Philosophy* (Edinburgh, 1872). See chapter 14.
113 A. Chitnis, *The Scottish Enlightenment and Early Victorian English Society* (London: Croom Helm, 1986.) The six included George Birkbeck, Lord Brougham, James Mill and Lord John Russell.

114 K. Haakonssen, *Natural Law and Moral Philosophy* (Cambridge: Cambridge University Press, 1996).
115 Veitch: *Life*, Chapter II; CW X, p. liv.
116 F. D. Maurice, *Modern Philosophy* (London, 1862).
117 M. Brown, *Creating a Canon: Dugald Stewart's Construction of the Scottish Enlightenment* in *History of Universities, Vol. XVI (1)* (Oxford: Oxford University Press, 2000).
118 P. B. Wood, *Dugald Stewart and the Invention of "the Scottish Enlightenment"* in P. Wood (ed.), *The Scottish Enlightenment: Essays in Reinterpretation* (Woodbridge: University of Rochester Press, 2000).
119 K. Haakonssen, *Introduction* to D. Stewart,: *Collected Works*, (Bristol: Thoemmes Press, 1994).
120 A. Broadie, *The Scottish Enlightenment: an Anthology* (Edinburgh: Canongate, 1997).
121 A. Herman, *The Scottish Enlightenment – The Scots' Invention of the Modern World* (London: Fourth Estate, 2002).

Supplement A – *The Writings*

1 DS: Preface to *Three Biographical Essays*; CW X, pp. 1–2.
2 DS: EPHM II, Advertisement; CW III, p. 3.
3 Cockburn: *Memorials*.
4 Sir J. Mackintosh, *Journal*, 16 November 1811; R. J. Mackintosh, *Memoirs of the Life of Sir James Mackintosh* (Boston, 1853).
5 J. R. Guild and A. Law, *Edinburgh University Library 1580–1980* (Edinburgh, Edinburgh University Press, 1982).
6 DS: Diss, Part Second, Section 4; CW I, p. 341.
7 DS: EPHM II, Chapter III, Section 1; CW III, p. 192.
8 Sydney Smith to Francis Horner, 1816; Lady S. Holland, *Memoir of the Reverend Sydney Smith* (London, 1854).
9 *Quarterly Review*, Vol. 6, October 1811.
10 J. K. Ingram in *Palgrave's Dictionary of Political Economy* (London, 1899).
11 *Scots Magazine*, September, 1810.
12 Thomas Carlyle to Robert Stewart, 12 February 1817; NAS GD1/719/14.
13 DS: PAMP II, Note D; CW VII, p. 383. Translation in CW XI, p. 224.
14 DS: Pol Econ, Part First, Book Second, Chapter II, Section iii; CW VIII, p. 371.
15 *Edinburgh Review*, Vol. 46 (October 1827): *State of German Literature (fn.)*. This article was subsequently published among the *Critical and Miscellaneous Essays of Thomas Carlyle* (London, 1899).
16 J. Johnstone, *Samuel Parr, with Memoirs of his Life and Writings and a Selection from his Correspondence* (London, 1828).
17 DS to 6th Marquess of Lothian, 23 October 1815; NAS, Lothian Muniments.
18 DS: Life of Robertson, Section IV; CW X, pp. 173–7.
19 *Edinburgh Review*, Vol. 2 (April 1803).
20 See chapter 14, note 77.
21 *Edinburgh Review*, Vol. 2 (April 1803).
22 DS: Life of Robertson, Section III; CW X, p. 150.

23 DS: Life of Reid, Section III; CW X, p. 319.
24 See P. B. Wood, *The Hagiography of Common Sense: Dugald Stewart's Account of the Life and Writings of Thomas Reid* in A. J. Holland, *Philosophy, its History and Historiography* (Dordrecht: D. Reidel, 1985) and *Dugald Stewart and the Invention of "the Scottish Enlightenment"* in P. B. Wood (ed.) *The Scottish Enlightenment: Essays in Reinterpretation*; and M. Brown, *Creating a Canon: Dugald Stewart's Construction of the Scottish Enlightenment* in *History of Universities, Vol. XVI (1)* (Oxford: Oxford University Press, 2000).
25 S. Romilly to E. Dumont, 9 January 1802; Romilly (ed.), *Memoirs of the Life of Sir Samuel Romilly, written by himself, with a selection of his correspondence* (London, 1842).
26 DS: Pol Econ II, Part First, Book Second, Chapter IV, Section V; CW IX, p. 253.
27 DS: Diss, Part First, Chapter II, Section 1; CW I, p. 87 fn.
28 DS: Diss, Part Second, Section 2; CW I, p. 273.
29 DS: PE, Part First, Essay Second, Chapter II, Section 2fn; CW V, p. 118. This, however, was in 1810. DS must have made another attempt to come to terms with Kant, to whom he does pay some attention in Diss.
30 DS: Diss, Part Second, Section 7, fn. to heading; CW I, p. 389.
31 DS: EPHM I, Introduction – Part I; CW II, p. 46.
32 DS: PE, Preliminary Dissertation, Chapter I; CW V, p. 18.
33 DS: OMP, Introduction, Paragraph 9; CW II, p. 7.
34 DS: PE Preliminary Dissertation, Chapter II, CW V, p. 41.
35 DS: OMP, Introduction, Paragraph 8; CW II, p. 7
36 DS: EPHM I, Introduction – Part II; CW II, p. 58.
37 DS: OMP, Introduction, Paragraph 11; CW II, p. 8.
38 DS: EPHM I, Introducion – Part I; CW II, p. 8.
39 T. Reid, *Essays on the Intellectual Powers of Man*, Essay I, Chapter I (Edinburgh, 1863).
40 F. Jeffrey in *Edinburgh Review, Vol. III* (January 1804).
41 DS: PE, Preliminary Dissertation, Chapter II; CW V, pp. 23ff.
42 Ibid., p. 35.
43 DS: Life of Robertson, Section I; CW X, pp. 120–1.
44 D. Hume, *An Essay concerning Human Understanding*, Section 8, Part 1.
45 DS: *Life of Smith*, Section II; CW X, p. 34.
46 Ibid., p. 33. DS is referring to Smith's *Considerations concerning the First Formation of Languages* which was appended to *The Theory of Moral Sentiments*.
47 DS: PE, Part First, Essay Fifth, Chapter I; CW V, p. 149.
48 Ibid., pp. 153–4.
49 DS: PE, Part Second, Essay First; CW V, p. 191ff.
50 DS: PE, Part Second, Essay Third, Chapter IV; CW V, p. 383.
51 DS: PE, Part Second, Essay Third, Chapter II; CW V, p. 340.
52 DS: PE, Part Second, Essay Third, Chapter III; CW V, p. 366.
53 DS: PE, Part Second, Essay Fourth, Chapter I; CW V, pp. 384–9.
54 DS: PE, Part Second, Essay Third, Chapter IV; CW V, pp. 370–1.

Notes to pp. 254–8

55 DS: EPHM II, Chapter I, Section 1, Subsection 1; CW III, pp. 33–4.
56 DS: EPHM II, Part Second, Chapter II, Section 2; CW III, pp. 45–7.
57 DS: PAMP II, Book Third, Chapter III, Section 1; CW VII, p. 121.
58 DS: PAMP I, Book Second, Chapter V, Section 1; CW VI, p. 295.
59 DS: PAMP II, Book Fourth, Chapter V, Section 4; CW VII, p. 362.
60 DS: OMP, Part Second, Chapter I, Section 6, Article 3, Paragraph 218; CW VI, p. 35.
61 J. W. Ward to Mrs S., 8 (February 1814); S. H. Romilly, *Letters to "Ivy" from the first Earl of Dudley* (London; Longmans Green, 1905).
62 DS: PAMP I, Book Second, Chapter III; CW VI, pp. 237–8; and PAMP II, Book Third, Chapter IV, Section 2; CW VII, pp. 207–10.
63 Ibid., p. 208. It is possible that DS met Bligh in October 1795 when the latter was in port at Leith and Mrs Bligh came there for a short time to see him. He had also been in Edinburgh in 1782, when Boswell met him. This was probably while the ship of which he was then an officer, the Cambridge, was undergoing repairs. Bligh's father-in-law, Richard Betham, had been a close friend of David Hume and Adam Smith. See G. Kennedy, *Captain Bligh – the man and his mutinies* (London: George Duckworth, 1989).
64 DS: OMP, Part Second, Chapter I, Section 6, Article 1, Paragraph 177; CW VI, pp. 22–3.
65 DS: PAMP I, Appendix, Section 1; CW VI, p. 343.
66 DS: OMP, Part Second, Chapter I, Section 7; CW VI, pp. 36–42.
67 DS: PE, Part Second, Essay Fourth, Chapter I; CW V, p. 388.
68 DS: OMP, Part Second, Chapter II, paragraph 246; CW VI, p. 44.
69 DS: OMP, Part Second, Chapter II, Section 3, Paragraph 391; CW VI, p. 91.
70 DS: PAMP II, Book Fourth, Chapter IV, Section 4 (5); CW VII, p. 350.
71 DS: OMP, Part Second, Chapter II, Section 1, Article 1, Paragraph 251; CW VI, p. 46.
72 Ibid. Paragraph 270; CW VI, p. 54.
73 Ibid., Article 2; CW VI, pp. 60–8.
74 Ibid., Article I (1); CW VI, pp. 47–51.
75 DS: PAMP II, Book Fourth, Part I, Chapter II; CW VII, pp. 256–9.
76 DS: Pol Econ, Part First, Book Fourth; CW IX, pp. 330–1.
77 W. M. Humes and H. M. Paterson (eds.), *Scottish Culture and Scottish Education* (Edinburgh, John Donald, 1983).
78 Francis Horner to DS, 6 April 1805; EUL, Xerox Phot. 1717. DS refers to this letter in Pol Econ, Part First, Book Fourth; CW IX, pp. 341–2.
79 DS: EPHM I, Introduction – Part Second, Section 1; CW II, p. 59.
80 Ibid.
81 DS: PE, Preliminary Dissertation, Chapter II; CW V, pp. 51–2.
82 DS: EPHM I, Introduction – Part Second, Section 1; CW II, p. 59.
83 Ibid., p. 62.
84 DS: Diss., Part Second, Section 1; CW I, pp. 249–50.
85 DS: PAMP II, Book Fourth, Chapter III; CW VII, p. 276.
86 DS: PAMP I, Book First, Chapter II, Section 1; CW VI, p. 134.
87 Ibid., pp. 134–5.

88 J. Walker, *Notes taken on Moral Phlosophy Lectures delivered by Dugald Stewart, 1778–79*; EUL, Gen. 2023.
89 DS: EPHM I, Introduction – Part Second, Section 1; CW II, p. 60.
90 DS: EPHM I, Part First, Chapter IV, Section 7; CW II, pp. 217–19.

Supplement B – *Stewart's Written Words*

All quotations are from the works of DS.

1   EPHM I, Part First, Chapter V, Part II, Section 1; CW II, p. 313.
2   Ibid., Chapter VI, Section 8; CW II, p. 423.
3   Ibid.,Section 6; CW II, p. 407.
4   EPHM II, Part Second, Chapter IV, Section 5; CW III, pp. 328–9.
5   EPHM I, Part First, Chapter V, Part II, Section 1; CW II, pp. 311–12.
6   Diss, Part Second, Section 1; CW I, p. 216.
7   EPHM I, Part First, Chapter V, Part II, Section 2; CW II, pp. 325–6.
8   Diss, Part Second, Section 3; CW I, pp. 291–2.
9   Pol Econ, Part Second, Chapter I, Section ii, Subject 3; CW IX, p. 399.
10 EPHM I, Part First, Chapter V, Part II, Section 2; CW II, p. 332.
11 PAMP I, Book First, Chapter II, Section 5; CW VI, p. 164.
12 Life of Reid, Section II; CW X, pp. 278–9.
13 EPHM I, Part First, Introduction – Part II, Section 2; CW II p. 79.
14 Ibid., p. 86.
15 Ibid., Chapter I, Section 3; CW II, p. 109.
16 PE, Part Second, Essay First, Part First, Chapter IV; CW V, p. 227.
17 EPHM III, Part Second, Chapter II, Section iv; CW IV, p. 165.
18 Diss, Part Second, Section 6; CW I, p. 384.
19 Pol Econ, Part Second, Chapter II, Section i; CW IX, p. 404.
20 PE, Part Second, Essay First, Part First, Chapter VI; CW V, p. 246.
21 EPHM I, Part First, Chapter IV, Section 6; CW II, p. 209.
22 Diss, Part First, Chapter II, Section 2; CW I, p. 117.
23 EPHM III, Part Third, Section iii; CW IV, p. 220.
24 EPHM II, Part Second, Chapter III, Section 2; CW III, p. 208.
25 Diss, Part Second, Section 4; CW I, p. 335.
26 Diss, Part Third, Concluding Chapter; CW I, p. 523.
27 EPHM III, Part Third, Section 5; CW IV, p. 238.
28 Ibid., p. 240.
29 Ibid., pp. 241–2.
30 Ibid., p. 245.
31 EPHM I, Part First, Chapter V, Part II, Section 3; CW II, p. 337.
32 PAMP I, Book Second, Chpter V, Section 1; CW VI, p. 299.
33 PAMP II, Book Fourth, Chapter IV, Section 3, Sub-section 1; CW VII, p. 310.
34 Diss, Part Third, Chapter; CW I, p. 510.
35 Pol Econ, Part First, Book Fourth; CW IX, p. 332.
36 Diss, Part Third, Chapter; CW I, p. 497.
37 EPHM III, Part Second, Chapter I, Section i; CW IV, pp. 6–7.
38 Ibid., Chapter II, Section ii; CW IV, p. 136.
39 PAMP II, Book Fourth, Chapter IV, Section 4, Sub-section 5; CW VII, p. 173.
40 Diss, Part Third, Concluding Chapter; CW I, pp. 489–90.

Further Reading

Writings about Stewart's philosophy are numerous. Some of the standard nineteenth-century accounts are still useful – in, for example,

A. Bain, *Mental and Moral Science* (London, 1868).
Sir J. Mackintosh, *On the Progress of Ethical Philosophy* (Edinburgh, 1872).
Sir L. Stephen, *History of English Thought in the Eighteenth Century* (London, 1881).

Of more recent publications the following is a limited list of those which I have found particularly helpful.

A. Broadie, *The Scottish Enlightenment* (Edinburgh: Canongate, 2001).
A. Chitnis, *The Scottish Enlightenment – a Social History* (London: Croom Helm, 1976).
A. Chitnis, *The Scottish Enlightenment and Early Victorian Society* (London: Croom Helm, 1986).
P. Flynn, *Enlightened Scotland* (Edinburgh: Scottish Academic Press, 1992).
S. A. Grave, *The Scottish Philosophy of Common Sense* (Oxford: Oxford University Press, 1960).
S. A. Grave, *Dugald Stewart* in *Encyclopedia of Philosophy* (New York and London, 1967).
K. Haakonssen, *From Moral Philosophy to Political Economy: the contribution of Dugald Stewart*, in V. Hope, *Philosophers of the Scottish Enlightenment* (Edinburgh: Edinburgh University Press, 1984).
K. Haakonssen, *Natural Law and Moral Philosophy* (Cambridge: Cambridge University Press, 1996).
D. Winch, *The System in the North: Dugald Stewart and his Pupils* in S. Collini, D. Winch and J. Burrows, *That Noble Science of Politics – a study in nineteenth century intellectual history* (Cambridge: Cambridge University Press, 1983).

Index

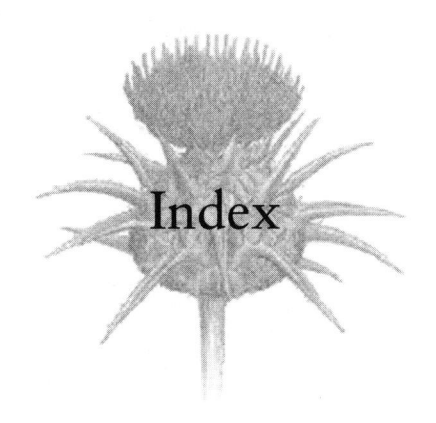

Abercromby, Alexander, Lord (1745–95), 88–90
Abercromby, General Sir John (1772–1817), 174
Aberdeen, George Hamilton Gordon, 1st Earl of (1784–1860), 144
Aberdeen University, 16; King's College, 22; Marischal College, 22; Philosophical Society (Wise Club), 22
Abbotsford, Border Region, 78, 192, 212
Act of Union, 3, 37
Adam, Alexander (1741–1809), 16–17, 25, 151
Adam, Mrs Alexander, 151
Adam, James (1730–94), 52
Adam, John (1721–92), 81
Adam, Robert (1728–92), 1, 52, 74, 81
Adam, William, Lord Chief Commissioner (1751–1839), 1, 2, 23, 85, 191
Adams, President John (1735–1826), 73
Addington, Henry (1st Viscount Sidmouth) (1757–1844), 139
Addison, Joseph (1672–1719), 265
aesthetics, 2, 248, 252, 253–4
agriculture, 157, 263
Aiken, Dr (song collector), 61
Aikin, John (1747–1822), 92
Akenside, Mark (1721–70), 167
d'Alembert, Jean Le Rond (1717–83), 248
algebra, 31, 111
Alison, Rev. Archibald (1757–1839), 21, 23, 33, 34, 42–3, 45, 52, 62, 65, 68, 70, 71, 72, 73, 82, 84, 85, 94, 101, 112, 119, 122, 149, 150–1, 156, 174,
253; *Essays on the Nature and Principles of Taste,* 174
Alison, Sir Archibald (1792–1867), 84, 51, 156, 158
Alison, Mrs Dorothea, *née* Gregory (d.1830), 52, 53, 68, 71, 84, 117
Alison, Mrs Margaret, *née* Gregory, 237
Alison, Dr Wiliam Pulteney (1790–1859), 151, 237, 238, 143
Allahabad, India, 147, 173
Allen, Frances, 120
Allen, Dr John (1771–1843), 141, 170, 179
America (United States of), 5, 42, 52, 67, 75, 135, 156, 192, 214, 239, 244, 255, 168
American revolution, 2, 29, 31, 33, 42, 44, 45, 71, 75, 96, 114
Amiens, France, 42
Amiens, Peace of, 139
Amsterdam, Netherlands, 40
Ancram, Lord: *see* Lothian, 6th Marquess
Andover, Hampshire, 119
antiquities, Roman, 69
anthropology, 20
Arbuthnot, ? Robert, 70, 72, 74
Arbuthnot, Sir William, 72
architecture, 3, 99–100
Argyll, Archibald Campbell, 1st Duke of, 7
Argyll, Archibald Campbell, 3rd Duke of (1682–1761), 8
Argyllshire, 6
Aristotle (384–322 BC), 248
arithmetic, 167, 181
Arkwright, Richard (1732–92), 66

Index

Arran, Isle of, Ayrshire, 53, 119
Arrochar, Argyll & Bute, 119
art/drawing, 3, 96, 107
d'Artois, Charles Philippe, Comte (King Charles X) (1757–1836), 180
Ashbourne, Derbyshire, 119; Blackamoor Inn, 119
Ashburton, Anne, Lady, *née* Cunninghame, 131–2
Ashburton, John Dunning, 1st Baron (1731–83), 96
Ashburton, Elizabeth, Lady *née* Baring (1744–1809), 96, 99, 114
Ashburton, Richard Barré, 2nd Baron (1782–1823), 96–7, 98, 99, 101, 106, 107, 108, 110, 111, 114, 118, 119, 123, 131–2; *Genealogical Memoirs of the Royal House of France*, 132
Ashburton, Devon, 114, 175
Asse (Asch/Aalst), Belgium, 40
Astronomical Institution, 196
astronomy, 2, 30, 31, 32
Athens, Greece, 4; Choragic Monument of Lysikrates, 229–30
Austen, Jane (1775–1817), 167
Austerlitz, Battle of, 139
Australia, 244; Australian National University, 245
Ayr, Ayrshire, 11, 46, 56
Ayr Bank, 117
Ayr, River, 11, 56, 66
Ayrshire, 27, 38, 46, 50, 59, 60, 61, 69, 79, 81, 119, 144, 178, 179, 181, 188

Babbage, Charles (1792–1871), 197–8, 199, 207, 208, 209, 212, 214, 217, 221, 234
Babbage, Mrs Charles, 197, 198, 212, 234
Babbage, Edward Stewart (1820–21), 198, 209
Bacon, Francis (Baron Verulam) (1561–1626), 19, 206, 251, 252
Bahamas, 191
Bahia, Brazil, 221
Ballantine, John (1743–1812), 56, 59
Ballochmyle, Ayrshire, 117–18
Bankhead, Lanarkshire, 130–1
Bannatyne, Andrew (b. 1798), 237, 240
Bannatyne, Dugald (1755–1842), 21, 43, 66, 118–19, 234, 240, 243
Bannatyne, Dugald John (b. 1805), 240
Bannatyne, Neil (b. 1696), 21, 43
Bannatyne, Sir William Macleod, Lord (1743–1833), 118
Barbauld, Mrs Anna Letitia, *née* Aikin (1743–1824), 92, 93
Barnard Castle, County Durham, 99

Bath, Somerset, 101, 234, 235
Beaufort, Admiral Sir Francis (1774–1857), 194
Bedford, John Russell, 6th Duke of (1766–1839), 152, 195
Belsches, Williamina (1776–1810), 93
Belfast, County Antrim, 24, 28, 38, 87, 145, 146, 180, 198; Academical Institution, 198; Cabin Hill, 146
Belhaven & Stenton, John Hamilton, 2nd Baron (1752–1708), 37
Belhaven & Stenton, William Hamilton, 7th Baron (1765–1814), 36, 37, 66
Ben Cruachan, Argyll & Bute, 119
Ben Ledi, Stirlingshire, 153
Bengal, India, 178, 196
Bentham, Jeremy (1748–1832), 114
Berkeley, George (1685–1753), 247, 248
Berlin, Germany, 140, 173, 235, 236, 237; Royal Academy, 179
Berwick-upon-Tweed, Northumberland, 52
Birkbeck, George (1776–1841), 97, 219
Birmingham, West Midlands, 119
Black, Adam (1784–1874), 224; Black, A. & C., 241
Black, Prof. Joseph (1728–99), 31, 60, 122
Black Watch Regiment, 20
Blacklock, Thomas (1721–91), 51, 54–5, 56, 57
Blair, Rev. Prof. Hugh (1718–1800), 20, 93
Blair, Sir James Hunter (1741–87), 46, 70
Blair, Sir John Hunter, 70
Blair-Adam House, 191
Blackwood's Magazine, 201
Blake, William (1757–1827), 167
Bligh, Captain William (1754–*c*.1817), 255
Bohemia, 85
Bombay, India, 116
Bo'ness (Borrowstoneness), Falkirk, 149, 174, 214
book-keeping, 110, 167
Borders, Scottish, 60, 91, 99
Boroughbridge, Yorkshire, 99
Boston, American Society of, 179
Boswell, Sir Alexander (1775–1822), 210
Boswell, James (1740–95), 5, 45, 50–1, 80, 210; *Journal of a Tour to the Hebrides with Samuel Johnson,* 50–1
botany, 110
Botany Bay, Australia, 85
Boulogne, France, 42
Bourbons, 43
Bowditch, Nathaniel (1773–1838), 192

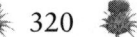

Index

Bowles, Rev. William Lisle (1762–1850), 195
Bowness-on-Windermere, Cumbria, 114
Bowood House, Wiltshire, 101, 180, 194–95, 212, 234
Boyd, Prof. John, 6
Braxfield, Robert Macqueen, Lord (1722–99), 85
Bridges, James, 242
Brighton, Sussex, 234
Bristol, 51, 245
Britain/British Isles/United Kingdom, 37, 73, 85, 119, 126, 181, 214, 244, 245, 257; constitution, 73, 88, 264; government, 26, 29, 31, 33, 52, 85–6, 90, 122, 126, 134–5, 136, 137, 143
British Library, x
Broadie, Prof. Alexander, 245; *The Scottish Enlightenment: an Anthology*, 245
Broadlands, Hampshire, 104, 115, 119, 123, 124, 142
Brodie, Deacon William (c.1741–88), 65, 75
Broster, Mr (speech therapist), 216
Brougham and Vaux, Henry Peter, 1st Baron (1788–1868), 16, 17, 91, 109, 111, 122, 130, 168, 220, 243
Brown, Dr Michael, 244
Brown, Prof. Thomas (1778–1820), 5, 91, 129, 148, 149, 151–3, 161, 167, 198–9, 205–6, 241, 242
Bruce, Prof. John (1745–1826), 29, 46
Brussels, Belgium, 40
Brydone, Mary, *née* Robertson, 38–9, 212, 227
Brydone, Patrick (c.1741–1818), 39; *Tour through Sicily and Malta*, 39
Buccleuch, Henry Scott, 3rd Duke of (1746–1812), 39
Buchan, David Steuart Erskine, 11th Earl of (1742–1820), 150
Buchan, Henry David Erskine, 12th Earl of (1783–1857), 111
Buonaparte, Napoleon (1769–1821), 97, 119, 139, 141, 182
Burger, Gottfried August (1747–94), 92; *Lenore*, 92
Burgoyne, General Sir John (1722–92), 29
Burke, Edmund (1729–97), 44–5, 67, 84, 139; *Reflections on the French Revolution*, 84–5
Burney, Fanny (Mme d'Arblay) (1752–1840), 167
Burns, Gilbert (1760–1827), 54
Burns, Mrs Jean *née* Armour (1765–1834), 63–4

Burns, Robert (1759–96), 5, 38, 54–64, 75, 76, 79, 90, 118, 121, 164, 167, 168–69; *Kilmarnock edition*, 54, 55, 56; *The Vision*, 55; *Edinburgh edition*, 56; *The Brigs of Ayr*, 56; *On Turning up a Mouse with his Plough*, 56; *On the Mountain Daisy*, 56; *The Lament*, 56; *Lines on Meeting with Lord Daer*, 57–8; *For W. Creech*, 60
Burntisland, Fife, 105, 113
Bute, John Stuart, 3rd Earl of (1713–92), 8
Bute, Isle of, Argyll & Bute, 6, 7, 27, 34, 66, 81, 115, 234
Butler, Lady Eleanor (c.1739–1829), 100
Buxton, Derbyshire, 210
Byron, George Gordon, 6th Baron (1788–1824), 37, 167, 180

Cadell, Robert (1788–1849), 179, 211, 221
Cadell, Thomas (1742–1802), 71, 82, 83; Cadell & Strachan, 211
Caesar, Gaius Julius (100–44 BC), 8
Cairnmuir, Border Region, 145, 146
Calais, France, 39, 42; Dessein's Inn, 42
Calcutta, India, 142, 174
Cambrai, France, 39
Cambridge, Philosophical Society of, 179
Cambridge University, 79, 95, 109–11, 112, 113, 115, 134, 135, 221; St John's College, 116, 120, 140; Trinity College, 101
Campbell, Thomas (1777–1841), 5, 78, 101, 112, 120, 149, 153, 165, 167, 184, 237, 239, 243; *The Pleasures of Hope*, 101; *Ye Mariners of England*, 112; *Hohenlinden*, 112; *Gertrude of Wyoming*, 149
Campbeltown, Argyll & Bute, 6, 7, 119
Canning, George (1770–1827), 98, 136, 220
capital punishment, 32, 75, 90
Carlisle, Frederick Howard, 5th Earl of (1748–1825), 31
Carlisle, Cumbria, 99, 110, 114, 119, 176
Carlyle, Rev. Dr Alexander (1722–1805), 7, 8, 19
Carlyle, Thomas (1795–1881), 130, 221, 241, 249, 250
Carron Ironworks, 45, 150
Catholic Church, 69, 190
Catholic emancipation, 33, 87, 143, 165
Catrine, Ayrshire, 10–81 *passim*; 144, 169, 178, 231, 233, 240, 241
causation, 44, 126–7
Cervantes Saavedra, Miguel de (1547–1616): *Don Quixote*, 19

321

Index

Chalmers, Rev. Thomas (1780–1847), 159, 242
Chantilly, France, 42
Chantrey, Sir Francis Leggatt (1781–1841), 177
Cheltenham, Gloucestershire, 119
chemistry/chemists, 31, 111, 214, 258
Chesterfield, Philip Stanhope, 5th Earl of (1755–1815), 39
China, 225
Chomeley, Mrs Francis, 119
Christison, Prof. Alexander, 111
Church of England, 21, 23, 34
Church of Scotland, 6, 7, 55, 125–30, 176; Evangelicals, 127–29; General Assembly, 9, 17, 33, 128–30; Ministers' Widows Fund, 11; Moderates, 5, 125–9; Presbytery of Edinburgh, 126; puritanism in, 3; Synod of Lothian and Tweeddale, 128
church history, 208
Cicero, Marcus Tullius (106–43 BC), 156, 249–50, 256
Classics/classical literature, 96, 110, 167, 203
Cleghorn, Prof. Hugh (1752–1837), 68–9
Cockburn, Henry, Lord (1779–1854), 2, 16, 25, 87, 90, 109, 122–3, 154, 156, 159–60, 161, 162, 169, 170, 171, 210, 227, 229, 242, 248; *Memorials of his Time*, ix, 15
Colburn, Zerah (1804–1839), 181
Coleridge, Samuel Taylor (1772–1834), 167
Collins, William (1721–59), 167
Condillac, Etienne Bonnot de (1715–80), 248
Condorcet, Marie Jean Antoine Nicolas de Caritat, Marquis de (1743–94), 57, 87, 89, 91
Constable, Archibald (1774–1827), 78, 130, 151, 166, 167, 172, 176–221 *passim*
Constable, Thomas (1780–1881), 166, 243
Constant de Rebecque, Benjamin, Baron (1767–1830), 43
conveyancing, 200
Cook, Capt. James (1728–79), 255
Corehouse, George Cranstoun, Lord (1771–1850), 75, 92, 122, 130, 132, 193, 202, 212, 213, 223–4, 225, 228, 229, 233, 237–8, 240; *The Diamond Beetle Case*, 76
Corehouse Estate, 193, 228, 233, 234
Corsica, 92
cotton textile industry, 66, 80

Court of Session, 87, 229
Cowes, Isle of Wight, 120
Craig, Sir James Gibson (James Gibson) (1765–1850), 201
Craig, William, Lord (1745–1801), 88–90
Cranstoun, Hon. George (d. 1788), 76, 77–8, 81
Cranstoun, George: *see* Corehouse, Lord
Cranstoun, Henry (1757–1843), 78, 118
Cranstoun, Mrs Maria, *née* Brisbane (d. 1807), 76, 78, 83, 145
Cranstoun, Mary Anne, *née* Whiteefoord, 118
Cranstoun, William, 3rd Lord, 81
Cranstoun, William, 5th Lord (d. 1726/7), 76
Creech, William (1745–1815), 60, 63
Crinan Canal, Argyll & Bute, 119
Cruickshank, Alexander, 225
Cruickshank, of Langley Park, 225
Cudworth, Ralph (1617–88), 248
Cullen, Prof. William (1710–90), 19, 38
Cumnock, Ayrshire, 34, 70, 71, 81, 184, 188–89
Cunningham, Alexander (1763–1812), 63
Cunninghame, Margaret Nicolson, *née* Cranstoun, 78, 79, 112, 124, 131–2, 218, 233
Cunninghame, William (c.1731–1805), 78
Cunninghame, William (son of above) (1763–1805), 78, 82, 124
Cupar, Fife, 119
Currie, Dr James (1756–1805), 62, 64; *Life of Burns*, 64

Daer, Basil William Douglas, Lord (1763–94), 36, 37, 38, 40, 42, 45, 57–8, 71, 73, 87, 110, 122, 140, 212
Dale, David (1739–1806), 80, 257
Dalkeith, Midlothian, 212
Dalmeny Park, West Lothian, 177
Dalzel, Prof. Andrew (1742–1806), 25, 27, 28, 29–30, 32, 39, 43, 44, 47, 52, 76, 83, 90, 91, 122, 123, 141, 193, 196, 239; *History of Edinburgh University*, 141–2
Dalzel, Mrs Anne, *née* Drysdale (1751–1829), 52, 177
Dalzel, John (1796–1823), 193
Dalzel, Mary, 239
dancing, 96, 110
Darwin, Erasmus ((1731–1802), 247, 248
Dauphiné, France, 70
Davidson, Alexander, 214
Davie, Dr George Elder, 244
Davy, Sir Humphry (1778–1829), 178, 183

Index

Davy, Lady Jane (1780–1855), 178
Debarry, Rev. (Lord Henry Petty's tutor), 97
Declaration of American Independence, 29, 42, 70
Delft, Netherlands, 40
Denholm, Border Region, 91
Derbyshire, 104, 178
Dessein, Pierre Quillacq, 42
Devon, 195
divinity, 6, 49, 126, 127, 208
Donington, Leicestershire, 178–9
Dorset, 31–2
Douai, France, 39, 68–9; Scots College, 69
Dougalstown, Dunbartonshire, 38
Douglas, Hon. John (1765–97), 71
Douglas, the Ladies, 119
Dovedale, Derbyshire, 119
Dover, Kent, 39, 42, 71
Dow, John, 242
Drennan, Mrs Sarah *née* Swanwick, 145–7
Drennan, William (1754–1820), 21, 28–9, 38–9, 87–8, 106, 142, 145–7, 180–1, 193; *Letters of an Irish Helot*, 87; *Address to the Volunteers*, 87–8; *When Erin First Rose*, 146
Drummond, Agnes, 185
Dryburgh, Border Region, 222
Dublin, Ireland, 87, 146, 221
Dudley, John William Ward, 1st Earl of (John William Ward) (1781–1833), 98–9, 101, 102, 115, 120, 132, 140, 163, 164, 165–6, 180, 188, 208, 210–11, 220, 221, 224
Dudley and Ward, William Ward, 3rd Viscount (1750–1823), 98
Dumfries, Dumfries & Galloway, 38
Dumfriesshire, 61
Dumbarton, Dunbartonshire, 38, 178, 193
Dumont, Pierre Etienne Louis (1759–1829), 83
Dunbartonshire, 38
Duncan, Rev. Henry (1774–1846), 91, 220
Duncan, Lady (Scots lady in Bath), 235
Dundas, Henry: *see* Melville, 1st Viscount
Dundas, Robert Saunders (1771–1851), 143
Dunfermline, Fife, 119
Dunglass Castle, Dunbartonshire, 193
Dunlop, Mrs Frances of Dunlop, *née* Wallace (1730–1815), 61, 79, 90
Durham, County Durham, 176
Dyke, Great, Netherlands, 40

East India Charter, 179
East India College, Haileybury, 201

East India Company, 21, 44, 102, 139, 225
economics, 2, 109
Edgeworth, Frances Maria (1799–1865), 212
Edgeworth, Harriet (1801–89), 212
Edgeworth, Henry (1782–1813), 116–17
Edgeworth, Honora (1791–1858), 212
Edgeworth, Lovell (1775–1842), 97, 108, 116
Edgeworth, Maria (1768–1849), 5, 97, 108, 116, 152, 163, 194–95, 212, 232, 257; *Moral Tales*, 108; *Helen*, 232
Edgeworth, Richard Lovell (1744–1817), 116, 257
Edgeworth, Sophia (1803–37), 212
Edinburgh, 1–240 *passim*; Ainslie Place, ix, 225–7; Ann Street, 239; Argyle's Square, 80, 93; Arthur's Seat, 80, 106; Barnton, 66; Bonington, 80; Botanic Gardens (old), 110; Botanic Gardens (new), 221; Braid Hills, 16, 60; Bridges, The, 74, 75, 227; Callander's Entry, 93; Callander House, 117–18, 149, 161; Calton Hill, 2, 227, 229, 230; Canongate, 45, 93, 117, 118; Canongate Churchyard, 227, 230, 239, 241; Castle, 4, 16, 123; Charlotte Chapel, 102; Charlotte Square, 111; College Wynd, 76; Cowgate, 16, 17; Cowgate Episcopal Chapel, 112; Cramond Regis, 66; Davidson's Mains Park, 66; Drumsheugh, 50, 62, 80; Fish Market Close, 190; Frederick Street, 92; George Square, 76; George Street, 103; Grange (House), 82, 83; Grassmarket, 122; Hay Street, 43; Heriot's Hospital, 68; High Church, 20; High Street, 75, 227; Howard Place, 211; Infirmary Street, 14; Lady Yester's Church, 168; Leith Walk, 110; Lothian House (Hut), 93, 95, 97, 98, 101, 102, 106, 107, 108, 111, 112, 116, 117, 118, 120, 144, 162; Merchiston, 16; Newington Road, 80; New Town, 4, 97, 118, 225; Nicolson Square, 43; Old Greyfriars Church, 17; Old Town, 118; Palace of Holyroodhouse, 4, 180, 211; Panmure House, 45; Parliament Close, 74; Potter Row, 43; Princes Street, 74, 185; Queensferry Road, 66; Rankeillor Street, 144; Register House, 74; Rose Street, 102; St Andrew Square, 118; St Bernard's

Index

Well, 230; St Cuthbert's Church, 129; St Giles Cathedral, 75; Sciennes Hill House, 60; Stewartfield (House), 80, 93, 118; Stockbridge, 230; Trinity Church, 124; Warriston (House), 234, 239; West End, 80; Whitefoord House, 117–18, 137, 162
Edinburgh, bugesses of, 15, 27
Edinburgh Gazette, 135, 223, 233, 237, 240
Edinburgh High Scool, 14–17, 25, 74, 87, 106, 151
Edinburgh Review, 5, 87, 109, 130, 163, 187, 243, 250, 251
Edinburgh Town Council, 9, 10, 15, 25, 26, 27, 28, 31, 46, 49, 74–5, 124, 126–7, 153, 169, 196, 200, 201, 203, 227
Edinburgh University (Town's College), 1–242 *passim*; common hall, 30; Dialectic Society, 85; General Convention, 83; houses in, 10, 17, 25, 27, 32, 43, 49–50; library, x, 65, 83, 228, 248; Literary Society, 75; mace, 65, 75; Old College, 74–5; Senatus Academicus, 27, 30, 126, 196; Speculative Society, 26, 27, 28–9, 43, 60, 97, 121; teaching accommodation, 27–8; teaching system, 9, 18, 25, 28, 48–9, 162, 168; Teviot Chambers, 10, 43
Edmonstoune, Miss (of Corehouse), 193
education, 2, 97, 102, 153, 169, 248, 255, 256–8, 265; adult education, 219–20, 257
Eildon Hall, Border Region, 222
Elder, Lord Provost Thomas (1737–99), 75
Elliot, Lady Charlotte ('Lotty') (d. 1899), 234–5, 240
Elliot, Lady Frances Anna Maria ('Fanny') (Lady Russell) (d. 1898), 234, 236, 239, 242
Elliot, Hon. George Francis Stewart ('Doddy') (1823–1901), 212–13, 236
Elliot, Gilbert: *see* Minto, 2nd Earl
Elliot, Hon. Henry George (b. 1817), 235
Elliot, Hon. Capt. John Edmund (1788–1862), 182, 216
Elliot, Lady Mary (d. 1874), 234, 235–6, 238
Ellisland (Dumfries & Galloway), 62
Emerson, Ralph Waldo (1803–82), 241
Emmett, Thomas Addis (1764–1827), 87
Encyclopaedia Britannica, 178, 182–83, 188, 199, 208, 247
Endsleigh House, Devon, 195
engineering/civil engineering, 157

England, 5, 34, 53, 93, 95, 103, 110, 112, 122, 140, 148, 178, 179, 180, 182, 194, 197, 211, 213, 234, 235, 239, 264; language/accent, 250, 261; universities, 95, 152
English Channel, 39
Enlightenment (Scottish), ix, 2–4, 7, 29, 44–5, 121, 125, 169, 178, 245, 253, 257, 258
Ermenonville, France, 74
Erskine, Hon. Henry (1746–1817), 59, 111
Esdale, Mr (candidate for moral philosophy chair), 99
ethics, 20, 22, 247, 252, 256
Eton College, Windsor, 195, 235
Etruria, Staffordshire, 51
Euclid (fl. 300 BC)/ Euclidian geometry, 8, 30, 45, 107
Europe/'The Continent', 3, 39, 66, 68, 71, 75, 86, 89, 101, 122, 126, 139, 214, 247, 257, 268
Exeter, Devon, 192, 195, 215, 234, 243

Falkirk, 177
Falkland, Fife, 119
Falls of Clyde, Lanarkshire, 193
Farquhar, Robert, 15
fencing, 110, 113
Ferguson, Rev. Prof. Adam (1723–1816), 5, 20, 21, 31, 32, 39, 40, 46, 47, 49, 60; *Essay on the History of Civil Society*, 20
Ferguson, Sir Adam (1771–1855), 60
Ferguson, James (1710–76), 17
Fergusons of Raith (Robert Ferguson, 1771–1840), 47
Fettes, Lord Provost Sir William (1750–1836), 125–7
Fielding, Henry (1707–54), 15, 167; *Joseph Andrews*, 15
Fife, 60, 119, 176, 210
Finlayson, Rev. Prof. James (1758–1808), 123, 126
Flanders, 40; Parliament, 39
Florence, Italy, 4
Fontenoy, Battle of, 20, 40
Forbes, Peggie, 144
Forbes, Sir William (1739–1806), 63
Forfar, Angus, 225
Forth, River, 29, 60, 105, 150
Foston-le-Clay, Yorkshire, 135, 176
Fountains Abbey, Yorkshire, 99
Fox, Charles James (1749–1806), 36, 67, 85, 135, 138–9, 141, 156, 175, 232
Fox, Miss (sister of Lord Holland), 211
France, 5, 39–42, 44, 57, 68–70, 71–4, 81,

Index

82, 84, 85, 88–9, 95, 106, 122, 134, 140, 163, 182, 224, 241, 267; Chamber of Deputies, 43; Estates General, 70, 71, 72, 73; government, 29, 139, 141; language, 39, 68, 72, 96, 140, 172, 224, 241, 248, 263; National Convention, 84; Philosophical Society, 179
Frankfurt, Germany, 140
Franklin, Benjamin (1706–90), 42, 44, 52, 67, 68, 137, 165
Free Church of Scotland, 159
Freemasonry/freemasons, 4, 42, 50, 53, 57, 73, 75, 93, 121, 196; Canongate Lodge, Edinburgh, 50, 59; St James's Lodge, Tarbolton, 57, 60; St Andrew's Lodge, Edinburgh, 59
free will, 247, 255
French, the, 263–4
French revolution, 2, 57, 69, 70, 71, 72–4, 84, 125, 141, 161, 24, 267
Friday Club, 122–3, 150

Gaelic language, 20
Geneva, Switzerland, 70, 172–3
geography, 15
geology, 105, 122
geometry, 8, 12, 24, 25, 30, 108
George III, King (1738–1820), 26, 67, 143, 163, 174, 175, 185, 198
George IV, King (Prince Regent) (1762–1830), 72, 175, 176, 178, 180, 211, 220
de Gerando, Marie Joseph, Baron (1772–1842), 141, 179, 182
Germany, 40, 112; language, 92, 251; philosophy, 251
Ghent (Gent), Belgium, 40
ghost stories, 209
Gibbon, Edward (1737–94), 82
Gibson, Principal William (1738–1821), 69
Gibraltar, 198
Gillies, Robert Pearse (1788–1858), 13, 137, 155, 162, 165
Gilmer, Francis Walker (1790–1826), 214–15
Gilsland, Northumberland, 119
Glasford, Henry, 36, 37–8
Glasford, John (1715–83), 37–8
Glasgow, 21–4, 45, 66, 94, 101, 118–19, 173, 178, 179, 181, 198, 234, 243; Anderston, 8; Chamber of Commerce, 118–19; Gallery of Modern Art, 78; Queen Street, 78; Saracen's Head Inn, 45
Glasgow tobacco lords, 38, 78

Glasgow University, 6, 7–8, 12, 21–3, 37, 43, 44–5, 67, 76, 87, 125, 201, 202, 208; College Chapel, 45; Literary Society, 22, 121; Snell Foundation, 21
Glen Shira, Argyll & Bute, 119
God, 55, 126, 128, 247, 256, 261
Godwin, William (1756–1836), 189; *Political Justice*, 189
Goldie, Prof. John, 8
Gordon riots, 33
Goval, Abbé, 68
Graham, James Gillespie (c.1771–1855), 5
Grampian Mountains, Perth & Kinross, 174
Grant, Elizabeth of Rothiemurchus (Mrs Smith) (1797–1885), 132, 195
Grant, Sir John Peter of Rothiemurchus (1774–1848), 195
Grant, Sir John Peter (son of above) (b. 1807), 195–6
Grant, Principal (of Scots College, Douai), 39
gravity, law of, 252
Gray, Thomas (1716–71), 167; *Elegy Written in a Country Church-yard*, 167
Great Malvern, Worcestershire, 119
Gregory, Prof. James (1753–1821), 30, 52, 68, 94, 146, 147, 191, 199
Gregory, Prof. John (1724–73), 52, 53; *A Father's Legacy to his Daughters*, 52
Greece, 90; language and literature, 15, 16, 18, 25, 43, 107, 111, 123, 215, 248; mathematics, 8; philosophy, 31
Green, ? Amos, 100
Greenfield, Thomas, 144
Greenfield, Rev. Prof. William (d. 1827), 92, 123
Greenwich Observatory, 208
Grenville, William Wyndham, 1st Baron (1759–1834), 135, 139, 141, 143
Greville, Charles Francis (1749–1809), 102
Greville, Robert Fulke (1751–1824), 102
Grey, Charles, 2nd Earl (1764–1845), 85, 235, 243
Grose, Capt. Francis ((1730–91), 62
Guyot, M. (tutor to brothers de Lessert), 70, 73–4

Haakonssen, Prof. Knud, 243, 245
Halkett, Dunbar Stewart (1817–c.1886), 191
Halkett, John (b. 1768), 191
Halkett, Lady Katherine, née Douglas (1778–1848), 180, 191, 240

Index

Hallancey, Mrs (at Eton College), 235
Hamilton, Archibald, 9th Duke of (1740–1819), 149, 153, 196
Hamilton, Alexander, 10th Duke of (1767–1852), 196, 253
Hamilton, Elizabeth (1758–1816), 114–15; *Letters on Education*, 114; *Memoirs of the Life of Agrippina, the wife of Germanicus*, 115
Hamilton, Sir William (1788–1856), 199, 201, 202, 203, 232, 241, 242
Hamilton, Lanarkshire, 119
handwriting, 110
Hardie, Charles Martin (1858–1916), 60
Harrogate, Yorkshire, 176, 240
Harrow School, 37, 104, 107, 112
Hartley, David (1705–57), 247, 249
Harvard University, USA, 241
Hastings, Warren (1732–1818), 67, 102
Hatton House, Midlothian, 44
Hawthorne, Nathaniel (1804–64), 241
Heaphy, Thomas (1775–1835), 143
Henderson Alexander, 221, 234
Henderson, Margaret, *née* Miller (1783–1862), 184, 189, 196, 211, 216, 221, 234
Henning, John (1771–1851), 160, 161
Herman, Prof. Arthur, 47, 245; *The Scottish Enlightenment – the Scots' Invention of the Modern World*, 245
Herschel, Sir William (1738–1822), 67
Heslington, Yorkshire, 176
Hicks Beach, Michael, 100
Hicks Beach, Michael (son of above), 100, 102, 103
Hicks Beach, William, 103
Highlands, Scottish, 60, 61, 110, 178, 192, 211
Hill, Prof. John, 27
history, 15, 20, 51, 68–9, 157, 164, 253
Hobbes, Thomas (1588–1679), 256
Holland, Elizabeth, Lady (1770–1845), 101–2, 152, 178, 190, 207, 209
Holland, Henry Richard Fox, 3rd Baron (1773–1840), 101–2, 141, 170, 179, 190, 211
Holland, Henry Edward, 4th Baron (Lord Henry Fox) (1802–59), 209
Holland, Sir Henry (1788–1873), 152
Holland, Saba, Lady *née* Smith (1802–1866), 113, 176, 227
Holland, 40; Dutch coffee house, 263
Home, Alexander, 10th Earl of (1769–1841), 69
Home, Jane, Lady (d. 1787), 50, 66

Home, Rev. John (1722–1808), 67; *Douglas*, 67
Hope, Louisa Dorothea, Lady (d. 1836), 180
Hoppus, John (1789–1875), 243
Horner, Anne ('Nancy'), 177, 187–8
Horner, Francis (1778–1817), 91, 102, 109, 123, 130, 135, 138, 148, 158, 159, 162, 168, 169, 170, 173, 174, 175, 178, 179–80, 181, 183, 187–8, 189, 190–1, 196, 206, 231, 250, 251, 257
Horner, Leonard (1785–1864), 189, 190, 193, 197, 206, 214, 232
House of Commons, 44, 134, 136, 137–8, 201, 243
House of Lords, 138, 140
humanity (subject of), 18, 27, 67
Hume, David (1711–76), 20, 43, 55, 109, 126, 128, 129, 173, 176, 248, 253, 254, 255
Hungary, 85
Hunter, Rev. Prof. Andrew (1743–1809), 127
Hunter, Prof. Robert, 18
Hutcheson, Prof. Francis (1694–1746), 7–8, 21, 125
Hutton, Charles (1737–1823), 105
Hutton, Dr James (1726–97), 60, 122
hydrostatics, 65

idealism, 247
India, 139, 142, 173, 178, 182, 216, 225, 231, 233
induction, 251–2
industrial revolution, 2, 38, 45, 66, 79–80, 169
internationalism, 261
Inveraray, Argyll & Bute, 118–19
Ireland, 5, 100, 104, 146, 180, 214, 221
Irish, the, 116
Irish Volunteers, 87
Irving, Washington (1783–1859), 192

Jackson, Rev. Thomas (Prof. Jackson) (1797–1878), 183, 207–8, 212, 218, 221
Jacobite rising (1745), 4, 8, 26, 122
Jamaica, 55, 196
James VI and I, King, 33
James, William (1842–1910), 241
Japan, 244
Jay, John (1745–1829), 42, 52
Jedburgh, Border Region, 38
Jefferson, President Thomas (1743–1826), 67, 70, 71, 73, 214–15, 232, 241
Jeffrey, Francis (1773–1850), 2, 87, 109,

326

Index

114, 122, 130, 173, 192, 202, 210, 217, 242, 252
Jeffrey, George, 87
Johnson, James, 61; *Scots Musical Museum*, 61, 63
Johnson, Dr Samuel (1709–84), 50–1; *Journey to the Western Islands of Scotland*, 50
Jones, John Paul (1747–92), 29
Joseph II, Emperor (1741–90), 40
Joseph, Samuel (d. 1850), 161, 229
Jouffroy, Simon-Théodore (1796–1842), 224
jurisprudence, 2, 20, 256

Kames, Bute, Argyll & Bute, 7, 118
Kant, Immanuel (1724–1804), 3, 251
Keith, Hester Maria ('Queeney'), Viscountess, *née* Thrale (1764–1857), 217
Kellie Castle, 225
Kenley, Shropshire, 101
Kent, 72
Ker, Lord Henry Francis Charles (1800–82), 190, 213–14
Keswick, Cumbria, 114
Kilmarnock, Ayrshire, 181
Kingswells (? King's Well Inn, Ayrshire), 45
Kinnaird, Perthshire, 149
Kinneil House and Estate, Falkirk, 53, 149–50, 151–235 *passim*
Kintyre, Mull of, Argyll & Bute, 7, 119
Kirkcaldy, Fife, 47
Kirkcudbright, Dumfries & Galloway, 55, 110, 192
Knight, Richard Payne (1750–1824), 170, 251
Knutsford, Cheshire, 119
Kraken, 27

Lafayette, Marie Joseph Yves Gilbert du Motier, Marquis de (1757–1834), 42, 232
Laing, James, 169
Lainshaw, Ayrshire, 78, 82, 112, 124, 132
Lake District, English, 99, 176
Lamb, Frederick (3rd Viscount Melbourne) (1782–1853), 105
Lancashire, 119, 178
Lancaster, Joseph (1778–1838), 257
Langholm, Dumfries & Galloway, 120
Langley Park, Angus, 181, 191, 212, 225
language(s), 91, 247, 252, 253, 264
Lansdowne, William Petty, 1st Marquess of (Lord Shelburne) (1737–1805), 52,
67, 95–7, 98, 101, 106, 120, 130, 141
Lansdowne, Henry Petty-Fitzmaurice, 3rd Marquess of (Lord Henry Petty) (1780–1863), 97, 98, 101, 102, 111, 113, 114, 130, 132, 134, 135, 136, 177, 194, 205, 207, 208, 211, 215, 217, 220, 221, 222, 223, 224, 228, 234, 243
Lansdowne, Louisa Emma, Marchioness of, *née* Fox-Strangeways (1785–1851), 195
La Rochefoucault-Liancourt, François-Alexandre-Frédéric, Duc de (1747–1827), 72–3
Latin language and literature, 7, 14, 15, 16, 18, 25, 30, 107, 111, 145, 193, 230, 248, 251
Lauderdale, James Maitland, 7th Earl of (1718–1789), 44
Lauderdale, James Maitland, 8th Earl of (Lord Maitland) (1759–1839), 25, 39, 44–5, 97, 105, 139–41, 142, 197, 229, 232
law/civil law, 21, 101, 202, 256, 264–5
Lawrie, Alexander, 135
Lawrie, Rev. George (1722–99), 54–5, 56
Lee, Rev. (Principal) John (1779–1859), 168
Leiden, Netherlands, 40
Leith, Midlothian, 16, 29, 80, 131, 211
Leonardo da Vinci (1452–1519), 120; *The Virgin of the Rocks*, 120
Leslie, Prof. Sir John (1766–1832), 51, 126–30; *Properties of Heat*, 126
de Lessert, Benjamin, 70
de Lessert, Stephen, 70
de Lessert, Mme (mother of above), 73
Leyden, John (1775–1811), 91
Liberal Party, 243
Lille, France, 40
Lind, Dr James (1736–1812), 67
Lindsay, Capt. Alexander (1788–1822), 225
Lindsay, Alexander (son of above), 225
Lindsay, Amy, *née* Cruickshank, ix, 225
Linlithgow Palace, West Lothian, 212
Lisbon, Portugal, 199
Lichfield, Staffordshire, 108
literature, 3, 43, 170, 203–4, 248
literary criticism, 2, 20
Literary Journal, 168
Liverpool, Robert Banks Jenkinson, Earl of (1770–1828), 177, 220, 221
Liverpool, Merseyside, 64, 119, 236
Llangollen, Denbighshire, 100; Ladies of, 100, 166.

Index

Lochgilphead, Argyll & Bute, 119
Locke, John (1632–1704), 247, 248
Lockhart, John Gibson (1794–1854), 48, 75, 201
logic, 18, 19, 46, 48, 123, 126, 242, 243, 247, 252
Lomond, Loch, Argyll & Bute, 45
London, 33–250 *passim*; Adelphi Hotel, 43; Admiralty, The, 235; Hanover Square, 104, 112; Holland House, 102, 135, 140; Lincoln's Inn, 148; Mayfair, 102; National Gallery, 120; National Portrait Gallery, 160; Pall Mall, 241; Royal Institution, 123; Russell Square, 194; Thames, River, 181; United Service Club, 241; Westminster Abbey, 182; Westminster Hall, 67; Westminster School, 96, 97; Wimpole Street, 240; Woolwich, 221
London, Elizabethan, 4
London University, 243
Lothian, William Ker, 3rd Marquess of (d. 1767), 76
Lothian, William Henry Ker, 4th Marquess of (d. 1775), 93
Lothian, William John Ker, 5th Marquess of (1737–1815), 38, 93
Lothian, William Ker, 6th Marquess of (Lord Ancram) (1763–1824), 36, 38, 39–43, 50, 76, 77, 83, 93, 118, 148, 185–6, 190, 198, 211–12, 213, 250
Lothian, Henrietta, Marchioness of, *née* Hobart (1762–1805), 213, 214
Lothian, Harriet, Marchioness of, *née* Montagu (1780–1833), 148, 190, 238
Lothian, John William Robert Ker, 7th Marquess of (1794–1841), 213, 221, 225–6, 229, 231, 238
Lothian, Cecil, Marchioness of, *née* Chetwynd (d. 1877), 238
Lothian, William Schomberg Henry Ker, 8th Marquess of (1832–70), 238
Loudoun, Ayrshire, 54; Castle, 79
Louis XVI, King (1754–94), 42, 69, 72, 89, 215
Louis XVIII, King (1755–1824), 180
The Lounger, 58–9
Low Countries, 39, 191
Luther, Martin (1483–1546), 268
Lyon, Lord, King at Arms, 144
Lyons, France, 190

McCulloch, Prof. John Ramsay (1789–1864), 243
Macdonald, Ranald George, 132

Mackenzie, Henry (1745–1831), 5, 15, 58–9, 60, 63, 122, 166, 167, 174, 175, 176–77, 197; *The Man of Feeling*, 58; *Surprising Effects of Original Genius*, 59
Mackenzie, John of Delvine, 37
Mackenzie, Dr John (*c.*1755–1837), 55–8, 59
Mackintosh, Sir James (1765–1832), 49, 67, 110, 116, 170, 177, 183, 187, 199, 200–1, 208, 243, 248
Mackintosh, Catherine, Lady *née* Allen (d. 1830), 177
Macknight, Rev. Thomas (*c.*1762–1836), 124–6, 199
Maclaurin, Prof. Colin (1698–1746), 8–9, 24, 27, 30, 43
Maclaurin, Mrs Colin, 10
MacLea, Rev. Archibald (1838–1824), 34, 53, 66, 81, 188
MacLea, Isabella, *née* McLeod (d. 1812), 118
McLehose, Mrs Agnes ('Clarinda') (1759–1841), 61
McTier, Martha, *née* Drennan (1742–1837), 28, 38, 87
Madeira wine, 133
Maitland, General Sir Thomas (*c.*1759–1824), 196–7
Malmesbury, James Harris, 1st Earl of (1746–1820), 112, 115–16
Malta, 196, 198, 200, 203, 205
Malthus, Rev. Thomas Robert (1766–1834), 150; *Essay on the Principle of Population*, 150
Manderton, Lord Provost John, 199–200, 203
Marie-Antoinette, Queen (1755–93), 42, 89
Marseilles, France, 69
Mary, Queen of Scots (1542–87), 253
Maryland, USA, 38
Maskelyne, Nevil (1732–1811), 44
mathematics/mathematicians, 2, 3, 9, 12, 24–5, 27, 32, 37, 45, 47, 50, 52, 70, 78, 90, 98, 110, 123, 124, 197, 200, 247, 254, 258, 263, 264
Matheson, Alexander, 16
Mathews, Charles (1776–1835), 218
Mauchline, Ayrshire, 56, 60, 61
Maurice, Rev. Prof. Frederick (1805–72), 244
mechanics, 65
Mechanics Institutes, 219
medicine (subject of), 21, 28, 49, 52, 67, 91, 107, 202, 248, 260
Mediterranean, 196, 206

Index

Melbourne, William Lamb, 2nd Viscount (1779–1848), 105, 243
Melrose, Border Region, 222; Abbey, 100
Melville, Henry Dundas, 1st Viscount (1742–1811), 33, 74, 90, 125, 137–8, 143, 166, 203
Menton (?Menstrie), Clackmannanshire, 132
Mill, James (1773–1836), 91, 156, 168, 201
Mill, John Stuart (1806–73), 91, 241–2; *Autobiography*, 241
Millar, Prof. John (1735–1801), 21, 45, 87, 105; *The Origin and Distinction of Ranks*, 21
Miller, Capt. Dugald Stewart (d. 1914), 236
Miller, Major James (d. 1815), 184
Miller, Janet ('Jenny'), *née* Stewart (1752–89), 11, 34–5, 70, 81, 124, 184, 221, 236
Miller, Marjory (1781–1805), 124
Miller, Matthew (1787–1833), 221, 236
Miller, Dr Patrick ('Peter') (1782–1871), 106–7, 192, 195, 215, 234, 243
Miller, Robert, 93
Miller, Rev. Thomas (1740–1819), 34–5, 70, 81, 184, 188–9, 196
Miller, Col. William ('Willy') (1785–1852), 107, 123, 124, 221
Milton, John (1608–74), 156, 167, 262
Minto, Sir Gilbert Elliot, 1st Earl of (1751–1814), 111, 112, 130, 142, 143, 147–8, 173–4, 175, 182
Minto, Anna Maria, Countess of, *née* Amyand (1752–1829), 111, 123, 132, 138, 143, 149, 150, 160, 162, 167
Minto, Gilbert Elliot, 2nd Earl of (1782–1859), 39, 71, 111, 112, 124, 175, 176, 182, 185, 186, 196, 213, 215–16, 218, 220, 222–3, 223–4, 226, 228, 229, 230, 231, 234, 235, 239, 243
Minto, Mary, Countess of, *née* Brydone (1786–1853), 39, 175, 212, 217, 218, 222–3, 231, 234, 235, 236–7, 240
Minto, William Hugh Elliot, 3rd Earl of (Lord Melgund) (1814–91), 235
Minto House, Border Region, 111, 119, 138, 147, 189, 216, 222–3, 234, 237, 239
Mitchell, Mrs Christian *née* Gordon (d. 1821), 176
Mitchell, Rev. Donald (1749–1811), 176
Mitchell, James Errol (1795–1869), 176–7, 219, 247

Mitchell, Jane G. (1787–1861), 176–7, 219
Moffat, Dumfries & Galloway, 119
Moira, Francis Rawdon-Hastings, 2nd Earl of (1754–1826), 178, 182, 195
Moira, Flora Mure Campbell, Countess of, and Countess of Loudoun in her own right (c.1780–1840), 178
Monboddo, James Burnett, Lord (1714–99), 30–1, 67
Moncrieff Wellwood, Rev. Sir Henry (1750–1827), 129, 185
Montagu, Mrs Elizabeth, *née* Robinson (1720–1800), 52
Montesquieu, Charles de Secondat, Baron de la Brede et de (1689–1755), 68
Monteviot House, Border Region, 38, 83, 148
Montgolfier, brothers (Joseph Michel, 1740–1810; Jacques Etienne, 1745–99), 42
Montrose, Angus, 150, 181, 212
Moore, Thomas (1779–1852), 5, 167, 179, 195, 217–18, 234
moral philosophy, 2, 18, 20, 21, 45–6, 48–9, 75, 88, 91, 94, 109, 123, 149, 151–3, 157, 167, 169, 170, 174, 198, 199–204, 254–6, 266, 268
Moravians, 40
Morayshire, 176
Morellet, Abbé André (1727–1819), 141
Mossgeil Farm, Ayrshire, 54, 56, 61
Muir, Thomas (1765–98), 85
Muir Mackenzie, Alexander (d. 1835), 36, 37
Murray, John (1778–1843), 219
Murray, Sir John Archibald (1779–1859), 123, 170, 177, 179, 181, 210, 217
Musselburgh, Midlothian, 216
mythology, 15

Napier, Francis, 7th Baron (1758–1828), 75
Napier, Macvey (1776–1847), 161, 163, 173, 179, 183, 191, 199–200, 201, 202, 203, 204, 205, 208, 210, 212, 219, 224, 226, 230
Naples, Italy, 140, 190; Royal Academy, 179
National Library of Scotland, x
Nasmyth, Alexander (1758–1840), 5, 53, 150, 160
Nathaniel (prophet), 58
natural law, 256
natural philosophy, 19, 20, 44, 51, 65, 110, 124, 156
Navy Pay Office, 78

Index

Necker, Jacques (1732–1804), 70, 180
Netheravon, Wiltshire, 100
Neuchatel, Switzerland, 70
Newbattle Abbey/Park, Midlothian, 38, 118, 186, 198, 211, 212, 213, 225–6, 240
Newbury, Berkshire, 119
New Forest, Hampshire, 119
New Lanark, Lanarkshire, 80, 257
New Machar, Aberdeenshire, 22
Newry, County Down, 87
Newton, Sir Isaac (1642–1727), 8, 12, 23, 26, 30, 252, 266
Newtonian Club, 30, 121
Niger, River, 109
Nimes, France, 69
Northamptonshire, 52, 74
Northumberland, 101
Norwich, Norfolk, 92

Oban, Agyll & Bute, 119
optics, 30, 107
Oxford, 33
Oxford University, 18, 21, 95, 98, 109, 201, 202; Balliol College, 23, 33, 43
Oyster Club, 122

Paine, Thomas (1737–1809), 84–5
Palmer, Rev. Thomas Fyshe (1747–1802), 88
Palmerston, Henry Temple, 2nd Viscount (1739–1802), 104–8, 111, 112
Palmerston, Mary, Lady, *née* Mee (d. 1805), 105, 107, 111, 112, 113, 119, 123, 124
Palmerston, Henry John Temple, 3rd Viscount (1784–1865), ix, 99, 104–13, 115, 116, 118, 119, 120, 123, 124, 127, 130–2, 133, 134, 140, 142, 143–4, 145, 162, 180, 208, 220, 222, 223, 225, 226, 230, 233–4, 236, 237, 243
Paris, France, 39, 40–2, 52, 69, 70, 71–4, 86, 116, 117, 118, 139, 140–1, 182, 183, 214, 215, 232, 235; Bastille, 73; Notre Dame Cathedral, 42; Pont Neuf, 74
Paris, Treaty of, 42
Park, Mungo (1771–1806), 108, 255
parliamentary reform, 38, 87
Parr, Dr Samuel (1747–1825), 94, 153, 183, 188, 190, 192, 197, 198, 217, 250
Passy, France, 42
pathology, 156
Paul, Col. H., 101
Pennsylvania, USA, 42

Penrith, Cumbria, 119
Pentland Hills, Midlothian, 164
Perceval, Spencer (1762–1812), 136, 175
Perth, Perth & Kinross, 199
Perthshire, 37, 150
Petty, Lord Henry: *see* Lansdowne, 3rd Marquess
Philadelphia, American Society of, 179
philology, 2, 248, 253
philosophes, 87
Philosophical Society of Edinburgh, 30, 43, 121
philosophy (of mind), 2, 3, 32, 43, 170, 173, 178, 193, 218, 224, 243, 247, 251–2, 254, 257, 259, 262–63 (*See also*: moral philosophy); Scottish School of Common Sense, 254
physics, 214
Physiocrats, 109
physiognomy, 267–8
Pillans, Prof. James (1778–1864), 214
Pisa, Italy, 190
Pitt, William (1759–1806), 39, 67, 125, 134, 137, 139, 156, 251
Plato (*c.*428–*c.*348 BC), 180
Playfair, Prof. John (1748–1819), 12, 46, 47, 52, 90, 105, 107, 111, 122, 123, 124, 125–7, 129, 130, 152, 156, 168, 176–7, 178, 179, 181, 192, 196, 201, 229; *Illustrations of the Huttonian Theory of the Earth*, 105
Playfair, William Henry (1789–1857), 2, 5, 229, 230
Poker Club, 122
political economy, 109, 111, 140, 159, 170, 243, 248, 250, 256
political philosophy/science/theory, 2, 20, 22, 244, 247, 248, 252
Ponsonby, Sarah (1755–1829), 100
Pope, Alexander (1688–1744), 167
Portland, William Henry Cavendish-Bentinck, 3rd Duke of (1738–1809), 143
Portobello, Midlothian, 181, 185, 236; Brighton Crescent, 237, 240; High Street, 237; Marshall's Lodgings, 185; railway station, 240
Portpatrick, Dumfries & Galloway, 247
Portsmouth, Hampshire, 120
Powerscourt, Richard Wingfield, 4th Viscount (1762–1809), 36–7
Prestonpans, East Lothian, 38
Prévost, Prof. Pierre (1751–1834), 70, 91, 172, 214
Price, Richard (1723–91), 71, 73, 249
Priestley, Joseph (1733–1804), 247, 249
Prince Edward Island, Bahamas, 7

Index

Princeton University, USA, 114
Prior, Matthew (1664–1721), 146
professors, appointment and remuneration of, 9, 26
Prussia, 85, 141
psychology, 2, 20
Purgstall, Jane Anne, Countess, *née* Cranstoun (*c.*1760–1835), 78, 92–3, 97, 133
Purgstall, Wenceslaus Gottfried, Count (d.1812), 97

Quarterly Review, 76, 78, 165, 173, 249

Raeburn, Sir Henry (1756–96), 5, 83, 160, 215
Ramsay, George, 66–70
Ramsay, Jean, *née* Hamilton, 66
Ramsay, William (1732–1807), 66
Rankin, Councillor, 125, 127
Raynal, Abbé Guillaume Thomas-François (*c.*1712–96), 69
Reform Act, 243
Reformation, 268
Reid, Prof. Thomas (1710–96), 4, 21–2, 23, 81–2, 94, 176, 205–6, 241, 248, 252, 255, 256; *Inquiry into the Human Mind*, 21, 114; *Essays on the Intellectual Powers of Man*, 94
religion, 157, 224, 254, 261
Rembrandt van Rijn (1606–69), 40
rhetoric (and belles lettres), 20, 22, 93, 123, 221, 242
Rhine, River, 15
rights of man, 3, 33
Ripon, Yorkshire, 99
Robert (Stewarts' servant), 119, 143, 185, 212, 236
Robertson, Rev. Principal William (1721–93), 5, 17, 19, 20, 33, 38, 43, 46, 50, 52, 59, 63, 74–5, 76, 82–3, 91, 102, 125, 126, 255; *History of Scotland*, 17, 83, 113, 114; *History of Charles V*, 83; *History of America*, 83; *Historical disquisition concerning the Knowledge which the Ancients had of India*, 83
Robertson, William ('Willie'), Lord (1754–1835), 16, 17, 27, 28, 39, 40, 45, 46, 83, 122
Robison, Prof. John (1739–1805), 44, 65, 110, 124
Roebuck, Dr John (1718–94), 150
Rogers, Samuel (1763–1855), 170
Roman Catholic Church: *see* Catholic
Romantic Movement, 5, 167, 204
Rome, Italy, 53, 60

Romilly, Anne, Lady (d. 1818), 177, 194
Romilly, Mrs Elizabeth Amelia Jane, *née* Elliot (d. 1892), 243
Romilly, Sir Samuel (1757–1818), 82, 83–4, 85, 135, 138, 173, 177–8, 194, 201, 206, 251; *Observations on the Criminal Law of England*, 173
Romsey, Hampshire, 104, 119
Roseberry, Neil Primrose, 3rd Earl of (1729–1814), 177
Rosneath, Argyll & Bute, 8, 10
Rosslyn, Charlotte, Countess of, 138
Rothesay, Isle of Bute, 6, 7, 10, 34, 53, 66, 118, 234
Rothiemurchus, Highland Region, 132, 195
Rousseau, Jean Jacques (1712–78), 73, 74
Roxburghshire, 111
Royal Bank of Scotland, 66
Royal Commission on the Scottish Universities, 168
Royal Edinburgh Volunteers, 90
Royal Engineers, 142
Royal Society, 126, 214
Royal Society of Edinburgh, 1, 43–4, 45, 52, 53, 94, 113, 116, 121, 146, 176, 177, 192, 196, 198, 231; Council, 177; Literary Class, 37, 44, 45; Physical Class, 44; Transactions, 82
Rubens, Peter Paul (1577–1640), 40
Russell, Prof. James (1754–1836), 19, 20
Russell, Lord John (1st Earl Russell) (1792–1878), 144, 152, 155, 177, 195, 242, 243
Russia, 67, 139
Rutherfurd, Andrew, Lord (1791–1854), 230
Ruthwell, Dumfries & Galloway, 91

St Amand (Abbey), France, 68
St Andrews, Fife, 119, 189, 126
St Andrews University, 47, 69, 208, 242
St Germain-en-Laye, France, 42
St Mary's Isle, Dumfries & Galloway, 110, 123, 179, 180, 211
St Petersburg, Russia, 140; Imperial Academy of Sciences, 179
Salem, Massachusetts, USA, 192
Salisbury, Wiltshire, 119
Sands, Mrs Ann, *née* Stewart (b. 1716), 7, 10
Sands, William, 10
Sandwich, Kent, 180
Sanskrit, 215
Saratoga, Battle of, 29
Scarborough, Yorkshire, 115
Schiehallion, Perth & Kinross, 105

Index

Schloss Hainfeld, Austria, 97
Schloss Riegersburg, Styria, Austria, 97
science, 3, 5, 128, 248
Scotland, *passim*; ballads, 61; jury court, 1; militia, 90, 122; parish schools, 4, 257, 267; parliament, 93; philosophy, 244, 247, 254–5; Scottish accent/Scotticisms, 28, 57, 140, 250, 260–61; universities, 4, 9, 18, 96, 105, 109–10; 137, 157
Scots College, Douai, France, 39
The Scotsman, 164, 199, 202, 203, 210, 227, 230
Scott, Miss (DS's travelling companion in 1808), 119
Scott, Mrs ('the Lady') (DS's travelling companion in 1808), 119
Scott, Prof. Robert Eden (1770–1811), 174
Scott, Sir Walter (1771–1832), 2, 5, 16, 60, 75–6, 91, 92–3, 122, 136, 138, 141, 159, 164, 166, 167, 184, 192, 193, 201, 211, 242; *Origins of the Feudal System*, 75; *On the Manners and Customs of the Northern Nations*, 76; translations, incl. *William and Helen*, 93; *Health to Lord Melville*, 138; *Waverley Novels*, 167; *Waverley*, 184; *Guy Mannering*, 184; *The Antiquary*, 90, 184; *Rob Roy*, 193; *Tales of my Landlord*, 193; *The Heart of Midlothian*, 8, 193; *Ivanhoe*, 217; *Kenilworth*, 207; *Redgauntlet*, 16; *Tales of the Crusaders (The Talisman)*, 217; *Woodstock*, 218; *The Surgeon's Daughter*, 233; *Journal*, 159
Scott, William Robert, 244
Scottish National Portrait Gallery, 160–1, 195, 215
Seizer (Harry Temple's dog), 108
Selborne, Hampshire, 101
Selkirk, Dunbar Douglas, 4th Earl of (1722–99), 38, 110
Selkirk, Thomas Douglas, 5th Earl of (1771–1820), 110, 119, 122, 123, 179, 191, 192, 211
Selkirk, Border Region, 60
Selkirkshire, 108
Seward, Anna (1747–1809), 166
Seymour, Lord Webb (d. 1819), 102, 109, 122, 148, 179, 196
Shakespeare, William (1564–1616), 58, 117, 156, 167; *Julius Caesar*, 58
Sheen, Derbyshire, 104
Shelburne, Lord: see Lansdowne, 1st Marquess
Shelley, Percy Bysshe (1792–1822), 189

Sheridan, Richard Brinsley (1751–1816), 67, 85, 140
shooting (sport), 107–8, 174
Shropshire, 101
Siddons, Mrs Sarah née Kemble (1755–1831), 156
Signet Library, 91, 179
Silliman, Benjamin (1779–1864), 5, 136–7, 160, 163
Simson, Prof. Robert (1687–1768), 8, 12
Sinclair, Sir John (1754–1835), 15, 22; *Statistical Account of Scotland*, 15
sinecures, 135–36, 221–23, 233, 237
slavery, 32–3, 45, 92
Slough, Berkshire, 67
Smith, Prof. Adam (1723–90), 4, 8, 12, 21, 22, 38, 39, 44–5, 47, 59, 71, 72, 82, 109, 141, 150, 158, 169, 244, 253, 255; *An Inquiry into the Nature and Causes of the Wealth of Nations*, 5, 82, 141; *Essays on Philosophical Subjects*, 82
Smith, Catherine Amelia, née Pybus (d. 1852), 103, 113
Smith, Rev. Sydney (1771–1845), 100, 102–3, 109, 113, 119, 120, 122, 123–4, 130, 135, 162–3, 165, 173, 176, 227, 249, 251; *The Letters of Peter Plymley*, 165
Smith, Mr (carriage hirer), 189
Smith, Mrs (wife of above), 189–90
Smollett, Tobias (1721–71), 4, 38; *The Expedition of Humphry Clinker*, 38, 53
Society of Friends of the People, 85, 87
Socrates (469–399 BC), 58
Somme, France, 40
Southampton, Hampshire, 120, 234
Southey, Robert (1774–1843), 167
Spain, 29, 241
de Staël, Mme. Anne Louise Germaine, née Necker (1766–1817), 43, 180, 232, 255
Staffordshire, 126
Stark, John, 181, 190, 205, 218, 224
Stephen, Sir Leslie (1832–1904), ix
Sterne, Laurence (1713–68), 42; *A Sentimental Journey through France and Italy*, 42
Steuart, Prof. George, 18
Stevenage, Hertfordshire, 182
Stevenson, Prof. John, 19, 20, 21
Stewart, Archibald (d. 1752), 10
Stewart, Archibald (d. in infancy, 1751), 11
Stewart, Mrs Christian, née Aird, 10, 11
Stewart, Christian (1758–1837), 11

332

Index

Stewart, Rev. Dugald (1674-1753), 6-7, 10, 11, 34

Stewart, Prof. Dugald (1753-1828), *passim*; appearance, 117, 146, 160-4, 215; character, 5, 17, 23, 28-9, 32, 34, 37, 58, 61-3, 64, 69, 78, 90, 91, 97, 101, 108, 113, 115, 117, 118, 130, 131, 132, 138, 142-3, 144, 145, 146, 148, 149, 151, 153, 155-71, 177-8, 181, 188, 191, 201-2, 206, 208-9, 217, 222-3, 227, 244; political views, 29, 32-3, 73, 84-5, 85-91, 135, 138, 169, 175, 182, 202; health, 11, 19, 32, 124, 146, 148, 151, 152, 161, 164, 173, 177, 178, 179-80, 181, 185, 186, 191, 192, 193, 194, 195, 198, 200, 206-12, 214, 216, 217, 218, 219, 225-6; infancy, 6, 11-12; at Edinburgh High School, 14-17; at Edinburgh University, 17-21; at Glasgow University, 21-3; teacher of mathematics, 24-30, 37, 45-6, 107, 108; teacher of moral philosophy, 31-3, 45-7, 48-9, 51, 81, 89-90, 91, 97, 99, 102, 107, 110, 111, 151, 155-60; teacher of political economy, 109, 111, 113, 115, 140, 158-60, 170, 242; teacher at summer courses, 80-1, 113; first marriage, 21, 43, 52-3; second marriage, 76-8, 79-241 *passim*; Freemasonry, 50, 57, 60, 93, 121; membership of clubs and societies, 30, 32, 43-4, 52, 121-3; resident students, 36-8, 43, 95-9, 102, 104-8, 109-10, 111, 112-13, 115, 120, 123-24, 140; journeys, 27, 32-3, 39-43, 52-3, 66-70, 71-4, 82, 99-100, 105, 110, 113-14, 114-15, 119-20, 123, 130-1, 145, 146, 149, 173, 176, 178-9, 181, 188-9, 191, 192, 210-11, 212, 222-3, 224-5; as host, 91-2, 93, 102, 108, 117, 136-7; as author, 63, 81-2, 83, 94, 116, 145, 153, 172, 175, 178, 179, 180, 182-3, 189, 190, 217-18; income, 26, 37, 38, 46, 106, 123, 135-6, 176, 183, 208, 211, 219, 221-4; coat of arms, 144-5; places of residence, 25, 27, 43, 49-50, 80, 93, 95, 117-18 149-50; retirement, 148-9, 151, 152-4, 172, 200-4; death/funeral, 226-7; will, 224, 231, 233, 242; memorials, 1-2, 228-30; reputation, ix, 2, 170-1, 179, 219, 241-5; style, 248-51. <u>Writings</u>: *Dreaming*, 22-3, 26; *The Causes and Effects of Scepticism*, 26; *Taste*, 26; *The Conduct of Literary Instituions with a View to Philosophical Improvement*, 26; *Cause and Effect*, 44; *Nature and Object of Natural Philosophy*, 44; *EPHM I*, 63, 81-2, 86, 114, 128, 172, 197, 215, 220, 246; *Life of Smith*, 82, 86, 175, 211, 246; *OMP*, 49, 83, 84, 111, 193, 224, 246-7, 248; *Life of Robertson*, 83, 93-4, 113, 114, 175, 211, 247, 250, 251, 253; *Life of Reid*, 94, 113, 114, 116, 175-6, 211, 247, 251; *Short Statement of Facts*, 128, 130, 242, 247; *PE*, 145, 149, 172-3, 175, 183, 192, 241, 247, 249; *EPHM II*, 175, 178, 179, 180, 181, 182, 247, 249; *Diss*, 182-3, 185, 187-8, 190, 191, 205-6, 207, 208, 230, 241, 244, 247, 249, 250; *EPHM III*, 182, 206, 215, 217, 218, 219, 247; *PAMP*, 219, 224-5, 231, 247, 249; *CW*, 232, 243, 245, 247; *Pol Econ*, 115, 242, 248; Letter about Burns, 64; *On an Unfortunate Lady*, 167; translations, 172, 224

Stewart, George (1791-1809), 81, 99, 106, 118-19, 124, 143, 145, 146-8, 156, 160, 172, 213

Stewart, Helen, *née* Bannatyne (1756-1787), 21, 43, 46, 50, 53, 65, 150, 160

Stewart, Helen D'Arcy, *née* Cranstoun (1765-1838), ix, x, 2, 18, 63, 76-241 *passim*; family background, 76-8; appearance, 78, 142, 161, 165; character, 76, 78, 101, 105, 111, 117, 131-3, 143, 145, 151, 165-6, 175, 177, 184, 187, 194, 197, 221-3, 226, 228, 233, 235, 237; as 'Euphrosyne', 79; as 'Ivy', 98-9, 140, 165, 188; health, 115, 118, 148, 173, 175, 189, 195, 197, 198, 211, 218, 222, 224, 225, 236, 237, 239; *The tears I shed must ever fall*, 76-7

Stewart, James, 7

Stewart, James (of Stewartfield), 80

Stewart, Mrs Janet, *née* Craig (1693-1725), 10, 11, 145

Stewart, Mrs Janet, *née* Bannatyne (d. 1761), 7, 10, 11, 43

Stewart, Prof. John, 13

Stewart, Maria D'Arcy (1793-1846), 83, 114, 124, 143, 145, 149, 151, 160, 166, 173, 177, 178, 180, 184, 185, 188, 189, 192, 195, 207-9, 211, 212,

333

Index

216, 217, 218, 222–3, 225, 226, 228–40, 242
Stewart, Mrs Margaret, *née* Stewart, 7
Stewart, Mrs Marjory, *née* Stewart (*c*.1720–1771), 10
Stewart, Prof. Matthew (1717–1785), 7–13. 19, 24–5, 26, 27, 30, 46, 49, 50, 52, 55, 125, 127; *General Theorems of considerable use in the higher parts of Mathematics*, 9; Essays, 12; Tracts, 12; *The Distance of the Sun from the Earth determined by the Theory of Gravity*, 24
Stewart, Matthew, 34
Stewart, Col. Matthew (*c*.1784–1851), 36, 46, 53, 66, 69–70, 71, 74, 78, 91, 95, 99, 102, 106, 108, 110, 111, 113, 114, 115, 118–19, 120, 141, 142, 146, 147–8, 150, 156, 160, 162, 163–4, 182, 189, 190, 192, 196, 198, 200, 202–3, 205, 206, 208, 215–16, 223, 225, 226, 230–3, 240–1, 242; army career, 142–3, 147, 173–4, 178–9, 190, 196–7, 200, 215; deterioration of personality, 216, 230–3; *Memoir of the late Dugald Stewart, Esq.*, ix, 231; *Account of the Life and Writings of Dugald Stewart*, 232; tracts on Indian affairs, 231
Stewart, Rev. Robert, 7
Stewart, Robert (1713–61), 7
Stewart, Robert (1731–87), 7
Stirling, Stirlingshire, 214; Castle, 97
Stirlingshire, 150, 185
Stockholm, Sweden, 140
Stuart, James Francis Edward ('the old Pretender') (1688–1766), 42
Stuart, James of Dunearn (1775–1849), 210
Sudbury, Derbyshire, 52, 119
Sulivan, Hon. Elizabeth, *née* Temple (1790–1837), 144
Sulivan, Lawrence (1783–1866), 102, 120, 123, 130, 143–4
Switzerland, 39, 70, 150

Talleyrand-Périgord, Charles Maurice, Duc de (1754–1838), 139, 141
Tarbolton, Ayrshire, 57
Tassie, James (1735–99), 5, 160
taxation, 248, 251
Taylor, William (1765–1836), 92
Telford, Thomas (1757–1834), 149
Temple, Hon. Henry: see Palmerston, 3rd Viscount
Temple, Hon. Sir William (1788–1856), 112, 120, 123, 124, 133, 140

Teviot, River, 148
theology, 20, 22, 51, 126
The Times, 227
Thoemmes Press, Bristol, 245
Thomson, James (1700–1748), 167
Thomson, Prof. John (1765–1846), 156, 226
Thomson, Thomas (1768–1852), 130, 177, 179, 192, 196, 207, 209, 212, 219, 228, 229
Thorvaldsen, Bertel (*c*.1770–1844), 229
Tooke, John Horne (1736–1812), 249
Tories, 102, 134, 135, 136, 210, 223
Toulouse, Battle of, 134
Tournai, Belgium, 40
travel, 259–60
trigonometry, 30, 142
Trinidad, Trinidad & Tobago, 192
Tulliebole, Perth & Kinross, 185
Tweeddale, Border Region, 146
Turner, Charles (1774–1857), 160
Tytler, Alexander Fraser: *see* Woodhouselee, Lord
Tytler, Ann Fraser, 164, 166
Tytler, Patrick (Peter) Fraser (1791–1849), 164; *History of Scotland*, 164

Ulster, 7
United Irishmen, 85, 87
universal male suffrage, 87, 88
utilitarianism, 114, 255
Utrecht, Netherlands, 40

Van Dyck, Sir Anthony (1599–1641), 40
Vaughan, Bernard (1751–1835), 52–3, 67
Veitch, Prof. John (1829–94), ix, x, 31, 43, 45, 80, 92, 109, 158, 167, 171, 185, 241, 243, 244; *Memoir of Dugald Stewart*, ix, 31, 185, 243
Verdun, France, 139
Vernon, Henry Venables-Vernon, 3rd Baron (1747–1829), 119
Vernon, Miss (cousin of Miss Fox), 211
Versailles, France, 42, 72, 73, 74
Victoria, Queen (1819–1901), 241
Victoria University, Canada, 244
Viking remains, 27
Virginia, USA, 38; University of, 214–15
Voltaire, Francois Marie Arouet de (1694–1778), 150

Wales, 100, 123, 135
Walker, Prof. Josiah (1761–1831), 32, 67, 258
Wallace, Prof. William (1768–1843), 197
Ward, John William: see Dudley, Earl

Index

Wardrop, Dr James (1782–1869), 176
Warwick, George Greville, 2nd Earl of (1746–1809), 102, 105
Warwick, Henry Richard Greville, 3rd Earl of (Lord Brooke) (1776–1853), 102, 105
Warwick, Warwickshire, 102; Castle, 101, 102
Warwickshire, 102
Washington, President George (1732–99), 31, 85
Water of Leith, 80, 130
Watson, William Stewart (1800–70), 59
Watt, James (1736–1819), 150
Watt, Robert, 90
Wedderburn, Sir David, 218
Wedderburn, Lady (wife of the above), 221
Wedderburn, James (1782–1822), 202
Wedgwood, John (1766–1844), 51, 120, 177
Wedgwood, Josiah I (1730–95), 51
Wedgwood, Josiah II (1769–1843), 51–2, 55, 120, 177
Wedgwood, Josiah III (1795–1880), 52
Wedgwood, Thomas (1771–1805), 51, 55, 120, 126
Wellesley, Richard Colley, 1st Marquess (1760–1842), 139
Wellington, Arthur Wellesley, 1st Duke of (1769–1852), 98, 184, 221
Western Isles, 50
West Indies, 190
West Linton, Border Region, 145
West Lothian, 180, 194, 195
Westminster Confession of Faith, 126
Whigs, 45, 85, 87, 90, 91, 95, 102, 104, 111, 112, 126, 134, 135, 136, 137, 139, 143, 153, 175, 178, 182, 183, 196, 199, 201, 201, 210, 220, 221, 235

Whishaw, John, 206
whist, 264
White, Gilbert (1720–93), 101
Whitefoord, Sir John (1734–1803), 117–18
Wicklow, County, Ireland, 37
Wigton, Dumfries & Galloway, 87
Wilkie, Sir David (1785–1841), 5, 150, 161, 162, 185, 191, 215
Williamson, Mr (teacher of Classics), 107
Williamstrip Park, Gloucestershire, 100
Wilson, Prof. John ('Christopher North') (1785–1854), 199, 201–5, 211
Wiltshire, 101, 195
Winchester, Hampshire, 120; School, 102
Windsor, Berkshire, 67, 120
Wingfield, John, 37
Wolcot, John ('Peter Pindar') (1738–1819), 67; *The Lousiad*, 67
Wollstonecraft, Mary (Mrs Godwin) (1759–97), 94; *A Vindication of the Rights of Woman*, 94
women, 264, 265–66
Wood, Prof. Paul, 244
Woodhouselee, Alexander Fraser Tytler, Lord (1747–1813), 51, 63, 107, 160, 164
Woodhouselee, Ann, Lady née Fraser, 164
Woodhouselee, Midlothian, 164
Worcester, Worcestershire, 119
Wordsworth, William (1770–1850), 11, 85, 167

Yale University, USA, 136
Yarmouth, Francis Charles Seymour-Conway, Earl of (3rd Marquess of Hertford) (1777–1842), 139, 141
York, Yorkshire, 99, 114, 115, 120, 176; Archbishop, 9; Minster, 99–100
Yorkshire, 114, 176
Young Poker Club, 122